THE
INTELLIGENT
DESIGN
OF
COMPUTER-ASSISTED
INSTRUCTION

THE
INTELLIGENT
DESIGN
OF
COMPUTER·ASSISTED
INSTRUCTION

RICHARD VENEZKY

The University of Delaware

LUIS OSIN

Centre for Educational Technology, Ramat Aviv

Longman
New York & London

The Intelligent Design of Computer-Assisted Instruction

Longman, 95 Church Street, White Plains, N.Y. 10601

Associated companies:
Longman Group Ltd., London
Longman Cheshire Pty., Melbourne
Longman Paul Pty., Auckland
Copp Clark Pitman, Toronto

Executive editor: Raymond T. O'Connell
Development editor: Virginia L. Blanford
Production editor: Janice Baillie
Cover design: Renée Kilbride-Edelman
Text art: Fineline, Inc.

Library of Congress Cataloging in Publication Data

Venezky, Richard L.
    The intelligent design of computer-assisted instruction / Richard
Venezky, Luis Osin.
        p.   cm.
    Includes bibliographical references (p.   ).
    1. Computer-assisted instruction.   I. Osin, Luis.   II. Title.
LB1028.5.V44   1990
371.3'34—dc20   90-33778
                                                 CIP

ISBN: 0-8013-0390-7

ABCDEFGHIJ-MU-99   98   97   96   95   94   93   92   91   90

To: Plato
    Quintilian
    Aquinas
    Erasmus
    Comenius
    Pestalozzi
       and
    Dewey,

whose visions on education are the foundation from which springs
hope for the children of the future.

Contents

PART III: System Design

Acknowledgments

The authors want to thank the professionals in the field whose experience, openness, generosity, and cordiality allowed this book to be based on the real world. The visits to their centers, and the rewarding conversations held with them, enriched our knowledge, and, we hope, some of their insights will reach our readers. Prominent among them are: Donald Bitzer, Bruce Sherwood, Esther Steinberg, and Jack Stifle at CERL (University of Illinois at Urbana-Champaign);   Jack Brahan at the National Research Council of Canada;   Bertram Bruce, Alan Collins, Wally Feurzeig, Mario Grignetti, Paul Horwitz, Ray Nickerson, John Richards, and Andee Rubin, at Bolt, Beranek & Newman, Inc.;   John S. Brown and Richard Burton at Xerox PARC;   Dustin Heuston, Peter Fairweather, and Andrew Gibbons at WICAT;   Fred Hofstetter and Bonnie Anderson Seiler at the University of Delaware;   Alan Lesgold at LRDC (University of Pittsburgh);   Arthur Melmed at the National Institute of Education;   Judah Schwartz at the Educational Technology Center (Harvard University);   Graham Scott at the Ontario Institute for Studies in Education;   Bruce Sherwood at Carnegie Mellon University;   Patrick Suppes and Barbara Searle at Computer Curriculum Corporation, Inc.;   Robert Tinker at T.E.R.C.

Thanks for the careful reading of the chapters or topics in their field of specialization to Robert Calfee (Chapters 2 to 5), R. Timothy Smith (Chapters 1 to 4), Joe Lipson (Chapter 4), Ludwig Mosberg (Chapter 5), Yoav Cohen (Chapter 9), Amos Wulkan (Chapter 10), Miki Bareket and Hila Sela (Chapter 11), and Hanan Yaniv (Hypermedia); and to the many students in the CAI programming courses at the University of Delaware who provided critical comments on earlier drafts of many of these chapters.

Introduction

Wherein the Reader Is Introduced to the Authors and Learns of Their Attitudes Toward Computers and Education

> *"In the seethe of this, in the doing of that, terms, abstract, concrete, third dimension, fourth dimension—bah. Don't bother me."*
> —John Marin's dismissal of the complexities of Cubist theory, quoted in Barbara Rose, *American Painting in the Twentieth Century* (1980)

You, dear reader, could be eating napoleons now in a French cafe or reading one of Italo Calvino's Italian folktales or better yet, listening to one of the Brandenburg Concertos while supine and motionless on a soft couch, your portable, all-weather laptop safely tucked away in the office. Why, with so many other things to do, should you plow on with this text? What pleasures can you expect, what new knowledge might you gain, what confirmation of firmly held opinion? Your time, like ours, is no doubt limited and your patience for repetition, platitude, and technohype easily strained. Let us tell you then what the remaining pages will reveal and how it is that we justify the destruction of yet another patch of North America's precious forests.

This text attempts to define a relatively new field—computer-assisted instruction. We present its terminology, its history, its methodologies, paradigms, and algorithms, and its raison d'etre. In this effort we are as concerned with psychological and pedagogical underpinnings as we are with computer science concepts, rituals, and mysteries.

But this text is also a "how-to" book. By the end, you should feel competent to design instructional software or, if that task seems too large an undertaking, to assess the design of software presented for your use. Like a master chef learning to produce a sauce bearnaise, you will not learn by rote; instead, you will be led through enough of the chemistry of the culinary arts that you will be able to predict whether soybean margarine is an acceptable substitute for cold butter or basil for tarragon in the standard bearnaise recipe. We are concerned with how to write good courseware, but we assume that a necessary and reasonable base for this skill includes an understanding not only of computer capabilities but also of instruction, classrooms, and learners.

Ah, you are probably saying to yourself, yet another of those instant guides to learning theory—100 years of rat and pigeon-prancing bound into two chapters of disconnected half-truths. No, none of that here. Something on learning, yes. But we do not provide an exhaustive academic review of the empirical literature. Rather, we include only what we feel is directly relevant to instructional design, filtered through our own interpretations. We are neither comprehensive nor unbiased. Some of the last hundred years of experimental psychology speaks to the problems encountered in on-line instruction; much does not. Our role is to reduce this material to its essential form and to structure it for your benefit. The core of this text deals with instruction: what it is, what the instructional designer has control over, and what techniques can be used with computers to gain this control.

Defining a field like this has its difficulties, in spite of almost 40 years of productivity from universities, industry, research laboratories, and schools. Even the label for the field itself is problematic. For several decades the term *CAI—computer-assisted (or aided) instruction*—was acceptable to most participants, with *CAL (computer-aided learning)*, *CBE (computer-based education)*, and a slew of lesser contenders holding the runner-up positions. More recently, *ICAI—intelligent CAI*—has been adopted by most of those drawing on artificial intelligence techniques in on-line instruction, partly to distinguish their work from the more mechanical aspects of traditional CAI. Others, focusing more narrowly on a specific form of instruction, have opted for *ITS—intelligent tutoring systems*.

While recognizing (and applauding) the contributions of ICAI and ITS work, we see the need for a general title for the field, a title that can represent the full range of activities related to on-line instruction, from the simplest drill lesson to the most comprehensive intelligent tutoring system, yet at the same time remain neutral toward instructional strategy. For these reasons we will stick with CAI as a general descriptor, but with the continual reminder that intelligent design is critical to all good instruction, no matter what techniques are employed in its implementation.

But beware! This book is not a celebration of the marvels of digital wizardry, nor is it a paean for either computers or cognitive science. No teacherless classroom is forecast here, no conjuring of quantum leaps in instructional prowess. This text is a blueprint for evolution, not revolution. We hold that computer-assisted instruction can have a meaningful role in teacher-directed elementary, secondary, and postsecondary settings, and in industrial and home learning. With decreased hardware costs and more efficient processes for generating courseware, computers will become a major support element in all educational systems. Much of this support role, however, will not be directly instructional but will be spent in management, testing, grading, scheduling, and communicating. All courseware should be built on intelligent models of subject matter, learners, and instruction, but this does not rule out testing and practice,[1] multiple-choice questions, or browsing. As instructional or diagnostic techniques they have both theoretical and practical support.

Education is a social need. Modern, information-based societies are heavily dependent upon education, both for practical and philosophical reasons. As society has become more bureaucratic and more technical, the amount of information that any citizen must process has increased. Whether for pleasure, business, or ordinary citizenship, more facts, forms, and decisions confront us each day than ever confronted our parents. To prepare us for this burden, we turn to our schools. But the desire to educate everyone to higher and higher standards has become the Gordian knot of public education.

Computers alone will not solve this problem, but even with today's technologies and finances they offer considerable hope for improvement over existing conditions.

---

[1]The more traditional *drill and practice* is redundant. Drill is, by definition, practice (see your Funk and Wagnall's). Therefore, we use the more descriptive title *testing and practice*.

Part of this hope derives from what computers can do more efficiently than humans, such as store and access student records, evaluate constrained responses, and provide quick access to local and remote databases and other electronic resources. But part also derives from the potential that computers have for improving teachers' abilities to teach without computers. By providing instruction with well-defined skill relationships, we attune teachers to the abilities that are ostensibly important for a subject area and to the prerequisites for learning any one of them. By reporting on the skill mastery of individual students, we attune teachers to specific individual needs, and by providing interesting and instructive simulations, games, and tutoring, we encourage teachers to consider alternatives to drill and lecturing.

Nevertheless, these benefits will not emerge Athena-like from the body of just any clever courseware delivered to the classroom door. Courseware, like an office building, must be designed to fit a specific environment. The visual and functional integration of an office building into its locality is paralleled by the curricular and physical integration of courseware into classroom, factory, or home. When on-line instruction is not designed for easy integration, neither students nor teachers nor the national economy will profit.

By this point you might have sensed that this text is strongly concerned with cognitive abilities. These are the foundation upon which we build courseware and also the primary concern of our more theoretical interests. To be a little more precise, this text is concerned mostly with the on-line teaching of cognitive skills—that is, of subjects like math, science, automotive diagnosis and repair, banking, and football scorekeeping—topics that can be characterized by mental skills and procedures. We have only a passing interest in motor skills such as typing, tank driving, and airplane flying, and in affective skills such as attitudes toward alternative lifestyles. This is not to say that the latter two areas are not important for education. They are ignored here only because the former generally requires specialized equipment with which neither of the authors has had experience, and the latter has yet to be explored sufficiently through on-line techniques. Within the realm of cognition instruction, we have a wide range of interests: instruction, diagnosis, testing, management, and all the ways to implement these on-line, including simulations and games.

Having navigated this far, you may have a sense of whether or not this text is for you. Let us be more direct. We are writing for a fairly wide audience, centered on courseware designers and their supporting specialists: programmers, subject area specialists, and instructional gurus. For those interested primarily in the principles and context of instructional design, Part I ("Overview"), Part II ("Instruction"), and perhaps Part V ("Outlook") may provide sufficient repast. For those interested mainly in implementation, the meal consists of Part III ("System Design") and Part IV ("System Implementation"). But we do not discourage others from trying our wares: policymakers, administrators, salespeople, and others who might want to peek under the hood of the CAI engine, to learn something more about this field than can be garnered from a journal article.

We should note here that the authors have separate areas of specialization and recognizably different writing styles. We have not tried to disguise our identities through verbal homogenization. Richard Venezky wrote the Introduction and parts I, II, and V; Luis Osin wrote parts III and IV. But the organization of the text, the definitions, the approach to treating the different topics, and the various opinions stated are all joint responsibilities.

Some chapters in the text are fairly general, requiring little in the way of technical knowledge, while others are meant for specialists in the field. To help you decide where to venture, each chapter begins with an overview that indicates, among other things, any assumptions we make about the readers of that chapter. Technical vocabulary is usually defined where it first appears; a glossary is also available at the back of the book. You will also find a complete list of references at the back of the book. And since so much of the information in this field is transmitted through the activities of professional organizations and other interested groups, we have listed these in an appendix along with a listing of the better-known newsletters and journals.

This, then, is what we're about. You should, after reading this book from beginning to end, be able to design courseware that incorporates the principles of appropriate instruction and the knowledge that research has provided over the years about how children learn. From the Contents listing you can see what we include and how we sequence this information. But don't feel bound by our ordering (unless your instructor insists upon it). Start with the last first, if you prefer, and see what our view is of the school of the future. Or begin at the beginning. We wish you well.

PART I
Overview

The first section of this text is both warm up and first movement. From basic introductions to instruction, learning, and technology, we saunter through a few scenarios involving computer-assisted instruction and introduce the basics of courseware design, implementation, and delivery: courseware types, support systems, authoring environments, delivery mechanisms, and a few other components. All of this is Chapter 1. From there we proceed to a tutorial on technology (Chapter 2), meant for those who might need a basic explanation of CPU, bus, and peripheral, and then conclude the preliminaries with the grand and glorious history of on-line instruction (Chapter 3).

CHAPTER 1

Learning, Instruction and Technology
Whereby Some Common Experiences Are Created and Inductive Instruction Begins

> *"These School Books . . . have received the cordial endorsement of the most intelligent and successful teachers throughout the Union. They combine the rare advantages of superior intrinsic merit, typographical beauty, cheapness, and extensive uniformity of adoption and use."*
> —McGuffey's New High School Reader (1857)

INSTRUCTION DEFINED

The platform, the bedrock, the stage upon which this book rests is instruction, so we will set out a few directions now on how to engage this topic. To begin, *instruction* is defined as *planned learning experiences. Learning* is an increase in accessible knowledge or ability. An increase in inaccessible knowledge or ability might, in some distant and abstract world, appear as learning, but inaccessible means not assessable, untappable, and therefore not of practical value. *Planned* means deliberate, but not necessarily in a preprogrammed, step-by-step fashion. Planned still leaves room for student control and random generation of problems, but within the constraints of specified learning goals and instructional modes. Corrective or evaluative feedback is essential to most forms of cognitive learning, but it is not a sine qua non for instruction. Furthermore, not all learning occurs through instruction.

Types of Learning

Unstructured and Undirected. The young child, for example, does an enormous amount of learning through unstructured interaction with the environment. Driven primarily by innate tendencies (e.g., curiosity, hunger), the child attempts to grasp at the various objects within his perceptual field and thereby acquires information on solidity, texture and weight, depth of field, and the muscle movements needed to grasp and move objects to specific locations (e.g., the mouth). This type of learning is unstructured and involves no overt instruction.

Unstructured and Directed. A second type of learning is also unstructured, but is directed toward acquisition of knowledge. When you breathe on a glass plate to see if it fogs over, or when you throw grass into the air to determine which way the wind is blowing, you are attempting to learn through experimentation. But you usually do not carefully structure the sequence of ideas or skills you explore; instead, you are driven by curiosity or some immediate need. A more extreme case involves the attempt to learn a new language by listening to the "natives." This type of learning sometimes takes on many of the features of traditional instruction, such as rehearsal and assessment, but it usually remains unstructured. That is, you rarely if ever select a particular sequence of vocabulary or grammatical patterns to learn under these conditions, nor do you operate from any particular model of the skills required to learn the target language.

Structured and Directed. A third type of learning, the one with which we are primarily concerned here, is learning-oriented and structured. By *structured* we mean *planned;* by *learning-oriented* we imply the existence of *learning goals,* that is, specific knowledge or skills. This form of learning differs from the curiosity-driven form mainly in the extent of its structure. Planned learning activities are usually extended over time, rather than being singular and spur of the moment.

These three types of learning can be represented by the 2 × 2 diagram shown in Figure 1.1, in which the fourth cell (non-learning-oriented but structured), representing what we often feel is wrong with our colleagues and neighbors, is labeled *ritual* for lack of a more suitable term.[1]

Instruction, therefore, involves goals and procedures. Goals might be quite broad (e.g., learn to speak and understand French) or quite narrow (e.g., learn what was the first book printed in England with movable type) or anyplace in between. For the design of computer-assisted instruction we require only that goals be defined specifically enough that their degree of attainment can be measured. In other words, we require that learning goals be stated in terms that allow for evaluation of goal attainment. What qualifies as structure (that is, what sets of procedures fit the definition of "structured") is the concern of Chapter 3. For the present we need only know that well-structured instruction, regardless of delivery mechanism, is built on (1) a model of the knowledge that is being taught, (2) a model of the learner, and (3) a theory of instruction that specifies the range of procedures that are effective in assisting learners to master a particular knowledge base.

Corrective Feedback

Instruction without corrective or evaluative feedback is not only possible but common. Instruction manuals for appliances are typical examples. "To play, load the tape cassette into the holder with the exposed strip of tape toward the buttons. Close cover and press play." If the tape plays, the intrinsic feedback is sufficient not only to signal success, but also to fix learning. If the tape fails to play, the situation becomes a little more complex since the specific nature of the fault is not indicated by the failure. *Intrinsic feedback,* such as the tape's playing or not playing, is feedback that is inher-

---

[1]Joseph Campbell (1972) has written that "The function of ritual . . . is to give form to human life. Not in the way of a mere surface arrangement, but in depth" (p. 43). Rituals are not performed so that the performers or observers can acquire new knowledge or skills. Instead, they are enacted to unite people with each other and with their past, to resolve anxiety and uncertainty, and to provide constancy amidst change. Ritual has also been defined as communication without information.

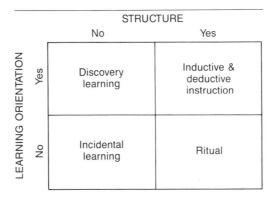

Figure 1.1. Types of Learning Experiences

ent in the task itself, as opposed to externally provided or *extrinsic feedback,* which is given by an instructor, intelligent computer program, or equivalent. A student can also obtain extrinsic feedback by checking an answer key.

Nevertheless, for almost all cognitive learning, instruction is enhanced by evaluative feedback. In many cases it is essential, if any learning is to occur. Translation of a foreign language is a prime example of the latter situation. Any number of incorrect but plausible readings might be assigned to a sentence in a foreign language; without evaluation of the response from a person knowledgeable in the language, little learning is possible. Where the learner can easily provide her own feedback, such as in rote memorization tasks, feedback plays a minor role as a corrective mechanism. But as learning tasks become more complex, feedback becomes more important. We will say much more on feedback in later chapters, including different reasons for giving feedback, different types of feedback, and when its use is counterproductive. One of the biggest challenges in the design of on-line instruction is providing evaluative feedback through analysis of student performance. For quantitative areas, such as basic mathematics and algebra, this is usually possible within the range of abilities of current technology, but for areas in which natural language responses are the norm in live classrooms, the task is much greater.

ORGANIZATION OF INSTRUCTION

Consider for a moment all the different types of courses of which you are aware. Most will no doubt be delivered within traditional educational institutions: schools, colleges, universities, and the like. But courses are also given by a variety of other institutions such as trade schools, unions, hairdressing institutes, driving schools, and clown colleges, and in a variety of locations, including churches and synagogues, community centers, hospitals, and the like. Some of these places are, by definition, associated with a well-defined range of courses (e.g., grade school, hairdressing institute); others are simply locales where courses of almost any content might be offered, subject only to the tastes of the administrators and the limitations of equipment and space. Thus a church basement might be used for a preschool or a religious school, or for community courses on sewing or adult literacy training, or for almost anything else that would not be offensive to the primary function of the organization.

Since our purpose in discussing types of courses is to present the range of opportunities for on-line instruction, we will divvy up this domain first by course content and then by context. For the latter we will indicate the traditional setting for the course category, list a few of the more common nontraditional settings, and in general leave unstated that almost every course imaginable might be taught in a military setting, and every one that doesn't require special equipment might be arranged for home delivery. The categories that follow are derived in part from traditional classifications and in part from our own organization.

Preschool Education. In this category we place all that is taught in preschools, nurseries, and kindergartens, except where the regular grade school curriculum is involved (e.g., initial reading instruction). Much of what is done at this level is not structured by lessons and courses, but some is, even if done loosely. Thus, a kindergarten might have a formal prereading program, taught within a lesson structure, or alternatively, a preschool teacher might do units on such topics as colors, shapes, sizes, and letters. In the United States, the traditional setting for a kindergarten is the elementary school, but preschools are located almost anywhere that appropriate heat, light, and shelter can be found: homes, industries, storefronts, straw huts, and so forth.

Arts and Sciences Courses. In this category we place all the general curriculum for elementary and secondary schools and that which is labeled "Arts and Sciences" (or some reasonable facsimile thereof) at the college and university level. For courseware design, a division should be made between elementary- and secondary-level courses on one hand, and postsecondary courses on the other. The former are designed for a heterogeneous student population, where entry-level abilities and motivational levels vary wildly. The latter are directed toward a more selective audience where entry-level abilities are often used for student selection and where motivational differences are smaller.

Some parts of the traditional arts and sciences curriculum, such as foreign languages, are taught outside of schools and colleges in businesses and industry, military bases and institutes, community centers, and the like. Other parts, such as literacy and basic mathematics, are taught in remedial form to adults in libraries, prisons, night schools, and the like. These courses have many characteristics that differentiate them from courses with the same subject matter taught for children, but they are arts and sciences courses nevertheless.

Professional and Semiprofessional Training. In this category we place specialty courses found in typical medical, law, and nursing schools, as well as courses for teaching (a semiprofession) and the ministry. By specialty courses we mean the courses that are strongly tied to the profession itself, such as diagnosis courses in medicine, torts courses in law, and sermon writing courses in ministry training. In contrast, many courses required in professional schools are indistinguishable from traditional arts and sciences courses, for example, history of medicine (or law or whatever), comparative anatomy, religions of the world. These courses are usually taught in colleges, universities, theological seminaries, or hospitals, but a night law school, for example, might hold courses in almost any setting suitable for lectures and discussion.

Religious Training. Courses taught by churches and synagogues in their religious schools are often similar to arts and sciences courses (e.g., history, language) but differ in that religious doctrine generally is infused within each subject area. In addition, songs, prayers, and chants, as well as special rituals are taught.

Job-Oriented Training. The core of this class combines motor skills with thinking: truck and car driving, plumbing, hairdressing, clowning, and fighter plane piloting are a few examples. These courses are taught in technical colleges and institutes, in industry (on-the-job training), and in special "schools." The periphery of this class includes motor skills acquired usually for recreational or other private use: sewing, knitting, and cooking being the prime examples. These latter courses are taught in homes, stores, and other locales concerned with the products involved, or at the multitude of places where continuing education occurs: community centers, night schools, prisons, hospitals, and the like.

Personal Skills. Self-control, leadership, wellness, parenting, and relaxation are all subjects for a special category of courses, aimed toward people who want to improve their abilities to cope with themselves and the world around them. Some of these topics are found in executive training courses; others tend to be associated with clinics and personal or family counseling. Some, however, have become standard fare for community schools, YMCA/YMHA programs, and other forms of adult education.

Incidental and Occasional Training. Besides formal courses, workshops, and other structured approaches to instruction and learning, briefer and more casual forms exist. Consider, for example, a word processor that has on-line help and training. At the point of peak frustration over formatting of footnotes on the page, you might press the help key and encounter an interactive tutorial on the mysteries of the footnote command, complete with questions and feedback. Not many word processors have this level of on-line help, but it does occasionally appear. This is what we call *incidental and occasional training.* It occurs only on demand and usually within a highly constrained situation where the information taught is immediately needed. Other examples include the "How-to-Order" sections of product catalogues, instructions for filling out a particular tax form, and equipment user manuals.

A Note on Terminology

The term *courseware* is used in both a broad and a narrow sense. Technically, courseware is software, but to distinguish instructional systems from other types of software systems, the term courseware has quietly been adopted. We use *courseware* to mean software that engages directly in instruction. Instructional tools like word processors and database systems are not gathered under this label here. *Lessonware,* a neologism of more recent vintage, applies to segments of courseware that teach single lessons. Given the impreciseness of lesson and course in everyday use, lessonware and courseware might often be confused. Except under duress, we will avoid the term *lessonware.*

TECHNOLOGY AND INSTRUCTION: AN INTRODUCTION

Since the next chapter explores in depth the topic of technology and instruction, we insert here only a placeholder for this later presentation. The point of the classification scheme offered under the heading "Organization of Instruction" was to define the range of application of on-line instruction. What should have emerged from that discussion was that CAI is not limited to courses taught in schools and colleges; instead it has an enormous range of potential application, from formal academic courses to on-line repair manuals and computer-user guides. Furthermore, the computer role in any of these applications might vary from a complete course to some limited course component, such as practice problems, lab simulations, or interactive demonstrations with tutoring. Coupled with the instructional components might be a variety of student supports, such as word processing, databases, mathematical routines, electronic mail, and graphic programs, as well as teacher supports, such as course management, curriculum and course planning, grading and reporting, and communications. (These supports do not qualify by themselves as instruction, however, unless they have planned sequencing and corrective feedback. They are, nevertheless, sometimes listed as *instructional systems* in courseware catalogues.)

The range of technology involved could also vary across all conceivable sizes of computers, input-output devices, and storage media. Voice, touch, mouse, keyboard, and eye-blink input are all potentially usable, as are voice, graphic display, and print output. Videodisc, CD-ROM, local-area and remote networks, satellite transmission, and electronic blackboards are also available for incorporation in such systems. As with so many other areas of technology application today, we are more limited by our imagination than we are by the technology itself.

A Few Scenarios Involving On-line Instruction

"Example is better than precept" says an old Latin proverb. Edmund Burke, writing at the end of the eighteenth century, stated "Example is the school of mankind, and they will learn at no other." Modern psychology gives some cause for doubting the universality of the second half of this statement, but, nevertheless, we present here examples and not precepts. What follows is the beginnings of a common database that readers and authors will share, several scenarios that display the full range of concerns of this text for on-line instruction, management, and instructional support. These scenarios are situated in elementary schools, but might be transformed, mutatis mutandis, to other settings. In the final chapter a second set of scenarios is presented, representing projected settings five years or so from now. Some patience will be required on your part because at best you will receive half a loaf from each description. The descriptions are brief, emphasizing (where appropriate) educational goals, environment (i.e., types of learners, place in curriculum, usage, physical setting, related resources), delivery system, instructional modes, user-system interaction, and instructional management. The important point here is not the marvels of the lessons described, but rather the varieties of usage for on-line instructional materials.

Scenario 1—Casual CAI. Imagine a modern, open-pod elementary school with three units of about 150 students each, kindergarten through sixth grade, lots of space, carpets on the floor, audiovisual equipment and microcomputers everywhere. Now focus on the fifth-grade math class in pod A, which is taught with a popular math textbook, part of a K–6 series. Instruction for all three groups in the class is prescribed by the teacher's guide, with pretests, posttests, and plenty of activity sheets. Calculators and computers are mentioned in the student textbook, and occasionally BASIC code is shown, but the only students who regularly use microcomputers for math are those from the top and middle groups who finish their seatwork early. For them awaits a selection of math games, including some that drill on basic arithmetic operations and some that require slightly higher levels of cognition. The games are run on stand alone microcomputers with no recording of results.

A connection between the topic of the current math program and the topic of any game a student might select is often no closer than lightning is to a lightning bug. Computer work is unmonitored, except that help is available if a disk won't load or a strange error message appears on the screen. Students appear to enjoy the programs, and a few have become highly proficient at flying around the world by doing rapid multiplication or popping weird animals back in their cages through rapid identification of geometric shapes. The math teacher also likes to play some of these games, but rarely mentions them in math class.

Scenario 2—Integral CAI. Gaze now at P.S. 7 in a major American metropolis. Eighth-grade students regularly use computers for their language arts class, which focuses on writing. While the majority of the computer use on the 25 non-networked microcomputers is with a word processing package, several programs are assigned for introducing and practicing grammar concepts. Students work each unit on their own until they feel they understand it. They can then attempt the mastery test, which the teachers themselves prepared on ditto masters. Students who master these tests proceed to the following units; those who fail may either redo the related CAI lessons once or be tutored by a teacher, using one of several available reference books. Teachers describe the on-line grammar lessons in class and suggest how to use them for self-study. Each one displays a menu of specific grammar objectives upon entry, and shows a summary of student performance on exit. This summary can also be printed. A teacher option allows entry onto the program diskette of teacher-generated quizzes. Several have been prepared by the teachers in the language arts group.

Scenario 3—The Works. Finally, take the subway across town to the new Dolley Madison High School and observe the microcomputer network that was installed earlier this year for instruction. Fifty workstations are connected to the ring network, along with a large file server that stores courseware, student and class records, utility programs, and several large databases (e.g., dictionary, encyclopedia). Several of the workstations have videodisc players connected to them, and the central file server has a CD-ROM drive. Students from algebra, history, and biology II regularly use these materials for either introductions to topics, practice, or review and assessment. Performance data are automatically posted to central files, which teachers can monitor from terminals on their own desks. When students sign-on, they are informed where they are in the on-line lessons and what they should do next. Messages can be routed to teachers, administrators, or other students. Special requests for on-line assistance can also be posted for peer tutors who spend a half hour per day, three days each week, giving on-line assistance.

Teachers and administrators can access student and class records, review courseware, generate reports, make student assignments, and develop their own on-line materials using special authoring facilities. Not many do this, but one history teacher has become adept at using the test generator and does all of her history tests on-line now, and a biology teacher has developed two lab simulations that introduce students to lab exercises and teach them what equipment they need. Several others have taken summer courses in HyperCard® and Pascal and have begun to generate lessons. Administrators use the system regularly for grade reporting, competency skill management, and attendance records. Parents and students with the necessary equipment outside of school can dial into a bulletin board maintained on the system for homework assignments, school news, and extracurricular schedules.

Some Categories for On-line Materials

Complete Systems. While these scenarios represent only a part of the on-line instructional world, they give us a foothold for classifying what now exists. The last system described (Scenario 3), represents a complete CAI system, that is, one that has authoring, archiving, delivery, and management components. With such a system, courseware developers can design, implement, and test courseware; students can be instructed online; and teachers and administrators can monitor student progress, obtain student and group reports, and assign materials to students. Such systems are expensive to build and maintain, and consequently few exist today. The earliest of any note was PLATO, followed by TICCIT®. (The history of these is described in Chapter 3.) Most CAI materials available for purchase now, however, fall into the categories that follow.

Curriculum-based Programs. Scenario 2 (Integral CAI) is an example of what we call curriculum-based programs, that is, courseware that is by design or adaptation an integral part of complete courses or curricula. The computer role in a particular course or curriculum may be extensive or minimal; but rarely will it be the only component. (By *course* we have in mind such things as third-grade mathematics, high school-level biology, college physics I, the U.S. Army's introductory course on electronics, a home-study course on stocks and bonds, and the like. A fuller exposition on courses, curricula, and so forth, awaits the reader in Chapter 4.) What is critical for a course is a coherent set of skill goals, with appropriate instruction, review, and assessment. Some curriculum-based materials are available, particularly for elementary mathematics, and many textbook publishers are beginning to provide on-line practice and assessment materials to accompany textbook programs.

Skill-based Programs. Scenario 1 (Casual CAI) represents how the majority of the CAI materials listed in the current courseware catalogues are used. These materials usually focus on one or more skills without regard for the other trappings of the courses in which these skills might be taught. Programs that offer practice in spelling or addition and subtraction often fit into this category, as do most so-called educational games. They are designed specifically for designated skills and might be used in many different courses and in a variety of different ways. Admittedly, a curriculum-based CAI program and a skill-based one might be identical, but the development procedures will be quite different.

Support Systems. Finally, to round out our classification scheme, we define a class of on-line support systems (or utilities) for CAI: management of instruction, test scoring, reporting, authoring, and the like. Many of these are marketed as stand-alone packages, usable with a wide range of approaches to instruction. In other cases they exist as components of specific instructional systems, such as with TOAM or PLATO.

SUMMARY

Instruction requires planned learning experiences, where learning is defined as an increase in accessible knowledge or ability. Planned, however, still allows student control of some facets of the instruction, along with random generation of problems or scenarios. Feedback is essential for most forms of instruction, but is not always required for learning to occur.

In most instructional settings (e.g., schools, military, industry), instruction is organized into courses that, for present purposes, we class as preschool, arts and sciences, professional and semiprofessional, religious, job-oriented, personal skills, and incidental and occasional training. These course types are characterized by particular audiences, locales, and content. Technology can play a role in facilitating instruction in each of these categories, varying from minor support to full delivery. The uses of technology in the schools today represent this variation, especially in the span from casual CAI on stand-alone microcomputers to complete course delivery on a networked system.

CHAPTER 2

Wherefore and Why Technology and Instruction?

> *Professor: To resume: it takes years and years to learn to pronounce. Thanks to science, we can achieve this in a few minutes.*
> —Eugène Ionesco, *The Lesson* (1958)

This chapter begins with a summary of technology—not just any old technology but the technology that supports on-line, interactive instruction. In the last century the hot technologies in education were the blackboard, the globe, and the wall chart. With solid-state electronics, satellite transmission, digital recording, and many other wonders of the twentieth century, much has changed—but not everything. From technology we move to instruction, building on the definition given in the first chapter to give a sense of which components of instruction might be enhanced by an infusion of technology and which audiences might be candidates for such arrangements. Finally, we arrive at the issue of *Why Technology?* which we approach with what the late Margaret Mead called "disciplined subjectivity." Rounding out the discussion are some brief comments on problems that technology engenders when mixed with education. If you are at all conversant with hardware and software terminology, you probably want to skip ahead to the section labeled "Design," although you might be curious enough to want to see how we trip over our own feet trying to define computer technology in a limited space.

WHAT IS TECHNOLOGY?

A 1982 Office of Technology Assessment report listed nine technologies that it felt could have a significant impact on education: cable, satellite, digital telephone, broadcast, computers, mass storage, video transmission, videodisc, and information services (U.S. Congress, 1982). Of these, our core interest is with interactive technologies and therefore with computers and the components that support computers, such as mass storage and videodisc. Cable, satellite communications, and other transmission technologies, while applicable to on-line instruction, receive only casual mention hereafter. For talking about computers, we establish a general set of taxonomies and some common language. The reader should be aware, however, that this technology is rapidly changing, so that techniques and capacities should be taken as indicators of today but not necessarily of tomorrow. Our concern with on-line instruction (which implies *interactive instruction)* involves *hardware, software,* and a design and implementation *process.* These together comprise our technology of interest.

Hardware

Since we have already arrived at the time when microcomputers can be configured easily from basic components selected from a catalogue, it is important to have some general understanding of what these components are. A computer, of whatever size, is generally composed of

1. a central processing unit (CPU), which is characterized by the number (in millions) of instructions it can execute in a second (MIPS)
2. random-access memory (RAM), generally stated in thousands or millions of bytes or characters (kbytes or mbytes)
3. remote storage, generally sized in the millions-of-bytes range (mbytes)
4. input and output (I/O) devices (e.g., keyboard, mouse, video display, printer)
5. a channel or *bus* that allows all of these components to communicate gracefully with each other.

A simple sketch of these components and their relationships is shown in Figure 2.1.

A variety of refinements could be added to this description. A CPU, for example, might have a full set of instructions, or it might have a reduced set (RISC), thus allowing cheaper construction but requiring software to do more. The data bus might have 8, 16, or 32 bits of addressing capability, besides other specialized functions; and it might be designed to be compatible with one or another of the current bus standards. Random-access memory, which allows addressing at a byte (i.e., character) level, might have restricted sections that are extremely high speed (cache memory) or that contain

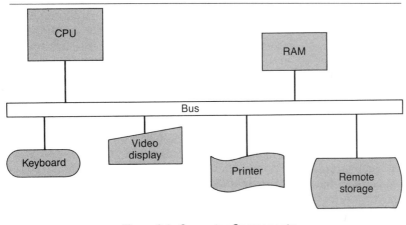

Figure 2.1. Computer Components

permanent instructions and data and therefore can be read from but not written to. This latter type of memory is called read-only memory or ROM to distinguish it from random-access memory or RAM. Remote memory is generally mass storage that must be addressed in blocks of many characters but that can hold millions of characters at a cost significantly lower than RAM. Remote storage technologies, such as hard disk, floppy disk, CD-ROM, and optical disk, are characterized by capacity (in bytes), access time (the time to move a read/write head to where reading or writing should start), and data transfer rate. A medium-priced hard disk for a Macintosh II℠, for example, has 80 mbytes of storage, an access time of 28 msecs, and a data transfer rate of 250 kbytes per second. A 12-cm CD-ROM, for comparison, holds more than 550 mbytes, which is equivalent to more than 270,000 typewritten pages. (This capacity translates to 700 floppy disks with 800 kbytes each.)

Through clever hardware schemes, remote memory can be treated as if it were local memory, that is, as *virtual memory*. The advantage to this bit of electronic *trompe l'oeil* is that the programmer can write code for a much larger RAM space than actually exists. The system shuffles blocks of memory content back and forth from remote storage to RAM, so that whatever the program requires will be present without the programmer having to make overt calls for it. The use of virtual memory not only speeds up program operation but also simplifies program design, particularly for large programs.

Common input devices include a keyboard (which is standard for almost every general purpose computer sold today), optical scanner, voice recognition circuit, touch screen, mouse, and various magnetic or optical media: tape, diskette, hard disk, optical disk, videodisc, CD-ROM. Common output devices include visual-display unit, voice and sound unit, plotter, and magnetic/optical storage. To these can be added the not-so-common I/O devices, such as prosthetic and robotic systems. Of all of these devices, the visual-display unit (hereafter called a *VDU)* is the most common and also the most critical for instructional output. The characteristics of VDUs that are important for instructional applications are the same as for most other applications: graphic quality, generally given in terms of resolution in dots, or *pixels,* per inch; color or gray-scale range; and overall size. (Note that technical terms like *gray scale* are defined in the glossary at the end of the book. Terms that are critical for understanding ideas presented are also defined when they are introduced, although a few may have slipped through our highly attentive proofreading.)

Some of these technologies have presented capabilities that extend beyond just a quantum leap in storage capacity. The videodisc, for example, has opened a new capability for interactive video. Because TV frames can be retrieved rapidly from a videodisc, alternative video sequences can be developed dynamically, based upon student responses. A demonstration of an assembly process for a backyard swing set, for example, might repeat a particular section when the viewer fails to correctly answer a question about it, or it might shift to a different approach upon detection of a particular misconception about the assembly process. A CD-ROM, because of its enormous storage capacity, can bring resources such as dictionaries, encyclopedias, and newspaper archives to on-line instruction. As one example, the thirteen volumes of the *Oxford English Dictionary* have recently been made available on two CD-ROMs, and work is proceeding on integrating into this database the recently complete four-volume supplement.

Types of Computers. In the early 1980s, perhaps, one could draw reasonably clear distinctions among the various sizes of computers. At the peak of Mt. Parnassus were the supercomputers, followed in descending capacity down the slopes by mainframes, minis, and then micros (i.e., microcomputers). Each class of machinery could be assigned ranges of prices, speeds, and throughput capacities that for the most part had little overlap. Now, however, the world of computer hardware has become more complex. Yes, supercomputers still exist, and they become bigger, faster, and generally more expensive each year. But super-minicomputers also exist as do array processors and other extenders for mainframes that give them many of the characteristics of supercomputers. Then, too, microcomputers have grown both bigger and smaller at the same time, so that on one hand are the powerful workstations that are equal to the minicomputers in power and on the other are the lap computers that are truly micro in size but not in capability. Finally, multiple processor systems have been developed, wherein batches of microprocessors, operating in parallel, rival mainframes in throughput for certain types of problems.

Configurations. A second complication for squeezing computers into neat categories is that both machines and components can be tied together in networks, thus allowing interprocessor communications, data sharing, and even distributed processing. A cluster of 16 workstations might, for example, share a single, large hard disk and some specialized I/O devices such as a digitizer and plotter. For most serious on-line instructional applications, networking is essential. With networks, large libraries of courseware can be accessible to individual workstations via high-speed transfer, and central collection of student data is facilitated. For the present we are distinguishing between fully coupled and partially coupled networks. The former refers to systems that are permanently coupled at reasonably high transmission rates (called *baud* rates), while the latter refers to systems that do not have permanent connections or that operate at such low speeds that transmission of graphics, for example, cannot be done in real time. Typical of the latter are workstations coupled through telephone connections. A teacher might dial into a central system, download a course, and then disconnect from the central system and operate in a stand-alone mode.

A typical instructional network is shown in Figure 2.2. In this system, 32 workstations are connected in a *ring* network with several specialized systems or *servers*. One server, for example, is a database system that retrieves information on request from large data files. Another executes a powerful mathematics program. Student workstations send requests for services to these servers and receive information back from them. In a well-integrated system, these requests are hidden from the student; that is, the student has no way of telling whether a particular operation is performed locally or at a remote site. A second type of network, called a *star* system, is shown in Figure 2.3. Here, all communications to and from workstations are processed by a central system, in contrast to the configuration shown in Figure 2.2, where each workstation can communicate directly with any other workstations or with any server.

Software

A second area of computer technology is software, which consists of *systems* programs such as *operating systems* and *compilers,* as well as *utilities* for such tasks as screen

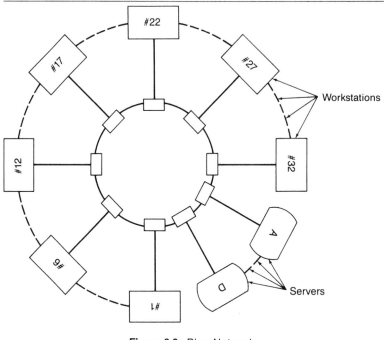

Figure 2.2. Ring Network

management and data reduction. An operating system can be viewed as a resource manager. It interprets user requests, keeps track of storage allocations, monitors the operation of I/O devices, locates needed utilities and assigns tasks to them, and does other things to ensure that the system is used as the user requests it to be. The most popular operating system for scientific workstations and for minicomputers, UNIX®,

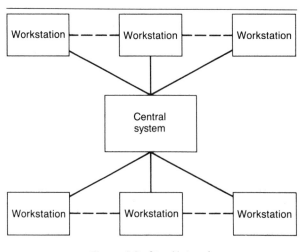

Figure 2.3. Star Network

has been under continual development since 1970 and is being used with increasing frequency on microcomputers.

UNIX, like most of its newer competitors, allows *multitasking,* that is, it allows the user to run more than one task at the same time. For example, a user might start up a program that converts Word Perfect® files to XYWrite files and set it to work on a long document. While this is grinding away, the user might initiate his favorite database program and start searching for his stock investments for the coming week. When the second program is started, the operating system might divide the VDU screen in half horizontally and give the upper half to the conversion program and the lower half to the database program. These separate screen areas or *windows* would function independently of each other, although some operating systems might allow transfer of data from one area to the next, either directly or via an intermediate file or *scratchpad.*

The style or manner of interaction between user and system is mostly a function of software, although hardware components such as cursor movement devices (e.g., mouse) and monitor characteristics are also important. Two basic interaction styles exist: a text/command style and an icon/menu style. The former dates from the La Brea Tar Pit period of computing and involves the typing of commands like

copy A:curricula\necromancy\spring90 spring91

The latter, pioneered through the Xerox Star® and the Apple® Macintosh, employ a desktop metaphor with icons that are pointed to and dragged around the screen, and pull-down menus from which selections are made by mouse operation or key presses. Associated with, but not restricted to, the icon style are overlapping windows that appear on the screen to enclose information for separate tasks and components of tasks. New software technology includes graphics and window managers that facilitate the placement, moving, and resizing of graphic images and windows.

Programming Languages. What is called *applications programming*—the writing of programs such as spreadsheets, word processors, statistical packages, and the like—is generally done in high-level programming languages, such as Pascal or C. These languages have commands that relate to the task being done rather than to the instruction set that the hardware can execute. For example, in Pascal one can write:

total: = total + 1;   {which means "add one to *total*"}

For a particular computer, the equivalent machine instructions are:

lda t1

ini 1

sta t1

The first instruction (lda t1) transfers the contents of storage location t1 to an operational register called the accumulator. The second instruction (ini 1) increases the contents of the accumulator by one, and the third instruction (sta t1) stores the new value of the accumulator back into storage location t1, destroying whatever was originally stored there. These instructions are in assembly language form, which is close to the actual machine code of the computer, but still rife with alphanumeric mnemonics, such as t1 and lda. A program called an assembler translates this code into the binary patterns that the computer actually responds to. For example, the second instruction above might appear to the running hardware (after the assembly process) as 0101100000000001.

Authoring Languages. Programs written in languages like Pascal or C are reduced by compilers or interpreters to the form the computer can execute. Instructional programs, or *courseware,* can be written in standard high-level programming languages, but most designers find these languages unsuitable for large-scale development work. Therefore, a class of languages, called *authoring languages,* has been developed over the past 25 years, with names like COURSEWRITER®, TUTOR, and PILOT. Most of these languages restrict the user to a limited subset of the utilities available on a computer, but some allow inclusion of programs written in other languages so that, at least in theory, anything that the computer will allow can be incorporated in courseware.

Object-Oriented Programming. Several new developments in systems programming may totally alter the procedures used in the future for developing courseware. The first of these is object-oriented programming, which has been around since the language SIMULA was introduced in the 1960s (Dahl & Nygaard, 1966), but which has only recently been seriously applied to a wide range of programming tasks. Object-oriented programming centers around objects and classes of objects and the messages they exchange. Once a class of objects is defined, instances of the class of *objects* can be created, each of which has all the properties of the class, plus (potentially) all the properties of the superclasses of the current class. The properties of an object include its defined variables (called *instance variables),* the messages it can receive, and the actions it takes upon each message (i.e., its *methods).* Among other virtues, object-oriented programming allows and encourages modularity and software reuse.

Hypermedia. A second new direction is seen in the rising popularity of hypermedia systems. Hypermedia or hypertext is another old idea that has finally emerged in full-fledged, usable systems, such as GUIDE, NoteCards, HyperCard, and Xanadu (Conklin, 1987). In its simplest form, hypertext is a mechanism for creating nonlinear texts, that is, texts where in addition to the normal, linear sequence of sentences and paragraphs, alternative paths that potentially link every object (word, sentence, paragraph, etc.) to every other object in the text, or to objects outside the text, are also possible. A novel, for example, might be coded so that the activities for each character are connected. A reader, on encountering a character of interest, might then jump through the story, following this character's appearances. Unusual words, foreign phrases, and idioms might be connected to definitions, and certain actions or statements might be annotated with interpretive notes. The presence of these notes and alternative routes might be signaled by icons within the text. Pressing designated keys might then either pop up windows with definitions or comments or replace the displayed material with material to which it is linked.

Of special note is the Macintosh HyperCard system that integrates hypertext concepts with a database structure and with primitive object-oriented capabilities. The basic unit in HyperCard is the screen image or *card,* which is more like a dynamic database record than a traditional filing card. A card can contain visible fields, hidden fields, and buttons. A field can contain text and graphics, and the graphics can be animated. Scripts, written in a language called HyperTalk℠, can be associated with a stack of cards, an entire card, a card field, or a card button. A script defines the actions to take when particular messages (e.g., click, double click) are received by an object (e.g., button, field). Thus a help button might be scripted so that pointing to it with the mouse and clicking once will bring up a window with a brief help message, while pointing to it and double clicking will bring up a different window with an extended message that can be scrolled, and that queries the user and interprets his responses. Cards are organized into stacks that can be traversed either linearly or through any other route the stack creator has defined. Standard facilities are provided for searching on card fields, sorting cards, creating dialogues with a user, and for many other functions that are useful in courseware design.

Authoring Systems. Authoring languages generally facilitate such operations as presenting a question to a student, reading and evaluating a response, and selecting the next question, problem, or task. But writing the sequence of instructions for an instructional unit is just one of many tasks required in the intelligent design and implementation of courseware. Courses and shorter stretches of code need to be tested and debugged, student responses need to be collected and analyzed, graphics generated, and reports constructed for teachers and others. The total collection of system routines, compilers, and other utilities, when interconnected to create a total working system, comprise an *authoring system.* Ideally, all courseware will be developed within a rich authoring environment that facilitates design, coding, testing, and revision.

WHY TECHNOLOGY AND INSTRUCTION?

Now, finally, we arrive at the central issue for this chapter: Why introduce technology into instruction? In case the warnings of Chapter 1 went unheeded, let us clarify immediately that the answer is not that we anticipate a revolution in education as a result of intelligent teaching systems or that the teacher-proof school is the answer to our literacy/numeracy/science problem. To be honest, there is little hard evidence that on-line instruction can make a big difference in the amount or quality of learning when comparisons are made to equally well resourced alternatives. Levin, Glass, and Meister

---

Design

    Hardware and software are both tools and technologies, to be used well or not so well, according to the adeptness of the implementers and the designers. *Systematic design* is also a tool and a technology, drawing on psychology, education, content area studies (e.g., mathematics, science), computer science, and upon years of experience by courseware developers. But it is no more a guarantee of good courseware than *liberté, égalité, fraternité* are of good government. Instead, as the remainder of this book teaches, it provides a systematic, logical base for development and improvement of principled instruction.

(1984) claim, for example, that for math and reading drill, peer tutoring is more cost-effective than CAI. Why, then, invest in technology for solving educational problems? We believe there are four reasons, any one of which could justify an investment in CAI.

Reasons for Using Technology in Education

Reason 1: New Capabilities. Computer technology can provide instructional experiences in areas that are either too expensive or too dangerous or too inaccessible to provide otherwise. Consider, for example, the potential for simulation that high-power computers and good color graphics systems provide. Students could experience travel and everyday life in outer space, experiment with dangerous chemicals and chemical processes, observe long-term effects on human and animal populations from alterations in reproductive or environmental conditions, and engage in complex stock market and legal interactions—without risk to life, limb, national solvency, or the environment. For some areas, such as flight training, the advantages of simulation are well established. For other areas, the potential is obvious, but much work remains to be done in the design of realistic and educational simulations.

A second new capability is in access to large databases. Without computer storage and retrieval techniques, instruction that centered on data-bound fields, such as demographics and meteorology, had severe limitations. Now, almost any imaginable type of problem involving large masses of data can be prepared for student solution, so long as the data are accessible on-line. Students can be asked to compare population characteristics across different geographic areas or census periods, plan art exhibits that draw upon the entire holdings of major North American and European museums, and test hypotheses about climatic change over extended periods of time.

Another capability derives directly from the color graphics potential of modern display equipment. Visualization of physical processes and of mathematical equations is a rapidly developing field. The potential to present multiple representations simultaneously makes this area especially important to CAI. Consider, for example, the power of a display containing a complex formula plus a color representation of the equation in three dimensions, with the added capability of allowing the user to enter values for the variables or to change the values of constants and see their immediate effects. Its importance to such new areas as chaos studies has been documented; in other fields, considerable work is underway in developing improved visualization techniques. We do not yet understand the full implications of visualization for instruction, but we do have some understanding of its importance in the advancement of science and technology (e.g., Ferguson, 1977), and some promising studies of its role in specific types of learning (Goldsmith, 1984; Willows & Houghton, 1987; Houghton & Willows, 1987).

Different in kind from the capabilities described above is the potential of on-line instruction to adapt to different learner, content, and pedagogical characteristics. For example, in rapidly changing technological fields, new device characteristics can be incorporated more quickly in on-line instruction than they can in print materials. Consider an automotive repair course. As each new automobile is produced, its characteristics can be entered into data tables and made available on-line for instruction that is developed around such tables. Obviously, when an entirely new concept is involved, such as in the switch from a carburetor to a fuel injection system, new instruction will need to be generated. Similarly, with generators that can utilize standard data to produce instruction in alternative formats, more variety can be entered into an on-line instructional system than would be possible with printed materials.

We have judiciously avoided the term *individualization* up to this point because of the confusion and distemper it often engenders. To some, knowingly or unknowingly, the ideal schooling has each child in a separate cubicle, working at his own pace for the entire day, advancing as far in each subject as his abilities and motivation will allow. This is what some mean by individualization. Others, including the majority of educators, have a more sober view of the degree to which instruction can or should be adapted to individual needs and abilities. For this text individualization will be value free. It will refer to *any* adaptation of instruction to an individual's needs or abilities. Computers offer a unique ability to store information about students and to interpret this information in terms of parameters in instructional programs. The resulting individualization might apply as well to students who are working in groups on common objectives as it does to students working independently on different objectives.

Individualizing to advance students at their optimal rates is desirable in some instructional contexts and not in others. A refresher course in industry on filtering techniques might have no other goal than to impart the course content as quickly as possible and, therefore, individual rates of advancement are appropriate. But elementary and to some degree secondary schooling has many other goals besides imparting curricular knowledge, including social, ethical, and emotional ones. Having each child always advancing at his own pace in subject areas without regard for interaction with others is seldom desirable or practicable. This does not rule out other approaches for adapting instruction to individual needs, or even occasionally allowing, within practical limits, advancement at individual paces. But it does remove complete individualization as a desired goal of schooling. Therefore, while at various places we discuss methods for adapting instruction to individual needs and abilities, we try to avoid any implication that complete individualization is a necessary goal of schooling.

Reason 2: Access. Computer delivery of instruction can reach remote areas where teachers can be sent only infrequently. It can also bring educational access to certain types of handicapped students and to homes. These advantages assume the existence of quality courseware that can be used profitably under the operating environments implied. For example, a world history course that is to be delivered to remote villages in Alaska must not only present and explain concepts and information but also be coupled with human instructors who, perhaps via telephone or electronic mail, can critique written work and answer student questions. Similarly, students with communications handicaps might, through prosthetic devices, be able to interact with computer instructional systems and thereby receive more hours per day of instruction than would be possible without technological assistance.

For home study and continuing education, on-line instruction is a potential benefit, but the advantages are only slowly being realized, due to equipment expense and courseware faults. In theory, people who are homebound could have access to almost any on-line course developed in the world. When problems of language differences, prerequisites, and courseware quality are factored in, some advantage remains, but its size is difficult to determine.

Reason 3: Efficiency. Assessing the efficiency of instructional methods is challenging, requiring careful control of variables that are often difficult to measure (e.g., student and teacher motivation, degree and quality of program implementation). For CAI, evaluation is further complicated by the limited number of sites in which this approach is institutionalized to the same degree as traditional methods or in which the separate contributions of CAI and non-CAI to learning can be identified. The results of many years of comparing CAI to other methods of instruction were summarized recently by Ross and Morrison (1988):

> Although the above qualities (interactive responding, personalized feedback, etc.) provide CAI with significant "face appeal," the fundamental question is how well it actually teaches. Research findings on this topic have generally been supportive . . . , but are not (and will probably never be) sufficiently strong or consistent to proclaim CAI as "better than traditional methods . . ." A more reasonable interpretation is that CAI possesses different delivery capabilities than lectures or textbooks, and thus will have advantages in some situations and disadvantages in others. (p. 227)

In business, industrial, and military settings, where instruction tends to be expensive and changing technologies require frequent changes in instructional content, online instruction has proven to be cost-effective, compared to available alternatives (U.S. Congress, 1988, pp. 74ff; Kulik, Kulik, & Shwalb, 1986). The case for elementary and secondary applications is more problematic to evaluate. Some studies (e.g., Ragosta, Holland, & Jamison, 1982; Kulik, Bangert, & Williams, 1983; Hawley et al., 1986) have found advantages for CAI over traditional instruction, while others (e.g., Clark, 1983; Levin et al., 1984) have found CAI less effective than other alternatives (e.g., peer tutoring). Cost-effectiveness is difficult to measure for formal schooling and tends to vary with teacher ability and attitude, student ability, and subject matter. It is also difficult to establish an agreed-upon value for quantity and quality of learning.

At the college and university level, on-line instruction appears to be cost-effective for certain types of short courses (e.g., library usage) where personnel costs can be reduced. When good courseware becomes as available as good textbooks, the cost-effectiveness of on-line instruction will probably improve. Until then, efficiency will be achieved in some areas, remain a goal for some, and perhaps never be realized in others.

Reason 4: Discipline. The struggle to produce good courseware has already begun to have a positive side effect, and this is in advancing the study of instruction itself. The very act of reducing instruction to something well-enough specified to be delivered by computer requires an understanding of learning and instruction that goes beyond what has been empirically established. From the uncertainties revealed in this design process come new research questions that focus attention on both practical and theoretical issues. Derek Bok (1985) recognized this possibility in reviewing the future role of technology in higher education.

> In the end, therefore, with all the exaggerated claims and the media hype, we can still look upon the new technology with cautious enthusiasm. At the very least, universities should manage to use technology to engage students in a more active process of thinking and problem solving that will help them learn more effectively. At best, the new

machines may also be a catalyst to hasten the development of new insights into human cognition and new ways of helping students learn. (p. 38)

Problems with Using Technology in Education

Our cold-sober, no-hype approach to this topic leads us, finally, to opening for the reader's consideration a number of potential problems with technology in education. One is that it is a discipline in which broken promises stand out like dried cornstalks in the winter fields. After the first decade of experiments in CAI, Oettinger (1969) coldly stated, "The technology-there-is fails in the schools-as-they-are. No one can tell for sure how to marry the technology-that-could-be with the schools-that-might-be" (p. 219). Suppes had promised that we would have "the personal services of a tutor as well-informed and responsive as Aristotle" (Suppes, 1966; cited in Bok, 1985, p. 32), but no such capabilities have materialized in the intervening 20-odd years and none appears to be within easy reach. In a generally upbeat report on technology and education, the Office of Technology Assessment in 1982 could, at best, say that information technology was "beginning to play an important role" and that it "holds significant promise" (U.S. Congress, 1982, p. 4).

Six years later this same agency, while noting that new interactive technologies "have already contributed to important improvements in education . . .", projected only a "steady but slow improvement in software (i.e., courseware), and spotty access to the technology by children" (U.S. Congress, 1988, p. 4). For interactive technology to realize its potential for improving education in the United States, this committee claims "A more focused effort to substantially expand the use of technology in education and attain more fully integrated applications across the curriculum will probably require new strategies and perhaps new authority" (p. 5).

Then, too, there is less than universal agreement on the virtues of on-line instruction. For example, some worry that at the elementary and secondary levels, it will divorce learning from social, moral, and emotional experience, and that it bears little relationship to creativity, intuition, and feeling (Cuban, 1986). This is certainly possible, but these same problems can result from overly mechanical human teaching, from inconsiderate administrators, and from overemphasis on factual learning. On-line instruction should not be viewed as an alternative to human instruction, but as one of many options for enhancing human instruction. If social, moral, and emotional experiences are considered important for schooling, then it is the responsibility of educators to ensure that they occur throughout the school year. Computers, if overused, could limit the time available for such learning but, like all other educational experiences, that is a result of human decision processes and not something intrinsic to computer instruction.

Further problems result from (1) the relatively high expense of both hardware purchase and courseware development, (2) the need to retrain teachers on the use of interactive technologies, and (3) the lack, particularly in elementary and secondary schools, of good courseware that can be integrated easily into the existing curriculum. Finally, we should note that the state of the art in educational psychology is far from what is desirable for planning effective on-line or off-line instruction. Few (if any) well-proven theorems, algorithms, or even heuristics exist for determining what is best for teaching topic x to student y under conditions a, b, and c. But we are not totally ignorant in this field, either. From a careful reading and reflecting on the research literature, and from teacher expertise and common sense, a reasonable beginning can be made on most topics. Then what is required is careful testing, evaluation, and revising, with enough of these cycles to converge on an acceptable solution. What the rest of this book tries to do is to raise the quality of the first attempt so that the number of revision cycles required will be minimal.

THE WORLD OF EDUCATIONAL TECHNOLOGY TODAY

The state of the art in on-line instruction is represented by two types of systems. In one, called *curriculum-based programs,* a complete course or major part of a course is implemented, along with all the management components required to make the course usable in an organized educational setting: sign-on, record keeping, student assignment, reporting, and so forth. Usually these systems involve multiple terminals and are hardware-dependent. They also tend to be expensive, and therefore few have been introduced.

The second type of state-of-the-art system is the research-based program that incorporates artificial intelligence techniques to extend the capabilities of instructional programs. Such systems usually originate from research laboratories in both universities and industry, run on high-powered workstations, and incorporate few aids for instructional management. Their goals are usually not immediate, practical implementation, but advancement of understanding. Unfortunately, funding for experimental work in on-line instruction has been severely limited over the past decade so that relatively few such systems have been developed and tested.

In the valley between the two thinly populated peaks just described reside the thousands of CAI programs advertised in the trade and professional journals and in the educational courseware catalogues. These are, for the most part, snippets of courses: lessons on specific topics, drills, games, a few simulations, and a few database-centered programs. While the general impression of this lot is none too good, its quality has improved in recent years as teachers have become more familiar with the capabilities and problems of computers and as professional organizations have begun to stress courseware quality. EDUCOM, for example, has an Educational Software Initiative (ESI), which distributes and publicizes a reference list of exemplary courseware.[1] Various other academic and professional organizations serve this field, including the Association for Computing Machinery (ACM), through their Computer Uses in Education special interest group (SIGCUE); the Association for the Advancement of Computing in Education (AACE); the International Society for Technology in Education (ISTE); and the National Educational Computing Conference (NECC). (See the appendix for a more complete list.)

An industry centered around on-line instructional materials has begun to form, including courseware specialty houses, courseware divisions within computer companies and textbook publishers, and other groups scattered across a variety of other es-

---

[1]EDUCOM is a nonprofit consortium of almost 600 colleges and universities, plus about 120 corporate associates. Established in 1964, its primary goal is to facilitate the introduction, use, and management of information technology. To this end it sponsors conferences, workshops and seminars; issues various publications, including a quarterly, *EDUCOM Review;* and maintains various task forces and consulting groups.

tablishments, including the military and educational consulting firms. Journals like *Electronic Learning* and the *Journal of Computer-Based Education* have gained a wide circulation, as have various newsletters and bulletin boards that serve the field. This may not yet qualify as a booming field, but it is certainly healthy and expanding.

SUMMARY

The interactive technologies that are important for on-line instruction include computer hardware and software, plus systematic design processes. Allied to computer hardware are new technologies for data storage, including CD-ROM and optical disk. Transmission technologies, like satellite communications and cable, might augment on-line learning but are not central to it. The important software technologies include graphics managers, authoring languages, authoring systems, and hybrid systems like HyperCard that combine features of databases, hypertext, and object-oriented programming.

On-line instruction should be considered for all types of instruction: formal courses, short courses, workshops, sales training, product maintenance training, and even on-line help. It should be considered not only within formal educational settings such as elementary and secondary schools and colleges, but also for instruction in prisons and museums, business and industry, military bases, community centers, and the like, and it should be considered for components of instruction (e.g., practice, testing, review, explanation) as well as for whole units (e.g., courses).

Technology should be considered in instruction for (1) capabilities that are generally not available otherwise, such as simulating travel to the moon or operation of a chemical-processing plant; (2) improved access to instruction for persons in remote or inaccessible areas or for handicapped or elderly persons; (3) increased efficiency, which can be realized in some but not all settings where on-line instruction is tried; and (4) advancing our understanding of teaching and learning.

CHAPTER 3

A History without Victories
Beginning with the Emergence of CAI from the Slimy Ooze of Programmed Instruction

> *"I know the present only through the television screen, whereas I have direct knowledge of the Middle Ages."*
>
> —Umberto Eco, *New York Times Book Review* (1984)

Having direct knowledge of the Middle Ages today is a remarkable feat, but direct knowledge of the first CAI programs is available to many. These programs emerged not in the late Ice Age but at the same time that Nabokov's *Lolita* was becoming a best seller and just a few years after the English runner Roger Bannister broke the 4-minute mile—in other words, in the late 1950s.

By the middle of 1987, over 2 million personal computers had been installed in elementary and secondary schools, leaving only 4% of America's public schools without computers, according to an article in the *Wall Street Journal* (Bulkeley, 1988). And according to a National Assessment of Educational Progress computing survey, released in April 1988, 87 percent of all 11th graders in the United States could correctly identify pictures of a keyboard and a floppy disk. Schools are awash in magazines, newsletters, and promotional materials on hardware and software, and new courseware announcements arrive with a frequency approaching nuclear resonance.

Yet the same article that reported on the penetration of computers into the public schools also reported that the heralded computer-learning revolution had yet to arrive (Bulkeley, 1988). "The potential of these machines as pedagogical tool remains largely untapped," reported another recent survey (Fisher, 1988, p. D1). The reasons given for this disparity between physical presence and instructional impact sound oddly familiar: limited access by students, limited machine power, poor teacher training, lousy instructional software, and incomplete integration of computers into the curriculum. There is more than a grain of truth to these plaints, yet taken together they do not fully explain the failure of computers to revolutionize schooling. We suggest that deeper problems exist, centered on the concepts of learning that have driven most courseware development in the past and on the models of school achievement (or lack thereof) assumed by computer learning enthusiasts.

In this chapter we lead the reader on a tour through recent computer time, beginning with the primordial sea of mechanical teaching machines, and wending forward to the bit-mapped, multi-megabyte workstations of today's school of tomorrow. This

> **Some Terminology**
>
> Words have been spoken for a hundred thousand years or more; dictionaries are a creation of the last 2000 years, and the need to define terms is of even more recent origin. Nevertheless, clarification of terminology is needed here. In the Introduction we bandied about the "C" terms: CAI, CBE, CAL, and ICAI. Here we examine a little more carefully the term *courseware*. For the present we won't be too fussy about what qualifies as courseware. A system that tries to teach introductory college physics definitely does, while a Pascal compiler by itself definitely does not. Help messages, such as one finds under certain operating systems and on-line documentation (e.g., the *man* command under UNIX) represent the gray transition zone from noninstruction to instruction. On the one hand, these features have an educational function; on the other hand, they are generally totally passive, acting more as information retrieval than instruction. In this text we restrict courseware to mean those programs that are educational in intent and allow student interactions, at least at the level of asking or answering questions.

ambit will pass through a number of recently identified periods in the evolution of computer-based learning, pausing long enough in each to observe its accomplishments, its failures, and its perceptions of why the revolution had not yet arrived. The belief in an inevitable computer-learning revolution and the rationalization of its failure represent the constants across all the periods traversed. Our denouement, contained in a brief concluding section, reflects on the failings of the past but at the same time creates sufficient optimism about the future for the reader to justify continuing into the succeeding chapters.

THE AGES OF CAI

Computer-aided instruction emerged from the slimy ooze of programmed instruction and teaching machines in the late 1950s and since then has zigged and zagged through four distinct phases in its search for acceptance in education. Each phase is marked by its attitudes toward hardware and software needs, toward the psychology of learning, and by its interpretations of the barriers to wider adoption in the schools and colleges.

The early Pleistocene of CAI, labeled here the Age of Engineers, extends from 1958, when the earliest applications of computers to teaching were considered, until 1961, when the first conference on application of digital computers to automated instruction was held (see Coulson, 1962). This is an age characterized primarily by hardware issues and, in particular, by how to connect terminals, slide projectors, and other input-output devices to computers for practical interaction.

The Age of Acronyms extended from 1962 until 1967. During this period, increased government and military funding led to the initiation of several major CAI projects, which were characterized as much by their clever acronyms (e.g., CLASS, PLATO, SOCRATES, SAID) as they were by their computational and psychological orientations.

Third was the Age of the Titans, in particular, PLATO and TICCIT, which received extensive funding, publicity, and critical assessment during this time. Major evaluation studies, carried out by the Educational Testing Service and published in the late 1970s (Murphy & Appel, 1977; Alderman, 1978), marked the end of this era of inflated expectations and provided a basis for a more sober and perhaps more productive assessment of the potential role of CAI in instruction.

The present age, the Age of Small Wonders, began in 1977 with the manufacture of the first complete microcomputers and continues through the present day. It is marked by a major shift in school attitudes toward CAI and a substantial revival of industrial interest in producing CAI hardware and software. These ages, with their major and minor themes, are presented below.

THE AGE OF ENGINEERS

Machines for teaching did not originate with modern digital computers, but instead with mechanical testing systems used by psychologists for studying learning. Mechanical devices that presented questions printed on a paper roll and that scored multiple-choice responses were developed in the 1920s by S. L. Pressey at Ohio State University (Pressey, 1926; Benjamin, 1988). In Pressey's original device, as well as in later versions that he and others developed, the student could not advance to the next frame (i.e., question) until the correct response was given to the current frame (Pressey, 1926). (See Figures 3.1 and 3.2.) Little (1934) reported on studies of learning done with a similar contraption that allowed true and false responses, kept a cumulative count of tries, and allowed the student to recycle through the questions until she answered each question correctly on a single pass. This procedure was used twice each week for administering a pretest on material to be taught in traditional classes (and laboratory sessions) for an undergraduate educational psychology course.

Mechanical and electrical devices for testing and for self-instruction continued to

Figure 3.1. A self-scoring, multiple-choice device exhibited by Pressey in 1924–25. (From S. L. Pressey, A simple apparatus which gives tests and scores—and teaches. Reprinted in A. A. Lumsdaine and R. Glaser, eds., *Teaching Machines and Programmed Learning. A Source Book* (Washington, D.C.: National Education Association, 1960), pp. 36, 38. Copyright 1960 by the National Education Association. Reprinted by permission.)

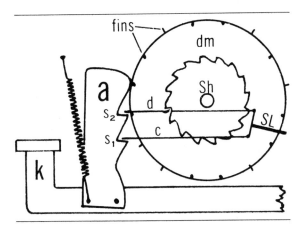

Figure 3.2. Schematic diagram of Pressey's device. (From S. L. Pressey, A simple apparatus which gives tests and scores—and teaches. Reprinted in A. A. Lumsdaine and R. Glaser, eds., *Teaching Machines and Programmed Learning. A Source Book* (Washington, D.C.: National Education Association, 1960), pp. 36, 38. Copyright 1960 by the National Education Association. Reprinted by permission.)

be developed and tried out through the 1930s and 1940s (Pressey, 1950), but until Skinner's seminal work on programmed instruction and teaching machines in the 1950s, widespread interest in mechanical aids to instruction was lacking. Skinner, who had developed a widely accepted theory of learning based on techniques originally designed for training rats and pigeons, became interested in the early 1950s in machines that could implement his approach to instruction. Earlier he had developed the Skinner box, a device that contained (originally) a rat, a lever for the rat to push, and a mechanism that released a food pellet when the lever was pushed. His theory of *operant behavior* (or *operant conditioning*), derived mostly from studies of rat and pigeon behavior in the Skinner box, was then applied to human learning (Skinner, 1954, 1963).

In operant conditioning, a stimulus is presented and maintained until a correct response is made. Then a contingent, reinforcing stimulus is presented. In teaching machines a question typically represents the initial stimulus and a correct answer, the response. Reinforcement comes in telling the student she is correct. Notice, however, that if an incorrect response is given, contingent reinforcement does not occur and therefore (in Skinner's theory) no learning takes place. This led Skinner and others of similar persuasion to reduce learning programs to short, easy steps that minimized the possibility of error. This narrow view of learning based on a black-box, input/output learning theory, dominated instructional psychology in the 1950s and well into the 1960s, although cogent criticism of it did appear (e.g., Pressey, 1959).

Of interest here is not, however, the failings of operant conditioning as a psychological theory or practical scheme for instruction but rather the direct line of development from teaching machines to computer-aided instruction. From programmed instruction, which was the title given to the design of short-step sequences based on Skinnerian conditioning, came programmed textbooks (Reid, 1969), a flood of mechanical teaching machines, and then, by the late 1950s, computer control of the many variations of programmed instruction that developed from the orthodox Skinner view. Of particular importance in this expansion of programmed instruction was the work on branching initiated by Crowder (e.g., Crowder, 1963).

One of the earliest uses of computers in instruction occurred in the late 1950s at IBM's Research Center where an IBM 650 computer was used to simulate a teaching machine (Rath, Anderson, & Brainerd, 1959). A six-part program for teaching the basics of binary arithmetic was developed, using a single typewriter entry station. At about the same time, a computer-controlled slide projection system for a teaching machine was being developed in California at Systems Development Corporation (Coulson & Silberman, 1962) and an on-line program for teaching analytic geometry was being developed in Massachusetts at Bolt Beranek and Newman, Inc. (Licklider, 1962).

Even in these early experiments, which were viewed mostly as extensions of teaching machines, more eclectic learning psychologies were employed. In a series of three on-line courses developed at IBM in the early 1960s, for example, student histories were kept in the form of error buckets that retained the addresses of items that had been missed a given number of times during instruction. Subsequent instruction could mix review items with new items (Uttal, 1962). By this time the IBM 650 system, originally used for teaching binary arithmetic with a single, student "inquiry station," had been expanded to a 20-station system and new courses developed in stenotype, psychological statistics, and German reading. The decision logic for the statistics program allowed for various types of on-line help, alternate problems, and variable negative feedback based on the number of errors the student had made.

Although this period was dominated by hardware problems and characterized by an unbridled enthusiasm for the potential of computers to individualize instruction, some cautionary words were occasionally uttered. For example, while most enthusiasts of technology in education were riding the surge of the post-Sputnik criticism of traditional education in the United States, Pressey, the inventor of the teaching machine, was offering a more balanced view to a conference on automatic teaching.

> It is not enough that in the experimental situation the proposed new methods work well. They must do so in the average situation where they are to be used and with average people there; and they must there be sufficiently better than the methods and materials these same people have been using, that a changeover is both warranted and feasible. (Pressey, 1959, p. 196)

Confusion of statistical significance with educational significance, nevertheless, has continued to the present day. What Pressey rightly observed was that being better by itself did not necessarily justify the adoption of a new teaching method, be it CAI or any other. To merit adoption, the method had not only to prove itself worthy in normal instructional situations (i.e., show ecological validity), but also to be so much better than existing methods that the institutional costs and anxieties of change could be justified. The *fallacy of statistical significance* results from the failure to recognize this reality. Change in education is usually expensive and is rarely done willingly just to gain a few percentage points of advantage over the status quo.

When the Age of Engineers drew to a close in the early 1960s, CAI had barely emerged as an entity separate from the mechanical implementation of programmed instruction. Improved hardware and software were seen as major needs, particularly in servicing many users (i.e., students) at once. Skinnerian psychology dominated, although many minor and one or two major deviations had developed. The primary barriers to school adoption were seen as high costs and teacher resistance, although a few recognized that the lack of an adequate research base on school learning was also a barrier (Gentile, 1967). Most assumed, however, that the product was ready, if only the consumer would believe what she was told and not what she saw.

What was not realized, except by an unassertive few, was the fragility of the empirical support for most of the psychological assumptions that drove courseware development at the time. In a brief but devastating review entitled "Taps for Teaching Machines,'' Feldhusen (1963) analyzed the research support for the cardinal principles of programmed learning: active, overt learner participation, small step size, immediate feedback, reinforcement of correct responses, and so forth, and in all cases found meaningful exceptions. That is, he found reasonable conditions under which the absence of one or another of these variables did not result in reduced learning.

Instead of the uniformly enthusiastic reports of learner gains and learner excitement for programmed instruction produced by Skinner et al., Feldhusen (1963) found reports of student boredom and of what was called the "pall effect." One observation of note was that materials written to ensure 90 to 95 percent correct response rates were so inherently simple that learners didn't need feedback to reassure them of giving correct responses. But as Bergson noted, faith is not in moving mountains, but in not seeing that mountains move.

Many psychologists as well as educators and computer programmers continued to find the principles of programmed instruction attractive in spite of their discredited support. These same people seem to have assumed that the majority of the variance in school achievement could be accounted for by variables that teachers could control. Others, like Stephens (1967), suggested otherwise, but the belief that school achievement can be radically altered by simple, quick fixes resides deep within the human soul. Each succeeding age was to make this same mistake, and then to rationalize its failures with variables other than the ones that were truly significant.

THE AGE OF ACRONYMS

Several CAI projects started in the late 1950s and early 1960s were, by the middle 1960s, unfettered by their teaching-machine origins. One of these, the PLATO project, began at the University of Illinois as a "research project in the field of teaching machines" (Bitzer, Braunfeld, & Lichtenberger, 1962, p. 205). PLATO (Programmed Logic for Automatic Teaching Operations) initially allowed experiments with only a single user; PLATO II, developed in the early 1960s on the University of Illinois–designed system, the ILLIAC, allowed two users, as shown in Figure 3.3. PLATO III, installed in late 1964 on a CDC 1604, was a true multi-user system that utilized an extended version of FORTRAN as an authoring language for instructional programs. It also allowed for a variety of instructional modes, including games and simulations. The developers of PLATO clearly disassociated PLATO III from the teaching-machine camp.

> Without wanting to underrate the usefulness of computer-based systems for such role learning situations as arithmetic drill and practice, we think it important to dispel the notion that computer-assisted instruction is limited to this type of application or is, in effect, an automated version of the Skinner teaching machine. The teaching strategies developed for PLATO III are so far removed from this approach as to represent a totally different concept of the role of computer-based systems in education. (Alpert & Bitzer, 1970, pp. 1583ff)

Other major projects of the period with proper acronyms included SAID (Speech Auto-Instructional Device) at the University of Michigan, CLASS (Computer-based Laboratory for Automation of School Systems) at Systems Development Corporation,

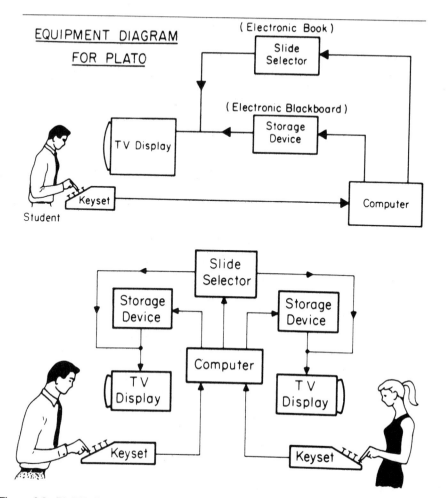

Figure 3.3. PLATO II (From D. L. Bitzer, E. R. Lyman, and J. A. Easley, Jr., 1966. The uses of PLATO, a computer controlled teaching system, *Audiovisual Instruction* 11(1), p. 18. Copyright 1966 by the Association for Educational Communication and Technology. Reprinted by permission.)

and SOCRATES (System for Organizing Content to Review and Teach Educational Subjects). Two projects without acronyms, however, were considerably more influential in shaping the direction of CAI.

The first of these was a project started at the Institute for Mathematical Studies in the Social Sciences at Stanford University under the direction of Patrick Suppes and Richard Atkinson. Using primarily drill approaches, the Stanford project was the first to do extensive field testing of CAI materials in a school setting (Suppes & Morningstar, 1969; Atkinson, et al., 1971). This work began on a PDP-1 Computer but changed in 1965–66 to an IBM 1500 system that the Stanford Project had helped IBM design. While this system was placed in a number of university research settings, IBM discontinued support of it in 1970. Experience gained from the Stanford experiments has been incorporated in the materials now sold commercially by Computer Curriculum Corporation, which was started in late 1967 by Suppes, Atkinson, and Wilson.

But the most innovative work of this period, and perhaps of all four periods, was done at Bolt Beranek and Newman, Inc., in Cambridge, Massachusetts, where cognitive processes rather than reinforcement theory formed the psychological base for instructional experimentation. Beginning with experiments on the graphic display of simple functions, systems were developed for teaching medical diagnosis, military strategy, and decision making in business and management. Work originated by Feurzeig on children's problem-solving techniques, and continued later by Feurzeig, Bobrow, and Papert, led to the development of LOGO, a language designed to foster problem-solving abilities in children. This tradition was continued into the period to be discussed shortly with the efforts by Carbonell to utilize artificial intelligence techniques in CAI, and later with experiments on computer coaching.

The Advent of Authoring Languages

With the development of large-scale systems such as CLASS and PLATO, the programming bottleneck became more evident. One hundred or more hours of programming was typically required for each hour of delivered CAI. Given the simplistic notions of instruction that dominated the early CAI system, the majority of the early lessons were based on *frames,* in which a small amount of explanatory text was presented, a question asked, and then another frame selected on the basis of the response. To facilitate this form of lesson, a number of authoring languages were developed in the middle 1960s, all based on frame-by-frame instruction. The best known of these included PLANIT (SDC), COURSEWRITER (IBM), and CATO (University of Illinois). A typical question frame in PLANIT, entered interactively via teletype, could look like this. (Designer responses are underlined. Everything else is generated by PLANIT.)

- FRAME 1.00 LABEL = *MATH*
- 2. SQ.
- *?*
- 2. SPECIFY QUESTION
- *HOW MUCH IS 3 SQUARED?*
- *
- 3. SA.
- *A+9*
- *B 6*
- *
- 4. SAT.
- *AF:PRETTY GOOD B:4*
- *BR: DON'T ADD. TRY AGAIN.*
- *−R:NO. TRY AGAIN.*
- *
- *−C:COUNT=COUNT+1*

In this frame a question is specified in part 2, correct and anticipated incorrect answers in part 3, and corresponding actions to take in part 4. Data storage is extremely limited as is data manipulation outside of simple mathematical functions. The main power of languages like PLANIT and COURSEWRITER came in their frame management and answer-judging capabilities. The latter included phonetic and keyword matching for verbal responses and algebraic matching for quantitative (formula) responses.

In the late 1960s the PLATO Project developed TUTOR, an authoring language that incorporated features of assembly and compiler languages as well as extended answer-judging facilities. Although initially limited by its restricted data storage facilities, TUTOR developed eclectically over the next 15 years to include, among a plethora of other features, better data storage, based on the FORTRAN common model. By the 1970s, three major approaches to authoring languages had developed: (1) standard programming languages, of which BASIC was and is still today the leader; (2) frame-oriented systems like PLANIT, TUTOR, and PILOT; and (3) template systems like TICCIT. The latter utilizes a rather rigid deductive approach to instruction whereby authors specify which of a small set of frames they intend to use, and then submit required categories of information. Instruction is almost exclusively deductive, proceeding from rule or principle to example.

PILOT, which is similar in structure to PLANIT and COURSEWRITER, was developed by John Starkweather at the University of California Medical Center for simulating psychiatric interviewing. This system grew from an earlier CAI-like language, COMPUTEST, and was further developed by several other people in the San Francisco Bay area. An early version was developed at Dartmouth in 1970, and current versions, some of which allow intermixing of BASIC code, are available for microcomputers.

BASIC is a variation on FORTRAN and is extremely popular in grade school and high school computing classes. According to one of its authors, it first appeared at 4 A.M. on May 1, 1964, at Dartmouth College, the invention of John Kemeny and Thomas Kurtz (Kemeny & Kurtz, 1984). BASIC, unlike Pascal or C, is highly forgiving of programming excesses, such as the mixing of arithmetic types and the failure to declare small arrays. What it provides in control and data declaration freedom, it takes back in answer judging, which must be coded from scratch.

While programmed instruction dominated the instructional approaches at the beginning of this period, a wide variety of approaches could be found by 1967 when this era was summarized in a special issue of the *IEEE Transactions on Human Factors in Electronics*. Simulations, games and tutorial dialogues had been designed, along with an oversupply of drill exercises. Articles in the special issue of the *IEEE Transactions* described the PLATO, CLASS, and BB&N projects, gave an example of an early version of LOGO, used for programming pig Latin, and surveyed available hardware systems. Feurzeig (1965), in presenting the LOGO example, even suggested that "English students at many levels may some day be using this and similar languages" (p. 87).[1]

LOGO has a long and interesting history, both as an instructional environment (i.e., microworld) and as a focus for controversy over both the value of discovery-oriented approaches to engendering higher cognition in children and the appropriate methodologies to apply to the evaluation of nontraditional instructional methods. In

---

[1]A slightly different orientation to the development of LOGO is presented in Papert (1980).

general, studies of LOGO classrooms have failed to find systematic advantages for this system as a facilitator of cognitive abilities. Its discovery-oriented approach has not resulted in major changes in the behavior of either teachers or students who have used it (Pea, Kurland, & Hawkins, 1985; Pea, Soloway, & Spohrer, 1987). Papert (1987) blames the failure to find more consistent positive results in part on the evaluation methodologies used, but others find little favor in this argument (Pea, 1987; Becker, 1987). In addition, Becker (1987) points out that in a 1985 survey of instructional uses of school computers, nearly three quarters of all elementary-level teachers using LOGO were not using it for regular instruction but for enrichment. The average LOGO classroom had only three computers for 21 students and was three times more likely to contain high-ability than low-ability students.

Zinn (1968), in summarizing CAI up to the end of this period, emphasized the high cost of producing courseware: $200,000 to $2,000,000 for 100 hours of adjunct material for a one-year course. He also stressed the need for tools for author and researcher, a need that yet remains to be met adequately. High costs, inadequate courseware, and lack of teacher acceptance were seen as the main barriers to wider use of CAI.

Yet, just as Pressey in 1959 had cautioned about the outcomes that were required for CAI to be useful, so did others in this period examine CAI critically. Perhaps the most penetrating criticisms were made by an educator, Philip W. Jackson, in the Horace Mann Lecture at the University of Pittsburgh in 1967. Jackson (1968) asserted that many advantages of individual instruction delivered by a teacher, including physical and psychological proximity, and the communication of feelings, could not be duplicated by a computer. He also pointed out that graded school systems and not teachers were the greatest barriers to meeting individual differences in learning and that immediate reinforcement, particularly on errors, could be counterproductive. But perhaps his most enduring warning was that "the greatest intellectual challenge of our time is not how to design machines that behave more and more like humans, but rather, how to protect humans from being treated more and more like machines" (Jackson, 1968, p. 66).

THE AGE OF THE TITANS

While center stage in the CAI drama was occupied from the late 1960s until the late 1970s by two heavily funded CAI systems, PLATO and TICCIT, which are described shortly, other influential work also was done in the wings and antechambers. Therefore, to label the years from 1968 through 1976 as the "Age of the Titans" risks doing an injustice to a number of important contributions. We therefore describe these other themes before presenting the heavyweights.

Artificial Intelligence in CAI

One important line of development during this period, which has already been briefly described, was the application of artificial intelligence techniques to CAI. In the middle 1960s, attempts were already being made to develop generative systems for CAI. Uttal (1962) had used an equation generator to create mathematical problems in one of the earliest CAI lessons on record, and Uhr (1967) had developed SNOBOL programs on an IBM 7090 to generate instructional programs directly from books. But the first application of artificial intelligence techniques directly to instruction occurred in Carbonell's SCHOLAR, which used a semantic net to store geographical information (Carbonell, 1970). SCHOLAR could either teach or test a student, or allow a student to ask it questions. This mixed-mode approach to instruction had been used earlier at BB&N in the SOCRATIC system, which taught medical diagnosis (Swets & Feurzeig, 1965). Using rudimentary natural-language analysis and inferencing, SCHOLAR was successful, not so much for what it did as a CAI system but for the influence of its techniques on later work in CAI. (For further information on SCHOLAR, see Chapter 8.)

While attempts were made to continue SCHOLAR after Carbonell's untimely death, particularly with the WHY system (Stevens & Collins, 1977), emphasis in the application of AI techniques shifted to computer coaching, a term coined by Goldstein (1977). A variety of systems developed at BB&N, MIT, and elsewhere (e.g., SOPHIE, WUMPUS, BUGGY, West Coach) explored both the range of application of coaching in CAI and principles to be employed for effective use of this approach to instruction (Sleeman & Brown, 1982). Most of these systems focused primarily upon diagnosis of student skill deficits or misconceptions (i.e., bugs). Representation of expert knowledge in the form of skill graphs or even lists became the framework upon which student models were constructed. Thus the expert-novice paradigm was translated into an instructional guide, both directly in terms of the superordinate-subordinate skill relationships in the expert model and more subtly in the elimination of intervening skill configurations that might represent correct intermediate stages of competence but differ structurally from the expert model.

By updating the expert model with information derived from student performance on specific tasks, the current status of the student relative to the expert model could be maintained. In West Coach, for example, information about the student's knowledge of specific features of the game was obtained through responses to randomly generated problems that required those features for optimal solution (Burton & Brown, 1979). In contrast, BUGGY had the ability to generate problems containing specified features (e.g., single-column borrow) and could simulate response behavior for specified student bugs (e.g., borrow but not decrement) (Brown & Burton, 1978; Burton, 1982). Although the abilities of these programs to instruct directly were limited, they demonstrated a profitable direction for CAI that helped move at least a segment of the field beyond simple frame-by-frame courseware. Many of the ideas from these systems have influenced present-day courseware design. Since several of these systems will be discussed in considerable detail in later chapters, this genre of CAI will not be explained further here. Nevertheless, the limited space devoted to them should not detract from their importance, which was large.

Authoring Languages

A second line of development focused on the design of authoring languages and authoring environments. Some new languages were developed (e.g., NATAL-74®), some old ones were overhauled (e.g., PILOT, COURSEWRITER), and even a few regular programming languages were beefed up to do graceful response handling and branching (e.g., FORTRAN/MIL). The most interesting of the new languages was NATAL-74, whose design was sponsored by the National Research Council in Canada. NATAL-74 is a block-structured language, similar to ALGOL, that requires type declarations and fairly standard control structures, but has extensive answer-judging facilities and even a frame mode for less experienced programmers (Brahan & Godfrey, 1984). At the same time the PLATO system was expanded to a full authoring environment, incorporating not only the authoring language TUTOR, but a screen editor, debugging and tryout aids, on-line documentation, a management system, library facilities, mail, bulletin boards, and more yet.

Evaluation

A third important minor theme of this period was the continued development and testing of courseware. Representative of the contributions to educational evaluation made by CAI projects was the work done at the University of Alberta by Hunka, Romaniuk, and their colleagues in developing and applying new techniques for formative and summative evaluation (e.g., Romaniuk, 1978). What was especially remarkable about the Alberta courseware development was the quantity and quality of material produced, even though the only hardware available for most of this period was an IBM 1500 system.

The Titans Themselves

While CAI development and testing continued not only in the United States and Canada but also in France, England, West Germany, Israel, and a few other nations, primary attention was centered on the PLATO and TICCIT projects, and, in particular, on the NSF-sponsored evaluation of these two systems.

Background: PLATO and TICCIT. PLATO's infancy was described above, from its nativity through its early childhood as an ILLIAC (PLATO I-II) and then a CDC 1604 system (PLATO III). Plans for PLATO IV were begun in the late 1960s and included development of a flat plasma display panel to replace the conventional CRT display, and a new language, TUTOR, to replace the CATO system developed for PLATO III. Although originally configured as a 4,000-terminal system, PLATO IV at the University of Illinois operated through most of the 1970s with 1,000 terminals connected to twin CDC 6500s. The plasma display terminal which was constructed at the Computer-based Education Research Laboratory (CERL) in Urbana, Illinois, had a keyboard and a rear-projection microfiche projector. This latter contraption, as well as an auxiliary audio system, was driven by compressed air. Neither proved to be reliable or practical and in time were quietly retired.

PLATO IV's main successes during this period were in (1) connecting hundreds of remote sites, including research laboratories, universities, and schools, into a central system, and (2) developing an extensive library of instructional materials. While the quality of a large segment of this curricular mass is questionable, there were clearly exemplary materials developed, including some well-known math games (e.g., West, Darts) and genetics and chemistry lab simulations. The plasma panel, which could be programmed as a 512×512 dot matrix or as a 32×64 character display, allowed (for its time) interesting mixtures of text and graphics, and was flicker-free and stable—qualities difficult to match at the time.

Where the expectations of PLATO's designers were not met, however, was in the design of courseware. Contrary to the assumptions that drove the design of TUTOR, teachers rarely became good PLATO programmers. After an attempt to teach community college instructors to design their own courseware failed, the PLATO project was forced to hire a professional staff to meet its obligations to the NSF evaluation study. This same lesson has been learned over and over at other PLATO sites and at almost every other type of CAI installation, even with authoring languages far easier to learn than TUTOR.

TICCIT, in contrast to PLATO, joined the CAI procession relatively late, being conceived at MITRE Corporation in 1968. From its start it focused on demonstrating low-cost, multiuser CAI, with off-the-shelf components. Staff members at MITRE Corporation developed the technical concept for TICCIT, while researchers at the University of Texas and at Brigham Young University developed the instructional model and courseware. During 1972, the directors of the University of Texas TICCIT Project moved to BYU, where the TICCIT courseware development continued. (For further information on the history of TICCIT, see Bunderson & Faust, 1976, and Morton, 1976. Instructional issues related to TICCIT are discussed in Merrill, 1980, and Merrill, Schneider & Fletcher, 1980.) The original TICCIT system, shown in Figure 3.4, consisted of twin Nova 840 processors, 128 color TV receivers, keyboards, videotape players, and various other peripheral devices (disks, etc.).

Initial courseware efforts were concentrated at a community college level with precalculus mathematics and English composition and grammar. The instructional model for TICCIT courseware was built on the assumption that instructional methods are independent of course content. Courses are first divided into units, then units into lessons, and then lessons into segments. Each segment included a single rule or generalization that was explained in four different styles. Explanations were supplemented with instances and practice problems. Different types of orientation and help materials were also available on-line. Students could select topics to study, as well as difficulty levels, instructional sequence, and pace. In contrast to the PLATO project, however, courseware development in the TICCIT project was done by teams composed of content specialists, instructional designers, and programmers. This approach appears to have yielded a smooth and reasonably consistent production of courseware. (For more information on the TICCIT instructional model, see Chapter 8.)

Beginning in 1972, MITRE Corporation was funded by the National Science Foundation to develop and demonstrate the TICCIT system at community colleges. Systems were eventually installed at two such sites, and evaluation studies were done during the 1975 and 1976 school terms. At the same time that NSF was initiating the TICCIT community college project, it initiated a similar project with the PLATO project—to complete the development of PLATO IV and to demonstrate its application to elementary and community college-level instruction. After several false starts, evaluation of PLATO in five community colleges and in four elementary schools began in the fall of 1974. Both evaluation studies were directed by the Educational Testing Service (ETS).

Evaluation Results. Due to the complexities inherent in the initial implementation of instructional systems based on new technologies, both evaluation studies present interpretation difficulties.[2] In neither case was a completely stable instructional procedure demonstrated for the CAI courses. And since none of the courses utilized CAI exclusively, the results reflect not only CAI per se, but the admixture of CAI with lecture

---

[2]The results given here are derived from the final reports on the TICCIT and PLATO evaluations, issued by Educational Testing Service. See Murphy & Appel (1977); Swinton, Amarel, & Morgan (1978); and Alderman (1978).

and laboratory sessions. Furthermore, we have little information on the quality of the CAI materials themselves. The evaluation design selected by ETS might have been appropriate for well-institutionalized methods but had serious limitations with methodologies that were still being developed as the evaluation was proceeding. This design was a traditional comparison of instructional methods, pitting CAI courses against the same courses taught with lecture sessions.

The results yielded limited support for CAI, especially when considered against the considerable instructional support given to the sites in which the CAI systems were installed. PLATO at the community college level was found to have generally favorable effects on student attitudes toward CAI learning, but no effect on student attrition and no effect on learning. In more precise terms, students achieved no better in PLATO courses than they did in comparable lecture courses, nor did they tend to complete PLATO courses at a higher rate than they completed lecture courses. At the elementary level, outcomes varied by subject area. The PLATO elementary mathematics curriculum was successful in an "add-on" mode, leading to large achievement gains in grades 4–6 and moderate positive attitude changes in grades 4 and 5.

In contrast, the elementary reading curriculum had a negative impact on first grade reading achievement (pilot year) and on kindergarten reading readiness (demonstration year). No effects on attitudes were found. Part of the failure of the reading curriculum was attributed by the evaluators to curriculum design flaws, in particular, to a discrete and slow-moving succession of skills that failed to emphasize meaning. Part also appeared to result from implementation flaws (e.g., not involving teachers sufficiently) and from hardware failures, particularly with auxiliary equipment. In reviewing both the mathematics and reading results in the full context of elementary schooling, the evaluators concluded that "Without considerable cost reduction, we do not see PLATO IV as an economically viable delivery system for elementary schools, even when provided lessons as attractive and effective as those developed by the PLATO elementary mathematics groups" (Swinton, Amarel, & Morgan, 1978, p. 25).

TICCIT had a generally negative impact on student attitudes and a uniform and largely negative impact on course completion. For example, the course completion rate for traditional lecture sections in mathematics was 50 percent while for comparable TICCIT sections it was 16 percent. In general, only the better prepared students survived the TICCIT courses. Among the course survivors, TICCIT students tended to score higher on the achievement tests given at the end of the courses, but this advantage was 5 percent or less for English and slightly over 10 percent for mathematics, hardly overwhelming support for a major change in instructional methods.

In summary, neither system reached that level of significance that Pressey suggested as necessary to justify a change in school practice. What might have happened had the CAI courses gone on for several more years, with continual adjustment and improvement, cannot be determined. Neither system has gained entry to elementary or secondary schooling, and manufacturers have moved away from the large or midi-machine configurations for CAI to microcomputer delivery—as demanded by the current age, the Age of Small Wonders.

The Age of the Titans ended with a whimper, which was better than the end of the Age of the Titans in classical Greek mythology, but not much better.[3] Computer

---

[3]For a brief account of the overthrow of the Titans by Cronus's children under the leadership of Zeus, see Dan S. Norton and Peters Rushton, *Classical Myths in English Literature* (New York: Rinehart & Co., 1952).

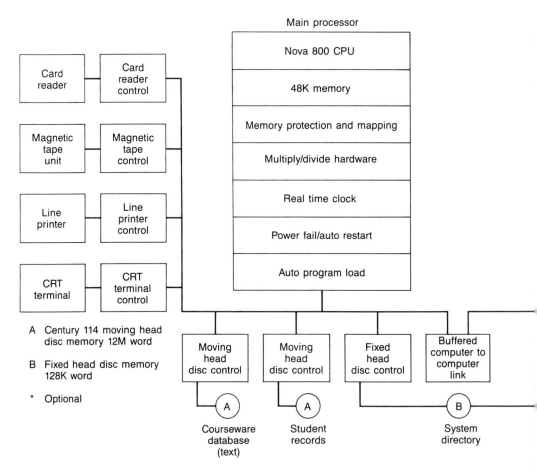

Figure 3.4. TICCIT System Block Diagram (From R. P. Morton, 1976, The Variety of TIC-CIT systems—An overview, *SIGCSE Bulletin 8*(1), (SIGCUE Topics Vol. 2), p. 145. Copyright 1975 by Association for Computing Machinery, Inc. Reprinted by permission.)

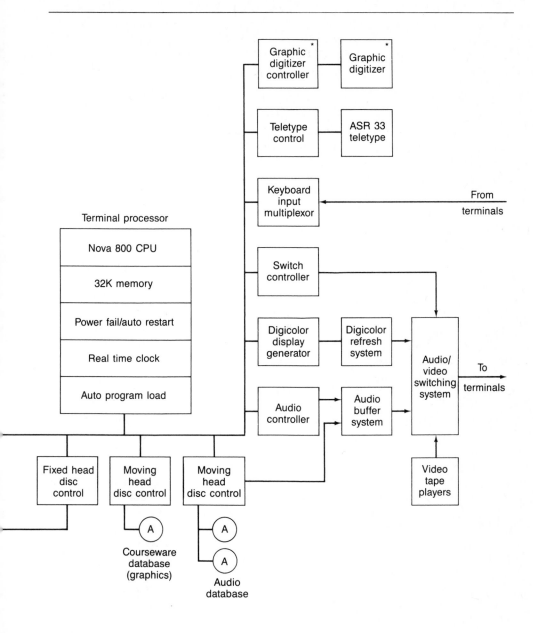

hardware and software were no longer portrayed as barriers to CAI acceptance, and instructional models were no longer restricted to black-box types, yet acceptance of CAI was still relatively low, for reasons that were seldom examined adequately. One obvious cause was that CAI was overhyped and oversold as a stand-alone answer to education's ills. The failure of TICCIT and PLATO to engender significant improvements in achievement was especially disastrous against this background of exaggerated promise.

But a second and perhaps more fundamental barrier was that teachers were not ready to have computers in the classroom, regardless of their value. As Clifford (1973) points out, most innovations reach education through cultural diffusion. Teachers, principals, and others are part of the masses and, as such, bring popular cultural values into the schools. So long as computers were seen as giant brains, attended to by a technological elite, there was little hope that teachers would be comfortable with them as classroom colleagues. But all of this was changed by the Age of Small Wonders.

THE AGE OF SMALL WONDERS

When the stage lights darkened on the Age of the Titans, Control Data Corporation, the University of Illinois, and several other universities were developing PLATO courseware. Hazeltine, a few community colleges, and a few military installations were developing TICCIT lessons, and several other CAI products were making small dents in the educational marketplace, including those of CCC and DEC. More minicomputer systems were to come, but what began as a small trickle in 1977 had become a flood by the early 1980s and has continued to surge across the globe. This is the onslaught of microcomputers, which, in every flavor, size, and configuration, have come marching into schoolhouses. CAI has started a second (third?) renaissance, with courses and lessons by the thousands now being advertised.

What has brought computers into the schools and what has stimulated CAI, however, has not been innovations in CAI itself, or new evidence of its merits. Those reams and reams of courseware catalogs now being published are testimonials to an unparalleled, ill-conceived, and often sloppily implemented pretense to instruction. Instructionally sound courseware, usable in the context of an established curriculum, is rare. No, the microcomputer has yet to engender a quantum increase in usable CAI. Instead, it has found its way into the home and the office through low prices and adequately implemented word processors, spreadsheets, and the like. Its commonplaceness, as represented by its appearance in cartoons, incidental news items, and interior design photographs, as well as its presence on the discount department store shelves, is what has changed the attitudes of teachers. From its acceptance in mass culture, particularly in the United States, the microcomputer has entered the classroom, carried by parents, students, and teachers alike. Once again cultural diffusion was the transmission route from innovation to education.[4]

The technical revolution that made the computer possible began in the late 1960s with the development of manufacturing techniques for multicomponent microelec-

---

[4]The extent of microcomputer usage in schools was surveyed in the mid–1980s by the Center for Organization of Schools at Johns Hopkins University. See Becker (1986, 1987) for a summary of results. More recent but less extensive data are reported by Bulkeley (1988) and Fisher (1988).

tronic circuits on single *chips*. In 1959 each circuit component required its own chip. By 1964 10 components could be packed on a single chip; by 1970 1,000 could fit in the same area; and by 1976 32,000, with only a modest increase in cost over the one-component chip (Abelson & Hammond, 1977). This dramatic reduction in the cost-effectiveness ratio made microcomputers possible, but the transition from chip to computer required several years of microprocessor development.

Intelligent Tutoring Systems

While the microcomputer blitz has focused attention on small and relatively powerless computing systems, the academic community has continued to explore applications of artificial intelligence to interactive learning, using relatively powerful workstations. The line of development that began in the Age of the Titans with SCHOLAR, BUGGY, and West Coach has continued to flourish. Over the past decade tutoring systems have been developed for such areas as introductory programming, geometry, and LISP programming. These are not full instructional systems but rather practice environments, in which greater or lesser degrees of tutoring are offered. All of these systems share a number of features, which include:

1. Expert model. All tutoring systems embody in one form or another a model of an expert (or competent performer) for the skills being taught. Generally, this expertise is encoded as *production rules* or as a *procedural network*. (See the Glossary for definitions of these terms.)
2. Student model. A representation of the student's abilities, generally based on some isomorphism to the expert model, is kept and is updated as part of the system-student interaction.
3. Error (bug) detection. A set of defined errors or bugs is included in almost all tutoring systems. These may be defined by rules (i.e., faulty rules) that, for example, generate the result of subtraction with borrowing but without decrementing, or by lists. In West Coach, the main errors of interest were not arithmetic errors, but failures to use specific features ("issues") of the game, such as shortcuts or parentheses.
4. Tutoring discipline. Since the tutoring component tends to be the weakest part of most of these systems, the tutoring disciplines tend to be ad hoc sets of rules for deciding when to tutor. The tutoring itself usually amounts to little else than telling the student what has been done wrong or what the correct response should be.

Although some of these systems are based on recognizable psychological principles, others appear more idiosyncratic. Few are concerned, for example, with the sequencing of instruction, other than in the selection of specific problems to present. Nevertheless, the diagnostic networks are often quite sophisticated and the resulting systems could be used (in some cases) as laboratories for studying problem-solving behavior.

Evaluation

Some studies of the effects of computers in the classroom, as well as of the effects of learning environments such as LOGO, have already been discussed in this chapter.

Other major evaluation studies done in the 1980s include the meta-analyses by Kulik and colleagues (Kulik, Kulik, & Cohen, 1980; Kulik, Bangert, & Williams, 1983; Kulik, Kulik & Shwalb, 1986) and the work of Clark (1983), Clements (1986), and Salomon and Gardner (1986). Experiments in using computer networking to teach writing skills have been in progress for several years at the University of California–San Diego, and systems for fostering writing skills have been developed by Bolt Beranek and Newman, Inc., and the Bank Street College of Education. Apple Computer has introduced HyperCard for the Macintosh (Goodman, 1987), and organizations like Brown University's Institute for Research in Information and Scholarship (IRIS) have experimented with hypermedia systems for organizing instructional information (Yankelovich et al., 1988). New authoring environments have appeared (e.g., Course of Action®), sound synthesis of acceptable quality for most learners has been developed, and networks have become commonplace. Finally, new chips with remarkable qualities have continued to appear, bringing more power and flexibility to microcomputers at tolerable increases in cost.

Yet with all of this progress, several of the problems that have plagued this field over the last 30 years have remained. Computers are still being touted as the prime movers of a schooling revolution, raising expectations beyond where promises can be delivered, and much courseware continues to reflect an outmoded and mostly discredited psychology. School achievement does not result from a simple set of variables that the school (or a clever courseware designer) can manipulate. Instead, it results from a complex configuration of factors, some not well understood, that are distributed across school, home, community, and society in general. Effective instruction must be flexible, attuned to the changing needs and abilities of the learner, and designed within the school's total instructional environment.

There are valid reasons for assuming that computers can assist in some aspects of present-day instruction and may, with significant improvements in courseware, make major contributions to schooling in the future. But continued promises of a schooling revolution are bound to disappoint. What is needed is a more sober assessment of the potential of any instructional innovation to raise achievement scores or to effect any other desired outcome of schooling. With such limited but still worthy expectations, attention can turn to the task of designing good courseware, which is what the succeeding chapters are about.

SUMMARY

CAI slithered from the cocoon of teaching machines and programmed learning in the late 1950s but has yet to totally shed the traces of its psychological ancestry. The field has passed through four distinct ages, each characterized by different attitudes toward hardware and software, by varying allegiances toward particular theories of learning, and by different rationalizations for the lack of wider acceptance in established instructional settings. The ages of CAI include (1) the Age of Engineers, (2) the Age of Acronyms, (3) the Age of the Titans, and (4) the Age of Small Wonders.

Accurate and generalizable evaluation of CAI is difficult because of the general inability of experimenters to control all potentially significant variables in natural instructional settings. Nevertheless, at its best CAI has shown an ability in particular settings to accelerate the pace of learning. It has not yet, however, shown an ability to induce levels of learning beyond what can be achieved through traditional means.

The touting of CAI as a revolution in instruction sets expectations beyond what can reasonably be accomplished in complex organizations like schools. With more modest goals, CAI can be a cost-effective approach to instruction in a wide variety of learning contexts.

PART II

Instruction

In educational texts, the psychology of learning is generally treated before instruction is discussed. Similarly, review articles on instructional psychology usually devote themselves primarily to the empirical literature on learning, with a small amount of concluding space reserved for instructional implications. Here we reverse the traditional ordering for two reasons. First, the design of instruction depends upon considerably more than the psychology of learning, as we hope will become clear before the concluding pages are reached, and second, an instructional framework will help organize the psychology of learning and make it more meaningful and easier to digest. Therefore, we present our views on instruction first (Chapter 4), followed by an interpretation of the psychology of learning (Chapter 5), or at least of that segment of the field that we think is most relevant to the design of instruction. With these two chapters to buoy the reader's confidence, we then move to instructional design (Chapter 6).

CHAPTER 4

The Mysteries of Planning
Learning Experiences

By the end of the last tour we were attracting small animals backstage because I was hitting notes that only they could hear.
—Rock singer Steve Perry, quoted in *Hit Parade Yearbook* (1983)

THE NEED FOR GOOD INTENTIONS: APPROPRIATE INSTRUCTION

In Chapter 1 we defined *instruction* as *planned learning experiences* and added the further proviso that corrective feedback was required if anything more than memorization was desired. A second proviso is that the learning experiences be planned with a particular audience in mind and that the planning be appropriate for that particular audience. Consider for a few moments the vocabulary teaching practices of some 10th-grade social studies teachers. Generally at this level vocabulary is assigned for self-learning. That is, students are told that they are responsible for knowing the meanings of new words that they encounter in their readings. Techniques might be suggested for recording and learning new words, quizzes and tests might be given on them, occasional discussions and explanations might be provided, but the primary burden for instruction is still relegated to the learner. Does this qualify as instruction and would it if done in first or second grade?

To answer these questions we need to introduce a slightly fuzzy modification of the original query. At issue, we think, in this and in many similar cases, is not "What is instruction?" but "What is *appropriate* instruction?" Most people would probably agree that high school students can and should look up words in a dictionary and monitor their own learning of vocabulary. First and second graders, in contrast, are not capable of doing this. Thus, we have appropriate instruction for high school students and inappropriate instruction for first and second graders. Whether or not the approach to vocabulary instruction just mentioned qualifies as *instruction* in an absolute or philosophical sense is not of interest here. As with proverbial noises in the unmonitored forest, our definition of appropriate instruction requires consideration of both the phenomenon itself and its intended audience.

This latter point can be made clearer by a further example. Consider a prize-winning lecture on seventeenth-century New England witchcraft, one in which the material is so cleverly sequenced and presented, where motivational devices, analogies,

53

and summaries are so well applied that students and colleagues who hear the lecture all agree that exceptional instruction has been witnessed. That is, everyone capable of following the lecture agrees on assigning the label "exceptional instruction." But what would students in another country think of the lecture if they did not understand the language of the lecturer? What would these people gain from the lecture? Would they agree that the lecture was exceptionally informative (or even mildly informative)? Here, we think, the situation is quite clear. Where the intended audience has little or no chance to learn from the activity or event, appropriate instruction has not occurred.

To sum up so far, appropriate instruction is composed of structured or planned learning experiences, generally with corrective feedback, that have a reasonable chance of resulting in some change of ability in the intended audience. Tutoring high school freshmen on wave mechanics or demonstrating de Morgan's theorems in English to monolingual speakers of Arapaho do not qualify as appropriate instruction. Notice, however, that "change of ability" covers motor skills such as bicycle riding and dulcimer strumming as well as chess playing, solving differential equations, and analyzing poetry. For the present we appeal to experience and tradition to decide the probability of a designated group of students learning from any particular instructional program. Later we will add some principles acquired from experimental psychology to these *desiderata*.

At this point we pause to consider the nature of what is taught, under the assumption that *how to teach* depends at least in part on *what is to be taught*. Those readers on the limited-time, executive schedule might want to skim and sample the following, treating it like a continental-style breakfast, and then dine more fully when we return to the structure of instruction. Those who prefer a seven-course meal, however, should proceed dead ahead.

CLASSIFICATION OF INSTRUCTIONAL OBJECTIVES

Aristotle was among the first to pursue seriously classification of the world's knowledge. Implicit in his work, as in the work of all taxonomists since, is the belief that there is order to the universe and that it can be revealed through proper classification and description (Sarton, 1952). Whether or not there is order in the world of instruction remains to be demonstrated. We pursue this holy grail of classification, nevertheless, in the hope that from our labels and terminology will emerge understanding that will lead to more effective teaching. The object of classification in the present case is to identify instructionally relevant commonalities across subject domains. For example, if we classified objectives strictly by subject matter (e.g., history, physics, mathematics, literature), we would gain little insight into the similarities or differences in instructional techniques required by the various areas. Certainly math and physics share a considerable number of basic objectives that could be taught with similar methods, as do other combinations of subjects.

The classifications that follow attend to the subject matter content of any course. This component absorbs the majority of instructional time and energy, but it should not be the only objective of good instruction. Two other sets of objectives should be considered, even though we offer little guidance here on teaching them. One is learning strategies, that is, the techniques learners should use to acquire, retain, and apply the subject matter. The other is attitudes and beliefs. Learners should be encouraged to adopt a positive attitude toward the subject matter and toward their abilities to understand it. In teaching reading, for example, there is little gain from teaching an extensive set of comprehension skills if the students acquire at the same time a distaste for the act of reading. For mathematics and science, on the other hand, some learners acquire negative attitudes about their own learning abilities for these subjects. Time spent building self-confidence in students may be equally important to time spent on algorithms and principles.

The most important attempt in recent times to classify cognitive objectives was carried out in the middle 1950s, promoted by the desire of test designers to have common classifications and terminology for writing test items. Published as *Taxonomy of Educational Objectives, Handbook 1: Cognitive Domain* (Bloom et al., 1956), the categories were ordered from the lowest level of learning outcomes to the highest, and included knowledge, comprehension, application, analysis, synthesis, and evaluation.[1] However adequate this classification may have been for the 1950s, it has only marginal utility today primarily because many of the psychological assumptions it is based on have been superseded.

An Alternative Approach

Alternatives to the Bloom et al. taxonomy have been developed from a variety of viewpoints (e.g., Gagne, 1965; Gagne & Briggs, 1974; Romiszowski, 1981), but none appears totally adequate for the approach to curriculum design presented here. Therefore, we offer yet another classification for cognitive skills, based upon a primary division between *declarative* and *procedural* knowledge. (Note, however, that we are not including motor, affective, or interaction skills.) By *declarative knowledge* we mean facts, labels, and other types of associations, the *what* of our knowledge store. In contrast, *procedural knowledge* is the *how to:* instructions and procedures for doing things—riding a bicycle, finding a square root, organizing an outline.

The taxonomy that follows is based strictly upon mental operations, although it does not attempt to predict how these operations might be done. Furthermore, the system attempts to account for different levels of complexity within the same basic operation. Skills are classed from the simplest to the most complex, with *logical thinking* representing the highest level. Because of the mental operation orientation, we use the label *knowledge* in a general sense; to be more specific, instead we posit two types of processes that account for information that a learner acquires: *associations* and *procedural operations. Association* is a multidimensional category that for simplicity we reduce to two dimensions, one for type of association (or relationship) and one for complexity. Three types of associations are identified: *categorical, logical/mathematical,* and *linguistic.*

Associations. Categorical associations include the following, ordered from simple to more complex:

> **1.** Labels of the form "George Washington is the subject of this picture" and "Our teacher's name is Ms. Smith."

---

[1]A sequel to this effort defined objectives in the affective domain (Krathwohl, Bloom, & Masia, 1964) and the psychomotor domain (Harrow, 1972).

2. Synonyms of the form "The capital of Liechtenstein is Vaduz."
3. Feature descriptions of the form "Mt. Everest is 29,202 feet high," and "The 1926 Model T Ford had its gas tank under the cowl."
4. Set memberships like "The duck-billed platypus is a marsupial" and "Carolingian uncials were a style of handwriting."
5. Concept definitions like "Feudalism as defined by Strayer is characterized by 'fragmentation of political authority, public power in private hands, and a military system in which an essential part of the armed forces is secured through private contracts.'"

Logical/mathematical associations include the following, also ordered from simple to complex.

1. Equivalence relationships of the form "$2 \times 2 = 4$" and "$8 - 4 = 4$."
2. Inequalities of the form "12 is greater than 6" and "A baby elephant is larger than a grown mouse."
3. Rules of the form "The same numeric operation can be performed on both sides of an equality without changing the equality itself," and "Any quantity to the zero power equals one."

Linguistic associations include the following, ordered also as above:

1. Memorization of verbal material for recall, such as "Casey at the Bat" or Pope's rhymed couplets.
2. Vocabulary equivalents in a foreign language.
3. Rules of the form "Initial *c* is pronounced [s] before *e, i,* or *y;* otherwise it is pronounced [k]."
4. Semantic relationships of the form "Wooden shoes are shoes made of wood, but track shoes are shoes worn for track and field sporting activities."

Associations are so named because they depend upon interrelationships among concepts for their significance. The labels *knowledge* and *fact* have acquired the sense of static elements that are stored and retrieved much like different grains and nuts in the grocer's bins. But we don't teach facts in isolation; instead, they occur as nodes in conceptual networks, to be learned in relationship to the categories and concepts that interrelate them. The height of Mt. Everest, for example, is meaningful only if geological formations and measurement scales are understood. In teaching this fact, it is also important to place Everest in comparison to other mountains, that is, to know that it is the highest of the earth's mountains, and that mountains range in height from several thousand feet to just under six miles.[2] Without this understanding, erroneous recall of the height of Everest could be 50 feet or 250,000 feet as easily as 20,000 feet.

Knowing something well requires more than memorization of isolated features.

---

[2]To be more precise, Mt. Everest is the highest mountain measured from the surface of dry land. Mt. Maunakea on the island of Hawaii is approximately 33,000 feet high, measured from its base on the ocean floor. On this and other commonly held fallacies, the reader is directed to Seymour Simon's text, *The Dinosaur is the Biggest Animal That Ever Lived, and Other Wrong Ideas You Though Were True.* (New York, Lippincott, 1984.)

And since some of memory is based on reconstruction, the ability to regenerate forgotten items from constraints and interrelationships, the teaching of "knowledge" needs to stress concepts and relationships as much as it does facts.

We have separated categorical, logical/mathematical, and linguistic associations because these three collections, although partially overlapping, seem to require different instructional procedures and appear to tap different forms of intelligence. Categorical associations range over most of the domains of history, philosophy, biology, sociology, art, music, and their related fields—in short, the humanities, and arts, and the nonmathematical portions of the social and biological sciences. These are typically taught through extensive reading, discussion, and writing, with the goal of requiring the learner to organize and manipulate the information at a deep cognitive level. Furthermore, associations in these areas are deeply embedded in basic procedural operations.

Logical/mathematical associations, on the other hand, are highly quantitative and, for the average learner, form the basis upon which procedural operations like ordering and evaluating are constructed. Multiplication tables and the number system are taught as primitive relationships, not as components of a larger network from which they can be derived. Teaching basic mathematical concepts usually evolves around visual representations (e.g., number line, pie-shaped area) and extensive practice, with the goal of automatic response for the most basic operations.

In contrast to these two categories, linguistic associations tend to draw on properties of natural language or its representation by script. Synonyms and antonyms, or equivalent terms in another language, draw on knowledge of language usage. Speakers of English, for example, recognize the difference in number between "The man worked," and "The men worked" from the forms of the nouns *man* and *men*. A Chinese speaker, reading or listening to his native language, would have to acquire number from context since the two utterances would be identical in Chinese. The network of interrelationships for linguistic associations is language itself, and therefore the teaching of linguistic associations requires particular attention to the learner's stage of language development.

Procedural Operations. *Procedural operations* are mental operations that require manipulation of objects, events, and associations. We feel ourselves on shaky grounds here in that the knowledge base for classifying mental operations could support a variety of different organizations. But since we have practical rather than philosophical goals in mind, we have developed a classification that appears to offer some advantage (however slight) over chaos for organizing the content of school-based and industrial-military subjects. In it we differentiate *basic* and *compound* procedural operations.

Basic procedural operations include:

1. Feature recognition: the ability to recognize features or attributes common to sets of objects, events, or ideas;
2. Identification (or instantiation): the ability to locate or identify instances of a concept or feature set;[3]

---

[3]This differs from set membership in that the present category requires the ability to identify an appropriate set of features for classifying something while set membership requires only the association of an entity with a superordinate label.

3. Rule application: the ability to apply a rule, given an appropriate context; and

4. Ordering: the ability to arrange a group of objects, events, or associations according to values within one or more of their shared attributes.

The *compound procedural operations* include:

1. Paraphrasing and summarizing: the ability to recognize the key elements in a text and to arrange them coherently in significantly fewer words than the original;

2. Organizing: the ability to extract attributes and values from a potentially large group of objects, events, or ideas and to arrange these into a structure that is revealing of the relationships among the objects or ideas;

3. Projecting: the ability to recognize trends within events and to project these trends beyond the currently available data;

4. Comparing: the ability to compare objects, events, and so forth, along one or more of their shared dimensions, using value metrics; and

5. Generalizing: the ability to extract a recurring pattern from members of a set and to use that pattern to predict the behavior of new set members.

Each of these could be arranged in varying degrees of complexity, so that no single one could be said to be more or less complex than another. Furthermore, in their most complex forms they are as challenging as any of the operations discussed in the next section, on *logical thinking*.

Logical Thinking. We define *logical thinking* as the productive use of associations and procedural operations that most often reveals itself in complex *problem solving, decision making, prediction,* and *evaluation.* We use these labels because they are common in the cognitive literature; they are not, however, precisely defined and mutually exclusive categories. Decision making, prediction, and evaluation, for example, could be classed as types of problem solving, and evaluation could be classed as a type of decision making. What we have in mind are truly complex problems of the scale of long-range weather prediction, evaluation of the performance of school districts, selection of national economic policy, and curbing the use of drugs. These, we claim, build on

- paraphrasing and summarizing,
- organizing,
- projecting,
- comparing, and
- generalizing.

These in turn rest on

- feature recognition,
- identification,
- rule application, and
- ordering.

And these build on associations. But from an instructional standpoint there is rarely an opportunity to traverse these in a strictly linear progression, traveling from associations to simple procedural operations to compound procedural operations to problem solving, decision making, and so forth. Most instruction requires a back-and-forth movement among these domains. One of the most challenging aspects of instruction is how to sequence all four domains so that learning in context is possible and integrated skills are acquired.

For example, the typical reference manual for a programming language is arranged in a linear sequence, beginning with the character set and moving through labels, constants, and the ilk, to commands and finally programs, with an occasional final section on applications, that is, problem solving. Instruction based on this ordering is usually tedious and painful for the students. Until the concept of a *program* is known, statements and data structures float like water droplets in space, unconnected to any known component of the universe. Similarly, variables, constants, and labels are homeless without the knowledge of statements and statement sequences.

Successful introductory programming courses typically introduce simplified concepts of *program, statement, data,* and *control,* before the minutiae of ranges, syntax, boundary conditions, and types are unloaded. Similarly, the teaching of almost any other school subject is a journey back and forth among the areas defined above. Associations require procedures, procedures require associations, and logical thinking requires them all.

Whether or not this organization is consistent and exhaustive we do not discuss further; instead we show briefly how it applies to commonly taught subjects. Consider, to begin, a typical middle school social studies course. Included among the course goals are (typically) *concepts* (e.g., the ideas of liberty, freedom, justice, and equality), *associations* (e.g., Greek civilization contributed the idea of democracy to humankind), *procedures* (e.g., drawing inferences from data), and *attitudes* (e.g., developing constructive attitudes toward conflicts).[4] In our scheme, a concept like *liberty* would be built first on positive and negative exemplars (e.g., rights of American citizens today versus rights of slaves in ancient Greece). These mostly would be categorical associations. Then, identification would be used, along with feature extractions to extend from the initial knowledge base to further exemplars. Finally, organization and generalization would be used to form the desired concept.

The associations desired appear as complexes of facts, often drawing on cause and effect relationships (e.g., The ability to produce surplus food led to changes in human life). Here we suspect that basic procedural operations are applied to associations to produce more complex associations. *Compound procedures,* like drawing inferences from data, depend heavily upon *projection, evaluation,* and *generalization.*

Basic mathematics provides another example of how associations, procedures, and problem solving are intermixed. A typical mathematics curriculum (e.g., sixth grade), mixes basic mathematical associations (e.g., large-number representation), simple and compound procedures (e.g., finding the interest on a simple loan), and problem solving techniques (e.g., using estimation to check the magnitude of a result). Drill on basic operations is mixed with practice in applying formulas and with solution of word problems.

Finally, we offer one more distinction: that between *subject* or *topic* and *skill.*

---

[4]These examples are taken from the sixth-grade teacher's guide for the New York State Education Department's *Social Studies Program,* published by the Bureau of General Education Curriculum Development in 1982.

Subject or *topic* refers to procedures, associations, or groups of these entities (e.g., elementary science, "the idea of liberty," or drawing inferences from data). *Skill* is reserved for operational definitions of topics, that is, topics expressed in a form that makes instructional outcomes testable. Skill means ability; to observe or test any particular ability we must know what we are looking for.

The topic *fractions,* for example, is taught at many different levels in the elementary school mathematics curriculum. But the skill in fractions expected at each grade level changes. At the lowest levels it might be definitional; knowing one-half and one-third applied to area and volume. At later levels addition and subtraction of proper fractions is required; then multiplication and division, with improper fractions and mixed numbers added to the domain of interest. A major task in instructional design is deriving skills from topics.

HOW IS INSTRUCTION ORGANIZED?

For ease of educational administration, instruction is organized into *courses* that contain a coherent sequence of topics and skills. A one-semester introduction to biology at the local high school, an on-line sequence of 20 lessons for learning to read and write the Cherokee syllabary, and a four-day workshop on means-ends analysis, are all examples of courses. A *curriculum,* on the other hand, is a slightly less well-defined entity generally referring to a group of courses that have coordinated difficulty levels and times of offering and that meet some programmatic end. For example, the third-grade curriculum at an elementary school might include courses in reading, arithmetic, social studies, science, gym, art, and music. Finally, a *program* is a collection of curricula that satisfies some broader educational objective such as preparation for working as a graphic designer or for certification as an accountant or for entering high school. We speak of the M.A. program in computer-aided design, or the grade school program at the Winterwilt Academy; but we might also use *curriculum* occasionally as a synonym for *program,* particularly if the program requires a year or less of study.

Since the concern of this text is with courses or their equivalent (module, workshop, etc.), we won't belabor the distinction between curriculum and program. Henceforth, *instructional design* and *course design* are used as synonyms. Furthermore, in this chapter we discuss a background for designing and implementing complete courses, even though on-line instruction might be used only for small portions of a course such as introducing new vocabulary or explaining editing procedures or practicing measurement skills. For the present we assume that a course is composed of discrete lessons, which themselves might contain games, debates, group discussions, simulations, tests, tutorials, or any of the other activities that characterize instruction.

For the present we won't attempt to offer a precise definition for *lesson,* other than to qualify that it is expected to have a well-defined beginning, middle, and end and to fit into a *session* or two or three. Thus *lesson* is a logical entity, defined by content while *session* is an event-driven entity, defined by assigned time, arrival/departure, or sign-on/sign-off. For convenience we also assume that lessons can be organized into *units,* thus giving three levels of instructional granularity: course, unit, and lesson, where lessons are realized (i.e., presented) in sessions. To define what goes on in instructional lessons, we switch to a functional analysis of instructional strategies.

INSTRUCTIONAL STRATEGIES

Consider an introductory course in BASIC programming. One approach to such courses is to imitate the typical reference manual and organize instruction from small pieces to big pieces, as mentioned in the previous section. Thus, the early lessons would present the character set, constants, variables, and expressions, while later lessons would build from commands finally to functions, subroutines, and programs. This is a bottom-up approach.

Another (and usually more humane) approach is to present material from the top down, starting with a simple program that is later analyzed into its constituent components: commands, labels, variables, and so forth. Commands are shown in their simplest and most common form initially, with layers of complexity added in later lessons. (In both this and the previous approach I have assumed that at some point commands, variables, expressions, and the like would be presented and explained, but this is not the only option for instructional mode.)

Yet another alternative would be to present large numbers of correct and incorrect, legal and illegal forms, and allow the learner to discover on his own what works. A command simulator might, on demand, parse commands left to right, showing how each command constituent would be interpreted. The learner would be encouraged to try out various types of commands to achieve particular goals. Guided problem solving would, therefore, replace the more traditional explanatory approach. These three options, although not exhausting the choices for organizing introductory BASIC courses, exemplify part of what *instructional strategy* means. To avoid potential confusion at this point we need to qualify that the traditional CAI labels *drill and practice, gaming, tutorial, simulation,* and the like, do not represent instructional strategies for courses. A complete course could not reasonably be built on drill alone or on games or simulations or coaching alone. In an explanatory sequence, for example, material must be introduced, explained, and practiced. *Drill, drill-type games, simulation,* and *coaching* provide or augment practice. Somehow, either through overt, direct explanation, summarization after discovery, or whatever other means can be found, introduction and explanation must be done. (On these more is in the offing.)

In total, *instructional strategy* refers to the grouping of students, sequencing of topics, modes of instruction (and *events* therein), and pathways through which individual learners are expected to travel in progressing from novices to graduates. In mastery learning, for example, students are taught (by whatever mode) a unit of material and then tested for mastery. Those who do not reach mastery on this first posttest are given extra help on the material and then retested, while those who did reach mastery either do enrichment activities or spend their time on other subjects until the reteaching and retesting of other students are completed. All of this is shown in Figure 4.1.

Other instructional strategies like tracking, team learning (Slavin, 1983), individually guided education (Klausmeier, Rossmiller, & Saily, 1977), and individually prescribed instruction (Glaser, 1976) are built on differing concepts of grouping, topic sequencing, instructional modes, and mastery levels. Not all of these, furthermore, have clear specifications for the variables involved. Mastery learning is neutral toward modes of instruction and topic sequencing. Tracking is mainly an organizational plan whereby students are placed in groups according to their abilities. How instruction is designed for each group is not mandated.

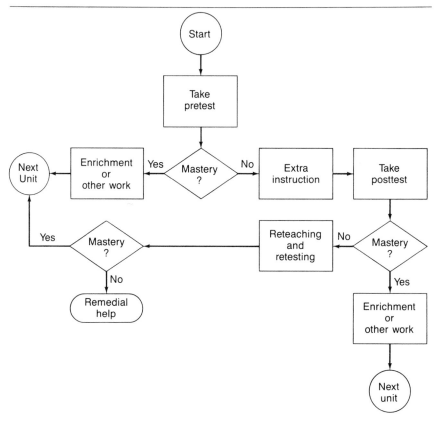

Figure 4.1. Mastery Learning

Since we are interested only in planned learning experiences, we will have nothing to say about instructional strategies built around discovery learning and other approaches that have minimal or no planning of instructional events. Furthermore, we have reserved for inclusion under the section *Instructional Tactics* a number of topics like *instructional delivery* and *instructional level* that might legitimately be included here. In general, we have tried to define under *strategy* those issues that are both global and general, and have left to tactics the particulars. That this division is occasionally arbitrary we admit.

Instructional Mode

The choice between an *explanatory* approach wherein associations and procedural operations are introduced and explained directly, a *demonstration* approach in which the application of these same abilities is shown, and a *problem-solving* approach wherein students are coached in applying rules and principles to solve problems is a question of *instructional mode*.

Explanatory Instruction. Most courses given in schools and colleges and most of the nondrill CAI materials now available employ an explanatory mode; that is, they teach by direct explanation. For most of the materials in this mode, a *teacher-directed* procedure is used: material is explained in a sequence selected by the instructor/designer. An alternative explanatory approach is the student-directed approach in which student questions trigger explanations. These two variations (and all the points in between) generally deliver similar explanations; the first, however, gives its explanations in a preselected sequence (which may or may not allow alternative paths for different students) while the second delivers an explanation only when it is requested.

Demonstration Instruction. In contrast to direct explanation, a demonstration approach depends on the application of a rule, principle, or process to initiate instruction. What is demonstrated might be a chemistry process, the steps in the solution of a geometry problem, the procedure required to start a Model T Ford on a cold morning, or anything else that can be shown in an instructional context. In general, a demonstration includes explanations either during the procedure (annotated demonstration) or afterward, but we withhold discussion of the complete sequence of events for an instructional mode until a later section. Drawing on Ohlsson (1985), we distinguish three major types of demonstration:

1. Abbreviated: present the step-by-step process or solution of a problem without justifying or explaining each step;
2. Annotated: state and explain each step; and
3. Interactive: a student specifies each step, and the tutor executes it (with or without elaboration).

Modeling as currently applied in the instructional psychology literature is a form of annotated demonstration in which the instructor thinks out loud in solving a problem or following a procedure (Collins, Brown, & Newman, 1986). Since modeling is usually done to demonstrate how a proficient problem solver approaches a particular task, it might include false starts, dead ends, and other unproductive steps as a means of showing that struggle, error, and indecision are all common and expected experiences. Modeling, in this sense, has been applied successfully to classroom instruction for mathematics (Schoenfeld, 1985), reading comprehension (Palincsar & Brown, 1984), and writing (Scardamalia & Bereiter, 1985). (Modeling also has another sense related to *simulating* a process through, typically, mechanical or electronic means. Thus, the Army Corps of Engineers used for many years a mechanical model of the San Francisco Bay to predict sedimentation and erosion effects. Now this type of modeling is usually done by computer.)

Problem-Solving Instruction. In contrast to the two modes just presented, problems might be presented that require new laws or relationships for solution. Students might either be tutored in how to solve them or have access, through a question-answer system, to an expert problem solver. A *simulation* (in the instructional context) is usually nothing more than a sequence of contextually related problem situations (see Chapter 8). A PLATO lesson called Tenure is an example of a simulation built around related tasks. A student is confronted with problems that must be solved in the first year of teaching, the object being to do well enough to receive tenure. A grading system must be established, discipline regulations instituted, and other educational decisions made, all within the context of a particular school, subject area, and type of principal. Simulations are related to experiments in that an experiment can be simulated. An experiment, however, offers limited opportunity for feedback and adjustment, while a simulation offers unlimited opportunity. The critical distinction between demonstration mode and problem-solving mode is that in the former an instructor carries the main burden of presenting material while in the latter the student is expected to be the principal actor.

Locus of Control

The instructional modes presented so far, with the possible exception of simulation, have assumed *instructor control.* Whether human, mechanical, or electronic, the instructor orchestrates the sequence of events that compose a mode of instruction. This does not preclude student involvement or even student direction of particular steps as, for example, when students are asked to demonstrate how to solve a problem. But even with frequent student involvement the instructor/machine remains in control. An alternative to instructor control is *instructor monitoring* whereby students, either individually or in small groups, are given assignments and then monitored while carrying them out.

Imagine, as an example, a lesson on endangered animal species wherein a team of six students is to develop a large chart showing characteristics of various endangered animals (e.g., size of population, natural habitat, dangers they face). The students might each study one of six animals independently and then regroup to draft a single report. The teacher would monitor the initial assignments to ensure a practicable work plan, check on the progress of individual students, and then help establish a model for recording each entry in the table. Student requests for help might be answered directly ("An aerie is a nest, usually in a difficult-to-access place") or by advice (e.g., "Have you tried the encyclopedia?") or through a minilesson, using either an explanatory or demonstration approach.

In a networked environment this lesson might be done on-line with students accessing bibliographies and other textual resources separately and then interacting on the drafting of the report. The teacher could be on-line also, actively monitoring but also available upon request through a "talk" mode.

Another alternative to *instructor control* is *student control,* whereby students plan their own instruction for a subject, drawing on the resources available (including instructors). A foreign-language course, for example, might allow students to select and pursue their own approaches to vocabulary learning, with audiotapes, vocabulary cards, and native speakers available on request. For student control to be a meaningful option for planned instruction, instructional options that are appropriate for the topics involved and the learners must be available. Finally, for completeness we define an *open* situation, wherein the instructor/machine plays no active role between initial assignment and grading. Most homework fits this category, although instructional assistance is often provided in the home by a sibling or parent. Homework, however, is usually not intended for introduction or explanation of a topic. Instead, it is most commonly employed for independent practice of procedures introduced within a formal instructional setting. When it is used for new topics, it usually involves the assignment of text materials that present the new materials within one of the common instructional modes. Without such assistance no true instruction occurs.[5]

One might be tempted to divide all instruction into teacher-directed and learner-directed categories, with perhaps a *mixed-initiative* category included as in Carbonell's (1970) system, SCHOLAR, and then to divide each class further into instructional modes. We resist this temptation because the instances where learner control most logically can occur involve teacher direction as the primary approach to instruction. For example, in some CAI programs students are allowed to select a topic of study from a menu of topics or the level of difficulty to be used in a topic presentation or some other aspect of instruction such as pace or amount of feedback. However, once these choices are made, instructional control resorts to the instructor/machine.

Even in a student-directed question-and-answer session, the instructor must select among a rather narrow list of modes for their responses. To a question like "How do I do square roots by hand?" one could either suggest self-instruction, that is, give no instruction directly (e.g., "Look it up in your textbook"), or one could provide instruction by explanation, demonstration, or problem solving. Therefore, rather than treating locus of control as a high-level division in our hierarchy of instructional approaches, we distribute it among several categories, but principally as an organizing and topic-sequencing issue.

Within this text the majority of our instructional emphasis is directed toward teacher-controlled instruction. Some attention is given, nevertheless, to *monitored instruction,* but no mention is made of *open instruction,* even though *learner control* of components of instructional sequences is discussed in various places.

Topic Sequencing

Mode is one component of instructional strategy; topic sequence is the other. As mentioned above, an explanatory mode for teaching an introductory BASIC course still allows several different organizations of the designated programming abilities. A bottom-up approach, although usually not recommended, is possible, as is a top-down approach. Each implies a different sequence of material. A foreign-language course offers an opportunity for a variety of different sequences of course components. One approach is to begin with intensive ear training and pronunciation drill, followed by common sentence frames and then vocabulary. An alternative is the grammar-first, speech-later model, in which parts of speech and syntactic patterns are inculcated before spoken utterances are allowed. This approach generally focuses more on reading and translation than does the first approach, which is more strongly oriented toward speaking and listening abilities. These differences, it should be noted, apply as much to explanatory approaches as they do to demonstration and problem-solving ones.

Topic sequencing can be viewed on a variety of levels. Consider, for example, the design of a fourth-grade mathematics course. At a macro level, fractions might be sequenced before area, but after multiplication of large numbers. At the next level of design, wherein the approach for teaching fractions is considered, another sequencing issue must be resolved. Will mixed numbers (e.g., $2\frac{3}{4}$) be introduced before finding the least common denominator? Will addition of fractions be introduced here or saved for

---

[5]Incidental learning, as in travel to foreign countries, might be considered a form of open instruction, especially if the journey begins with the parental request to "go out and learn about the world."

a later grade? And so on. Then, once these issues are resolved, sequencing reappears at the next level of refinement, lesson design. Will numerators greater than one be introduced by dividing an area (e.g., pie) into parts and then showing numeric representation, or should numeric representation be introduced first?

Instructional design can be viewed as a planning process applied recursively to each level of a course. Some decision like sequencing will appear at almost every level; others, like assessment, might have a more limited appearance.

INSTRUCTIONAL EVENTS

In the first part of this chapter we suggested that instruction could be viewed hierarchically from curriculum to course to unit and lesson/session. Within lessons one sequences instructional events (if more than one occurs) depending upon instructional strategy. For explanatory instruction these events include *introduction, explication, practice, review, test,* and *maintenance,* all named by the functions they serve.[6] New associations or procedures must first be *introduced.* This phase of instruction may be as brief as "one of the new vocabulary words for today is interdigitation" or as long as an entire session. Once introduced, a new concept needs to be explained. This might be done in a sequence of steps, built around an analogy or metaphor, or through one or more charts or graphs or through a simulated activity or in a variety of other ways. *Explication* should be the most creative part of instruction, the place where clever, incisive metaphors are invoked, crisp explanations constructed, and the learner tenderly led from darkness into light.

Practice is necessary, not because it makes perfect, but because it sets habits. Well-constructed practice will establish good habits; poorly built practice might not. In lower-level skill learning (e.g., basic math skills or letter-sound correspondences) the role of practice is not only to induce mastery of relationships but also to build automaticity in responding. There is reasonable evidence to conclude that the more automatic the lower level processing is, the better the learner will cope with the higher level demands of a task. If a new reader, for example, requires 2–3 seconds to recall each letter-sound correspondence in a word, the time required for sounding out even simple, monosyllabic words will probably be too long to allow easy integration of words into higher level meanings. (On the other hand, too much time spent on lower-level skills might result in insufficient attention to higher-level skills.)

In demonstration instruction, a topic, idea, or event is introduced, and then a demonstration performed. This might be followed by explication or by practice, that is, by the students taking turns attempting to do what the instructor did. Similarly, a problem-solving approach will have an introduction, problem solving, and then generally explication. Alternatively, students might struggle to solve a problem (with or without coaching). Then, the instructor might demonstrate how he does it before explaining the principle or rule involved. In these latter two modes explication is usually briefer than in explanatory mode because the demonstration or problem solving provides much of what an explanatory mode explication must achieve.

Practice, review, maintenance, and *testing* usually involve the same content; the first to help set habits, the second to inform the learner of his mastery of a topic, the

---

[6]The concept of instructional events presented here differs in kind from that of Gagné and Briggs, 1979.

third to maintain skills after they are mastered, and the last to inform the instructor (although the learner should also benefit from the testing results). Ideally, maintenance will occur through repeated application, but where application cannot be ensured, specific maintenance activities need to be designed. Finally there are *support* events, such as when the teacher gives out assignments or grades, counsels students on how to prepare for an exam, or explains the procedure for assigning students to laboratory sessions.

All of these events can be divided into four functional categories:

1. Initial teaching
   explanatory: introduction, explication, practice
   demonstration: introduction, demonstration, explication, practice
   problem solving: introduction, problem solving, practice
2. Assessment
   review
   testing
3. Maintenance
4. Support
   management
   guidance

The amount of time given to each phase or event, like so much else in instructional design, depends upon subject matter, learners, and instructional resources. Lower-level skills require mostly introduction and practice, while higher-level skills generally require heavier doses of explication. Assessment for young students should be more frequent than for older learners, and maintenance for frequently used skills can be much lighter than for skills not encountered in use so frequently.

In a later chapter we define different types of explication, practice, and demonstration that are relevant to on-line instruction. At this point coaching and other instructional techniques are defined.

INSTRUCTIONAL TACTICS

We begin our discussion of instructional tactics by summarizing the variables already mentioned that are part of an *instructional strategy*. Although all of these are discussed in Chapter 6 ("Instructional Design"), the discussion that follows here serves as an advance organizer for that chapter.

The Basics

Given the *topics* to be taught and the *level of difficulty* for each, a *sequence* for the topics must be defined. This sequence will depend in part on the *instructional mode*, which might be varied across a course, according to topic or some other design element. Students may have the same or different paths through the topics and may or may not control any part of the instruction.

Instructional Delivery. For a given audience and set of available resources (e.g., time, personnel), an instructional designer usually has some latitude in the selection of delivery approaches. A fourth-grade arithmetic course, for example, might assign guided and independent practice to aides and all other instructional events to teachers. In contrast, a course on new tax laws might have all explications and demonstrations on videotape, with independent practice delivered by computer. Selection of delivery approach is limited by certain practicalities, for example, number and type of personnel available, number and type of computers available, amenability of course content to nonlive presentation.

Development cost is also a constraint on video and computer delivery; good materials for these media are relatively expensive to produce. There is little research to guide the assignment of delivery means to instructional approaches. Most reports on CAI effectiveness focus on practice (e.g., Kulick, Kulick & Shwalb 1986), but the potential for CAI in problem solving and demonstration modes, in particular, has not been thoroughly investigated with high-quality, color graphics systems.

Adaptation to Individual Needs. The ability of instructional programs to adapt to individual needs rests heavily upon the type of individual diagnosis these programs are capable of doing. A lesson that marches inexorably from start to finish, rendering the same instruction regardless of a student's responses, has zero adaptability, whether delivered by human, video recorder, or computer. In contrast, an on-line practice lesson that maintains a dynamic model of the student's abilities based on the skills expected of a competent graduate of the course and updates the model with each response, has the potential to offer diagnosis in depth. Whether or not any lesson provides useful feedback or shifts in instruction based upon diagnoses of students will determine its true adaptability. Some programs such as BUGGY (Brown & Burton, 1978) have extensive diagnosis capabilities, but limited capacities for utilizing diagnostic information in instruction. Adaptive instruction must be capable of (1) gathering diagnosis information, (2) inferring from this information the specific needs of the student, and (3) adjusting instruction accordingly. Expert teachers are more capable than novices of detecting at the beginning of a class whether or not students mastered the material from the previous lesson and of adjusting their instruction accordingly (Berliner, 1986).

Adaptation to individual needs might be through change in content or rate of instruction, or through extra assistance, or through alteration in criterion levels for mastery. Thus, a student who fails to grasp a concept during initial presentation might be given an easier version of the concept (change in content), more time to review the same material (change in rate), individual tutoring (extra assistance), or may be allowed to progress to the next phase of instruction even though he failed to reach an assigned mastery level (alteration in criterion levels). Which of these might be best for any given instructional situation cannot be generalized. This decision depends in part on available resources and in part on diagnosis and instructional abilities.

Representation

Next in importance to the issues described above is representation scheme, an issue too often ignored in instructional design. Consider the paragraph below, which was used by Wright and Reid (1973) in a study on knowledge representation.

When time is limited, travel by rocket, unless cost is also limited, in which case go by space ship. When only cost is limited an Astrobus should be used for journeys of less than 10 orbs, and a Satellite for longer journeys. Cosmocars are recommended, when there are no constraints on time or cost, unless the distance to be traveled exceeds 10 orbs. For journeys longer than 10 orbs, when time and cost are not important, journeys should be made by Super Star. (p. 161)

The verbal text above represents one approach to presenting this information. But at least three reasonable alternatives exist: an algorithm in the form of a decision tree (see Figure 4.2), a decision table (see Figure 4.3), and a sequence of short sentences that paraphrase the original text such as these:

Where only time is limited
  travel by rocket.
Where only cost is limited
  travel by satellite if journey more than 10 orbs.
  travel by Astrobus if journey less than 10 orbs.
Where both time and cost are limited
  travel by spaceship
Where time and cost are not limited
  travel by Super Star if journey more than 10 orbs.
  travel by Cosmocar if journey less than 10 orbs. (p. 161)

Wright and Reid (1973) tested adults on their abilities to work problems based on information presented in the formats shown above. Each subject worked 36 problems in a single format, with errors and the time needed, either to read the problem or to find the solution, recorded. For difficult problems and the material continually avail-

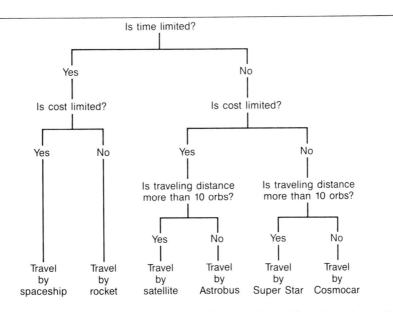

Figure 4.2. Decision Tree (From P. Wright and F. Reid, written information: Some alternatives to prose for expressing the outcomes of complex contingencies. *Journal of Applied Psychology* 57(1973):161. Copyright 1973 by the American Psychological Association. Reprinted by permission.)

Where only time is limited	If journey less than 10 orbs	If journey more than 10 orbs
	Travel by rocket	Travel by rocket
Where only cost is limited	Travel by Astrobus	Travel by satellite
Where time and cost are not limited	Travel by Cosmocar	Travel by Super Star
Where both time and cost are limited	Travel by spaceship	Travel by spaceship

Figure 4.3. Decision Table (Source: See Figure 4.2.)

able, the decision tree format yielded the fewest errors, but for easier problems all the nonprose formats were about equal, yet consistently better than the prose format. The decision table format produced the fastest solutions, however.

When the material was not continually available, error rates shot up above 50% for all formats. Under these conditions results were not so clear cut, but performance on the decision tree and decision table formats tended to deteriorate over trials while performance on the prose and short sentences formats tended to improve.

Other studies have also reported somewhat mixed results on knowledge representation formats, depending on the materials, the types of learners, and the amount of exposure given to each format. Coscarelli and Schwen (1979), for example, tested college-level chemistry students on algorithms presented as either flowcharts, lists, or standard prose. Although the list format was superior to the other two formats for the first two trials, the flowchart was clearly superior on trial 3, which involved highly complex data. By trial 5, however, the three modes were equal.

The bad news from these and other related studies is that no one has yet found a universal decision algorithm for selecting information representations. The good news, however, is that a variety of interesting formats are available and the best for any situation will depend upon the complexity of the information, the amount of exposure that students will have, and the task students will be required to perform.

The importance of this latter variable in the selection of a representation scheme is vividly shown in an example from Bruner (1966) concerning airline routes.[7] The data consist of airline connections among five Northeastern cities. One approach is to present the information as it might be extracted from a schedule; Boston to Concord, Danbury to Concord, Albany to Boston, and so forth. If a student who has memorized this list were asked "What is the shortest way to make a round trip from Albany to Danbury?" a considerable amount of information processing would be required. This processing load might be slightly reduced by listing the connections in alphabetical

[7]Bruner (1966, p. 46) attributes this example to Dr. J. Richard Hayes.

order: Albany to Boston, Albany to Elmira, Boston to Albany, and so forth, but neither approaches the utility of diagrams as shown in Figure 4.4.

Notice, however, that in the figure, *b* is slightly better than *a* for seeing that Elmira (E) is a trap and that there is only one way from Albany (A) to Danbury (D).

The options for representation discussed so far—flowcharts, tables, prose, graphs—are distinctly different structures for organizing information. Another dimension along which representations might vary is a metaphorical one, relating a new concept to an already acquired one. In the Lotus 1–2–3® documentation, for example, the electronic spreadsheet is likened to "a piece of ruled paper spread out on your desk," and the current display on the CRT is presented as a window that can be moved over the spreadsheet to show different scenes. Split-screen displays are explained by reference to two TV cameras sending images to separate monitor screens.

Motivation and Feedback

All students require motivation; the longer the course and the more complicated the material, the more motivation is needed. However, motivation must be appropriate for the age and social/cultural background of the learner. Repeated displays of the student's own name ("Natalie, you are right!" and "No, Marsha, that is not the answer") may, if not overdone, be motivating for younger students, but probably not for older ones. Games are basically motivational devices imposed on drill, where the motivation derives from the properties of the game itself: competition, randomness, and the like (Malone, 1981). Psychologists generally distinguish between intrinsic motivation, deriving from such natural human tendencies as curiosity and the desire "to know," and extrinsic motivation, which is based upon externally offered rewards.

For the design of CAI lessons, one must first judge the degree of intrinsic motivation a course might tap in the targeted student audience, and then decide how much, if any, extrinsic motivation is needed. The options for extrinsic motivators usually include game formats, humor, use of personal name, high-gloss graphics for variation in drill formats and feedback on progress. The last-named approach depends upon *achievement motivation,* that is, the desire to achieve. Unfortunately, this may not be present in all students.

Without feedback, little learning takes place. Sometimes a simple *yes* or *no, correct* or *wrong,* is sufficient feedback. At other times, a demonstration of the problem-solving procedure, step by step, is the most appropriate feedback. Intelligent teaching is diagnostic teaching, that is, based on feedback about learner needs. This feedback,

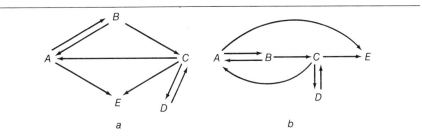

Figure 4.4. Diagrammatic Notation for Airline Routes (From J. S. Bruner, *Toward a theory of instruction* [Cambridge, MA: Harvard University Press, 1966], p. 47. Copyright 1966 by the President and Fellows of Harvard College. Reprinted by permission.)

ideally, will derive from student responses to instruction. As discussed above, a good CAI program generates, stores, and utilizes diagnostic information. Feedback and motivation are related; patterns of the former can produce positive amounts of the latter.

Difficulty Level

For a short period in the recent history of instruction, it was believed that the best instruction proceeded in small steps that minimized the chances for incorrect responses. The resulting curriculums, bound into the bland frames of programmed instruction, produced much boredom and little learning of anything above the factual level. The attitude today is closer to "No pain, no gain" than it is to the programmed instruction creed, yet there are limits to the returns that struggling will produce. Teachers learn through experience that with frustration little learning takes place but that with assistance students can handle more difficult material than they can independently. Difficulty level is controlled by two related variables: *content* and *pacing*. Content refers to the skills being taught: associations, procedures, and the like. The readiness of students to integrate the course materials into already acquired structures is a major determinant of difficulty level. But it is not the gap or distance between the student's current level of understanding and that required by the course materials that matters so much as the degree to which instruction provides bridges from the old to the new.

The transition from arithmetic to algebra, for example, requires the acquisition of a new (or extended) meaning for the equal sign, the use of symbolic values, and new approaches to problem solving (Matz, 1982). These concepts can be introduced gradually, carefully explained and practiced, and contrasted with arithmetic concepts. The new concepts could also be explained briefly and then applied, with little attempt made to wean old habits and build new ones.

Similarly, when a programming language is being taught at an introductory level, a slow, careful sequence is usually required with moderate content load. This approach appears to work fine for inexperienced programmers, but computer science majors can usually move at a significantly faster pace and handle a much higher conceptual load than is typically offered in such general courses. The selection of content and pace must be done in relation to the entry abilities of the learners as well as to their motivation and available study time. Within these constraints, pace needs to be adjusted according to the difficulty of the material being taught. The division of skills across lessons and the assignment of lessons to time slots also need to be guided by knowledge of skill difficulty. An even pace based on chapters, frames, lessons, or the like, seldom approaches optimal efficiency.

Interaction Style

"Style is the man himself," said Buffon.[8] So, also, does interaction style make a course, given that all else is done well. By interaction style is meant the relationship that is created between instructor and student by the tone of the messages presented and (for CAI) the *feel* of the screen displays. A course that elicits the student's first

---

[8]Compte George-Louise Leclerc de Buffon, a French naturalist of the eighteenth century, actually said, "Le style est l'homme même."

name and then proceeds to address the student by this name has a personality different from one that has no personal touches. A system that employs occasional humor, deprecates itself with comments like "I'm too limited to understand that," and is forgiving of obvious typing errors is perceived differently from a system that responds frigidly to all unrecognized responses with "Unrecognized input" or "Wrong."

Similarly, screen displays in unrelenting capital letters without borders or color create a feel different from displays that incorporate a full inventory of typographic and graphic devices. But all of this is not to say that a personal style incorporating humor and zippy, full-color windows is always desired over whatever the opposite of these qualities is. Repeated citing of a first name can become cloying, overuse of windows, distracting and cute animations, disturbing. On the creation of legible, readable, and aesthetically pleasing screen displays, a small but useful research literature is available (see Chapter 11).

Student Involvement

All things being equal (which they seldom are), academically engaged students learn more than those who are not so engaged. Exactly what "academically engaged" means and how it can be measured, however, are not easy to determine. Measuring the activity levels of particular areas in the cerebral cortex associated with learning might be one approach but an impractical one under current technological (and civil liberty) constraints. The alternative, which is advocated here, is to involve the student as actively as possible in the instructional process, with the hope that the added vigilance and attention required by this involvement will raise the probability of acquiring the instructional content.

One approach to student involvement is to ask students to perform particular activities (e.g., "Copy these words into your notebooks"); another is to provide opportunities for students, on their own initiative, to participate actively in the instruction, as for example, in question-answer sessions. Some of these opportunities for involvement result in students' controlling, to some degree, the instructional process; others, such as small-group discussions among students, result in a shift in the locus of control.

The lowest level of active student involvement occurs with questions or requests directed from the instructor/machine to the student. These may vary from "Press ENTER to continue" to requests for recall or problem solving (e.g., "How many oranges will be left at the end of the game?"). These might occur during an introduction, explication, simulation, demonstration, or instructor-led problem solving. In general, frequent attempts should be made during any extensive instructor presentation to involve the students and raise their levels of attention.

The next level of student involvement includes opportunites for questions directed from the student to the instructor. In a live teaching situation, these typically are open ended and may lead to smaller or larger shifts in the plan for the day or to guidance, such as "That is covered in the assigned reading for today." In on-line instruction, limits on the practicality of natural-language input constrain such requests to either present categories of assistance (e.g., "Press F1 for a definition, F2 for an example, F3 for a rewording of the principle") or to requests formulated from a constrained syntax and vocabulary (e.g., a key-word help system). Allowing backtracking to previous screens also fits this category.

Student interaction in pairs or small groups forms the third level of student involvement. In Slavin's (1983) team learning, groups of students, under the direction of a team leader, work together to solve a problem, produce a report, and so forth. For this to be productive, however, the instructor must have a well-developed work plan, complete with background materials and, if relevant, exemplars of what is expected to result from the team effort. In on-line learning, groups of students could interact using electronic mail, on-line conferencing, or interactive messages (e.g., "talk" in UNIX). A more sophisticated system for on-line team learning requires that students share a common problem window and be able to replay the interaction protocol at any time. Such a facility is highly desirable for simulations as well as for problem-solving sessions in which an instructor might monitor the group effort.

Finally, some brief consideration to contexts in which students act as instructors. Peer and cross-age tutoring are common examples of these in use today, as are, on a more limited scale, student modeling wherein students demonstrate how to solve a particular problem by thinking out loud (Palincsar and Brown, 1984). If the goal in using students as instructors is to enhance the learning of the student-as-teacher, then we might treat this as a form of practice. If, on the other hand, our goal is primarily to further the learning of the other students, then we are not changing any of the modes or methods outlined above. Instead, we are shifting, albeit temporarily, the role of student to that of instructor. However, since little experience has been gained from on-line student teachers, we can only suggest it as an interesting, but unproven idea for designers to consider.

These are the most important variables to be controlled within a particular instructional strategy. How these might be juggled for different instructional goals and different learners is the main content of Chapter 6.

SUMMARY

Appropriate instruction is composed of planned learning experiences, generally with corrective feedback, that have a reasonable chance of changing the learner's ability levels for the material taught. The goals of instruction in the cognitive domain are increases in both declarative and procedural knowledge, here labeled associations and procedural operations. The former is divided into categorical, logical/mathematical, and linguistic classes, while the latter is divided into basic and compound operations. Logical thinking, which is the long-range goal of most cognitive instruction, is the combined use of associations and procedural operations for problem solving, decision making, and the like.

Three instructional modes can be used to achieve these instructional ends: explanatory, demonstration, and problem solving. Each is defined by a particular sequence of instructional events, but within the same mode, topic sequencing, locus of control, instructional delivery, and adaptation to individual needs may vary considerably. For lesson design, primary importance is given to knowledge representation, motivation, feedback, interaction style, and student involvement.

CHAPTER 5

The Psychology of Learning
Shadows Cast on the Cave's Wall
from the Inner Workings of the Mind

I say moreover that you make a great, a very great mistake, if you think that psychology, being the science of the mind's law, is something from which you can deduce definite programmes and schemes and methods of instruction for immediate classroom use. Psychology is a science, and teaching is an art; and sciences never generate art directly out of themselves. An intermediary inventive mind must make the application, by using its originality.

—William James, *Talks to Teachers* (1989)

The statement above, originally delivered by William James to a group of teachers in Cambridge, Massachusetts, should be reread at the end of this chapter, lest the reader be misled on the powers and glory of psychology. This chapter is about the psychology of learning, or at least that part of the vast literature on psychology that could guide, inspire, or perhaps even constrain the instructional designer. The field of cognitive psychology, which is the subset of psychology that is of interest here, is important as a general guide for instructional design and is indispensable for certain specific decisions, but it is not so far advanced as to give complete directions to the instructor or curriculum designer, and even if it were, James's admonition would still hold. "A science only lays down lines within which the rules of the art must fall, laws which the follower of the art must not transgress; but what particular thing he shall positively do within those lines is left exclusively to his own genius," James continued (1899/1958, pp. 23–24), and we should heed.

Psychology is a vast field, encompassing such diverse matters as perception, psychophysics, clinical counseling, physiological psychology, and cognitive psychology. Furthermore, psychology, like the other social sciences, and perhaps all sciences, is bound by the tyranny of its own successes as codified in theories and experimental paradigms. Behaviorism, for example, which began in the early part of this century as a reaction to the perceived inconsistencies and contradictions of mentalism, dominated American psychology until after World War II. Its fundamental tenets were that the inner workings of the mind were not accessible and therefore should not be sought out. Only behavior could be observed, and thus the only legitimate approach to the study of human learning was through the outward manifestations of learning, in particular, responses to directly observable stimuli.

To Edward L. Thorndike, whose work had and continues to have a large influence on education, all learning could be explained by a series of laws: the Law of Readiness, the Law of Exercise, the Law of Effect, and so forth. These laws were based on the assumption that learning involved direct links between stimuli and responses, unmediated by higher cognitive processes. They also were assumed to be as important for human learning as they were for animal learning from which they derived. For Skinner, who subscribed to the basic Thorndike doctrine, the psychologist's role was to control behavior by manipulating the environment. Programmed instruction, which was the basis of the earliest CAI programs and which continues, sometimes in subtle forms, to influence CAI, was the direct outgrowth of Skinner's training studies with pigeons and rats. Small learning steps, positive reinforcement, and minimal opportunity for error were the processes through which any form of learning was to be built. *To understand learning* meant *to know how to control it.*

Today the study of the mind is back in favor. A variety of approaches, some old and some new, are used to probe the nature and limitations of memory, the role of imagery in learning and remembering, the acquisition of problem-solving strategies, and a variety of other cognitive issues. The newer spirit eschews grand theories of learning in favor of more focused attention to particular components of thinking—memory, problem-solving strategies, self-monitoring, and the like. We may be blinded at times by our own feelings of progress, but there are no dominating bullies as in the past around whom the field revolves. Perhaps the most important theme that has emerged from the newer study of cognition is the need to understand the concepts (and misconceptions) that students bring to a learning task and the representations that they use for this knowledge. Schema theory, runnable models, and the like, represent this new thrust.

What follows in this chapter is a highly selective summary of those aspects of cognitive psychology that are relevant to our interests in this book and, in particular, to those variables around which the last chapter ended—motivation, feedback, representation, and the like. No attempt is made here to be evenhanded or comprehensive; for those luxuries, the reader should consult recent works in the field, including Mayer (1983), Anderson (1985), and Klahr and Wallace (1976). Our goal is flavoring and mind-set, not specific guidelines. From this chapter the reader should gain a feeling for the issues the psychology of learning attends to and the kinds of questions the designer of learning systems should be asking. The next section presents an overview of learning, including developmental models. Subsequent sections focus on specific aspects of learning, including, among other topics, metacognition, memory, motivation, and feedback.

AN OVERVIEW OF LEARNING

Learning versus Intellectual Development

While we have spoken so far about learning, a distinction is made by psychologists between this entity and intellectual development, which is the true goal of most (but not all) school instruction. *Learning* involves the acquisition of associations and procedures (often called information or knowledge)—an accumulation of stuff in the mind. *Intellectual development,* on the other hand, implies an enrichment of the structures that control learning. Learning usually centers on specifics—circuit analysis, capitals of the states, stages in the economic development of a country or region, and so forth, while intellectual development centers on objects, classes, relationships, and structures.

The former begins with a fixed set of mental abilities and asks how these abilities might best be deployed for acquiring a particular topic, skill, idea, set of relations, or whatever. The latter asks how these very mental capacities might be extended, enriched, or improved. This distinction can be blurred, particularly when the term *learning* is applied to intellectual matters, such as the acquisition of problem-solving strategies. Nevertheless, the distinction of importance is between learning, in the sense of accumulating more and more knowledge, versus development of capacity for learning through acquisition of higher and more complex intellectual abilities. In this chapter we are interested in both phenomena.

Stages of Development. Observation of the enormous intellectual growth that the human species exhibits in passing from child to adult has led to a variety of theories about stages of intellectual development. These theories differ in the degree to which stages are bound to unalterable physiological mechanisms and in how the child progresses from stage to stage. Their importance for instructional design is in suggesting which strategies of instruction might be effective at different developmental stages. On one end are the *critical periods* models, which hold that humans, like many lower forms, pass through critical growth stages in which certain types of learning are facilitated and others not. Thus Lenneberg (1967) postulated that a critical period existed for learning a second language, extending perhaps to the age of seven. After this, due perhaps to a decrease in the plasticity of the brain, learning a second language is more difficult. More recent studies (e.g., Walberg, Keiko, & Rasher, 1978) appear to refute this notion. Similar ideas about learning stages based on physiological growth were advanced in the 1920s (e.g., Gesell, 1928), leading to the general concept of *readiness*. In the teaching of reading, for example, many psychologists held that until the child reached the mental age of 6.5 years, her ability to learn to read was not sufficient to ensure average progress. The evidence for this notion was derived primarily from correlational studies in which home background and schooling methods were not controlled.

Much more influential today, however, are the developmental models that have grown out of the work of Piaget and his colleagues and followers (e.g., Piaget, 1963; Patterson, 1977). Piaget postulated four major stages to account for intellectual development from birth to roughly 15 years of age: sensorimotor (birth to 2 years), preoperational (2 to 7 years), concrete operations (7 to 12 years), and formal operations (12 to 15 years). All children are assumed to pass through these stages in the same order, but not at the same rate. Each stage, and each of the various substages, is characterized by specific modes of thought and by specific mental structures. Thus, in the preoperational stage, which extends roughly from 2 to 7 years of age, the child acquires representational thought along with the ability to reflect on her own actions and on the past and the future. Most perception and thinking, however, is dominated by a central element; multiple features and multiple viewpoints are difficult to entertain.

Intelligence, according to Piaget, results from biological adaptation, but the modes of adaptation differ across the stages. Exactly how the child progresses from one stage or level to the next is somewhat fuzzy; nevertheless, the Piagetian model has led to a wealth of information on children's mental representations and on strategies for solving specific tasks. Its implications for the design of instruction derive strongly from Piaget's emphasis on learning as an active process, based on the child's probing of the environment. For the preoperational child, free collaboration, cooperation, and communication are critical components in a learning environment, as are concrete tasks.

Rule Learning. Other developmental psychologists, like Siegler (1986), while expounding developmental models, have chosen to focus more on the nature of the rules that children use at different stages to solve particular tasks. Siegler assumes that much of the child's understanding is rule-governed and that some rules have broad application, particularly to unify reasoning. Central to the construction and use of rules is the manner in which the child encodes a task or situation. A 6-year-old, for example, tends to use height alone to determine which of two glasses holds more water. In contrast, a 10-year-old will use two features, height and cross-sectional area, for the same task. Part of teaching the younger child to do the comparison properly involves leading the child to encode more than the height of the liquid.

Encoding is an important issue not just in Piagetian tasks, but in many other forms of learning and development. Consider, as an example, learning of decoding rules for reading. Some letters, like *c,* have several pronunciations (cf. city, coal, social, cello). In initial position the letter following *c* indicates whether *c* is hard as in *coal* or soft as in *city.* (*Cello* is an exception for which no rule applies.) In learning to read, children typically encounter many hard *c* words before any soft *c* ones, therefore they tend to generalize an invariant hard pronunciation for initial *c.* Only after encountering a number of soft *c* words do they begin to show variant pronunciations. Those who encode only the letter *c* and its first or most common pronunciation will generally not realize the basic importance of the following letter as quickly as those who encode not only the letter but its immediate orthographic environment. For those who have access to the letter following *c,* seeing that *e, i,* or *y* signals soft *c* while any other letter signals hard *c* should be easier than for those who don't have this information available.

Everyone engages in active encoding of the environment, which involves selecting certain features to encode and ignoring others. Learning what features to encode for a given experience and purpose is one way to view conceptual development. Even solving math word problems involves encoding. Part of what is known to trip up students in solving word problems is the presence of redundant or irrelevant information. Here the problem is to recognize that certain information is not to be encoded, that it is irrelevant to the solution of the problem.

In science learning, the role of incorrect rules or *misconceptions* is currently the object of considerable research. Both children and adults harbor misconceptions about how the physical world operates. Children, for example, generally assume before being taught otherwise that heat and temperature are identical. Instruction that attempts to bring the child to a realization that the two concepts are different might be more successful than instruction that ignores this common confusion and teaches the concepts sequentially. How tightly held such misconceptions are and how to alter them is only now being explored (Driver & Easley, 1978; Trowbridge & Mintzes, 1985; Hopp, 1985).

Memory and Learning

Memory has been a central object of psychological research since the influential list-learning studies of Ebbinghaus in the 1880s. However, Ebbinghaus wanted to explore memory without the influence of prior learning so he emphasized the use of lists of nonsense syllables and other unrelated units, a selection that directed and dominated memory studies until the 1930s when Bartlett published his works on memory for meaningful material (Bartlett, 1932). With the revival of cognitive psychology in the 1950s, studies of memory strategies and memory mechanisms increased dramatically and a variety of new concepts of memory developed. For many years memory was conceived as a three-part store: sensory memory; a short-term component (STM), with rapid decay and a small, fixed capacity; and a long-term component (LTM), with negligible decay and practically unlimited capacity. Information received through the senses came first into the sensory store and from there, through a variety of mechanisms, into short-term and then long-term memory.

More recent views of memory (e.g., Baddeley, 1986) replace the singular concept of a short-term memory with a multicomponent *working memory*. A central executive in working memory directs operations by controlling attention and selecting strategies for slave systems. The slave systems are memory stores specialized for particular types of data, for example, speech store, visuospatial scratch pad. These stores also have limited capacities and limited holding times. Information to be retained in working memory such as a telephone number, is recoded into a speechlike form and held in the speech store. To avoid decay of the information, the central executive directs an articulatory loop to periodically recycle it, thus restoring it with each cycle to its original intensity. This store-and-recycle mechanism is critical for holding information in working memory for more than 10–15 seconds.

Limits on working memory affect comprehension of speech and perception of moving scenes, as well as other types of input. However, capacity is enhanced by recoding. For adults, certain types of input are automatically recoded to a speechlike form when they are retained in working memory. Picture names and telephone numbers are typical of this class of input. Children, however, do not generally develop this ability until the age of 5 or 6 (Conrad, 1972). Some encoding also involves information in long-term memory; for example, when we transcribe a list of book titles from dictation, the ones we know are easier to retain in working memory than those we don't, because the former can be recoded in a brief form while the latter have to be held word for word. In other cases, such as in remembering a telephone number long enough to write it down, structural information from previous learning can be helpful. Anyone familiar with American phone numbers knows the basic structure of a three-digit area code, followed by three digits and then four more. Familiar area codes can be recoded as a city or state, which presumably requires less working memory space than three digits.

Structure also plays a major role in the retention of information in long-term memory. However, memory recall should be viewed not as a passive *find and retrieve,* but as imaginative reconstruction where items are partially recalled and partially rebuilt, either from specific or from general instructions. Studies of repeated recall demonstrate, for example, that information stored in long-term memory tends to be restructured over time to fit expectations. This could result from loss of specific information, which then is reconstructed based on related and therefore more common information. *Loss* in long-term memory is not conceived of as a decay loss as in working memory, but rather as loss of accessibility, whereby the routes for finding an item—its interconnections within the memory store—atrophy with disuse or become less accessible through interference from other material held in memory.

Images play an important role in long-term memory and a vast literature exists on the properties of visual images in learning and memory. Since classical Greek times memory enhancement methods have been taught and utilized. One of the oldest is the Method of Loci whereby a familiar room, floor, building, or even neighborhood is imagined, and items from a list assigned, one by one, to sequential locations in the scene. Recall then involves revisiting the scene and retrieving the stored items. Other imagery methods have been built, for example, around arbitrary associations of objects (paired associates). All of these methods work best for factual material and least for conceptual material. Children can be taught to generate images for facilitating learning and memory but generally not before the age of 8 or 9. However, pictures and high-imagery words do facilitate learning and memory even at the younger ages (Wittrock, 1986).

Patterns of Learning and Forgetting. If we prepared a list of foreign countries, each paired with its capital, and taught high school students with training/test trials to recall each capital when given the corresponding country name, we might obtain a learning plot such as shown in Figure 5.1. On each trial, the names of the countries are displayed one at a time on a VDU. The subject responds orally to each one with the name of its capital, then immediately sees the correct name displayed on the screen. A single trial consists of one pass (randomly) through all the countries. The percentage correct on each trial, as shown in Figure 5.1, increases gradually with trials and asymptotes at 100 percent. This *learning curve* is typical of incremental learning where a skill becomes gradually more proficient with practice. The slope of the learning curve and its asymptote will vary with task and learners but will retain a shape similar to Figure 5.1 for most associative learning.

A different type of learning curve is shown in Figure 5.2, where time to solve a decoding task (for a single subject) is plotted against trials. For the first eight trials, solution time decreases slightly, probably due to increased familiarity with the problem

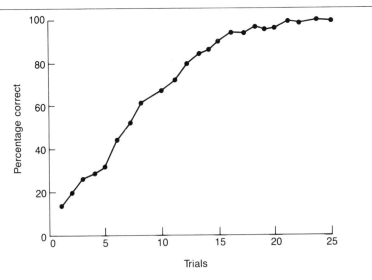

Figure 5.1. Learning Curve for Memorizing Capitals of Foreign Countries ($N = 140$)

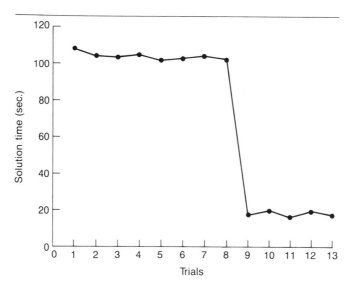

Figure 5.2. Learning Curve for Decoding Task ($N = 15$)

formats. Then, suddenly, on the ninth trial, solution time decreases dramatically and stays low for the remaining four trials. This type of learning is called breakthrough learning and is representative of many complex learning tasks where insight into a rule or pattern occurs in the course of problem solving. Breakthrough learning, which depends upon schema change, tends to endure for a longer time with disuse than associative learning, such as the country-capital type.

Decay of learning, also called *forgetting,* can also be plotted. Assume for the moment that all the subjects who mastered the country-capital list (i.e., scored 100% on two consecutive trials) were randomly assigned to 12 groups, numbered 1–12. With no prior knowledge or further testing, group 1 is called one week after completion of the initial trials and asked to do a single trial. Group 2 is called two weeks later, and so on through group 12. Assuming that the subjects did not rehearse after the end of the initial learning trials, we would expect the forgetting curve to appear similar to what is shown in Figure 5.3. Ebbinghaus (1913) found in the late nineteenth century that falloff in retention of meaningless materials fit a logarithmic curve. Since that time the same shape of forgetting curve has been shown to fit retention of many other types of materials, including numerals and meaningful words. The shapes of the learning and forgetting curves are important for both instructional planning and dynamic decision making.

Knowledge Representation. The manner in which knowledge is represented in memory has been a matter of concern at least since Bartlett's (1932) pioneering work on memory in which the concept of schema was initiated. A *schema* is a structure for interrelating knowledge. Information about schools, for example, might be held in a school schema, which would connect facts about teachers, students, classrooms, textbooks, report cards, and all the other objects, activities, and appurtenances of this topic. In reading about schools, we reference this schema to fill in missing information, make

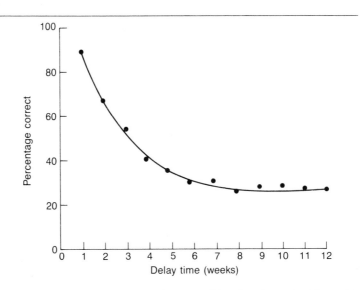

Figure 5.3. Forgetting Curve for Capitals of Foreign Countries (N = 132)

inferences, and test for validity. In the last chapter we discussed representation from the standpoint of the instructional designer, drawing particularly on Bruner (1966). Here we are concerned with the spontaneous representations that learners build with exposure to specific types of knowledge and, in particular, with how these representations differ from those held by experts in the field of concern.

Larkin (1983) has examined both novice and expert representations for force, mass, and acceleration problems in physics and found fundamental differences between the two. While naive subjects (novices) represented the physical systems strictly in terms of familiar entities and operations that worked in real time, experts supplemented this type of representation with another, built from fictitious entities like forces and momenta. In both cases the models were qualitative and runnable, but they differed in (a) the types of entities represented, (b) the rules of inference employed, and (c) the role of the physical environment in which they operated. The physical representations that were unique to the experts were time- and environment-independent, allowing solution plans that focused on abstract entities rather than often irrelevant real-world factors.

Similarly, Gott (1988–89), in reviewing work on electronic-circuit troubleshooting, points out that skilled performers in this domain use hierarchical device knowledge representations and can work back and forth across levels of abstraction in problem solving. Successful on-line training systems like Sherlock use problem space graphs as "cognitive model alternatives to a deep device simulation and runnable diagnostic expertise" (Gott, 1988–89, p. 140). Clancey (1986) distinguishes between a *behavioral* model, built of domain-specific situation-action patterns, and a *functional-qualitative* model, built of a general model plus a situation-specific model, which is derived from the general model by inference procedures. The transition from novice representation to expert representation may be domain-specific and might occur through successive approximations as suggested by White and Frederiksen (1987) or through radical schema change.

Metacognition

For years psychologists have been aware that part of intellectual development was the acquisition of monitoring or control abilities, specifically for control of learning and problem solving. More recently, a fancy term, *metacognition,* has been adopted for this and a few related abilities. The child who applies the last arithmetic operation taught to each problem in a practice set, regardless of its appropriateness, demonstrates lack of metacognitive ability. Similarly, the child who computes the area of a square and accepts a negative result displays the same deficit. Metacognitive ability refers to a range of control abilities, including task verification, solution planning, resource allocation, and solution checking. Metacognition applies to CAI design at several levels. In teaching any topic or skill, it is also desirable to teach how to monitor one's own acquisition of that topic or skill. This might lead to instruction in specific monitoring strategies, such as estimating the magnitude of a desired math problem solution or generating questions before attempting to read a social studies passage.

Knowledge of metacognitive abilities should also guide the extent of student control built into any lesson or course. TICCIT, for example, assumed that college-level students could make a wide range of decisions about their own learning, including what types of explanations they needed and when examples would be helpful. For lower-ability students, such decisions are often a source of added difficulty in a learning task. Little research exists, however, on the monitoring abilities of college students, although White and Smith (1974) have done a preliminary exploration of the amount of responsibility that students at this level can accept for instructional decisions. Studies done in several topic areas (e.g., Brown, 1978; Schoenfeld, 1985) show that certain metacognitive abilities can be taught overtly, resulting in enhanced problem-solving performance.

Part of metacognitive development may result from school experience. Younger children generally do not understand the relationship of school learning to out-of-school life nor do they recognize how they might control any of their own learning processes. As more experience is gained in classroom processes and as students are encouraged more and more to adopt good study habits, they may come to realize that even in solving specific problems they should be monitoring their own behavior. Vygotsky (1962) has proposed that higher-order cognitive skills, which would include metacognition, are acquired through an external-to-internal process. First, a skill is learned on a social level, generally through adult guidance or collaboration with more advanced peers. Then, through practice, it becomes internalized.

Metacognition involves skill, but it also involves attitudes and beliefs, in that the learner has to believe that she can acquire a certain body of material or solve a particular set of questions. The learner must also believe that further effort has a positive value. On this, more is said in the next section, "Motivation."

MOTIVATION

Motivation is considered important in most cognitive theories of learning, yet it tends to receive little attention in empirical studies. For instructional designers, the ability to motivate the learner may be more important than the specific instructional strategies adopted. Motivation is what drives the marathon runner to stay the course long after the body has called for surrender; it is what leads the problem solver to persist in the search for a solution when none appears to be available. Motivation provides both focus and intensity to behavior; it is the desire to reach a goal that transcends physical needs. For many learners, awareness of a task that requires solving is adequate motivation for working toward a solution. In more cognitive terms, an unsolved problem, an uncompleted task, a goal not yet reached, all evoke conflicting thoughts in the learner and drive her to resolve the conflict.

In contrast to these self-generated sources of motivation, behaviorists have stressed the role of external motivators—rewards and punishments—and a vast literature exists on the relative effects of chocolate candies, food pellets, and other treats on the immediate behavior of rats, pigeons, and college sophomores. These results have not been ignored by the many countries who openly offer large cash bonuses to their athletes for Olympic medals. Similar practices are common among middle-class parents who offer hard cash to their children for high marks in school or, alternatively, threaten removal of certain privileges for low marks. But for most sustained learning situations, the possibility of offering tangible rewards (or punishments) is quite limited, particularly on a day-by-day, problem-by-problem basis. We do not deny that motivation for learning can result from publicity on the importance of a college education for occupational success or on the economic advantages of graduation from high school. For many, these facts provide a continuing push for academic success; unfortunately, for others, they do not. But regardless of their value, they generally are not under control of the instructional designer or teacher nor are they always strong enough to sustain interest in every learning task. This, then, leaves us to search for those mental factors that can provide motivation for particular tasks within an instructional context, acknowledging at the same time that whatever can be done to provide more global motivation should be done.

Curiosity

Among the motivating variables that can be controlled is curiosity, which acts as a motivator by producing a moderately aroused state through novelty, surprise, or even complexity. Two types of curiosity have been identified: perceptual curiosity, which results from perceptual events, and epistemic curiosity, which results from cognitive events—discrepant thoughts, attitudes or beliefs, and is more important for long-term learning (Berlyne, 1960). To demonstrate the effects of curiosity, Berlyne & Frommer (1966) generated stories with varying levels of novelty and uncertainty and had them read to kindergarten and third- and fifth-grade children. The stories with high levels of uncertainty and novelty elicited the greatest number of questions from the children. The authors argue that novelty and uncertainty cause conceptual conflict and that the children's questions represent an attempt to reduce this arousal level. *Inquiry teaching,* which is built around attempts to engage the students in probing a subject area through their own questions, assumes cognitive conflict as a motivator. Its success depends, in part, on providing sufficient knowledge of a topic to arouse interest in understanding it further, but not leaving so much uncertainty that the students become overwhelmed by the difficulty of the task.

Epistemic curiosity, like other forms of cognitive motivation, does not have a linear relationship with problem-solving efficiency. Instead, the relationship has an inverted U-shape: efficiency increases as degree of motivation increases, but only to some maximum, defined separately for each learner. Then as degree of motivation in the learner increases beyond this maximum, problem-solving efficiency decreases. In this state, the learner is overaroused and can no longer control her behavior effectively (Hudgins, 1977). In practical terms, one must learn through experience how much uncertainty or novelty to provide to motivate most students but not to overwhelm them.

Attribution Theory

So far we have ignored that part of motivation that results from the learner's beliefs about ability, luck, and effort. *Attribution theory* holds that how people attribute their own successes and failures among these three variables affects their feelings about themselves and therefore their predictions of success on future tasks. These then control the amount of effort that is expended on a task. Much has been written on attribution theory and its effects on classroom learning. In the briefest terms, the more learners attribute success to their own efforts and the more positive they feel about their own abilities, the more effort they are willing to exert in learning. In creative writing, for example, many students believe that the great writers have some innate ability that allows them to whip out Pulitzer Prize-quality first drafts. When their own first drafts fail to astound their instructors, they often attribute their failure to lack of ability rather than lack of effort. For these students, a heavy dose of interviews with famous writers might produce a change in attribution, especially when they discover how often accomplished novelists rewrite chapters before allowing anyone else to see them.

Modeling of problem solving, such as is done by Schoenfeld (1985), provides a context for improving student attributions of success. Demonstrating that even mathematics professors go wrong occasionally in problem-solving techniques and that many problems require hours or even days and weeks to solve, may help remove the notion that good problem solvers immediately see how to solve a problem and proceed directly from first reading to solution. At issue is how to motivate students to sustained effort, assuming that you are teaching them techniques that, through effort, will usually result in success.

Attribution theory must be viewed with some caution, however. Younger learners have different views of themselves and of the world than do older learners, just as younger learners have different abilities to monitor their learning than do older learners. Some studies done with fifth and sixth graders show that positive feelings about one's abilities can be taught and that these improved attitudes can lead to higher success rates in learning. But whether or not the attributions of younger children could be as easily changed remains to be seen. Then, too, older people who have low self-concept do not modify their views quickly, even with success (E. Gagne, 1985). For them, success on a task is more often attributed to luck or task ease than to their own efforts or ability. Whether time spent on building positive attitudes toward their own abilities has any more value than just trying to teach specific abilities remains to be determined.

Instructional Level

The last paragraph raises an issue for which few empirical results are available to provide guidance. The question is what level of difficulty is optimal for learning, considering time, instructional effort, and motivation? We know very little about frustration, but observation and common sense indicate that when tasks become too difficult, learners not only quit trying to solve them, but also can experience extreme negative feelings, bordering on anger, and that these feelings interfere with future learning. To be less clinical, repeated failure is a real turn-off. On the other hand, to reduce all learning to little baby steps wherein success is nearly guaranteed is to make learning boring and unchallenging, as the programmed instruction school proved over and over in the 1960s and 1970s. Some challenge is necessary, not only for motivation but also for learner engagement. We tend to remember best those tasks we struggled with the most, and we tend to remember best those solutions that were the most difficult to discover. For lower-level learning (e.g., facts, multiplication tables), Brophy (1980; cited in Rosenshine & Stevens, 1986) suggests an 80 percent success rate as desirable when the material is new, but perhaps 95 percent for review. These figures derive mostly from correlational studies, however, and do not translate easily to higher-level instruction where an entire lesson might center on a single problem.

ATTENTION

Attention operates on both a global and a local level during learning. In the larger sense, we would like the learner throughout a learning task to attend to those elements of the task that are important for the learning goal and to ignore those that are not. Thus, in reading to understand the causes of the U.S. Civil War, the student should expend most of her energy on causal information and little on matters that are irrelevant to this goal, such as the personalities of the protagonists or the differences between North and South in oral traditions. Questions posed before reading or embedded throughout the text can help focus attention, but at a cost, as will be discussed below. At a more immediate level, sensory experiences present more information to the perceiver than can be processed efficiently. Through a variety of mechanisms, we select certain elements to encode and remember, leaving the others to decay into oblivion. Severe limits exist, however, on our ability to allocate attention overtly. A student confronted with an unfamiliar VDU display with 5–6 windows and a batch of supporting menus may not know where to look for specific information and consequently may miss important instructions. Or, confronted with unfamiliar visual and acoustical messages, may attend to one but not the other.

Psychological Framework

The psychological framework proposed for understanding attention includes two critical concepts that not all psychologists agree on: limited processing capacity and active perception. The former can be explained as follows: Imagine that the mind is composed of a fixed number of processors, where each processor has a different problem type or information form that it can handle. Furthermore, assume that tasks with which we are unfamiliar require these processors while overlearned tasks do not. Consider, now, what happens when we are confronted with two acoustical messages simultaneously. If we have only one acoustical processor, we can choose only one of the messages to attend to. In doing so, we rule out understanding the content of the other, although studies of dual-input processing (dichotic listening) show that we can often perceive presence or absence of input or gender of speaker on one acoustical channel while processing another one in depth.

Active perception is required when processing unfamiliar inputs, but with appropriate practice these inputs become increasingly familiar and tasks involving them can become more and more automatic and thereby require less overt attention. When we first learn to drive we desire as few distractions as possible so that we can focus or attend to the road, the other cars, the gear shift, and the other elements of automotive handling. In time, driving becomes so automatic that we not only can carry on conversations with others while driving, but we also generally do not recall many of the ordinary events that occurred while moving from starting point to destination. Similarly, people can be trained to become so automatic at tasks like copying dictated words that they can simultaneously read silently with reasonable comprehension (Neisser, 1976).

Automaticity

For learning and instruction, the significance of this aspect of attention is that certain low-level tasks, if overlearned, can become sufficiently automatic that they require little overt attention and therefore allow mental capacity to be allocated to other tasks. In problem solving, for example, if low-level tasks such as unit conversions and simple arithmetic operations are highly practiced, then the problem solver can devote the majority of her attention to strategies and monitoring. In reading aloud, the child who has not mastered decoding and word recognition will devote the majority of her energy to these tasks, and consequently less to comprehension than a child who has mastered the lower-level tasks. While attention alone is not a sufficient basis for selecting instructional strategies in arithmetic and reading, it does give a justification for practice on isolated skills.

Active Attention

The notion of active perception that was mentioned above is perhaps more of a theoretical than a practical matter. At issue is how unattended information is lost, or how selective attention works. One theory holds that we actively block out unwanted messages, perhaps by keying on one of their salient features (Treisman, 1969). The other, advocated by Neisser (1976) among others, holds that perception itself requires anticipation and exploration for information pickup and that without these active processes information is lost. In other words, information received through one of the senses comes first to a temporary storage buffer from which it must be actively removed and either recoded or rehearsed to be retained. Otherwise, it is soon lost. Thus, in a dichotic listening situation, the second of two acoustical messages is lost, not because of active blocking but from inattention. "We choose what we will hear by actively engaging ourselves with it, not by shutting out its competitors" (Neisser, 1976, p. 87). Studies of memory for complex visual arrays provide support for the active view of perception. In one set of studies Haith (1971) found that 5-year-olds could recall as much information from a briefly exposed array of eight unfamiliar objects as could adults, if the recall cue came soon after the array was exposed. But with longer delay times before reporting, the younger subjects' recall deteriorated more rapidly than did the adults recall. Further probing revealed that the 5-year-olds were not encoding the objects in immediate memory for recall, but the adults were. This result accords with recent views of memory that allocate an important role for rehearsal (see "Memory and Learning," earlier in this chapter).

For the more global case of attention, the mechanisms postulated above lead to the prediction that whenever the learner is provided with a strategy for narrowing attention during a task, utilization of that strategy will depress acquisition of noncued material. (If information pickup were strictly passive, then we would not predict failure to pick up noncued information.) Whether or not precuing facilitates pickup of the material relevant to the precues will depend upon the complexity of the task. For easy tasks where processing capacity is not strained, probably little enhancement will occur; with highly complex or difficult tasks, improvement is more likely. Some of these effects were demonstrated by Kaplan & Simmons (1974) who gave reading objectives to one group of readers *before* they read a passage, and to a matched group *after* they read the same material. Information relevant to objectives was learned equally well in the two cases, but other information was learned best in the postreading condition. We can assume from these results that the reading task itself was not overly taxing to the subjects involved, and therefore they were able to comprehend all the information in the passage. The precue, therefore, had a negative effect, depressing attention to material not related to the prestated objectives. Students who had no knowledge of specific objectives before the reading attempted to attend to and retain as much as they could.

PRACTICE

Practice does not make perfect; instead, it fixes habits. Practice an incorrect way to shoot free throws and that is what will be learned. On the other hand, the difference between expert and novice in many fields is seen as approximately 10 years of practice. Not genius; not innate ability, but years of hard work. Practice appears to have a variety of cognitive outcomes. One is to make a particular skill or process more automatic. One can explain verbally over and over the procedure for shifting from first to second gear in a car, but until the procedure is practiced repeatedly, the learner will not be able to do it smoothly and quickly. Practice allows the full set of psychomotor actions to be deployed in an appropriate sequence. Practicing long division achieves a similar goal: connection of a sequence of skills built around estimation, multiplication, and subtraction. Until they are put together to achieve a single goal, the learner will not know if she can solve long-division problems.

For learning associations (declarative knowledge), type of practice is crucial. Rote memorization, no matter how actively pursued, will seldom be as efficient for learning as attempts to organize and elaborate the information to be learned. Learning the names for different leaf margins provides a simple example for these practice options. Five types of leaf margins are shown in Figure 5.4. A botanist might learn these by rote, possibly with a mnemonic (e.g., "Some **w**ax **s**trawberries **d**on't **s**mile **l**ovingly"). A more efficient approach might be to create a branching diagram of the various margin types, as shown in Figure 5.5.

Part of the effectiveness gained organizing information derives from the resulting representation, which can potentially reduce long-term memory load. But part also derives from the cognitive operations invoked to create the organization and from the struggling that may have taken place before a satisfactory model was designed. The search for distinguishing features and for an organizational form can, by themselves, enhance learning.

The stages through which a learner progresses in practicing a procedural skill have

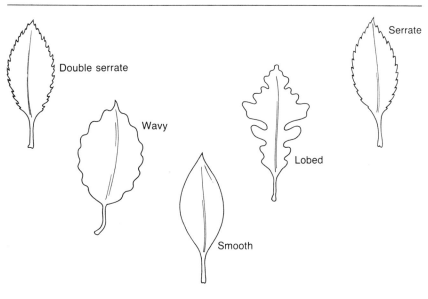

Figure 5.4. Leaf Margins

been mapped by Fitts & Posner (1967). First, the skill is encoded declaratively. That is, the learner verbalizes the actions to be taken. This is the verbal stage. Then, through practice, the learner detects and eliminates errors in initial understanding. The skill becomes procedural as the sequencing from step to step is learned. Finally, the skill becomes autonomous, that is automated and rapid. At this stage, particularly with overlearning, ability to verbalize steps may be lost.

Designing Skill Practice

In planning practice, three issues need special attention. The first is skill sequencing. If skills that are relatively independent are to be taught, is it best to teach each to

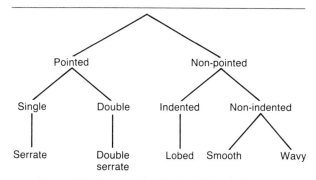

Figure 5.5. Organization for Leaf Margin Types

mastery before introducing the next, or should practice alternate across the skills, moving them in parallel toward mastery? For the ordinary classroom, the parallel approach is rarely used because of management difficulties; with computer-delivered instruction, however, it becomes a serious consideration. The parallel approach offers variety to the learner while at the same time forcing more attention to problem types than is achieved with single-skill practice, where the learner soon catches on that all the problems are of the same type. On the other hand, the parallel approach can become inefficient when each problem type requires considerable concentration from the learner. Then, the switching across problem types interferes with learning. In general, when the skills being taught are relatively simple, the parallel approach should at least be considered. But where skills are relatively complex, focused practice is probably the only effective option.

The second issue pits massed against distributed practice. Should practice sessions be relatively long and few in number or should they be short, with a larger number distributed over time? There is no simple answer to the question, although most experimental studies have concluded that distributed practice is superior to massed practice, particularly if motor skills are being learned (Ellis, 1978). The last issue concerns degree of overlearning (i.e., continuation of practice beyond mastery). We stated earlier that overlearning is important with some learning to ensure that procedures become automatic. The justification for this position came from considerations of mental capacity. Automatic skills required less mental capacity than nonautomatic ones. But Hudgins (1977), in reviewing studies on overlearning, finds that the increase in achievement from overlearning decreases rapidly beyond a point that varies with the type of learning involved. In one study involving memorization of words in a list, 50 percent overlearning (i.e., adding, after mastery, one half again the number of trials needed for mastery) was optimal for longer-term retention (about one month). Learning of meaningful material is also facilitated by overlearning, but too little is known about this topic to draw guidelines for instructional design.

Depth of Processing

If information in a text is to be learned for later recall, what is the best study technique? One approach is to reread the passage a sufficient number of times to reach the desired recall level. This is the most passive approach, but the one probably used most often. More active approaches involve underlining, note taking, and summarizing. For passages presented on a VDU, similar choices could be made; in addition, the lesson designer might highlight significant words or phrases for the student. Rickards and August (1975) examined several of these possibilities, using printed stories. The highest degree of learning resulted from the group in which students underlined words they thought were important. The next highest group read the stories with words already underlined by the teacher. Student underlining of unimportant words led to lower scores than no underlining at all. However, more recent studies have shown that the critical factor in study techniques is the degree to which they encourage deep processing. Those techniques, for example, that lead to organization and elaboration of material to be learned produce better results than those procedures that simply direct attention to particular items or features. (See Anderson and Armbruster, 1984, for a review.)

Lindsay and Norman (1979) make the same argument for memorization of word lists. Repeating the words over and over requires little depth of processing and therefore is not as effective a study technique as finding opposites for each word. This approach, however, is inferior to forming images of successive pairs, which in turn is inferior to creating a story that incorporates the words in their list order. The latter task requires the deepest processing, as measured by the number of associations that are created between the words themselves and between each word and information stored in long-term memory. Craig and Lockhart (1972) interpreted depth of processing in terms of degree of semantic (i.e., meaningful) processing, which they suggest requires the learner to relate knowledge held in memory (i.e., prior knowledge) to new information. Semantic encoding leads to better retention of information compared to shallower, more perceptual encoding.

Depth of processing, which is not always easy to define operationally, has also been advanced as a critical variable in determining achievement outcomes in cooperative learning of mathematics at the high school level (Corno, 1988). With group rather than individual incentives, lower-achieving students were not forced by group members to engage in appropriate problem-solving behavior and therefore did not acquire needed problem-solving skills. Depth of processing is one of the factors missing from the time-on-task models (e.g., Carroll, 1963; Denham & Lieberman, 1980). As Lindsay and Norman (1979) have demonstrated, students can be academically engaged and still not learn efficiently because of the learning method selected.

Nevertheless, active learning produces higher retention than passive learning, although results vary according to student abilities and types of difficulty levels of the materials to be learned. Wittrock (1981) has proposed a model of generative learning that assigns major importance in learning to organizing stimuli through active utilization of existing schemata, past experience, and information transformations. Sternberg (1985) incorporates similar notions in defining information-processing components of intelligence, which he divides into (1) performance components, (2) knowledge acquisition components, and (3) metacomponents. The performance components include encoding, inferring, mapping, and application. The knowledge acquisition components include, among others, selective encoding, selective combination, and selective comparison; and the metacomponents are the strategy construction mechanisms.

Response Mode

One of the choices that instructional designers are continually facing is what type of response to require for a particular task. The choices usually available are (1) constructed response; (2) multiple choice (including yes-no); (3) participation response (i.e., "press any key to continue"); (4) honor system (i.e., "think of an answer," but no overt response required); and (5) no response. Tobias (1982) claims that constructed responses facilitate achievement for new content, but that for familiar content, as in a review, no differences exist across the various response modes. The role of responses is to force the learner to actively engage herself in a task. Constructed responses are superior because they provide the highest potential focus on what is being taught. Multiple-choice questions, in contrast, encourage a focus on the question itself and, in particular, on the alternatives, which may allow a correct choice with limited knowledge of the topic of interest. Students who have a firm grasp of a topic will probably not profit from any manipulation of response mode; in fact, the more time or effort required for responding in such situations, the greater the potential for boredom. In contrast, the less-prepared student will generally profit from having to construct responses.

Feedback

In a learning situation, externally provided feedback might be (1) an evaluation of the correctness of a response (e.g., correct, nearly correct, wrong), (2) information on the speed of the response (e.g., too slow, 10 seconds), or (3) an evaluation of the procedure used for responding (e.g., step 3 was incorrect). Obviously, any combination of these might be employed, for example, "Your answer was correct, but it took you too long to produce and you reversed steps 5 and 6."

Besides providing corrective information, feedback is also potentially motivating (but not always so). Most people like to succeed, even in small tasks such as solving a math problem. Being told you are correct may increase your self-esteem and your desire to learn more. Being told you are incorrect creates an imbalance or tension, which you might strive to resolve by working harder to respond correctly. But as pointed out in an earlier chapter, not all learning requires externally provided feedback.

For cognitive learning, feedback has differential effects according to learner types. For slower learners and those with lower self-image, positive feedback can play a large reward function. However, overrewarding slower learners runs the risk in a classroom setting of reinforcing expectation differences (Weinstein, 1983). For average and above-average learners, feedback plays mostly an informational role. Therefore, it is most useful when a skill is first developing and decreases in value as the learner becomes more competent at a task. During initial learning, guidance not only on the correctness of an answer but also on the specific fault of an incorrect answer can facilitate learning. The same level of feedback on a review will probably have a mostly negative effect, in that the learner will be slowed from a normal pace and be forced to endure comments that are usually no longer needed.

On the timing of feedback, a somewhat misty picture has emerged from current research. Kulick and Kulick (1988), in a meta-analysis of 53 well-documented studies on feedback timing, found three different classes of results, depending on the learning content. For classroom quizzes or programmed materials (applied studies), immediate feedback was usually better than delayed feedback, although the average-effect sizes were not generally large (approximately 0.28 standard deviation). For learning of test content, immediate feedback was almost always inferior to delayed feedback, with average-effect sizes only slightly larger than in the first case (approximately 0.36 in favor of delayed). Finally, when learning was restricted to lists of words, immediate feedback was moderately better than delayed, but results were highly variable. In reexamining the experiments in which delayed feedback was superior to immediate feedback, the authors concluded (but not so convincingly) that delayed feedback was superior to immediate feedback only in highly restricted learning paradigms, that in general, immediate feedback was superior.

The argument for delayed feedback is that when an incorrect answer is given to a question, immediate feedback of the correct answer leaves the learner with two potential answers, both closely associated in time with the question. Either one might be recalled at a later time. With delayed feedback, however, the incorrect response may be forgotten by the time the correct one is provided. In the correct case, the delay does no harm in that the correct response is eventually presented. There is more to this story, however, in that what the learner does during the delay can determine whether the feedback enhances, is neutral to, or decreases learning (Wittrock, 1981). The active learner who continues to try to solve a problem while waiting for feedback is the one who receives the most advantage from the feedback.

TRANSFER

The immediate goal of instruction is change within the learner as to either associations, procedures, or attitudes. Knowledge thus imparted might serve any of four longer-term goals.

1. Rote reproduction. Poetry, prayers, and perhaps airline schedules are examples of material that is learned primarily for repetition in its original form. Many of us labored with ennui as elementary school students to entrust *Paul Revere's Ride* to memory, the sole purpose of which, so far as we could tell, was regurgitation under conditions selected to maximize potential embarrassment. Schedules and other tabular forms of data differ slightly from poetry and ritual incantations in that partial reproduction is more common than complete reproduction, but the general goal is the same.

2. Application. Many skills, from the very simple (e.g., locating a call number on a catalogue card) to the very complex (e.g., solving differential equations), are learned so that they can be applied to specific tasks. A real estate agent, for example, might learn how to solve power functions for that rare occasion when the monthly mortgage rate cannot be plucked from a table, and a chef might learn centigrade to Fahrenheit conversions solely for translating French recipes to North American standards.

3. Enablement of a more complex skill. Some skills are learned primarily as components of more complex skills. Addition of single-digit numbers, for example, has applications in the real world, but its inclusion in the mathematics curriculum is justified primarily as a step in learning to add numbers of arbitrary length. Complex tasks are often broken into simpler tasks and these learned separately before they are integrated into the more complex behavior. While the subskills may have importance on their own, the primary goal of learning them is usually the higher-level skill they enable.

4. Enhancement of learning ability. In spite of recurring controversies over the effectiveness of teaching general problem-solving skills, most psychologists and teachers go on believing in the human potential to acquire higher-order thinking skills through overt instruction. Study skills, such as note taking and outlining, as well as problem-solving strategies, such as estimation of the magnitude of the answer, are taught with the hope that they will *transfer* positively to subsequent learning situations. Promoters of programming languages like LOGO claim that learning their language will transfer positively to general problem-solving ability.

Transfer versus Application

Transfer is a general learning phenomenon, however, that is not restricted to structured situations. Any influence, whether negative or positive and whether planned or not, that the learning of one skill has upon the learning of a subsequent skill is labeled *transfer*. Thus, if learning Spanish makes the learning of French easier (by whatever metric), then learning Spanish transfers positively to learning French. Similarly, if learning Model-T Ford automobile repair makes the learning of present-day Mercedes Benz automobile repair more difficult, then there is negative transfer from the former to the latter. College students often find that the second semester of their freshman year is considerably easier than the first semester. Some things learned in the first semester transfer positively to second semester courses, whether they be study habits, expectations, or specific content.

We prefer to restrict the term *transfer* to situations where learning ability is influenced through prior learning of distantly related skills. Where directly related subskills are involved, we prefer the term *enablement,* and where abilities are learned for performance rather than learning ends, we prefer *application.* (Beware, however, that the research literature uses the term *transfer* promiscuously, applying it often to what we call application and enablement.) For symmetry, another term, *interference,* is required. *Interference* occurs when the learning of a skill depresses retention or use of a skill learned earlier. Thus, if performance in writing poetry decreased dramatically after learning technical writing, we would claim that learning technical writing interfered with poetry writing.

Advance Organizers

A special type of transfer is embodied by what Ausubel (1968) first labeled *advance organizers.* These are fundamental laws, generalizations, and the like, that are taught to facilitate the acquisition and retention of lower-order concepts. General principles of evolution, for example, might be taught to facilitate learning the phylogenetic ordering of plants and animals. The general understandings, if understood well enough to be manipulated by the learner, could provide scaffolding for the lower-order concepts, as well as a mechanism for generating information that is either not acquired or forgotten. Bruner (1960) summarized the value of theories as advance organizers thusly: "A good theory is the vehicle not only for understanding a phenomenon now but also for remembering it tomorrow" (p. 25). There is no general rule, however, that can be given for deciding when fundamental laws and principles should precede instruction in related concepts, or when the more specific material should be introduced first as stepping stones for the more general components.

Transfer is a critical element in instructional design, in that we want the ability to learn to improve as a result of all instruction. Viewed from a different perspective, it is inefficient to teach a subject solely for application or enablement. Transfer to subsequent learning should always be a goal. For instruction in thinking and problem-solving skills, transfer is the primary concern and one that should not be considered beyond present-day capabilities (Adams, 1989).

SUMMARY

The psychology of learning is not so far advanced that firm rules or prescriptions for instructional design can be generated. However, it can provide a guide for asking questions about the potential value of particular instructional plans and can create a mindset for reasoning about the answers to these questions.

Intellectual and emotional development can be described by stages of development, wherein particular mental structures and abilities are typically exhibited. With these models, however, questions remain on how the child can best be encouraged to move from one stage to another, and whether or not higher levels of reasoning can be taught at the earlier stages.

Part of intellectual development involves growth in the individual's ability to control her own learning processes. These metacognitive abilities can be improved with direct instruction.

Motivation to learn is an important issue in instructional design and should be considered at a local (i.e., task or lesson) level as well as at a global or course level. The main challenge in manipulating motivation is in finding those mechanisms that encourage the most long-term, self-generated motivation, but that, at the same time, do not risk either frustration or overarousal.

Attention capacity is limited; therefore, if lower-level components of complex tasks are overlearned, they will free attention capacity for higher-level operations.

Practice has a variety of cognitive consequences, one of the most important of which is to make sequences of operations automatic. In complex tasks, this frees attention capacity for higher-level operations.

Feedback has an information value and a reinforcement value. Both can enhance learning, but for average and above-average learners, the information value appears to be the most important. The content and extent of feedback should be considered in view of the learner's needs. Initial learning is enhanced more than review by extended or detailed feedback. The timing of feedback (immediate versus delayed) has a complex relationship to learning. Immediate feedback appears to enhance learning more than delayed feedback, but there are exceptions to this result and furthermore the learner's use of the delay time can influence the effectiveness of delayed feedback.

Transfer of learning should be a goal of all instruction, not just in the teaching of higher-level thinking skills. Transfer, however, should be carefully distinguished from application and enablement. Advance organizers are general principles, laws, and even theories, introduced to enhance the learning of lower-order concepts drawn from them. The transfer of learning that occurs with advance organizers can facilitate both initial learning and retention.

CHAPTER 6

Instructional Design
Being a Sketch of the Process

"When a designer creates a chair that is original in concept, it is enough to make his reputation for a decade. If it is possible to sit in it with anything less than acute pain, that is a bonus."

—Ralph Caplan, Cooper-Hewitt Museum Lecture (1976)

Similarities between chairs and instructional programs may be difficult to find, but the point of what Caplan says about chair design can also be true of on-line instructional programs—they can be elegant, attractive, and sophisticated and yet not teach. *Only the Best,* for example, lists the top CAI programs as evaluated by various professional organizations, including school boards and educational computing consortia, yet nowhere in this publication is any evidence on instructional effectiveness offered (Neill, 1989).

Some of the listed programs, when used properly, probably do increase learning, but some may not. Popularity guarantees instructional effectiveness no more than four legs and a tail guarantee a winning racehorse. What is needed as a first step toward instructionally effective on-line instruction is careful instructional design, which is what this chapter offers. We begin by defining the initial conditions from which instructional design originates. From here we provide an eclectic design process, something akin to a multiphase dance step, and then elaborate on its various stages. Finally, we arrive at lesson design and pause there long enough to present and explain a few examples and to describe some of the added demands of lesson design for computer-based instruction.

The instructional design process described here has eight steps that are defined and elaborated on throughout this chapter. The first six are, technically speaking, the design component; the last two are implementation, which is the concern of chapters 7–13, but they are included here for completeness. The steps are:

1. Task specification
2. Skill analysis
3. Learner strategies
4. Assessment design
5. Instructional strategy and tactics
6. Course organization

7. Design of model lessons
8. Development and evaluation

WHAT IS INSTRUCTIONAL DESIGN?

Instructional design is a process by which an instructional task specification is translated into an instructional program. This process draws upon (1) the instructional information given in Chapter 4, (2) the psychological information discussed and illustrated in Chapter 5, and (3) experience, to produce specifications from which a team of designers, writers, and programmers can develop an instructional program. Depending upon the competencies of those who will deliver the program, the instructional design may be sketchy or detailed. In the former case, which might be appropriate for an industrial course taught by subject matter specialists, a topic/subtopic sequence might be produced, along with a commentary on instructional modes to employ, decisions on instructional control, management, and delivery, along with sample lessons for each major variation on instruction. In contrast, CAI requires a detailed plan, including a complete sequence of scripts for an entire course, complete with specification of anticipated responses, procedures for diagnosis, and management.

As an example of a position between these extremes, Figure 6.1 shows a skill hierarchy for a sequence of lessons on writing Roman numerals, adapted from Dick and Carey (1978). Figure 6.2 shows the instructional strategies developed for the first objective to be taught, also adapted from Dick and Carey (1978).

These instructional strategies could be translated by experienced writers into either print or (mutatis mutandis) on-line lessons. Notice, for example, that the first topic to teach is recognizing and recalling seven basic symbols for Roman numerals. Experienced lesson writers, knowing the amount of time available for such a lesson, the abilities of the intended audience, and any physical limitations on page (or screen) space available, would decide on how many practice exercises to include, how difficult they should be, and whether or not the correct answers should be available to the students. An expanded plan would specify these exercises in more detail. (For example: "12 practice exercises, ranging from type A to type B. Show each Roman numeral at least four times and vary distractors from graphically dissimilar in the first few exercises to graphically similar in the last exercises.") Further detail would describe how practice would vary according to student parameters.

We conceive of the instructional design process in terms of a series of concentric circles where the process is applied first on the outer level for curriculum, reapplied for course decisions, then for successive units, again for lessons and finally, within lessons for specific sessions. Nevertheless, the most critical distinction is that between the overall instructional design for a course and the specific instructional designs for lessons. This distinction is much more than just a contrast between the general and the specific. On one hand, it is the difference between an overall military strategy and the specific tactics of each battle (or in this case, lesson) but also it is a difference between the outline of the action in a play and the specific dialogue and movements for any given scene. Furthermore, the instructional design for a course is typically based upon logic and past experience and seldom goes through the type of successive tryouts, pilot tests, and field tests for evaluation that a lesson does. A lesson, in contrast to a course, is the most visible part of instruction. It is the component that interacts most directly

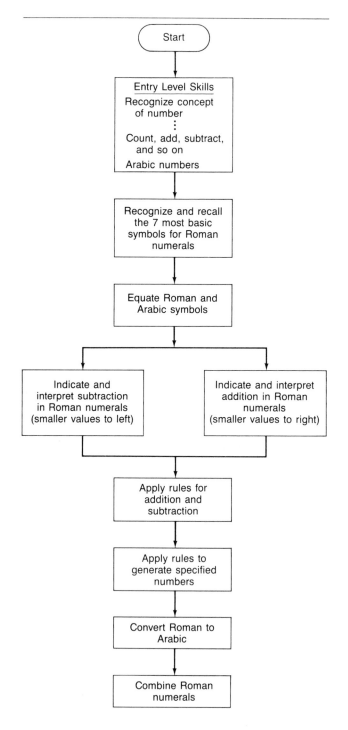

Figure 6.1. Skill Hierarchy for Roman Numerals

Introduction
>   *Objective:*   Recognize symbols for counting from 1 to 100.
>   *Prerequisites:* Arabic number skills: recognize, add, subtract.
>   *Motivation:*   Discuss why students should learn Roman numerals and what
>   they can do with them (e.g., outlines).

Explanation
>   *Content:*   1. Differentiate Arabic and Roman numerals.
>   2. Show that Roman numerals are letters.
>   3. Present the seven basic numerals: I, V, X, L, C, D, M.
>   *Examples:* 1. Arabic = 1, 2, 3; Roman = I, II, III.
>   2. Numbering for an outline.
>   3. Page numbers for a book preface.

Guided Practice
>   *Content:*   Recognition exercises, sequenced from simple to more difficult
>   such as, selecting the Roman numerals 1. (3, *, L); 2. (V, 6, P, M,
>   I, 4, 0).
>   *Feedback:*   Correct immediately: look for systematic errors.

Independent Practice
>   *Content:* Provide both recognition and recall problems.

Figure 6.2. Instructional Strategy for First Roman Numeral Objective

with the student and therefore, needs the most critical tuning to ensure its proper functioning. We will, however, begin by concentrating on course design and then present specific information on techniques to be used for lesson design. In the procedures presented here, we leave to the reader the decision on how much detail an instructional design should include. Our focus for this chapter is more on procedure, that is, the steps to be taken in a principled design process and the types of information that should be gathered.

DESIGN SYSTEMS

Berthold Brecht once said that "When everything is in the wrong place, that is disorder. But when you have nothing in all the right places, that is order." Most of the instructional design systems available today fit Brecht's description of order. They provide logical categories for making design decisions and sequence them in seemingly rational ways, but when instruction must finally be designed, there is no support from these systems for deciding on *how* to teach. Consider, for example, the Systems Approach Model described by Dick and Carey (1978, pp. 8–11).

1. Identify an instructional goal.
2. Conduct an instructional analysis.

3. Identify entry behaviors and characteristics.
4. Write performance objectives.
5. Develop criterion-referenced tests.
6. Develop an instructional strategy.
7. Develop and select instruction.
8. Design and conduct the formative evaluation.
9. Revise instruction.
10. Conduct summative evaluation.

Except for its overreliance on performance objectives (step 4), this is a reasonable overview of an instructional design process. Its failing is not in what it does, but in what it fails to do, which is to specify the *how* of instruction.

Expert-Novice Approaches

For the *how* of instruction we turn to some recent work based on expert-novice models and, in particular, to the work of Case and Bereiter (1984). As a result of developmental studies done in the 1970s, Case (1978) proposed a technology of instruction based on the following principles for teaching a new strategy.

   1a. Determine the spontaneous strategies used by students who do not have the skills to be taught (i.e., novices).
   1b. Determine the corresponding strategies used by experts.
   2a. Design instruction so that the limitations of the novices' strategies are apparent to them.[1]
   2b. Continue the instruction to demonstrate the correct strategy through guided discovery, didactic exposition, and modeling.
   2c. Provide an explanation of why the new strategy works better than the old ones and provide practice in using it, particularly with increasingly more complex situations.
   3. Minimize the load on working memory by simplifying the structure of the successful strategy and by controlling the number of novel cues or operations the student must attend to at any one time.

Further research on instruction revealed weaknesses in these principles and therefore in the resulting design strategy based on them. In particular, it was found that the strategies of experts were not always identical to the successful strategies used by children at different stages of development. Therefore, the design process was modified to the following (Case & Bereiter, 1984, p. 16):

   1. Identify the task to be taught and develop a task for assessing students' success or failure on it.
   2. Develop a procedure for assessing the strategies subjects employ on the measured task.
   3. Use this procedure to assess the strategies used by children at a variety of ages, both those where success is not achieved by current methods and those where it is.

---

[1]This idea is at least as old as the time of Plato. See, in particular, the dialogue between Socrates and the boy in Meno (*Dialogues of Plato,* trans. B. Jowett [New York: Random House, 1937], pp. 361ff).

4a. Devise an instructional sequence for "recapitulating development," i.e., for bringing students from one level to the next in the course of instruction.

4b. Keep the working memory load at each step within reasonable limits.[2]

  5. Once children's performance at one level becomes relatively automatic, move on to the next.

AN INTEGRATED APPROACH

The systems approach to instructional design provides a shell into which more specific design procedures can be placed. Case and Bereiter's (1984) rendition of an expert-novice model provides a basis for design of instruction for specific cognitive rules, principles, and strategies. To these procedures we add the diagnostic flavoring from the work of Brown & Burton (1978) and the instructional technology principles of Bruner (1966), to create the design process sketched below.

You might at this juncture feel overwhelmed with the prospect of petty paperwork and what might appear to be educational obfuscation. Listening to the Brandenburg concertos might be even more alluring as an alternative to developing instruction, with perhaps the hope that before the final coda, times will change and intuitive design processes will be in vogue. Don't despair. What we define is the full set of considerations that any major instructional design project could require. For many courses and lessons, only some of these steps will be relevant, and the answers to some categories

- TASK SPECIFICATIONS: Define the learning outcomes, audience, instructional environment, and development resources, as defined above.
- SKILL ANALYSIS: Define all the skills and subskills to be taught, their relationships to each other, and the relative difficulties of teaching each, based on past experience.
- LEARNER STRATEGIES: Determine the strategies used by successful learners, and by learners on entry to instruction. Find the more common errors and misconceptions that learners exhibit during instruction. Record attitudes and beliefs.
- ASSESSMENT DESIGN: Design sample assessment items or procedures for each major skill identified in the skill analysis.
- INSTRUCTIONAL STRATEGY AND TACTICS: Design instructional methods for each skill or skill group, using developmental data and error analyses to decide on instructional mode and on the size of each instructional step.
- COURSE ORGANIZATION: Organize the various instructional components designed into sessions, lessons, and units. Add support components to complete the initial design.
- DESIGN OF MODEL LESSONS: Develop exemplars of each lesson type.
- DEVELOPMENT AND EVALUATION: Develop and evaluate the course.

---

[2]The switch from minimizing working memory load (Case, 1978) to keeping this load within reasonable limits should be noted.

might be single words or short phrases. Furthermore, while our design procedure is geared for complete instructional systems, the on-line component may be narrowly circumscribed: practice for a particular set of skills, extension and enrichment for the early mastery group, or whatever. For the discussion that follows, we focus on *course* design. Reductions for design of smaller units or extensions for larger units (curriculums) will be left as an exercise for the reader.

Task Specifications

All instructional projects either begin with a well-defined set of task specifications or derive them prior to initiating design work. By a task specification we mean a description of the immutable givens for a desired course or lesson, that is, information about the objectives of the course, its intended audience, the environment in which it will be used, and the resources available for its development. For practical reasons we assume that these specifications, once defined, are unchangeable. In some cases this may not be true; further funds to cover development cost overruns may appear, and new equipment may be purchased by the intended audience. There is a difference, however, between planning for change and leaving success to chance. Clear, correct task specifications are critical to the success of any design project.

Learning Outcomes. Every course should have some learning goals, be they specific (e.g., apply the four basic arithmetic operations with one- and two-place integers) or general (e.g., appreciate chamber music). Whatever these are, they should be defined as precisely as possible in terms of associations and procedural operations, learning strategies, and attitudes. While we discourage the use of behavioral objectives of the form "The student will be able to select from four related alternatives in a vertical format the answer that correctly . . .",[3] we do suggest that where the outcomes of the course being planned are to be applied to a subsequent course or task, that this be part of the outcome description. Keep in mind, though, that an outcome description is not a detailed list of skills or attitudes, but a pointer to such a list, with the complexity levels and application abilities included.

Audience. A course is planned for a specific audience, which should be defined in terms of their general characteristics, entry level abilities, and learning characteristics. This might be as brief as "Average eighth graders who read on at least the 7.5 grade level," but generally will require more elaboration. By general characteristics is meant ages, grade levels, institutional status (e.g., members of gifted program, retained at grade level), and any other general characteristics that might influence instructional design (e.g., vision handicaps).

Entry-level abilities should include general abilities (e.g., reading ability) and also abilities specific to the content of the course, such as misconceptions about the topic. These descriptions should provide sufficient information so that the starting point for instruction can be defined.

---

[3]Our displeasure with behavioral objectives derives from their tendency to overemphasize both separate skills in narrowly defined contexts and observable behavior, at the expense of more general, integrated skills, knowledge representation, and learner strategies.

Learning characteristics refers to such matters as motivation and metacognitive level. For most school-based subjects there will usually be little to say here, but for industrial and military courses, these may be critical data for successful design.

Environment. All courses are delivered somewhere, whether in a school classroom, factory cafeteria, or library computer carrel. These environments make differing demands on instructional design because of the instructional resources they offer. A CAI course that is used in a 30-terminal resource center with teacher and aide present might take more liberties than one that must operate unattended. Similarly, designing for a network that can route messages between students and teachers, provide access to a large file of courses, and collect performance data is different from designing for stand-alone microcomputers, especially where one cannot assume even the presence of two floppy disk drives. These are the physical and human components of *environment.* Equally important is *time,* as measured by the amount available per student for the total course, for homework, and for access to any special equipment the course might require (e.g., electron microscope).

Development Resources. A kindergarten-through-eighth-grade basal reading program might cost $30–$40 million to develop *de novo.* An hour of field-tested CAI might cost from $2,000 to $20,000, depending upon the instructional methods employed and the delivery means engaged (e.g., CD-ROM, color graphics). How the costs of such systems (development and use) might be determined and how their cost-benefit and cost-effectiveness ratios might be analyzed are not discussed in this text, but should not be ignored. For the present we wish to state the obvious: Nothing comes ready-made or free. A budget for a development project may not be specified at the same time that learning outcomes, audience, and environment are defined, but we assume that in a rational world, a budget will be established prior to the beginning of serious development.

Skill Analysis

Skill analysis, like so much else in instructional design, is part science and part art. The most general strategy suggested for skill analysis is a top-down approach whereby skills are continually redefined in terms of their subskills until the skills assumed present at entry to the course are reached. If done with sufficient detail, this analysis should lead to a diagnostic network. Consider, as an example, the design of an adult literacy tutor. Imagine that the total system will include an optical reader, a workstation, and a speech-synthesis unit. The objective is to provide an open environment in which workers with low literacy skills can receive on-line tutoring with materials they bring to the system, or with precoded materials. Materials brought to the system would be scanned by the optical reader and then read to the user, with a minimum of prompting for user feedback. Precoded materials would be coded with a hypertext format so that common ideas, characters, and so forth, could be traced through the text, words could be related to their glossary definitions, and occasional questions could be asked to promote comprehension.

The skills the system would be able to teach are the following:

1. Reading strategies
   Previewing
      use of headings
      special typography
      graphics
   Monitoring
      question generation
      outlining
      note taking
   Vocabulary
      decoding
      context
      glossary
      dictionary
2. Text organization
   Headings
   Diagrams, charts, graphs, etc.
   Footnotes
   Paragraphs
3. Vocabulary
      technical terms
      abbreviations
4. Decoding
      prefixes and suffixes
      stress placement
      syllabication
      foreign decoding patterns (e.g., ch$\rightarrow$/k/)

These skills might be organized as shown in Figure 6.3, although other organizations are possible. What Figure 6.3 shows is both skills and skill dependencies. Critical subskills assumed to have been mastered already by users of the system are enclosed in dotted rectangles.

The final task here is to assign weights to each skill according to the difficulty we expect in teaching that skill to the anticipated audience. For this example we will define only two classes of difficulty: easy and moderately difficult, with the members of the latter class marked by asterisks in Figure 6.3. More difficulty levels are usually desirable, however. Mager and Beach (1967), for example, show four levels for an example from vocational instruction: easy, moderately difficult, difficult, and very difficult. These levels will generally be based on instructional experience, which means that four or five levels are about the maximum practical.

As a final note to this section we want to point out that while trees and other hierarchical schemes are often used to represent skills and their relationships, most large sets of skills do not fit the formal definitions of tree or hierarchy. To overcome these limitations, a variety of structures have been borrowed from mathematics and cognitive psychology, including types of networks or maps. Neil (1970; cited in Romiszowski, 1981) was the first to note the limitations of these newer schemes and in particular their inability to distinguish different types of skill relationships. Neil also ex-

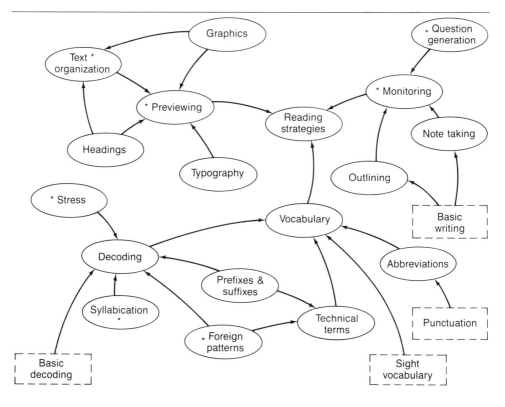

Figure 6.3. Skill Graph for Adult Literacy

pressed a need for construction rules that would encourage clear visual organization and presentation of the resulting model.

A formal structure that achieves these goals is a *directed graph*. A directed graph is composed of a finite set of nodes interconnected by arcs. The arcs represent directed relationships between nodes and may vary according to user definition. Figure 6.3, which shows the skills for teaching adult literacy, is a directed graph. This scheme might be extended by using solid arcs to indicate prerequisites that should be taught to all learners and broken arcs to indicate prerequisites that must be taught only to some learners. (Labeled arcs are what distinguish directed graphs from the quasi-tree diagrams used by Dick and Carey (1978) and others to show skill and subskill relationships.) Through labeled arcs, a rich set of relationships can be portrayed in a relatively uncomplicated manner. (Note, however, that the label "subskill of" has been omitted from all arcs in Figure 6.3.)

Learner Strategies

In the first step of the design process presented in this chapter, the desired learning outcomes and audience of a course are defined in general terms. In this step the abilities of a competent graduate of the course are defined in terms of strategies, attitudes, and beliefs, along with the misconceptions, errors, attitudes, and beliefs that either have been observed or are anticipated for novices. By *competent graduate* we mean someone who has successfully completed the course, as opposed to an *expert,* who might be at a level far beyond what the course attempts to achieve. The listing of common misconceptions and potential errors is critical not only for initial instruction, but also for diagnosis. Intelligent tutoring systems in particular depend quite heavily on these definitions.

For the adult literacy skills outlined above, we would anticipate errors and misconceptions like the following:

1. Overattention to the connected text, at the expense of headings, diagrams, and the like.
2. Failure to monitor comprehension.
3. Inflexibility in assigning letter-sound correspondences.
4. Guessing at words from their initial parts plus, perhaps, length.

For arithmetic operations misconceptions would center on such factors as failure to decrement in subtraction and not knowing how to propagate a carry in addition. These are what the ICAI literature calls *bugs* (see Burton, 1982). An approach to eliciting misconceptions in science is described by Stevens, Collins, and Goldin (1979).

LEARNING STRATEGIES refers to the strategies that the learner should adopt for self-sustained learning while ATTITUDES AND BELIEFS are what control our disposition toward the topic to be learned and toward our own ability to master the area. Learning strategies sometimes reduce to study skills, that is, techniques for obtaining and organizing information and pacing one's own way through course assignments. In a limited number of cognitive domains, such as memory, an extensive literature on learning strategies exists; for others, such as aesthetic judgments, a limited empirical base is available. For attitudes and beliefs, fairly general guidelines exist for building positive attitudes toward school-based subjects (see, for example, Schoenfeld, 1982, 1985).

For the adult literacy program, the learning strategies are captured in part by the reading strategies that are taught. Other learning strategies that should be suggested to students include (1) keeping a notebook for new vocabulary, (2) frequent rereading of articles, (3) daily review of the most recent additions to the vocabulary notebook, and (4) reading aloud to family or to a tutor. For attitudes and beliefs, the most important for adult literacy is that real improvement is possible for almost anyone, but will not occur immediately. One to two years of consistent work may be required before significant gains will be made. In other words, students should not be left with the belief that a few months of work will be sufficient to move from a stumbling, word-for-word reading style to that of an average high school graduate. One of the biggest problems in adult literacy is motivation, which is reflected in a high dropout rate from most programs. Retention might be improved if students were helped to adopt from the beginning a realistic attitude about their expected progress rate.

Assessment Design

The purpose of assessment design at this stage is not simply to build a final test for the course being offered, but rather to define as exactly as possible the types of knowledge that are expected to be acquired from the course. For each skill or subskill that is taught, the instructional designer should draft three or four typical test items that might be used to assess levels of competency in that particular skill. For example, in a course on plumbing the designer/instructor might consider items that would test the students' ability to diagnose faults in typical plumbing systems. This requires that the designer decide whether to assess this ability by showing typical blueprints of plumbing systems and asking for detection of faults (e.g., lack of adequate back venting) or by verbal descriptions of problems experienced in particular plumbing systems, to which the student would respond with a series of hypotheses about what might be wrong and a series of tests for ascertaining which, if any, of these hypotheses are correct.

Specific knowledge would also be assessed. For example, a plumbing course may have covered a variety of standard valves (e.g., standard globe, angle, gate valves). A student might be asked to recall information on the differences in water resistance that each of these valves might cause, or to order the valves from greater to lesser water resistance. If the student had learned the standard parts of a faucet, knowledge might be tested by requiring the student to label the various components (spindle, bonnet, packing, seat, washer, etc.) on a cross-sectional diagram or by providing labels and diagrams and requiring the student to connect them. Finally, the student might be required to produce a diagram of the standard faucet and to label it.

While we don't wish to belabor the design of test items for any particular course, we do want to ensure that the reader understands that the design of test items at this point is a step in the refinement of objectives of the course as much as it is an attempt to prepare for the final examination. The critical decisions concern the degree of specificity of each item and the particular paradigms to be used in assessing it.

Instructional Strategy and Tactics

Instructional strategy was defined in Chapter 4 as a combination of instructional mode, topic sequencing, learner grouping, and the pathways through which the learner might traverse the course topics. A course might be built on a single form of each of these elements or it may combine various forms of them. A high school algebra course, for example, might present an initial set of procedures and theorems by explanatory mode and then shift to demonstration and later to problem-solving modes. Similarly, all students might be required to study the same topics for the first part of a programming course. Then, according to backgrounds, they may pursue topic sequences that differ in degree of mathematical formality.

Student grouping patterns may also vary within a course. A civics course might group by individuals and pairs for one part of the course and then divide students into teams for a final project. In contrast, the sequencing of skills is unlikely to vary, given that most sequences are built, at least in part, on prerequisite dependencies. Along with strategy, some elements of instructional tactics are considered at a global level as well as at a local or lesson level. These include locus of control, instructional tone, assessment, and entry/exit techniques.

Tactics

Locus of Control. Will sequence, amount of practice, level of difficulty and other instructional variables be under designer (i.e., instructor or computer) control or student control? Many courses allow students to choose the skill they want to work on;

some allow the student to decide when he is ready to be tested; and a few, like TICCIT, allow the learner to direct the level of difficulty of explanations and examples.

Tone. Will the instructional tone be directive and serious, loose and somewhat humorous, flippant, or somewhere in between? Tone is not a well-defined variable, and is probably more important for computer-delivered instruction than it is for live instructors. Some CAI programs attempt to establish an air of humanness through repeated use of the student's name or through such messages as "I'll have to think a minute about that." Others try to relieve the potential tedium of computer-delivered instruction through colloquialisms (e.g., "great-job", "wow, that was super") or through cute, but often irrelevant animation and sound.

Tone is conveyed in part by overt mechanisms such as those just mentioned, and in part by syntax and general vocabulary (e.g., multisyllabic, latinate terms versus simpler one- and two-syllable words.) For planning a tone for CAI components of instruction, it is sufficient at this step to use terms like *serious, light, humorous, friendly,* and the like.

Assessment. How will the learner's progress be assessed during instruction and how will the results be utilized, either by the instructional system or the learner? And once all of this is defined, how will initial entry and follow-through components be designed? The former refers to the initial messages given to the learner when instruction begins, mainly for motivation, but also potentially for establishing outcome expectations and defining prerequisites, while the latter comprises the actions to be taken for students once they complete the program. On exit a student may have (1) failed to master the material, thus requiring remediation or reteaching, (2) successfully completed everything at an average pace, or (3) successfully completed the course at an accelerated pace. Many programs may not distinguish between these cases, but in any real instructional situation, something needs to be provided for students who complete course materials ahead of the standard or regular pace, be it no more than suggestions for enrichment activities.

Course Organization

At this point the nitty gritty decisions begin. First, the course must be divided into units, lessons, and sessions. This requires that the skills identified be organized with reference to the desired instructional strategies and tactics. If the learner is to control sequencing, then the design need not specify an order for major skills; in all other approaches, sequencing or partial sequencing is required. Once lessons are defined, lesson events must be specified, based upon instructional mode.

As the designer makes these decisions, delivery mechanisms can be selected, that is, which parts to do by computer, which by human instructor, and which by other means (e.g., print, audio, video), and how the different components will be synchronized. The next set of decisions concern initial placement and advancement, that is, how will learners be placed within the available instructional sequence and what criteria will be used to decide when to advance to the next lesson, skill, or module. For many courses (or lessons) all learners enter the instruction at the same place (i.e., the beginning) and all advance through the same path regardless of mastery level. More sophisticated systems have placement tests for new students and variable advancement criteria.

It is important to distinguish between course structure, as defined by units, lessons, and sessions, and the path or traversal of any student through the course. With or without computer delivery, students need not be constrained to follow the same instructional path. Some may show mastery on a pretest for a unit or lesson, and therefore skip over it. Alternatively, different paths might be defined for different learning styles, entry-level abilities, or interests (e.g., biology majors versus nonmajors taking a biology course to satisfy a distribution requirement). Other decisions must be made on types and amounts of feedback, motivational mechanisms, and (for CAI in particular) response modes (e.g., natural language, multiple choice, single words, or numbers). Finally, the type (if any) of management for the course must be designed. This includes sign-on, performance monitoring, exit and reentry, and reporting.

A Summary of the Instructional Design Process

Step 1: Task specifications
    A. Learning outcomes
    B. Audience
        1. General characteristics (age, academic level, etc.)
        2. Entry-level abilities vis-à-vis the course content
        3. Learning characteristics (motivation, etc.)
    C. Environment
        1. Physical characteristics
        2. Resources (time, people, etc.)
    D. Development resources
Step 2: Skill analysis
    A. Skills and subskills
    B. Skill dependencies
    C. Difficulty levels for learning each skill
Step 3: Learner strategies
    A. Abilities of the competent graduate
    B. Predicted or observed misconceptions and errors
    C. Learning strategies
    D. Attitudes and beliefs
Step 4: Assessment design
Step 5: Instructional strategy and tactics
    A. Strategy
    B. Tactics
Step 6: Course organization
    A. Course divisions (units, lessons, etc.)
    B. Delivery mechanisms
    C. Initial placement and advancement
    D. Feedback
    E. Motivation
    F. Response mode
    G. Management
Step 7: Design of model lessons
Step 8: Development and evaluation

Design of Model Lessons

With the decisions made in the preceding sections, the most practical next step is to develop model lessons to represent the main lesson types that will be used. These will usually reveal problems that will lead you to design revisions and rebuild the model lessons. In large expensive projects, model lessons are often used for internal evaluation of progress, and model lessons can occasionally be used with learners to assess complexity, pacing, difficulty level, and related issues (i.e., formative evaluation).

Development and Evaluation

Finally, give the entire course skin and flesh, all attached to the supportive structure established in the previous steps. For on-line instruction, specify screen displays; define all of this is defined, how will initial entry and follow-through components be ponents to allow programming to begin. The output of this process should be a design document or plan book that serves as a blueprint for developers. Then, evaluate.

LESSON DESIGN

In Chapter 4 we defined a lesson as a set of instructional events, generally taking no more than one to three sessions.[4] We define here four lesson types: new material, practice, review, and test. The most common lesson type is the first, that in which new material is introduced (and sometimes practiced). The second type is also fairly common, that is, where only practice is included. For example, a computer programming course may have one lecture session a week in which a large number of students hear a prepared lecture on one of the course topics. Then lab practice sessions are held with smaller groups, typically using graduate teaching assistants. In these sessions, students try to work problems with the assistance of the teaching assistant. The third type of lesson, the review type, is similar to the practice type, only (in general) we assume that less guidance is needed for students to do the work. Finally, we define a test lesson, that in which a test is given, and therefore no instruction or immediate feedback is given by the instructor.

Figure 6.4 shows a detailed lesson plan for a phonics lesson, adapted from several adult-literacy instructional guides. This lesson is intended for adult nonreaders and is meant to introduce a new letter-sound correspondence, that for the letter *m*. First, the letter sound /m/ is introduced, followed by the letter *m*. After letter and sound discrimination are practiced, blending is taught and practiced. The lesson ends with a review of what has been taught so far and an extension where the students practice writing the letter that they have just learned.

A slightly different approach to teaching this same topic is shown in Figure 6.5, which is a phonics lesson taken from a basal reading program intended for first grade students. In this lesson plan a four-step outline—recall, recognize, exercise, apply—is utilized. The recall step typically reviews material taught previously that relates in some way to the new material to be introduced. This step both allows the teacher to do a

---

[4]Alternative approaches to lesson design can be found in Gagné & Briggs (1979); Steinberg (1984); and Gagne, Wager, & Rojas (1981).

1. **Identify sound**

   Ask students to pronounce *map, moon,* and *monster,* and to then repeat several times the first sound in these words. Repeat the procedure for the final sound /m/ (e.g., Tim, room, aim).

2. **Identify letter**

   Write upper and lower case *m* on the board. Identify both name and sound. Ask students to write and say each several times. Give assistance in printing, if needed.

3. **Letter and sound practice**

   Write *m* plus four or five other letters on the board, repeating each several times. Ask students to identify each *m* and to give both its name and its sound. If further sound discrimination practice is needed, contrast different pairs (e.g., Sam/moon, monkey/map). Then ask students to produce words that begin with the sound /m/ and then to produce words that end with the sound /m/. Accept any word that ends with /m/ even if the spelling of the word ends with another letter (e.g., some, hymn).

4. **Blending**

   Write *mom* on the board and ask for the sounds of each letter. Say the sounds slowly; then blend left-to-right, adding one sound at a time: *m-o, mo, mo-m, mom.* Ask students to do the same, starting with the separate sounds. Ask for (oral) sentences with the word *mom.* Have each student blend the sounds to make the word and to then use the word in a sentence.

5. **Blending practice**

   Ask students to write *mom* in as many different ways as possible, using upper and lower case letters. Ask them to pronounce each word as it is written (e.g., mom, MOM, Mom, moM, MoM).

6. **Review**

   Review *M* and *m,* as well as the first vowel introduced, (*o*) giving the names and sounds. Ask students to invent their own image or mnemonic device for associating the letter *m* with the sound /m/. Discuss these in class. Repeat the blending of *mom* and the creation of sentences with this word. Ask students to help each other with printing and copying as they work in pairs.

Figure 6.4. Introducing the Consonant Pattern *m* → /m/

quick assessment of whether the students are ready for the new material and also provides a bridge from the old to the new. The explication that follows is built around the recognition step. This is followed by two types of practice: a teacher-guided exercise in which the letter-sound correspondence is practiced in isolation and then application of the correspondence itself.

In neither of these lessons is anything said about the typical anticipated student responses and how the teacher/computer should react to these. Nor is anything said about remediation for those students who don't acquire the lesson objectives through the normal path, or about management of the lesson. For example, in step 3 of the adult-literacy lesson plan, a student who responds "Yes, *Sam* and *moon* start with the same sound," might not be distinguishing acoustically between the /s/ and the /m/ sounds, or he may be comparing the /m/ at the end of *Sam* with the /m/ at the beginning of *moon.*

DECODING

Vowel: Decoding words with i(gh) *(ɪ high) (introductory instruction)*

Recall Briefly review short vowel *i* (ɪ dig) with consonant blends by writing these words on the chalkboard and having them read: *lift, list, sink, pink.*

Recognize Write *night, right,* and *tight* in a column and have them read. Ask pupils to say the words, listening for the vowel sound. Write *high* and read it. Slowly say all four words, and tell pupils that these words have the same vowel sound. Slowly say the words again. Point out that the letters *igh* stand for the long *i* vowel sound in each word and that the vowel sound and the letters may be at the end or in the middle of a word. Remind pupils that sometimes, in English words, two or more letters together stand for one sound. Help pupils sound out the words.

Exercise Write these column headings for the words on the chalkboard: *i, igh.* Then add these words to the appropriate columns:

i	*igh*
think	flight
sift	bright
mist	sigh

Challenge pupils to use what they know to decode the new words.

Apply Write *might* and have pupils sound out the word. Write *fight* under *might,* explaining that one letter has been changed to make a new word. Have pupils sound out both words. Then write these words, one by one, and have pupils take turns sounding them out:

fright	flight	light	slight
sight	sigh	high	thigh

Finally, write this sentence and have pupils read it: *A duck might take fright at a light in the night.* You may wish to have pupils write, tell, or illustrate a story beginning with this sentence.

Figure 6.5. A Phonics Lesson for Children (From T. Clymer & R. L. Venezky, *Ginn Reading Program,* Level 7, teacher's ed. [Boston: Ginn, 1982]. Copyright 1982 by Ginn & Co. Reprinted by permission.)

The teacher who is skilled at diagnosis will probably be able to ascertain the reason for the incorrect response by questioning the student and may then provide remediation. This remediation might, for example, begin with simple single-syllable words in which the letter *m* occurs at the beginning of the word, followed by single syllable words that have *m,* sometimes at the beginning, sometimes at the end, and sometimes not at all, followed then by multisyllabic words following the same sequence. This sequencing is sometimes referred to as a *lesson strategy,* using the term *strategy* that we applied in Chapter 4 to course instruction. Another example of a lesson strategy that is often used in elementary-level reading programs is to teach sound discrimination by starting with objects whose names begin or end with a particular sound, followed by pictures of the objects and finally just by the spoken words.

The full set of specifications for a lesson plan, therefore, includes a script with greater or lesser levels of detail that describes what the instructor is to do; some indication of the expected student responses, with indications of how to react to the expected incorrect responses; plans for remediation; and finally, management instructions.

Planning Diagnostic Lessons

The purpose of diagnosis, obviously, is to uncover those underlying misconceptions or faults that an instructor, or intelligently programmed computer, can remediate. This implies two phases. One is the building of the diagnostic system itself, and the second, which is equally important, is the building of the remedial instructional sequence that moves in what we hope is an effective manner from the point where the student is diagnosed as having a particular misconception to the point where the student can reenter the mainline of instruction. We define four steps in this process.

1. Gathering Data. Gather data on student performance from similar students under similar instructional circumstances. We cannot overemphasize the necessity of studying errors under *similar instructional circumstances.* For most students whom we attempt to teach, the instruction itself has a large bearing on the error patterns that the students make. For example, in reading instruction children taught by whole-word methods tend to make large numbers of substitution errors where the substituted word is inappropriate for the orthography of the word that was to have been read yet perfectly appropriate for the context. In contrast, students taught by intensive phonics methods often make substitution errors that are inappropriate for the semantic context but logical for the orthographic pattern of the target word (Barr, 1972).

Error data typically is collected through three methods. First, actual performance data can be collected from students. For example, Cox (1975) has described a large number of errors made in the four vertical arithmetic algorithms based on performances of 744 children in grades 2–6. In this case, students simply worked arithmetic problems and the results were evaluated and the errors then analyzed. The second approach, which attempts to get at a deeper level of student functioning, is through talk-aloud protocols. In this case students are asked to think out loud as they attempt to solve problems; their protocols typically are tape-recorded and later analyzed. This technique was popularized by the artificial intelligence group at Carnegie Mellon in the 1960s and 1970s (Simon, 1979) and is used extensively today, particularly for studying more complex problem solving. Finally, one can draw on published studies.

2. Analyzing Data. Analyze the performance data gathered in step 1 for underlying misconceptions. This step is particularly critical to the design of remedial instruction. Without an understanding of the incorrect strategies that children are attempting to apply, remediation can seldom be very effective. For example, many children mislabel lower case *b* and *d* when they are first learning the alphabet; if this were the only fact known, it would be very difficult to decide how to help children overcome this problem. The underlying fault potentially could derive from visual perception (as assumed for many years by remedial reading teachers), or it could result from a simple labeling problem. It could also be the persistence of prior experience in the child's environment up to the time that he begins to learn letters and numbers. Research has shown, for example, that orientation is not a feature that needs to be attended to for labeling prior to encountering letters and numbers. That is, a cup is still a cup whether the handle points to the left or to the right. Numbers and letters are the first objects in the child's environment in which orientation is critical for identification (Venezky & Pittelman, 1977). The types of remediation based upon this natural-development view are quite different from those that are developed by remedial reading teachers who assume the underlying problem in the *b-d* confusion derives from visual perception.

3. Reducing Errors. Reduce the various error types and underlying misconceptions that were developed in steps 1 and 2 to a reasonably small number that can be dealt with through differentiated remedial instruction. Defining 45–50 underlying misconceptions or error types is probably not helpful for instruction, whether live or computer delivered, if sufficient resources are not available to develop and test appropriate remediation for each. Therefore, the instructional designer has to set priorities by selecting from the total set of underlying misconceptions those that represent the bulk of the errors that children make and for which reasonable instruction can be developed.

4. Instruction. Finally the instruction itself for overcoming each of the faults delineated in step 3 must be planned. And that is what this chapter has primarily been concerned with.

Building and Testing Model Lessons

One purpose for building and testing model lessons is to ensure that the design specifications developed for a course can be realized. Another is to tune the specifications themselves. For many people, seeing a lesson in print or on a computer screen is critical for judging its coherence, length (in space or time), and its general appeal. To declare on paper that lessons will be informal, fresh, and easy to read requires only an elementary command of English spelling and syntax. To translate these noble aspirations into four-color images mixed with print on a VDU screen is a far more demanding task. Furthermore, the writers of a course are often not those who generated the instructional design. Therefore, model lessons become part of the design specifications, providing a tangible comparison for the implementers' efforts.

Model lessons, whether in print or in pixel glows, should incorporate all the critical design features that are common to the genre. For on-line instruction this requires special attention to the user interface: response modes, timing, graphic devices, and language, in particular (see Chapter 11). For print, graphic treatment, language, and lesson length are of comparable importance, along with coherence, legibility, and readability, which apply to all manners of delivery.

Once developed, model lessons should be reviewed and evaluated by the development staff and by external, experienced instructors. Usually, model lessons are submitted to several cycles of review and revision in-house before outside consultants/instructors are asked to review them. A few development projects end at this point; most, however, continue, albeit with greater or lesser degrees of redirection. Obtaining useful *student performance data* from model lessons is usually impossible, due to the difficulty of creating a meaningful instructional context in which single lessons can be inserted and where performance can be directly tied to lesson quality. But student opinions of lessons, especially of their aesthetic qualities, is readily available.

MAPPING THE COMPLETE COURSE

Once model lessons are approved, a development procedure for the entire course can be implemented. For large programs this requires management procedures for review levels, document (or program) control, and coordination across developers. At this stage, assessment and management components must be integrated with the instructional units, a teacher's guide or equivalent developed, and the entire package massaged into a deliverable form. For some programs this might require the design of teacher-training sessions, and the training of teacher trainers. In an ideal development world, units are developed, tested, and revised, with further testing done, if needed. For most projects on this earth, neither time nor funding is available for such careful evaluation. This is not to excuse the launching of instructional programs without adequate field test, but rather to warn that the ideal we advocate is both expensive and time consuming. Nevertheless, we urge that all programs be field tested before release, even if the field testing is abbreviated, either in time or in student population.

PLANNING FOR IMPROVEMENT

We are, admittedly, inconsistent in including this section at the end of the chapter when the processes it requires need to be considered in the early stages of design. Nevertheless, something must hold up the rear. For on-line courses, particularly those delivered over networks, opportunities exist for convenient gathering of course improvement data. Even for stand-alone microcomputer systems and for print programs, the developer can obtain cooperating sites where program performance data can be collected through teacher recording, observation, collection of student responses, and other means. All programs can be improved. For some, popularity and financial success lead to revisions; for others, revisions are required by design flaws and implementation problems that inhibit utility. Systematic developers will indicate, as part of the development process, issues for which field data are needed. These might vary from questions about timing of displays and menu lengths to the adequacy of major sections of instruction. We can provide no cookbook procedure for planning such data-gathering forays; instead, we suggest that all course developers indicate points where improvement data should be collected, just as car designers indicate chassis points for lubrication.

SUMMARY

The instructional design process that we advocate begins with *task specification*. This requires attention to learning outcomes, audience, environment, and development resources. *Skill analysis* is next, including skill dependencies and difficulty levels. *Learner strategies* are then defined, both for successful learners of the material to be taught and for students entering to this type of instruction. Strategies for the latter should include provision for the common errors and misconceptions of naive learners. Then, an *assessment design* is developed, including assessment items for each major skill defined in the previous step.

Instructional strategy and tactics are then designed and a *course organization* developed, dividing the knowledge to be taught into sessions, lessons, and (potentially) units. Finally, *model lessons* are designed and *development and evaluation* begun.

PART III

System Design

We now move from instruction and its principles and design to the specific design of computerized systems that may play an important role in the instructional process.

In Chapter 7, we examine the components and operation of a complete CAI system. In Chapter 8 we suggest taxonomies for courseware design, and in Chapter 9, algorithms for student assessment. Chapter 10 provides a clear analysis of systems for instructional administration. The principles presented in the previous chapters should provide a solid foundation for the concrete decisions that must be made in the design of effective and appropriate CAI systems. For the designer or user of CAI systems, much can also be learned from the experiences of living CAI systems, which, as adaptive organisms, have developed interesting survival strategies.

CHAPTER 7

A Complete CAI System

A good model is worth a thousand facts.
—New proverb

There is a tendency to view CAI, like its physical implementation suggests, as a confrontation between a student and a computer. Confrontation is not a good model, however, because CAI is neither a competition nor a spectator sport. Instead, we suggest that you consider for a moment, as an analogy, a stage play, perhaps one that you have seen recently, or that you greatly cherish. Except for some avant-garde works, the core of theater involves actors and actresses, performing from a script, for an audience. That is, the cast delivers the play, or script, to the audience. The play itself involves not only the verbal component delivered by the performers but also movements and gestures, scenery and other stage props, lighting, and sometimes music. All of this the audience experiences directly. But behind (and to the side and above and below) are the stage crew, director, musicians, costume handlers, and other support people who facilitate the performance.

At another and quite different level is the playwright, the author of the play, who may have developed the script through research and observation, but who no doubt wrote many drafts before offering the work for performance and then probably revised it after the initial rehearsals.

For the manager of a repertory theater company or the director of a high school play and others of similar responsibilities, the script of the play is just one of many contained in the library. In the planning for a single performance, or for a season, many scripts might be considered before decisions are made. And, finally, for most theater groups and theaters, there are administrators who schedule plays, arrange advertising, apply for grants, establish prices, print programs, issue reports to boards of directors and owners, and perform all the other activities necessary to ensure happy encounters between cast and audience.

In comparison, the core of CAI is an instructional system, something that interacts with a learner and that generally, but not always, follows a script. CAI also involves a verbal exchange, with movement, background, and even, occasionally, music. And like theater, CAI may have a support system, authoring facility, library, and administrative facilities. But surprisingly enough, the student is not the audience, he is the first actor. Furthermore we have a problem: the first actor does not master his lines, so the company must improvise to keep the performance going.

Let us not fool ourselves. This "improvisation" is carefully planned. Even when such a master of playwriting as Pirandello proclaims that *"Questa sera si recita a soggetto"* ("Tonight we improvise") there is a well-thought-out script guiding the performance. In the CAI environment it is the authoring team's task to organize the courseware (the "play") in such a way that the performance flows fluently for any possible student "interpretation."

Going a step further with the theatrical analogy, we may identify the behind-the-scene factors that contribute to the success of the play. The director is the head of the authoring team, the playwright corresponds to the subject matter expert who writes the instructional material, the set designer is the instructional designer, and the stage lighting is divided between the instructional designer and the graphics specialist. Our first actor has a coach: his teacher. What are the theatrical tasks corresponding to computer experts and programmers? They appear at two different stages and levels: in the first one, as architects and constructors; in the second one, as electricians, carpenters, and handymen. In the first, massive stage they have to build the theater and all its support facilities. In the second, permanent but less intensive, they are responsible for maintenance and for the development of all the improvements that the staff requests and technology permits.

Such an effort deserves, and indeed has, an audience. The first rows of the orchestra are occupied by school principals, followed by teachers; the boxes are filled with educational authorities and, perhaps, some politicians; the rest of the seats are taken by parents who worry about education and the future of their children. And finally, there are even critics: courseware evaluation organizations have multiplied, trying to provide guidance to a disoriented mass of spectators who would like a good show for their money.

We will not continue developing this parallel. The message is that the success of the "play" depends upon the collective effort of many agents and on many "rehearsals," including preliminary "tours." In the following chapters we are going to present all the facilities and activities needed to produce a "professional" CAI play. Don't feel intimidated by their complexity—once you know what the components are, you may select those you need to produce a show that will satisfy your audience.

FUNCTIONAL COMPONENTS

CAI systems of many types and sizes have been developed, as Chapter 3 has clearly shown. Some of these systems are presently serving the educational community, some constitute interesting museum pieces, and the rest found their way into the junkyard of oblivion.

As our first design step we present, in Figure 7.1, the block structure of what we call a complete system. Relative sizes are not necessarily meaningful in this diagram, nor are relative positions. All the possible communication paths are shown; however, like paths through a park, some are more heavily traversed. "Complete" is used here not to be presumptuous or to qualify other systems as incomplete, but rather to express a designer's position: A CAI system is not only an instructional delivery component,

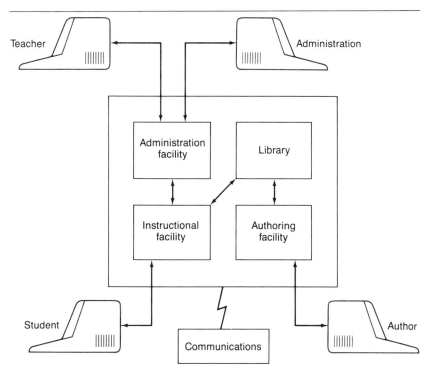

Figure 7.1. A Complete CAI System

but it also includes other important facilities, like administration and authoring. As we have said in the introduction, there is much more to a performance than just what happens on stage. Installations in the field may include different subsets of the complete system building blocks, as is shown later in this chapter.

Figure 7.1 depicts a complete system as including four main subsystems:

- The *Instructional facility* epitomizes the whole purpose of the system—the provision of instruction, the on-line facilitation of student learning. In practical terms, the core of the instructional facility consists of those programs that interact with the student at her terminal.
- The *Administration facility* is the repository of student, course, and statistical records that are necessary for the delivery of instruction and for the evaluation and improvement of instructional materials.
- The *Library* includes all the computerized instructional materials in any possible form, including courseware, tools, games, simulations, and other instructional programs that will be presented to the student or used by her.
- The *Authoring facility* serves primarily to create, update, and improve the library.

These facilities will be extensively described in following chapters (the Instructional facility in Chapters 8 and 9, the Administration facility in Chapter 10 and the

Authoring facility in Chapter 12). We have appended also a communications link, whose purpose is described later in this chapter.

A word of caution to our reader: the structure of the system we are describing is *our* view of how CAI *should* be organized and developed. It matches the structure of many existing instructional systems, some of them commercially available, but has nothing to do with many commercial systems that consist only of unrelated materials.

Instructional Facility

Let us now zoom into the Instructional facility, presented in Figure 7.2 with additional detail.

The Student Interaction. When a student starts a CAI session at a terminal, she must first identify herself. When the right to receive instruction is established, the student's record is retrieved from the Administration files in order to initialize the *student model*. The student model includes all the information that is kept about student background and student performance, needed for the system to decide the appropriate instructional steps.

As shown in the lower loop of Figure 7.2, the student may enter the CAI system

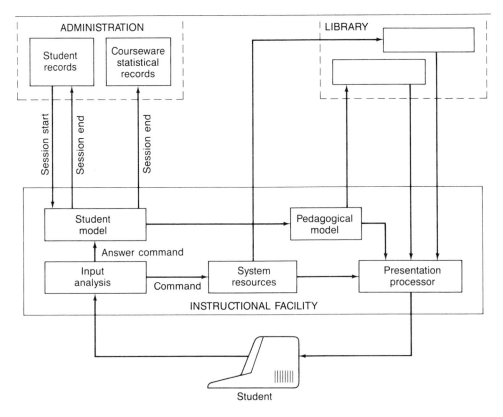

Figure 7.2. The Instructional Facility

to use system resources according to her inclinations; in this case, the student model determines only the student's access rights. A student model becomes really important if we want the system to select instructional materials that match the student's requirements and possibilities.

It is useful to distinguish, in the student model, between the relatively fixed psychological parameters relevant to the instructional process, and the variable state of the student's knowledge, which instruction is trying to improve. At its lowest level the student model may be nothing more than a record of which segments of the program the student has already seen in the current session. A more sophisticated student model might keep track of which problems a student has missed in a problem session so that appropriate review or reteaching can be planned. At an even higher level, information on the student's answer history, response time, learning style, and achievement might be accumulated over many terminal sessions and used for decisions not only on instructional content, but also on how long to wait for a response and what type of feedback to give on incorrect answers.

Few of today's systems incorporate a long-term student model, updated with system usage, but any system that conducts a meaningful dialogue with the learner must react to the learner's answers and requests during the session, and this is possible only if the program being used contains variables that reflect the learner's activity. We are not talking yet about implementation, so that the advantages of having a clearly defined structure that models the student are not discussed here. The point that we want to make is that, conceptually, all the information about the student that is used by the system during the dialogue should be labeled as *the student model.*

The Pedagogical Support. In the CAI systems we propound, the student model is analyzed by the *pedagogical model,* which in some sense mimics a teacher or, at least, a teaching strategy. If strategy is defined by the authoring team, then tactics are the domain of the pedagogical model. Adapting instruction to each student's state of knowledge and psychological parameters, establishing when mastery has been achieved in a specific area, deciding when and how remedial instruction is to be provided: these are pedagogical functions.

The concrete result of the analysis performed by the pedagogical model is expressed as a request to the Library. The *Library,* which is the system repository of knowledge, will then deliver a coded piece of information, or the script for a dialogue. This coded material is processed by the *presentation processor* for its presentation to the student. In some cases the pedagogical model may take a didactic decision that

---

NOTE: The student model, a conceptually vital component, is missing in many of the CAI systems used in schools today, with a double negative effect:

1. The pupil conducts a very shallow instructional dialogue with the system, because the system decisions are based on the minimal interaction being conducted, without considering the student's long-term performance or learning style.

2. In order for the students to receive instruction matched to their needs, the burden of making adequate assignments for each different student in each different subject falls upon the teacher.

does not require Library support, and this is expressed in Figure 7.2 by the arrow going directly from the pedagogical model to the presentation processor. Thus we enter the instructional loop that characterizes CAI: the student answers, the answer is analyzed and the student model is updated, the pedagogical model makes a pedagogical decision based on the updated student model, a new piece of information is requested and delivered by the Library, this information is presented to the student, and a new iteration of the loop is initiated.

Let's stop the description for a moment to emphasize what is probably the greatest potential virtue of CAI: pedagogical decisions are based on the state of a student model that is continuously updated as a result of the student's actual performance, in real time, within the instructional process. What a contrast with a lecture delivered to a large class!

The presentation processor encompasses two different levels of processing: at the highest it may include an interpreter to transform a courseware data structure into a script for interaction with the student; at the lowest, it is just the technical aspect of formatting and preparing the information for display.

At the end of the session the student record is updated in the *Administration* (permanent) file and performance statistics are stored in terms of frames (or appropriate instructional units) to be analyzed by the authoring team. The last element to be described in Figure 7.2, the *system resources,* expresses the possibility of the student using system resources (information, editors, calculators, etc.) on her own initiative, either independently of an instructional loop like the one just described or also to answer requests that were made to her within an instructional loop.

Administration Facility

Administration is an essential component of any large human enterprise. In the previous section we saw two examples of the functions performed by the Administration facility: one for student support and the other to allow for courseware improvement.

The Administration facility box from Figure 7.1 has been enlarged in Figure 7.3,

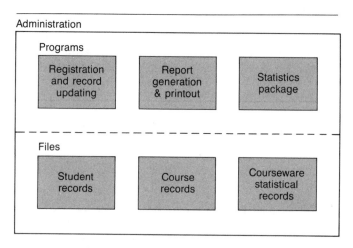

Figure 7.3. The Administration Facility

which details the main program packages and the files being used. Although the administrative processes may be similar in many cases, it is useful to distinguish between those functions related to student and course administration and those related to courseware administration.

Student and Course Administration Functions
- Creation, maintenance, and updating of student records
- Creation, maintenance, and updating of course records
- Test scoring
- Student assignments
- Report generation
- Instructional groupings

The student records are created and initialized with external information, while their updating is the result of the student's activities. At certain key instances, information is transferred from the student-records files into the course-records files (e.g., registration, completion, grades) and into the statistical-data files (e.g., test results). The course records are used for standard administrative purposes (certification, accounting, etc.), while the statistical data on test results allow for summative evaluation of the CAI courses. Reports on students' placement and progress are printed, to be used by teachers and administrators. The most important objective of these reports is to help the teacher plan her class activities and pupil support. Information on student interaction with courseware is very rich and extensive. A summary of it is stored in a student-history file when the corresponding instructional process is completed.

Courseware Administration Functions
- Creation, maintenance, and updating of unit/frame records
- Statistical processing of usage data
- Identification of possible irregularities
- Storage of unresolved student/computer dialogues

In a complete CAI facility detailed reports can be printed for the benefit of the authoring team and are essential for the continuing improvement of the courseware.

Library

The Library is our repository of knowledge. It constitutes the most critical CAI component for ensuring quality of instruction. The fruit of the creative work of the authoring team, improved through the experience of being presented to thousands of students and through constant upgrading, is there to be accessed where and when needed.

In many installations today a courseware library consists of a collection of diskette storage boxes. In a complete CAI system, the courseware resides in external on-line storage (usually hard disk), often under the control of a file server that handles access requests from many different workstations. PLATO had the earliest full, on-line library of courseware, but other large systems (e.g., TICCIT, WICAT, CCC, TOAM) soon adopted the same catalog approach. Today, as more and more microcomputers are being purchased with hard disks or are being connected into networks with file servers, the on-line library is becoming more important.

We envision such a library with courseware, lessonware, simulations, games and other instructional programs, an annotated directory, a set of related files for course improvement, a full complement of library maintenance facilities, and a powerful collection of software packages for instructional support.

Authoring Facility

A CAI authoring facility, whether as part of a complete CAI system, or as a separate facility, is as critical to the development of large-scale CAI programs as an interactive programming environment is to the production of mainline software. We delve extensively into this subject in Chapter 12. Here suffice to say only that courseware development requires not only CAI authoring systems but also general purpose and special purpose programming languages, software development and software management packages, support utilities, graphics packages, and all the other tools of modern software development. Furthermore, the environment should allow for development on powerful computers, with easy downloading to a student workstation for debugging and testing.

Communications

Communications may appear to be a luxury in a world populated by stand-alone microcomputers, but educational institutions are rapidly realizing the need for interconnecting student (and teacher) workstations. With any multi-user system, the need for tools to manage communications among users is obvious. This is an area that is not developed in the remainder of the book, but at least we can say that we envision three communication tools: a mail server, a talk facility, and a remote-access facility. The mail server handles local area mail, maintains mailboxes, and formats messages for transfer to other networks. The talk facility initiates and terminates direct communication links between active users on the local area network, and the remote-access facility provides file transfer, remote log-in, and other types of connections to remote users (e.g., other networks, dial-up stations).

Implementation

With present technology, the natural system architecture for a complete CAI system is based on a central computer with a powerful operating system, controlling the programs that execute all the central functions (administration, library requests, communications, etc.). The central computer is linked by a communications facility (e.g., a local-area network) to each one of the student terminals, consisting of a personal computer. This personal computer runs the programs that perform the functions of the instructional facility and sends requests for system resources, like library access, to the central computer.

OPERATION

The first section has shown the complexity of a full CAI system. The intention has not been to frighten you, but rather to raise your level of expectations and demands. Furthermore, it is important to point out that every installation has to be tailored according to the necessities and possibilities of its users. In particular, not every instructional environment that utilizes CAI among its pedagogical tools needs an authoring facility, and not every installation requires a communications facility. The purpose of the following sections is to describe well-established modes of operation so that they may serve as models to select or modify according to specific needs. We concentrate our analysis on two dimensions: the first considers how the authoring responsibilities influence the structure of the system, and the second deals with the options for installation and the possibilities for system growth.

Authoring Environments

One of the critical factors determining the complexity of a CAI system operation is whether the installation includes an Authoring facility and is responsible for courseware development or not.

In the following sections we examine three representative types of environment, each one with a distinct approach to the authoring requirements.

Integrated Authoring. An integrated environment is defined as one that possesses all the facilities of a complete CAI system as defined in the previous section, employs the personnel able to operate the system and develop courseware, provides instruction to a population of students, and supports the teaching staff in their educational activities.

The archetype for this conception was implemented by Donald Bitzer and his collaborators at the University of Illinois. As described in Chapter 3, experimentation started in the first PLATO system in the early 1960s and by 1968 Bitzer had defined PLATO IV as a system able to work simultaneously with up to 4,000 terminals (Bitzer & Skaperdas, 1970). The reasons for this system never fulfilling its full potential are of minor interest in this context; the important element is that the concept worked and, for many years, the University of Illinois PLATO system provided a creative environment and a center of attraction for anybody seriously interested in the field of CAI.

A natural integrated environment flourishes where three ingredients abound: students (or trainees), instructional developers, and money. PLATO at the University of Illinois enjoyed all three ingredients, although funding fluctuated through the years. Students were always there because the University of Illinois has an enrollment of some 40,000. Money was provided, during the most productive period, by very significant grants from the National Science Foundation (NSF) and the Advanced Research Projects Agency (ARPA), and by the contribution of computer resources form Control Data Corporation (CDC). (CDC continued this support when NSF funding ended, and markets PLATO commercially.) Some excellent instructional designers worked at the Computer-based Education Research Laboratory (CERL), where PLATO was developed, but an important element of the ideology was that the faculty would develop courseware for their students.

The infrastructure built for PLATO at the University of Illinois—a vast network that allows for communication among a community of scholars—constitutes a model worth studying. Authors would sit at the terminals and, using a very powerful (and hopefully very easy to use) authoring language named TUTOR, would develop lessons and courses for the students' benefit. If problems were encountered during development, on-line help was available both from very detailed on-line manuals and from the CERL staff, accessible by direct terminal-to-terminal conversation or electronic mail. Once a lesson was written, the author could test it by switching to student mode, and could debug it on-line. Students would study the available lessons at their convenience or, in the case of large classes, in allotted periods of time. A proctor would be available at each one of the large terminal rooms, but the communication channels were also open. The students could send messages, record doubts or abnormalities, request clarification, or point to courseware errors. If lucky, and the author was on-line or a consultant was available, difficulties could be solved on the spot, by direct terminal-to-terminal brief dialogue. (By "brief" we mean that only two lines were available for dialogue on the screen, one for each interlocutor.)

Instructors could obtain a variety of reports about student performance, according to different cross-sections and criteria. Statistical data about performance within their courseware would be accessible to the authors, to allow for courseware evaluation and improvement.

Everything sounds ideal. Nevertheless PLATO didn't change life dramatically at the University of Illinois. Courseware was developed but it was hard to prove that its use contributed significantly to the improvement of instruction. The faculty did not rush to participate in courseware development: it wasn't at all easy, it required different professional abilities than those characterizing the field in which each professor was an expert, and there was very limited academic recognition for the effort.

Besides universities, another natural environment for an integrated system is found in the large organizations that depend on continuous, or at least frequent, training of large numbers of personnel. In this case the trainees are there, the money is there, and the money can pay for the remaining ingredient: instructional developers. When compared with the university, the corporation seems a less "natural" environment, because the "authors" are inherent to the university, while in the large organizations authors must be added, because they are not part of the "production" process.

Let us argue in favor of the opposite standpoint, that large organizations with heavy training needs are in fact more natural clients than universities for integrated systems.

Our main reason is that trainees earn a salary, which is paid by the employing organization. Any increase in instructional efficiency translates immediately into measurable economic benefits. This allows for the consideration of an investment in instruction within the same policies that will try to optimize gains, and this is a language management understands. In effect, the objective of an instructional or training process is to bring a student (trainee) to a certain level of mastery. Improvements in instruction are not measured in terms of mastery (which is a given) but rather in terms of learner time or resources invested in the process. In the environment where learners' time can be measured in money, as well as resources, we have clear equations to justify investments that will improve instruction. For instance, if the training of workers in a factory requires an average of four weeks per year, and the incorporation of a CAI system reduces that to three weeks, then a week of average salary multiplied by the total number of workers may pay for the CAI system and leave a nice profit for the company.

Profit is not an objective of a reputable university. Furthermore, although universities do provide instruction, what characterizes an academic environment is the creation of knowledge, the establishment of truth, and the development of a thinking style that may be characterized by openness, honesty, and a scientific approach. This is not to say that instruction is not important: it is necessary for the perpetuation of the university in terms of its scholars, it serves the needs of the society the university is a part of, and it is a considerable source of income. But if economic resources are scarce and the university authorities are confronted with investing in a research facility or in the incorporation of prominent scholars on the one hand, or investing resources to shorten the time students must devote to their studies on the other hand, the decision will be clear.

Liberal arts colleges, community colleges, technical schools, and other postsecondary institutions differ from universities in their research involvement, and their decision considerations for adopting CAI may be nearer to those of the corporations.

Separated Authoring. Although not included in the concept of an integrated environment, it is a fact that in the actual implementations of this kind there is a tendency to use mainly in-house-developed courseware. If we assume that courseware development is at least as costly as book development, the parallel would be writing a book for use at just one university. This is clearly inefficient. The reasonable frame of mind (at least for some time) is to assume that the number of readers is larger than the number of writers, that the number of CAI learners is larger than the number of CAI authors, and that the number of CAI delivery facilities is larger than the number of CAI authoring facilities.

Since courseware development is very expensive and requires specialized personnel and facilities, the logical conclusion is: Have a little number of integrated systems where all the authoring is done and distribute the courseware over many CAI systems where delivery of instruction is the main function. This results in clear savings for production and development. Hardware and software can be standardized for the delivery systems (which are defined by the diagram of Figure 7.1 minus the Authoring-facility block), and the large investments required for authoring facilities and for courseware development can be amortized over a large number of users.

Conceptually it is possible to think of two ways of organizing this relationship between users and developers:

1. The users organize themselves and select development groups, or
2. A corporation organizes a venture, selects an educational or training market, defines the configuration of a delivery system and of a corresponding authoring facility, and starts developing courseware that caters to some basic educational needs and includes the educational administration programs that allow for controlling the learners' progress. The delivery systems (including courseware and administration programs) are marketed and, if successful, additional courseware is developed.

It seems that the second way is much easier than the first, because it is the only one found in practice.

An important feature of the separated environment (as opposed to the "free-coupled," described in the next section), is that the instructional administration and support are the same for all the facilities, which assumes a common approach to the organization of instruction. This is particularly important for courseware improvement, because statistics may be collected from many different installations, thus allowing not only for larger samples but also for a differential analysis based on installation parameters. For instance, in the school environment, performance results may be analyzed according to cross-sections that identify socioeconomic background or the language spoken at home.

Some inconveniences arise when the authoring and delivery environments are separated. At the delivery end, some of the personnel may resent the lack of authoring possibilities. Furthermore, local modifications of courseware are unacceptable if the advantages of general analysis of courseware performance and global improvements are to be maintained. At the development end, students are not an inherent component of the environment, and authors cannot always perform the frequent tests that would be ideal during development.

Free-coupling. Many schools bought personal computers either for reasons of prestige or with the expectation that the school staff would develop (in their free time!?) courseware that would be used by the students. This naturally resulted in an explosive growth of unutilized hardware. Nature abhors a vacuum, so many independent authors and, later, big publishers started producing courseware for all those personal computers. User consortia (including MECC and CONDUIT), and evaluation groups (Alberta's Clearinghouse, MECC, etc.) tried to guide consumers by evaluating courseware and sorting out the best materials; they discovered that much of what was offered was of questionable instructional quality. Surveys conducted in California and in Scotland in the early 1980s maintained that less than 2 percent of the materials examined were worthy of teachers' consideration.

To add to the difficulties of finding appropriate courseware, neither personal computers nor software were, until very recently, standardized. If, for example, a school principal found a well-developed piece of courseware, her school might nevertheless be unable to use it; the courseware had to match both the brand and the generation of the personal computers used in her school. Only in the last few years have the best publishers made serious efforts to solve the problems of quality and standardization, primarily by selecting authors more carefully, testing before publishing, and providing parallel versions of programs for the most widely used personal computers.

One problem remains in this type of environment, however, and its solution seems distant. Most free-coupled CAI systems lack an integrated concept of instruction, and few provide support for educational administration. As a result, students are not guided along a selected instructional path, but rather are diverted to a heterogeneous collection of courseware, with no actual assessment of intellectual progress. In this area, classical textbook-oriented instruction has advantages; a good textbook has clearly defined objectives, a balance of different topics, support activities, and even a teacher's guide. Students follow a well-defined path, and the teacher can control their progress.

Installation and Growth

In the previous section we established a taxonomy of installations according to their structure. The purpose of this section is to explore their evolution in time. We found in this orthogonal dimension three types of systems.

Research Environment. Computers, the information-processing machines, are a continuous challenge for researchers, who explore untapped possibilities and build layer upon layer of more and more sophisticated applications. It is natural for instruction, where the delivery, transfer, acquisition, and (sometimes) creation of information are essential tasks, to be a fertile field for such research. Cross-fertilization comes from the field of artificial intelligence—an unfortunate selection of name—where the challenge lies in developing the algorithms that allow computers to perform tasks that only humans were thought to be able to accomplish. Instruction delivery was once one of those tasks.

CAI research environments are typically universities (Stanford, Illinois, M.I.T., Pittsburgh, Carnegie Mellon, Brown, among others) and research organizations strong in the computational field, like Xerox PARC and Bolt, Beraneck and Newman Inc. (B.B.N.), to give just two of the best-known examples. Our concept of "installing a CAI system" does not apply to a research environment. The physical resources and the researchers are there, and the beginning of CAI research is just marked by somebody's decision to do it. The efforts of such research are geared not toward courseware production but rather, and wisely so, toward the development of tools, conceptions, and algorithms for their implementation.

Growth is related to the evolution of technology and to the increased possibilities opened by the tools (in the widest meaning of the word) being developed. Typically, the computer infrastructure is state-of-the-art, and the exciting and beautiful demonstrations of the examples being developed to exhibit research ideas will not run on economically feasible school installations. This does not detract from the immense value of the research, the fruits of which slowly but surely will benefit the whole instructional system.

Turnkey Systems. Schools and other organizations whose responsibilities include the delivery of instruction or training are usually not interested, and in most cases not prepared, for the development of computer tools. Their objective is to obtain the best facilities they can afford that will help in the instructional task. Catering to these needs are companies that study the customer instructional requirements and provide the type of CAI system that satisfies most of the customer needs. These companies are in charge of the system definition, its installation, and the training of the personnel that will operate it, use it, or be supported by it; they also provide maintenance and courseware updating. It terms of authoring, these systems usually match the separated environment classification previously presented, but it may well be that, in spite of not being interested in the development of computer tools, an organization is interested in the in-house development of courseware. In such a case, the needs analysis will determine that an authoring facility has to be included, and of course, a more complex type of training will also be required.

At a different level, turnkey systems suffer from the same lack of standardization that afflicts personal computers. Efforts are duplicated to an enormous extent as each company develops its own algorithms, tools, and in many cases, special hardware, in order to provide functions everybody needs. Competition prevails over cooperation which results in longer development time and courseware incompatibility. Clearly, we still do not know how to strike a balance between the healthy competition necessary for progress and the kind of public commitment that education deserves.

System growth is offered within each "family," and usually the companies that provide installations do worry about upgrading possibilities or at least upward compatibility. The recent tendency toward de facto standardization, or at least concentration of the vast majority of personal computers into a relatively limited number of models with well-defined characteristics, will certainly benefit education, by allowing for the use in one system of courseware developed for another. In effect, turnkey systems that were originally associated with proprietary hardware are evolving toward the production of courseware libraries and administration packages that may be run on standard equipment.

Incremental Installations. Many CAI systems are the result of haphazard decisions, often linked to an offer at reduced prices—or even the gift—of a small number of personal computers. Some of these installations will gather dust, essentially unused except for some game playing. Others may develop and grow, but only if somebody is interested and has appropriate skills; their growth may be measured in the richness of the courseware and software library and in the increase of usage time. When usage saturates the system possibilities, more hardware facilities may be added—more terminals, a fixed disk or a larger capacity one, a better printer, and so forth. The addition of carefully selected and adequately networked elements will bring good results, but even the successful system will not reach the level of services provided by turnkey systems. Such home-grown systems have, however, one element in their favor: their growth has been the consequence of a felt need.

This is the "school theater." If good plays are selected, and if invited experts are brought in to help, the outcome may be very enjoyable. If everything has to be developed in-house, even the play, it may be very motivating, but it will never deliver a first-rate performance.

SUMMARY

The structure and operation of complete CAI systems has been presented as a first step in the comprehension of the options available when designing or selecting a computerized environment to provide support to an instructional process.

The instructional, administrative, library, authoring, and communications facilities described coordinate their operation under the control of a powerful operating system, to create a rich educational environment.

Few systems marketed today provide all the functions we have described, but the educational use of computers is rapidly developing, as is network technology. Systems designed for the end of the twentieth century will certainly need more than the bare instructional functions to be successful. Already, teachers have become critical of software that does not provide instructor summaries of student progress. This is a first symptom of an impending major change in teacher style, strongly required in educational terms but that only now the technology is able to support. Reconciling the desire to have each pupil progress according to her possibilities and interests within a complex curriculum, with society's educational needs is a task that nobody can manage without adequate tools. The teacher has to add to her classical function of being a dispenser of knowledge, the very different and even more demanding tasks of being a guide, an advisor, and an administrator of instructional resources. These tasks require a computer support that cannot fall below that required for production in a sophisticated industry.

The production of courseware—a critical consideration—may be integrated within the instructional environment, or may be performed by external sources, either in terms of complete support or of independent packages.

And finally, this chapter has presented different possibilities for systems installations and upgrading.

In brief, analysis and classification of CAI systems was the theme of this chapter. The next chapter will do the same job for courseware.

CHAPTER 8

Courseware Taxonomies

Systematists will have only to decide (not that this will be easy) whether any form be sufficiently constant and distinct from other forms, to be capable of definition; and if definable, whether the differences be sufficiently important to deserve a specific name.

—Charles Darwin, *The Origin of Species,* (1859).

The word *courseware* appears in this chapter heading with the technical meaning it received in Chapter 2. This concept, which appeared in the sixties as a natural addition to the well-known computer terms *hardware* and *software,* denoted the instructional contents to be displayed to a student sitting at his computer-linked terminal (hardware) under the control of a stored program (software). The expanded use of personal computers brought a deluge of computer-delivered lessons, widely marketed, to be taken at school or at home; this development introduced another word, *lessonware,* to characterize these products. In addition to these two words we are using two more—*tools* and *microworlds*—to allow for more precise references within a computer-based instructional environment.

The importance of the taxonomy we have set forth lies in the fact that design techniques and required resources are very different for the production of courseware, lessonware, tools, and microworlds. With respect to the distinction between courseware and lessonware, it is important to emphasize that the difference in scale between

---

COURSEWARE: A complete course, entailing student instruction on a subject over long periods of time (usually one or more school semesters or academic terms). Progress through the course is determined by the student's (computer-controlled) performance.

LESSONWARE: An isolated topic, taught in a small number of CAI sessions (one, in many cases). In a class environment, the sequencing of lessons is a teacher or pupil decision.

TOOLS: Computational resources, placed in the hands of a student and under the student's control. These tools may be used for instructional support but, in many cases, they may be used independently of an instructional process. Examples are editors, dictionaries, and programming languages.

MICROWORLDS: Environments created for student exploration, providing the student with user-friendly sets of student commands.

---

courseware and lessonware does not imply an intrinsic difference in sophistication or quality among the instructional materials presented in the two types of packages. From the designer's standpoint the treatment is different in two aspects:

1. Logical, because courseware requires a much richer student model than lessonware, being that the courseware system is responsible for the student's progress over a large structure of knowledge.
2. Practical, because the tools and techniques required for lessonware development are simpler than those required for courseware.

To illustrate the different realities we are analyzing, let's compare two scenarios. In the first, a single author writes a lesson to provide practice in the use of a certain prefix. In a matter of days he decides on the examples to provide, the questions to ask, the possible student actions, and the system responses to those actions. In the closed and small universe of this lesson the author may directly specify all the system activities. In the second scenario, a team of 15 authors works over a period of five years to develop courseware for teaching reading comprehension, to be embedded within school instruction in grades 2 to 8. Development and management in the second scenario clearly have requirements far removed from those in the first.

We mentioned in the previous chapter that not every CAI environment requires a complete system. Similarly, you can develop lessonware without studying a lot about courseware—without, in other words, reading this chapter (or this book, for that matter). Nevertheless, we believe that the analysis presented here on the development of courseware will add insight about the development process, even to those who are interested in lessonware only.

INSTRUCTIONAL TAXONOMIES

In applying the principles of instructional design presented in Part II to the case of CAI, we find it useful to distinguish several dimensions where the author (or the authoring team) need to make concrete decisions. Since these decisions are interlinked, we do not provide a step-by-step procedure in this chapter. Rather, we think that by recognizing the multidimensionality of the process, your design may gain in modularity and neatness.

Extension

In talking about *extension,* which refers to the amount of instructional material covered and, correspondingly, to the time required to study it, we distinguish between:

- COURSES, which are large structures taught over long periods of time (years, terms),
- UNITS, which are parts of courses, like chapters in a book, (taught usually over weeks), and
- LESSONS, which are components of units, (taught usually in one computer session or in a small number of sessions).

These names are taken from educational practice (for lack of something better), but should be considered, in this taxonomy, simply as labels for identifying extension or duration and not for identifying instructional style or character. For example, a lesson could be a game, and a unit could be a simulation project. The reason we present extension first is that it restricts the applicability of the other dimensions of courseware. For instance, topology is critical at course level but is usually irrelevant at lesson level. Instructional interaction, on the other hand, is very relevant at lesson level but is rarely defined at unit or course level.

Topology and Traversal

Lessons are the building blocks of units and, as such, the building blocks of courseware also. In many cases lessons constitute the smallest instructional unit we want to refer to, but occasionally we are interested in a division of a lesson into smaller components. This may happen, for instance, if a lesson includes several instructional events and we want the pedagogical model to be able to decide when a learner should shift from one event to another. In order to have a unique denomination for the building blocks of all courseware and lessonware, we introduce the term *instructional block*. Lessons are formed by one or more instructional blocks. Thus, courses, units, and lessons are composed of instructional blocks, the smallest units we are interested in dealing with in this context.

The study of the contiguity between the instructional blocks in a piece of courseware, and of the relations between them, is called *topology*. From a topological standpoint, the contents of the instructional blocks are irrelevant.

The topological definition of a course may be viewed as a graph, where the nodes are instructional blocks covering the subjects of study to be taught in the course. See, for instance, the block diagram in Figure 8.1, taken from Koffman, 1972.

Any graph is composed of nodes (or vertices) that are connected by arcs (also called edges or branches) representing relations. The first and necessary relation represented in the example is the precedence relation that defines "prerequisite" conditions between blocks. For example, in Figure 8.1, the subject "Karnaugh maps" requires the previous mastery of the subjects "Decimal to bin-oct-hex conversion" and "Combinational design," the latter having several prerequisites of its own.

The actual instructional path that a student follows through the graph of instructional blocks is called a *graph traversal* or, simply, a *traversal*. Any traversal must respect the prerequisite conditions among the instructional blocks. Note, nevertheless, that this precedence relation does not necessarily define a complete ordering of the blocks. Additional relations may be added on the basis of pedagogical theories, instructional experience, or personal taste.

NOTE: We use the term *subject* to refer to an area to be taught. *Subject* and *topic* are often used interchangeably, perhaps with the connotation of subject covering a larger area and topic referring to a more specific one. To avoid ambiguity, we use the word *topic* to refer to each concept or rule or similar "knowledge constituent" involved in the teaching of a subject. (Things are not made easier by the fact that some topics are themselves subjects of study—but then nobody said that being easy is a virtue.)

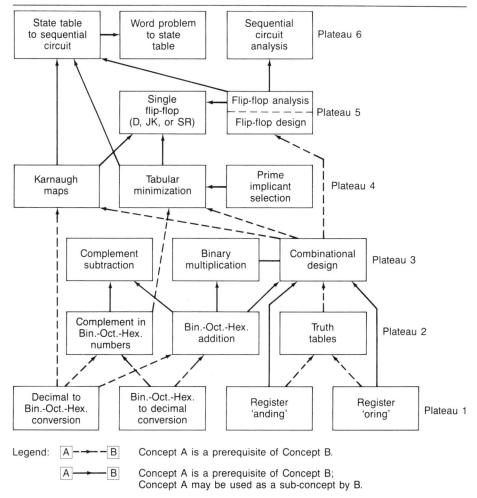

Legend: A ---▶--- B   Concept A is a prerequisite of Concept B.

A ——— B   Concept A is a prerequisite of Concept B;
Concept A may be used as a sub-concept by B.

Note: The relation "is a prerequisite of" is transitive
(A is a prerequisite of B, B is a prerequisite of C, implies A is a
prerequisite of C)

Figure 8.1. Precedence Relation Graph (From E. B. Koffman, 1972, A generative CAI
Tutor for Computer Science Concepts, *Spring Joint Computer Conference, AFIPS Conference Proceedings,* p. 381, Reprinted by permission.)

The author usually organizes his pedagogical strategy based on a traversal, selected by him *a priori,* one that satisfies all the necessary conditions of the topology,
and that will probably match the actual traversal of a student without learning difficulties. Such an *a priori* traversal will be called *canonical.* The author of the system must
consider possible student difficulties or initiatives by providing the means to traverse
the topology in many different ways besides the canonical. Furthermore, different canonical traversals my be considered for different types of students.

Let us now present *three basic topological structures: sequence, parallel sequences,* and *tree.*

Sequence Structure. In a sequence there is a clear, linear ordering of the instructional blocks (see Figure 8.2).

The label "Block i" stands for *instructional block i,* and will be shortened in the text as B_i.

The basic canonical traversal is well defined, with an implicit order of study that starts in the first instructional block (B_1) and finishes in the *n*th instructional block (B_n).

The distinction between canonical (*a priori*) traversal and dynamic (actual) traversal is required because the topological structures under examination (and the sequence in particular) are static organizations of knowledge that can support different pedagogical strategies. For each pedagogical strategy and for each particular student, each structure may be traversed in a different way, always respecting the prerequisite relations between blocks. This dynamic adaptation of different paths to different students may be provided for in various ways:

1. The author may match block parameters to fixed student parameters in such a way that each student sees only those blocks that match his particular profile.
2. Each student may be allowed to select the blocks he wants to study. (See "learner-directed" or "mixed-initiative" modes in the next section.)
3. According to his performance, as reflected in the variable parameters that represent student knowledge, a student may be recycled over blocks already seen or allowed to skip over blocks not yet presented.

The sequence structure of Figure 8.2, for $n = 7$, has the following basic canonical traversal.

$$B_1, B_2, B_3, B_4, B_5, B_6, B_7$$

The author may decide that the canonical traversal for a bright student may be restricted to:

$$B_2, B_4, B_6, B_7$$

A student characterized within the system as "bright", but caught unprepared in the subject in this sequence, may generate, because of remediation, the following *actual* instructional path:

$$B_2, B_1, B_2, B_4, B_6, B_2, B_3, B_4, B_5, B_6, B_7, B_5, B_6, B_7$$

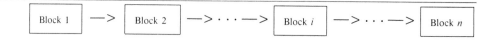

Figure 8.2. The Sequence Structure

Parallel-Sequences Structure. A parallel-sequences structure allows students to study several sequences simultaneously.

Figure 8.3 describes a course structure whose components are the previously defined sequences. Each sequence is built to teach a different subject within the course. What makes this structure different from the previous one is that the different sequences are not taught one after the other but in parallel. The student activity is switched constantly among the different parallel sequences, while progress is being controlled independently for each. The pedagogical model may increase or decrease the proportion of student activity in each sequence according to the student's performance. It may also provide for longer periods of uninterrupted activity in each sequence, if the student profile suggests that this strategy may be helpful—as it seems to be for low achievers.

Note that the distinction we made between static structure and dynamic traversal is essential to understand how a nonlinear static structure (like the one just presented, or the tree, introduced next) supports individual instructional paths, each one a sequence.

Parallel-sequences is the topological structure used by Professor Patrick Suppes from Stanford University for testing and practice in basic skills. It is also used in the TOAM systems; a detailed example for reading comprehension is presented in Chapter 13, in the section "TOAM's Testing and Practice in Reading Comprehension (RC)."

Tree Structure. A set of nodes is organized as a tree structure if the following conditions are satisfied:

1. There is one (and only one) node called *root.*
2. Every node may have *sons.* If node B is a son of node A, then node A is the *father* of node B.
3. The root has no father; every other node has exactly one father.

In Figure 8.4, B_1 is the root, with sons $B_{1,1}, B_{1,2}, \ldots, B_{1,k}$. Any of those nodes may have sons, and the figure includes those of $B_{1,2}$, denoted as: $B_{1,2,1}, B_{1,2,2}, \ldots, B_{1,2,p}$.

Trees are widely used in computer science, and very efficient algorithms have been

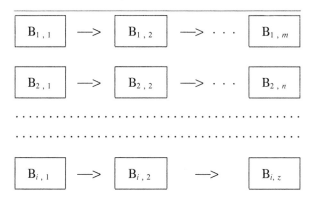

Figure 8.3. Parallel-Sequences Structure

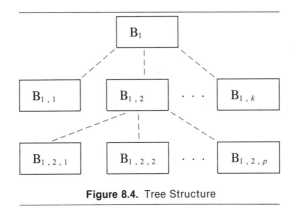

Figure 8.4. Tree Structure

built for their construction and their traversal. The instructional designer may enjoy the use of those algorithms, but it is the designer's responsibility to assign instructional significance, which is not inherent in the topology. The rest of this section describes two among the many possible ways to utilize a tree topology, the first one with an emphasis on organization and the second one with emphasis on prerequisite relations.

Organization Tree. Let us assume that a course comprises several units, and we want to organize its structure without imposing a preferred order of study among the units. The tree structure fits exactly this need: The root is the course, and the sons of the course are the units. Similarly, if every unit is composed of lessons, without a preferred order, then each lesson will appear in the structure as a son of its parent unit.

A concrete example of this idea can be found in the TICCIT courseware structure.

The TICCIT program (MITRE Corporation, 1974) advocated a systems approach, with CAI being one of the components of a global educational system. With such a system, a courseware structure was developed (see Figure 8.5) with a tree topology, a fixed assignment of instructional significance to the nodes in the tree, and with an underlying instructional method (rule, example, practice).

In this tree, a course includes a set of units, each unit includes a set of lessons, and each lesson includes a set of segments, each segment dealing with the primary instruction (according to the instructional method previously mentioned). In the canonical traversal the Course Introduction is presented, followed by a description of the Objectives of the different units. Then the units are studied, each one starting with a Unit Introduction followed by the presentation of the Objectives of its lessons. Moving down a level in the tree, each Lesson[1] starts with its own Introduction, followed by the presentation of the Segment Objectives. The primary instruction occurs at segment level.

Each Lesson ends with a Test, and each Segment failed in the test is reviewed. Other options at Lesson level are Fun (educational games) and AB (for students willing to obtain a high grade). Units finish with a Test also, and Lessons failed are reviewed.

Finally, there is a Course Test, and Units failed are reviewed. The actual (dynamic)

---

[1] In this section we have adopted TICCIT's terminology. *Lesson,* for instance, is used elsewhere in this book in a more flexible way. *Segment* is a term we have not defined and is part of TICCIT's terminology.

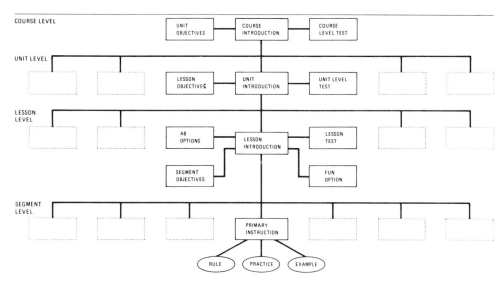

Figure 8.5. TICCIT Courseware Structure (From the MITRE Corporation, 1974, An Overview of the TICCIT Program, p. 29).

traversal would vary, both according to student performance and because of the several options that allow for student initiative.

This fixed (course-independent) topology reflects the TICCIT conception that the *way* subjects are taught can be viewed independently from *what* is taught. Although this conception is true for classes of courses, it cannot be applied universally. The evolution of the TICCIT system design, particularly as seen in the WISE system from WICAT Corporation, is toward increased freedom for the course developers.

Prerequisites Tree. Let us assume we have to design an instructional block to teach subject X. While writing the contents, we assume the learner is familiar with certain topics. This is always so, because subjects of study are taught assuming a learner's background. Nevertheless some of these topics may be unknown to some of the students. It is clear that we do not want to include the teaching of these other topics within the instructional block that teaches X. A possible structural solution is to define a tree where the prerequisites of X appear as its sons. Thus the designer may write instructional blocks for as many of X's sons as he considers necessary. The process is recursive: each son of X may have prerequisites that will become its sons. This approach was used by the Ontario Institute for Studies in Education (OISE), in its "Prerequisite Mathematics Skills Course" (Sakamoto, 1980). Figure 8.6 presents part of their CAN/CAI prerequisite math tree.[2]

The objective of the course is to teach the basic mathematics skills required for higher mathematics courses to those students who do not master them. For reasons of

---

[2]Although the uninitiated may think that "CAN" stands for Canadian, the fact is that the system developers were so tired of the proliferation of bombastic acronyms for CAI systems that their selection was "Completely Arbitrary Name."

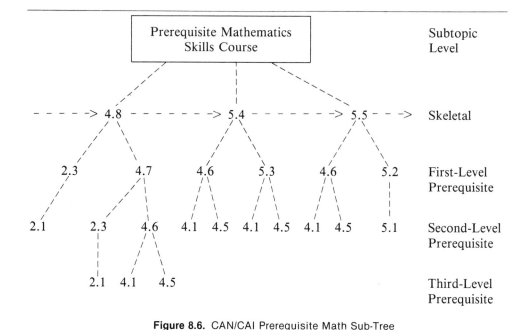

Figure 8.6. CAN/CAI Prerequisite Math Sub-Tree

efficiency, the system identifies precisely the subtopics where the learner's weaknesses reside. The subtree in Figure 8.6 presents, in the form <topic>.<subtopic>, subtopics belonging to the following topics:

Topic 2 – Factoring of Integers
Topic 3 – Handling of Signs and Common Fractions
Topic 4 – Equivalent Common Fractions and Reduction to Lowest Terms
Topic 5 – Complex Fractions

The student is tested in skeletal skills, in the succession shown by the dashed line, and if mastery is shown, he progresses quickly form one skill to the next. On the other hand, if the student fails at one skeletal skill, his mastery of the first-level prerequisites of this specific skill is tested. The algorithm continues within this strategy (a depth-first search) down the tree, until the student fails at a box without prerequisites. When this situation is reached, instruction is provided on the specific subtopic. These terminal nodes of the tree are called leaves—thus completing the peculiar image of these trees, with the root up and the leaves down.

The student may fail the test for subtopic Y and, nevertheless, succeed in the tests for each of the prerequisites of Y. In this situation (which usually depicts lack of skills integration), instruction is provided on subtopic Y. Once the prerequisites are mastered, the student moves up in the tree, receiving instruction in each of the subtopics failed. Student failures are thus dealt with at the most suitable level, and remedial instruction is always provided on a firm basis.

Directed Graph. Courseware authors may structure the courseware as they wish, without adopting any of the three topologies described above. Koffman's precedence-relation graph (Figure 8.1), describes a directed graph that is not a sequence, a parallel sequence, or a tree. The author's only obligation, when in charge, is to traverse the graph in a way that respects the existing precedence relations.

Locus of Control

In the previous section we analyzed topologies and their possible traversals; in this section our attention will be on who makes the decisions that determine the actual (dynamic) traversal. In this dimension of the instructional interaction, which deals with the *locus of control* problem, we distinguish three interaction styles: *prescribed, free,* and *mixed-initiative.*

Prescribed or Author-directed Interaction. In this kind of interaction the traversal path (as well as the use of system resources) is determined *a priori* by the author, in part rigidly and in part dependent on the learner's responses to proposed questions and (potentially) his response times. Two examples of this interaction system are the TOAM courseware and the CAN/CAI Prerequisite Mathematics Skill Course that was described above.

Free or Learner-directed Interaction. In this mode, the CAI environment is an open universe for the learner to explore. The computer resources (text files, graphics, data banks, programs) are manipulated by the student at his own initiative. This style applies more to tools and microworlds than to courseware as we define it. A programming language such as Papert's LOGO provides a well-known example of free learner activity. In terms of instructional design the drawback is that it is very hard to determine whether learning occurs, and even more difficult to measure it. The TICCIT implementation, in spite of its rigid topology and well-defined canonical traversal, is based on learner-directed interaction. In fact, it includes a Learner Control Command Language and a special functional keyboard based on this command language. The student may explore the course tree and receive instruction only in the blocks he selects. The student may even survey the course, unit or lesson under consideration by typing INTRO, thus receiving an overview of the instructional material. This exploration facility is also supported by an advisory program that, on request, provides suggestions on how to proceed.

The CAN/CAI system allows the regular students, once they have completed all the required topics, to switch to Learner Control mode, where they have access to any portion of the course. In this second mode the interaction style is free.

Although learner control in CAI seems very appealing, and blends with our convictions about individual freedom, the results of its application in particular instances have not been encouraging. As mentioned in Chapter 3, the application of TICCIT at the community college level showed an attrition rate of 84 percent for the mathematics course as compared with 50 percent for the control groups, and for the English courses, an attrition rate of 45 percent as compared with 34 percent for the control groups (Alderman, 1978). The results of White and Smith (1974), quoted in Chapter 4, have shown that the amount of student responsibility for instructional decisions must be correlated with the student's psychological parameters in order to achieve optimal learning. It may well be that a very high percentage of community college students in the TICCIT experiment were not prepared to cope with the responsibility of assuming full control of their instruction.

Mixed-Initiative Interaction. Mixed-initiative interaction mode is the eclectic answer to those situations that fall between the requirements for the author-directed and the learner-directed modes. In mixed-initiative interaction the learner is instructed in prescribed mode, until he requests a change to free interaction. The instructional dialogue then switches to learner-directed interaction, until his requests are satisfied, at which point the system reverts to prescribed interaction.

TICCIT could very easily work within this interaction style. A system built directly in this style (SMILE: Structured Mixed-Initiative Learning Environment), is described in Chapter 13.

Computer Integration

CAI is one among many instructional processes, and this last section dealing with instructional taxonomies is devoted to analyzing the possible functions CAI may serve, and how to integrate them within a larger instructional environment. A natural way to start is to refer to the instructional events defined in Chapter 4, indicating how and when CAI may by used.

Instructional events were classified as follows:

1. Initial teaching
    Introduction
    Explication
    Demonstration
    Problem solving
    Practice
2. Assessment
    Review
    Testing
3. Maintenance
4. Support
    Management
    Guidance

Computers may be used to carry out any one of these events, not always with the same efficiency or advantages. Let us group them according to computer implementation, with the proviso that we are going to generalize in order to present basic ideas, and that exceptions may be found in actual practice.

a. Introduction and explication
    The computer presents materials, usually not requiring active learner participation (except for acknowledgment of comprehension). It is possible to distinguish two submodes:

a.1 The explications are provided as a part of the instructional design (instructor control).

a.2 The explications are presented upon learner's request (in mixed-initiative or information-retrieval modes).

b. Demonstration

The computer shows how something is done. This is an excellent use of this medium, because a student may request repetitions as many times as he wants or needs, without any conflict with the teacher or the rest of the class. The videodisc technology has enriched this type of instruction by allowing for real imagery and, in the more sophisticated examples, for different perspectives or degrees of zooming.

c. Problem solving

Progress is being made in this area, but much more has to be done. There is no difficulty in a classical CAI dialogue, when the expected student activity is well-defined in terms of correct and incorrect predicted responses, but in open-ended situations there is a danger that must be avoided at all costs, that of stifling originality—that is, limiting those answers considered "right." Of course, there is the trivial possibility of not providing comments to the learner about what he is doing, but that is not much of a help in the classical CAI conception; on the other hand, this possibility is consistent with the exploration of a microworld or the use of a tool.

d. Practice, review, maintenance, testing

In these cases the student performs a clearly defined activity and the computer judges the performance. Practice, review, and maintenance are ongoing activities, the results of which should continuously affect the instructional process. Testing is usually done at isolated, boundary situations. The two classical examples for testing are:

d.1 Initial placement, where the system determines the point, within a course, at which the learner should begin his study.

d.2 End of unit or course, where the testing determines whether or not the student has mastered the topics and subtopics taught. The result in this case is either promotion to other instructional blocks or remedial instruction of the topics not adequately learned.

e. Management

According to student performance and to his pedagogical profile, the system decides on the next instructional steps or provides the teacher with information helpful for making those decisions.

f. Guidance

According to student performance and to his pedagogical profile the system provides him with information helpful for deciding on instructional matters.

We have described how computers may be integrated into the teaching process, based on our classification of instructional events. For completeness, we present in the box the definitions of terms frequently used in the CAI field.

There is no rigid separation between the computer uses defined in the list set forth; coaching may be done in a simulation or game environment; tutorial includes practice and may include simulations, and so forth.

In analyzing the taxonomies here presented, we need to recognize that some of the computer services described are particularly appropriate for a teacher-controlled

1. **DRILL AND PRACTICE:** The computer assigns exercises to a learner, usually according to a teacher's decision, and reports on the results (in most cases, percentage correct). (As previously noted, this term suffers from redundancy; either DRILL or PRACTICE suffices.)

2. **TESTING AND PRACTICE:** The computer determines the learner's initial placement, assigns exercises, determines when mastery is reached and switches to other topics or levels, and informs the teacher about the learner's progress and weaknesses.

3. **TUTORIAL:** The computer performs all the instructional functions required in explanatory mode: Introduction, explication, practice, assessment, and remediation.

4. **COACHING:** The computer assigns tasks for the student to practice, allowing him a high degree of freedom, and providing advice when an incorrect or inefficient tendency is detected.

5. **SIMULATION:** The computer is a tool for the user to experiment (or play) with in a closed universe, examine how the universe reacts or evolves, and learn from the experience. It is mainly used in demonstration or problem-solving approaches.

6. **GAME:** Simulation with competition, in an attractive (motivational) environment.

instructional evnironment, while others allow for teacher-independent study. We call *auxiliary* functions those used for teacher support, and *autonomous* functions, those adequate for independent study. We may envision a near future with schools making heavy use of auxiliary functions and homes making increasing use of autonomous instructional packages. This does not preclude schools making use of autonomous programs, particulary when they provide individualized instruction or allow for independent process.

It is clear that Testing and Practice, when available, does a better job as an auxiliary function than Testing and Practice performed independently. As explained in the case of TOAM (our Testing and Practice case study), pupils practice at an optimal level due to the permanent computer monitoring, without burdening the teacher with administrative tasks and decisions. The teacher is then free to assign his time to individual explanations and orientation. The cautionary "when available" is a reminder that not all subjects of study are amenable to equally efficient CAI. In many areas, and for a long time, teachers will continue to administer tests or to assign practice (with or without computers) as a standard component of their instructional planning.

Autonomous programs are particularly suitable, in the school environment, for pupils who have mastered all the requirements of the standard programs. In a class that allows for individual and differential progress there is a natural teacher tendency to devote most of his time to help those who are behind. Autonomous CAI allows the best pupils to progress independently of teacher activities. It naturally comes to mind that autonomous programs may serve an equally important role in providing tutorial instruction for weak pupils who stay way behind the mode (in statistical terms) of the class. Although this is true, experience shows that these pupils are less able to progress independently and will require, in any case, teacher attention.

COMPUTATIONAL TAXONOMIES

In this section we shift our focus from instructional to computational taxonomies. We will deal with program architecture in different aspects: granularity (to be defined), programming techniques, and system organization to deal with various pedagogical strategies.

Granularity

We propose the term *granularity* to refer to the structure and size of the components ("chunks") of an instructional dialogue. To clarify this point,, it is useful to refer back to the Instructional facility, described in Chapter 7 (pg. 122). The interlocutors in the instructional dialogue are the (real) student and the pedagogical model (implemented in programming code). Granularity refers to one of the characteristics of this programming code, and we distinguish two types: *discrete* and *continuous.*

In discrete granularity programs the script for the dialogue is prepared as a collection of (short) procedures, usually called frames. In each frame the universe (the environment for the dialogue) is restricted in such a way that the student actions are predictable, and a system response is included, in the frame, for each student action. In continuous granularity programs there are no frames; the universe of discourse is limited only by the resources available, and the system responses are determined by the totality of the state variables that define the environment, including those of the student model.

Examples of discrete granularity are most of the programs written using the classical programming languages, such as IBM's COURSEWRITER or PLATO's TUTOR, and also the TOAM programs that were described. Typical of continuous granularity are the simulation programs, where the user decides on how to explore the environment, and many of the artificial intelligence programs.

Programming Techniques

To introduce this taxonomy let us start by presenting, in Figure 8.7, a simplified view of the Instructional facility, where only the main logical components are displayed. Note that for consistency (and hopefully, elegance) of notation, the box that represents the Library and associated resources is labeled: "Knowledge Model."

Although any CAI system may be viewed as embodying the three models we described, very few are actually built on the basis of a clear structural separation into three modules. According to the programming techniques used to control the student's traversal, courseware will be classified into: address-oriented (AO), information-structure-oriented (ISO), and information-retrieval-oriented (IRO).

Address-Oriented CAI. The typical CAI frame, based on the programmed-instruction school of thought, and written in a COURSEWRITER-like language, can be described in the following sequence:

a. Presentation of Information
b. Question

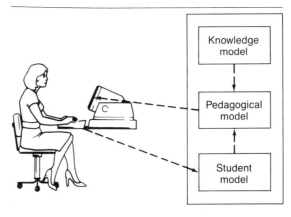

Figure 8.7. Modeling CAI

c. Answer Processing
    c_1. Expected answer 1
        Message 1
        Branching 1
    c_2. Expected answer 2
        Message 2
        Branching 2
        .
        .
        .
    c_n. Expected answer n
        Message n
        branching n

Usually, the correct answers are given first, followed by the incorrect answers. An example from a COURSEWRITER III manual is presented in Figure 8.8.

This example exhibits a frame (labeled "quest 1"), where a question is presented,

quest 1

qu   What is the product of 12 and 3?
ca   36
ty   Correct
br   quest 4
wa   15
ty   No, the answer you gave is the sum of 12 and 3.
       Try again.
un   You have not answered correctly.
       Make sure you use numeric input and try again.

Figure 8.8. Address-Oriented Example

several expected answers are described, and the corresponding messages and branching decisions are defined. The frame is divided into functional parts, each prefixed by a 2-character code, with the following meaning:

- qu: Text of the question to be presented
- ca: Expected correct answer
- ty: Text to be displayed (typed) if the student inputs the preceding expected answer
- br: Branch to a specified frame (in this case: quest 4), in correspondence with an expected answer
- wa: Expected wrong answer
- un: Text to be presented if the student answer is unanticipated (it doesn't match any of the previous expected correct or incorrect answers)

This frame structure is found also in TUTOR, PILOT, NATAL, and other languages. It exemplifies the intermingling, or the lack of modular use, of the three models we described. The knowledge model (KM) in used in the wording of the questions and in the prediction of the expected answers. The student model is very superficially used, because the main pedagogical decision (branching), embedded in the coding of the frame, is usually based on the student responses in the frame and almost never on long-term student history or on the student's pedagogical profile.

This type of CAI, where the system is just a slave of the author, blindly following his instructions (br quest 4) without "knowing" the reasons for the pedagogical decisions, has been called ad-hoc frame-oriented (AFO) by Carbonell (1970) and address-oriented (AO) by Osin (1976). The only property of a frame "known" by the system is its location or, in other words, its address. These systems are frequently used for lessonware development, but they are characterized by very low productivity when used for courseware development, because the author is burdened with the task of personally considering every possible state of a student, predicting every possible student answer, and deciding on the most appropriate system response, over a large universe of discourse, for each possible student action. The technological answer for courseware development must come from systems characterized by another Carbonell-coined term—information-structure-oriented (ISO) CAI—or from systems characterized by another Osin-coined term—information-retrieval-oriented (IRO) CAI.

Information-Structure-Oriented CAI. In well-defined ISO-CAI systems the three basic models are well-structured modules. The author's main task is to build the required knowledge databases; hopefully, the procedures able to traverse these databases searching for information or generating questions would have been developed by the system programmers team. The author should be able to design or select a pedagogical model that will make adequate decisions according to the student's model state variables, to his responses, and to his requests. Examples of ISO-CAI systems are SCHOLAR (which is discussed in the next section), TOAM, and GUIDON (Clancey, 1987). Those examples refer to systems with different levels of sophistication; the inclusion of TOAM should help to dispel the misconception that ISO is inevitably linked to AI (artificial intelligence) systems.

The Knowledge Model in SCHOLAR. Carbonell (1970) presented his SCHOLAR system in a seminal article that explicitly advocated the use of AI in CAI. He recommended the use of AI tools as a way to overcome the limitations inherent in AFO (ad-hoc frame-oriented) systems and to produce a richer, more flexible, and more natural instructional dialogue. An important contribution of SCHOLAR to CAI is the model-ing of the universe of discourse as a semantic net, following Quillian's (1968) ideas about a memory model. The memory model is a network (graph) of two kinds of nodes interconnected by associative links (arcs). For each word-concept there is one "type" or "patriarchal" node, which is the root of a tree composed of "token" nodes associ-ated by links. This tree corresponds to the dictionary "immediate definition," which Quillian calls "a plane." Each token node is either a word not defined in the model (referred to here as a "primitive") or includes a pointer to its type node (what Quillian terms an "out-of-the-plane" link). The richness, power, and potential applications of this representation are fascinating. The actual use, and the success, are related to the sophistication of the procedures used to traverse the network, find information, establish associations, and guide or help the user in finding answers to his questions.

Carbonell's work probes the application of the semantic memory model in the world of CAI. He selected, as a universe of discourse, the geography of South America. Being a good Uruguayan, he chose an area close to his heart. But the choice was also a neat example to disprove the hypothesis of Uttal and colleagues (1969) that generative systems (i.e., those generating their own questions) hinge completely upon algorithmic manipulation. He quotes Uttal: " . . . we must exclude verbally oriented subjects as possible items for generative curriculum" (pp. 194–195). Far more important in Carbo-nell's selection of Quillian's modeling technique as the basis of his work, was Carbonell's belief that:

> Storing information in a semantic network has distinct advantages for CAI and for other interactive man-computer systems generally. Assuming that human symbolic memory has an organization in the form of a semantic network, a machine using such an organization will be working with the same kind of information structures as a man. (p. 197)

SCHOLAR was implemented in LISP, an AI language designed for LISt Process-ing and most adequate for the network structure of the knowledge model. We repro-duce, in Figure 8.9, Carbonell's representation of a portion of the network, in terms of "planes" and "out-of-plane" pointers.

The representation includes some "LISPian" elements worth explaining. Let us concentrate on Argentina: its type node heads a plane, and is followed by a list of properties. Each property in SCHOLAR is a triplet:

name, tags, value

The tags are used by the programs that implement the instructional dialogue, and are not included in Figure 8.9. We do not deal with them in this summary. The name, or attribute, of a property may be:

1. A reserved word indicating a hierarchical link, like SUPERC in this example (standing for superconcept), whose meaning is that ARGENTINA is one in-stance of COUNTRY.
2. A primitive word (undefined as a plane in the system), like LOCATION. Primi-tive words are assumed to be known by the students.
3. A pointer to another type node, like LATITUDE is this example.

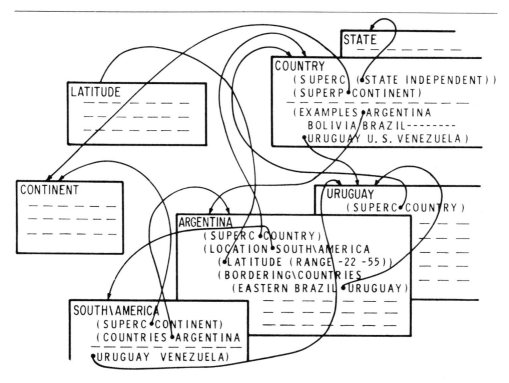

Figure 8.9. Representation of a Portion of a Network on South America. (From J. R. Carbonnell, 1970, *Mixed Initiative Man-Computer Instructional Dialogues,* [Cambridge, MA: Bolt, Beranek and Newman, Inc.] p. 19.)

The value of a property may be:

1. An atom (a word or number)
2. A pointer to a type node
3. A procedure
4. A property
5. Any sequence of the above.

The ARGENTINA example does not contain a type 1 property, the nearest to it being the property named RANGE, whose values is the pair of numbers $(-22, -55)$, a sequence of two atoms representing the latitude range of ARGENTINA (the $-$ indicates the Southern Hemisphere); an example of type 2 is the value COUNTRY for the property SUPERC; an example of type 4 is found in the property LATITUDE, whose value is the property named RANGE; an example of type 5 appears in the property LOCATION, whose value is a sequence of:

1. A pointer to SOUTH AMERICA[3]
2. The property LATITUDE with a given value

---

[3]In LISP this is written SOUTH/AMERICA, but we have decided to help our reader.

3. The property BORDERING COUNTRIES, whose value is a sequence of countries, and so forth.

The fact that the value of a property may be another property (or a sequence of properties) allows for multiple embedding. No examples of values of type 3 (procedures) appear in Figure 8.9, but the idea, though not quite developed in the original SCHOLAR, is very powerful and extremely rich in possibilities. An example proposed by Carbonell is a procedure for determining the climate of a place (when actual data is terms of temperature, precipitation, etc., are not included) by using other known geographical data (location, altitude, etc.)

Carbonell developed the procedures to use the knowledge stored in the graph in two types of dialogue:

TEST: SCHOLAR queries the student by generating questions in a specific topic.

QUESTION/ANSWER: The pupil may gather information from the system by asking questions about topics he is interested in.

One of the system features was the student's ability to switch modes, aptly denoted as mixed-initiative. Unfortunately Carbonell died suddenly in the early 1970s, without having the possibility of fully developing the seminal ideas presented in SCHOLAR.

Information-Retrieval–Oriented CAI. In AO systems the author is burdened with the complete specification of control, since the system has no access to content information. In ISO that burden has been lifted, but another one appears: the complete specification of content. An intermediate strategy is to identify the content information that is sufficient for control, thus avoiding the burdens of both AO and ISO systems. This strategy has been implemented in SMILE, a system described in Chapter 13, utilizing information-retrieval techniques. In IRO-CAI, the author's task is to classify the instructional blocks according to the pedagogical functions they serve over the universe of topics being taught. This information allows the system to make pedagogical decisions, for instance the definition of remedial loops according to the student's performance, and also encourages student initiative, because it is possible for a student to review or to explore topics according to his own requests.

The price to be paid for these services is measured in the investment of developing a full taxonomy of topics for the subject area being taught. We believe this investment is worthwhile, not only in terms of the CAI system functionality, but also because of several positive side effects:

1. It forces the author to make an in-depth analysis of the subject matter being taught.
2. The author receives from the development system a detailed analysis of each topic coverage in terms of instructional events, specifying the number of interactions or frames prepared for each type of event.
3. In terms of the learner's activity, it fosters metacognitive skills, both by a specific analysis of each failure, which is presented to the student, and by providing remedial tools that require the learner's self-analysis of possible knowledge weaknesses.

System Pedagogical Interventions

The reader may wonder why this section is included under computational instead of under instructional taxonomies. The reason is that what is examined here is not only the instructional mode but mainly the structure of the program that implements it. To be more precise, this section analyzes several variations, structural and functional, of the basic schema presented in Figure 8.7. According to mainly the intervention style of the pedagogical model, we distinguish four types: *fixed, tutorial, coaching,* and *open.*

Fixed. In this type of intervention the models in Figure 8.7 are very specialized: the model of knowledge contains information of a fixed kind, the pedagogical model acts according to a rigid strategy, and the student model contains only the basic information required for system control. The paradigm for this class is given by the Testing and Practice systems developed by Computer Curriculum Corporation, the Palo Alto-based company, and the Centre for Educational Technology or C.E.T. (within the TOAM system). Referring again to TOAM's Reading Comprehension program, the knowledge model is built according to a parallel-sequences topology, with 14 sequences of instructional blocks, each sequence compromising up to 70 blocks, and each block consisting of a sequence of 15 exercises. Each exercise is defined by a data structure whose arguments define the presentation modality, the texts to be presented by the system, and the system response to the student's answers. The same data structure is used for the 13,000 exercises included in the knowledge model. The pedagogical model has two main traversal algorithms, one for initial placement of a student and another for placement upgrading. The student model contains mainly performance data, used by the pedagogical model for the traversal decisions. All the traversal decisions are performed by the pedagogical model—there are no commands to allow for student control.

Note the reasons for these systems to be called "fixed":

1. Uniformity of data
2. Uniformity of function
3. Uniformity of control

Tutorial. For a system to deserve this denomination it has to be able to sustain a much richer instructional dialogue with the student than the one previously described. In functional terms it must be able to provide explanations and exercises; in instructional terms the pedagogical model should develop the required didactic sequences, furnishing introductions, explications, and practice, and being able to perform assessment in order to give remedial instruction as needed. A set of commands should allow the student to obtain control when the instructional environment permits it. Many of the programs developed by PLATO, TICCIT, and WICAT teams were inspired by the tutorial conception, and we will present an example of how the tutorial functions may be implemented when we describe the SMILE system.

It is natural that most of the efforts in tutorial CAI were invested in the classical subjects that are the mainstay of school curricula. We think that, in the future, CAI "tutors" may have an enormous impact in areas that are very poorly taught in today's educational systems.

Coaching. At this point we ask the reader to be temporarily satisfied with the definition for coaching presented on page 146. Later in this chapter an in-depth description is provided. Many of the ideas that are presented there are applicable to tutorial systems also.

Open. This type appears primarily for logical completeness. In the successive relaxation of system pedagogical interventions, starting from fixed and reaching the coach style, there is only one more step, which is not to intervene at all. Actually this type is used a great deal, because usually tools and microworlds have no underlying pedagogical model. In terms of our characterization of CAI systems, as presented in Figure 8.7, this type corresponds to a pedagogical model that just transmits the commands of the student, who has thus free access to the knowledge model (including all available system resources).

HEURISTIC INSTRUCTION

The classical school is strongly organized (although not necessarily successful) in deterministic subjects. There are textbooks, auxiliary materials, trained teachers, and a tradition for the teaching of mathematics, grammar, physics, and so forth. As a result, a school graduate is expected to be, and may even be, proficient in the areas learned. In contrast, the teaching of thinking is frequently ignored during the schooling process; for example, the techniques for analyzing a problem, for reducing its complexity, for organizing a search for a solution, are very seldom explicitly presented.

Not surprisingly, the initial utilization of CAI was in those same deterministic subjects; computer programs are algorithmically defined, and there is a tendency to apply them in algorithmic subjects. Nevertheless, there is no contradiction in developing algorithms for instruction in nonalgorithmic domains and this is what we intend to present. Two techniques will be described: *simulations,* as support for discovery learning, and *coaching,* to provide guided practice in heuristic[4] domains.

Modeling and Simulation

In many cases we have to deal with real systems whose complexity makes them hard to comprehend or to operate or to predict. When such a real system is affected by external events (which may or may not be under our control), we can record our observations, gathering a collection of behavioral data, correlated with the record of the external events that took place. A challenge that has motivated scientists for millennia is to "explain," reproduce and predict the observed behavior, by building a model[5] of the real system, consisting of a set of instructions for generating behavioral data, a mapping of the external events into input data, and a mapping of the model-generated output into real behavioral data. (See Figure 8.10.)

---

[4]*Heuristic,* in this section, satisfies its two meanings: the logical one, where it is used in opposition to algorithmic (i.e. in a heuristic process there are no predefined rules for reaching a solution), and the pedagogical one (the student is the agent in a discovery process).

[5]Ptolomeus, Copernicus, and Kepler built models of the solar system; Newton and Einstein built models of mechanics; the Greek word *atom* means indivisible, corresponding to the ancient Greek models of matter—today's models of the atom look like planetary systems in miniature.

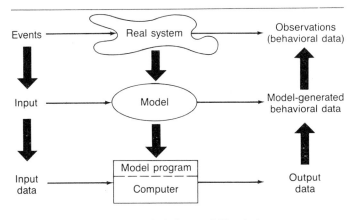

Figure 8.10. Modeling and Simulation

The gauntlet to raise is to build a simple and elegant model that, nevertheless, reflects the essential properties of the real system it tries to represent.

To check the validity of a model, we map a sequence of external events into input data, execute the instructions of the model according to the input data, and output the behavioral data generated by the model. If the mapping of the model-generated output points to the behavioral data that would have been produced by the real system (given this sequence of external events), then we have a presumption of validity. If this concordance subsists under any type of input, then the model is valid. A valid model may be used for predictive purposes, and here lies its importance.[6]

In practical terms, it is convenient to execute the model instructions by writing a computer program that automates this part of the process.[7] To run such a program, the input to the model has to be translated into input data for the computer program.

A computer *simulation* consists of running the model program, with a specific input data, and producing the corresponding output data. This output of the computer run has to be mapped back into behavioral data, in order to analyze the results in terms of the model and of the real system.

In an instructional process the most interesting application of simulations is to have the student generating the input data and observing the computer output. Probably the most widely known application is the flight simulator, which has professional and game versions. Simulations may be profitably used in teaching outside the CAI environment also; a lecturer may show students the effects of different economic policies (if the model is believable), the projections of population growth in underdevel-

---

[6]Kepler had modeled the orbit of Mars as a circle—according to the models developed by Copernicus—and had a set of observations, carefully measured by Tycho Brahe, to determine the orbit parameters. Based on a subset of these observations Kepler performed the calculations, which took him several years, and the orbit was determined. Then Kepler took another of Tycho Brahe's observations, to check whether it belonged to the calculated orbit. By a difference of 8 minutes of arc it did not. Conclusion: The circular model was not correct. Due to Kepler's genius and intellectual integrity (many would have dismissed the 8-minute difference as an experimental or computational error), he arrived at the elliptical model that we are still using.

[7]In this form, Kepler's calculations could have been computed in hours instead of years.

oped countries with or without birth control, the change in efficiency of a power station according to different usage parameters, and many more examples from varied areas of knowledge. The same models may be used in CAI, either in an open interaction mode without additional investment or in tutorial or coaching modes if the student activity is controlled.

Computational Structure. Let us assume that we want to study the evolution of a given system over time.

The modeler decides on what the components of the model are and for each component defines its state variables, that is, the variables that indicate the state of each component. The evolution of the model is given by the changes of its state variables over time.

After that, the modeler decides on a set of input variables and a set of output variables.

The computational process that determines the evolution of the system starts from an initial set of values for all the variables (at time 0) and executes two procedures:

1. A state-transition function (δ)
2. An output function (λ)

The state transition function computes the value at time $n + 1$ of all the state variables, as a function of the value at time n of all the state and input variables.

If we call:

S the vector of State variables
I the vector of Input variables
O the vector of Output variables
P a vector of Parameters

then, it is possible to visualize the first application of the state-transition function as:

$$S(1) = \delta[S(0), I(0), P]$$

meaning that the values of the state-variables at the time 1 have been determined as a function of the values of the state and input variables at time 0. The values of the parameters, used in the computations, are assumed constant all along the simulation process. A change in parameter values will produce a different evolution in time—and this is one of the possibilities that should be placed in the students' hands.

In general:

$$S (n + 1) = \delta[S(n), I(n), P]$$

There are two ways of defining the output function. The easiest (which we use) is:

$$O(n = \lambda[S(n), P]$$

Example: Predator-Prey Simulation

Based on an example presented by Lancaster (1976), and using Zeigler's (1976) organization, let us assume a closed environment where predators and preys coexist. The preys get their food from the environment and they themselves constitute the predators' food.

To model this peaceful universe we proceed as follows:

Components

- Population of predators
- Population of preys

Variables

- PREDPOP = predator population
- PREYPOP = prey population
- PREYPRED = prey eaten by one predator (in one year)

Parameters

- PREYGRT = prey natural growth rate
- CATCH = proportionality coefficient required to compute PREYPRED
- PREDGC = proportionality coefficient for predator growth.

Interaction Rules (on whose basis the state-transition function will be determined)

1. The number of prey taken by one predator is proportional to the population level of the prey.
2. The increase-ratio of the predator species is proportional to the consumption of food per individual.

These rules may be expressed as:

1. PREYPRED = CATCH.PREYPOP
2. PREDPOP($n+1$)/PREDPOP(n) = PREDGC.PREYPRED

State-Transition Function

From the previous expressions it follows that:
PREDPOP($n+1$) = PREDGC. CATCH.PREYPOP(n).PREDPOP(n)
and observing that the natural growth of the prey is reduced in the amount eaten by the predators, then:
PREYPOP($n+1$) = (1 + PREYGRT). PREYPOP(n)-CATCH.PREYPOP(n).PREDPOP(n)

Output Function

- PREDPOP(n)
- PREYPOP(n)

The output function, which provides us with the evolution of the populations in time, has a very interesting behavior, because of the interaction between the species.

An example of a simulation run, taken from Lancaster (1976) appears in Fig. 8.11. The upper graph shows the evolution in time of PREYPOP (n), measured in some arbitrary unit. The lower graph does the same of PREDPOP(n).

In a CAI environment the graphics specialist could provide a striking visual representation, by assigning two small, differently colored icons to predators and preys, and displaying every population level by a given density of icons distributed over the screen. The changes in population would then produce density and color fluctuations in the display.

With the specific selection of parameters that was done for this simulation, we observe that during the first year the predators keep the same population, at the expense of reducing the population of the prey. The result is that, the next year, the predator population declines because of lack of food, but so also does the prey population. Thus, the next year, the predator population has declined so much that the prey population starts to grow.

A growth in the prey population will eventually allow for a growth in the predator's population and the seesaw may continue.

A very illuminating result of this family of simulations is that a different selection of parameters may lead to catastrophic results. The predators may eat all the prey during one year and be extinct themselves during the next one.

This model does not include input variables. It is very easy to add a variable that would determine, for instance, the growth of natural resources (including food for the prey) in every year. This input variable would then affect PREYGRT, which would be moved to the VARIABLES area.

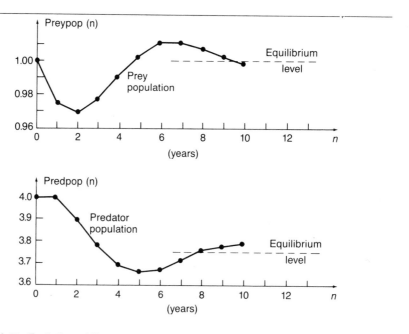

Figure 8.11. Evolution of Prey and Predator Populations Over Time. (Peter Lancaster, *Mathematics: Models of the Real World,* ©1976, pg. 58. Reprinted by permission of Prentice Hall, Inc., Englewood Cliffs, New Jersey).

meaning that the output at a given time is a function of the values of the state variables at the same time, the actual computation being influenced by the values selected for the parameters.

Model Dimensions. From our standpoint, models are programs and, as such, impose no limitations on their authors, other than to satisfy the requirements of the programming environment where their simulations are run.

To give a feeling for the variety of possibilities, let us start by characterizing the prey-predator example. This is a discrete-time model, meaning that the transitions from one state to the next are determined at fixed time periods. The period itself is not important in terms of the classification. In the prey-predator model the time unit was one year; in a physical model it could be a millionth of a second.

Two alternatives, each one in a different dimension, are possible. Instead of a discrete model, we can build a continuous model. A good example is presented in Chapter 13 (see the section, "Graphs and Tracks"), where the movement of a body, its velocity, and its acceleration are described by continuous graphs; the mathematical tools used (like integration and differentiation) were naturally conceived for continuous functions.

In another dimension, instead of a time-driven model, we can build an event-driven model. In this case the transitions in the state of the model are not determined at fixed periods of time, but rather when external events occur. The occurrence of such an event is defined by a change of values in the input variables. Strategic games, whether in management or in warfare, are modeled using this technique.

There is still a third dimension under the author's control. The prey-predator model is deterministic, meaning that once the parameters have been selected, the evolution in time has been completely defined. In other words, two simulations with the same initial values will produce exactly the same output. The alternative is to have probabilistic models where some events, or values, are determined using random variables. In this case, two simulations with the same initial values may produce very different outputs.

Consider a simple case: A roulette simulation. You, the player, are given a certain sum of money, which you can gamble at the roulette table. In every cycle the computer will produce a number between 0 and 36, with equal probability for each number (using a random-number generator).[8] You are "paid" by the computer according to standard roulette rules. Suppose that you decide to test a betting strategy, and you play for 10 minutes using this strategy. Win or lose, the next time you want to test the same strategy over the same period of time, that is, run the same simulation, the results may be totally different.

We have presented the components and the options for the creation of models and the running of simulations. Size has not been mentioned; the conceptual framework is the same whether you are dealing, on the one hand, with the popular Lemonade Stand simulation where you decide how many lemons to buy each day and how to price a glass of lemonade or, on the other hand, with Forrester's (1971) model of the world economy, where the population level is controlled by birth rate and death rate, which are influenced by food and pollution ratios, which are functions of capital investment and available resources, which depend on . . . , etc, etc.

---

[8]This is classical roulette. Some greedy establishments have two zeros on the roulette wheel.

You may be interested in knowing that Forrester's model predicts a catastrophe for the next century, due to overcrowding and pollution. This should provide, at least, food for thought.

Coaching

There may be differences in the amount and structure of the material to be learned in different fields, but the main difference we find in schools between algorithmic and heuristic domains resides in the different treatment of an essential component of the instructional process—practice. Learning by doing (or even the Piagetian: "to understand is to invent") is part of common educational philosophy. By the time we reach college we will have performed thousands and thousands of arithmetic operations, and solved thousands of problems and equations during our school instruction. This long and carefully graded training sequence, the result of long-time experience, is generally accepted as a necessary part of instruction. As a matter of fact, a CAI system for testing and practice improves the logistics and reduces the cost of this instructional component but does not introduce revolutionary conceptual changes: individual practice has been and continues to be, indispensable for learning.

School practice is so lacking in heuristic domains because standard schooling did not develop adequate techniques to deal with the critical element of *uncertainty*. All those thousands of exercises just mentioned included all the data required to apply a previously learned well-defined procedure.

Making decisions under uncertain conditions is a very different story. The uncertainty may be the consequence of incomplete knowledge about the present situation or, even less amenable to control, the result of being within a process where future events are unpredictable.

In trying to organize school practice in heuristic domains we must start by recognizing the characteristics of these domains:

1. The practitioner is confronted with a problem whose solution is not immediately apparent.
2. The process to find a solution is not algorithmically defined, and there is no certainty of success.
3. There is a theoretical basis that provides rules for action during the proces of searching for a solution or, at least, tools to restrict the number of acceptable decisions at any point in the process to a reasonable number.
4. Additional information is gathered throughout the process, thus allowing for the refinement of successive decisions.
5. It is acceptable to use a trial-and-error strategy, on the basis that success is always good and that errors may provide useful information, provided that no fatal errors and committed.

How should practice be structured for instruction in a heuristic domain?

- Very rich in terms of variety; many cases should be presented, to allow for the student to develop and internalize appropriate responses.
- Very open in terms of student decisions; the system cannot expect the student

to adopt optimal decisions at all points in the process— if it were so, the student would be an expert already.

What are the obstacles for implementation?

- Logistics: It is hardly possible to provide a trainee with thousands (or even hundreds) of TV sets for repair, with leeway to let him try, blow components, or even endanger himself, or to provide a medical student with a similar number of patients, allowing him to diagnose, provide treatment, and perform follow-up.
- Control: The training must be structured, so that the trainee or student receives adequate feedback and guidance. This is necessary in terms of both instructional efficiency and instructional guidance. Without adequate control, the learner would invest an inordinate amount of time in unproductive tactics and could even be fixated onto incorrect practices. The problem is that, due to the variety or even unpredictability, of the situations arising during the training, a personal tutor would have to be attached to each student every time a critical decision arises.

Enter CAI!

CAI is the natural answer when an instructional process demands many replications of given patterns, each time with different parameters. Let us consider what the prerequisites are for successful application of CAI in the heuristic domain under consideration.

1. The logical aspects of the performance should be separable from the physical dexterity required to execute the task. In other words, we will not use CAI to train a repairman in soldering nor to help a medical student stitch an abdomen.
2. The theoretical basis and the heuristics tools should be strong enough to allow for the construction of an algorithm to evaluate a wide range of possible decisions, whose performance may be ranked at expert level.

If the two prerequisites are fulfilled, we can refine our CAI models to provide training in nondeterministic fields such as those previously described. The refinement is as follows, with an asterisk indicating the main additions to the classical model:

KM — The knowledge model includes:
    a. Factual knowledge
 *b. "Expert" algorithm
    c. Models of tasks, with acceptable parameter ranges
    d. Present state of a selected task
SM — The student model includes:
    a. Personal parameters
    b. System history (tasks performed, with evaluation)
    c. Performance in the (presently) selected task
 *d. Evaluation of (c) as compared with the "expert"

PM — The pedagogical model includes:
  a. The criteria for sequencing the training on different tasks
  b. The definition of the proficiency required for each task
  *c. The criteria for giving advice or refraining from doing so ("coaching principles")

Thus, we can expand Figure 8.7 as shown in Figure 8.12.
The instructional process is as follows:

1. The pedagogical model selects a task to be presented to the student, based on the evaluation of the tasks already performed, on the criteria for task-training sequencing, and on the task proficiency required.
2. The selected task is initialized, by random assignment to its parameters of values within the acceptable ranges, and its initial state is stored as present state of the task.
3. The student makes a decision according to the present state of the task, and the record of his performance in the task is updated. The student decision may be to perform a direct action, or it may be a request for additional information (e.g., a lab report in the medical situation). Furthermore, the instructional designer may decide whether or not to allow for consultations (i.e., under which conditions to provide on-line advice or access to factual knowledge upon the student's request).
4. The expert analyzes the present state of the task and eventually, making use of

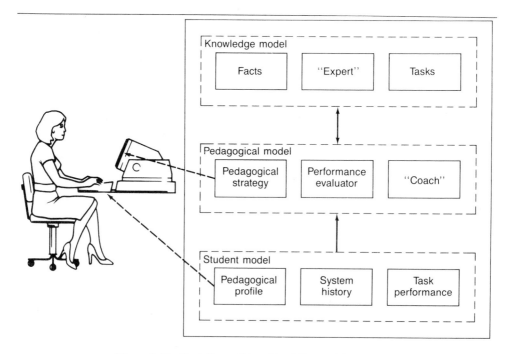

Figure 8.12. Modeling a "Coaching" Type of CAI System

the factual knowledge, produces a list of possible decisions, ranked from optimal to acceptable.

5. The state of the task is modified according to the student's decision adopted in step 3, and the updated state is stored.

6. The pedagogical model compares the student's decision with the list prepared in step 4 by the expert and stores its evaluation in the student model.

7. The pedagogical model analyzes the present state of the task, the student performance in the task, and its evaluation, and then proceeds according to one of the following possibilities:

   a. If the task is finished, an appropriate message is presented, the student's system history is updated, and the student selects whether to start a new task or to stop.

   b. Otherwise,

   If the student decision is very good, a congratulatory message is presented.

   If the move is acceptable, a proceed type of message is presented.

   If the move is poor and the coaching principles ask for it, advice is given. Go to step 3.

Areas where good experts were developed (independently of CAI applications) are natural candidates for the development of training systems. Two of the first seminal examples were SOPHIE (Brown, Burton, & Bell, 1974) and GUIDON (Clancey, 1979). SOPHIE, a SOPHisticated Instructional Environment for teaching electronic troubleshooting, uses as an expert a general-purpose electronic simulation program called SPICE (Nagel & Pederson, 1973). Many additional elements, including a superb front-end for natural-language processing, made SOPHIE an outstanding example of AI in CAI. GUIDON is a program for training diagnostic skills in the field of medicine. Its expert is MYCIN (Shortliffe, 1976), a program designed to provide advice or diagnosis and therapy for infectious diseases. It can be effectively used in training, because the "creation" of patients is a prerogative of the system. The pedagogical model in GUIDON is a separate module, including more than 200 tutorial rules. GUIDON's present state can be studied in Clancey, 1987.

We mentioned *coaching principles* earlier in this section, and the term merits explanation. Such an explanation will be clearer, however, in the context of a concrete example, and we provide this in our examination of "How the West Was Won" in Chapter 13. For the moment, we need only emphasize that a learner in a heuristic domain, contrary to one learning a subject like arithmetic, cannot be expected to make optimal decisions at every point in the instructional process. Like a good basketball coach, who will not interrupt his players at every nonoptimal move to instruct them, an effective CAI coach will allow the trainee to "play" at a suboptimal level without interruption, up to certain limits.

SUMMARY

This chapter has analyzed the structure, the components, and the pedagogical styles of computerized instructional materials, as well as the programming techniques that can be used to produce them.

The first part, dealing with instructional taxonomies, explored several dimensions.

In terms of extension, or duration, the sizes distinguished were: courses, units, and lessons. From a topological standpoint, that is, looking at the structure linking the instructional blocks without considering the contents of those blocks, several useful organizations were presented: linear, parallel sequences, and trees. All of them are particular cases of directed graphs. Any topological structure is a static organization, which can be traversed by different students in different ways according to their pedagogical profiles, their performance, and in some cases, their wishes. This last point is retaken in the next dimension: Locus of control, where the question of how the student traversal is decided was raised. Three possibilities were analyzed: prescribed (system decisions), free (student decisions), and mixed initiative (a mix of the previous two). Finally, the integration of the computer activities within the whole of the instructional process was discussed, in terms of both instructional events and current CAI jargon.

The second part was more directed to computational techniques. The first distinction was in terms of what we called granularity: discrete (frames) or continuous. In terms of programming techniques, three were analyzed: address-oriented (where all the branching is specified *a priori* by the author), information-structure-oriented (where the system includes a complete model of knowledge that allows for system decisions), and information-retrieval-oriented (where the branching decisions are made by the system based on information provided by the author in terms of frame contents). Ending this part, four types of implementations for different pedagogical interventions were presented: fixed, tutorial, coaching, and open, with increasing degrees of student freedom.

Finally, the third part detailed the techniques that may be used to develop two important (and not always well understood) types of instructional programs: simulation, where the student may explore the behavior of a model that reacts like a real system, and coaching, which provides an excellent answer to the problem of providing practice in heuristic domains.

CHAPTER 9

Algorithms for Student Assessment
Formalizing Instruction Evaluation

There is nothing more practical than a good theory.

The previous chapters have described and classified CAI systems but, as we promised in the Introduction, the purpose of this book is not only to give you a taste of what others have done, but also to allow you to graduate as a chef, ready to prepare your own gastronomical wonders. The teaching of culinary art is not performed by providing a set of recipes. The prospective chef is taught principles, components, and processes. Only when she knows the properties of baking, barbecueing, poaching, roasting, sauteing, scalloping, searing, shirring, simmering, steeping, stewing, and toasting, will she be able to select the best processes to implement her ideas. In this and following chapters we provide you with the description of several processes (much fewer in number than those required by a chef) that will constitute the building blocks for the CAI systems you are going to design. If you do not intend to be a chef yourself, at least you will be able to assess whether a CAI system you are being offered includes all the features necessary to satisfy your instructional needs.

In this chapter we describe processes of paramount importance in CAI practice, processes that fall under the common heading of *assessment*. Assessment is the basis for sound decision making. In the traditional classroom environment a large proportion of pupil assessment is largely informal, but in the CAI process this critical component of instruction has to be formally defined. When we compare the informal teacher's assessment with a well-designed computerized one, two main differences come to the fore:

1. The teacher is able to reach a depth of understanding of any one pupil's abilities and specific difficulties that no computer, in the foreseeable future, can approach.
2. In many subject areas, computers can provide an itemized assessment of the knowledge of every pupil in a class, with such detail that no teacher has the time to produce, and this assessment is naturally integrated within the computerized instructional process.

Assessment was introduced as a functional category of instructional events in Chapter 4, and further detailed in Chapter 8, where we distinguished between *testing,* which is performed at isolated, critical points in the instructional process such as at the beginning and end of courses, and *continuous evaluation,* which is performed within practice, review, and maintenance.

TESTING

Testing consists of the assignment of a set of tasks to be performed by a testee and the judgment of the testee's performance according to predefined criteria. For simplicity, in this context each one of those tasks is called an *exercise.*

In terms of content area, tests are divided between the cognitive domain and the noncognitive domains. This second type of testing, which deals with personality tests, attitude tests, interest tests, and the like, is not considered in this book.

Cognitive tests are further divided into aptitude tests and achievement tests. The avowed purpose of the aptitude tests is to predict how well an individual can learn; their most famous representatives are I.Q. tests. We deal only with achievement tests, whose more modest purpose is to measure what an individual knows in a given subject area.

Achievement tests may be unidimensional, their result being expressed by a number, or multidimensional, requiring a vector to describe their output. This last case reflects the situation where a test is measuring achievement in several topics (or skills) simultaneously. In the cases where the purpose of the test is to rank the population or to make binary decisions (like pass or fail), the various dimensions of the multidimensional test are assigned weights, and thus the test result is also converted into a number.

Another distinction found in the literature, which applies to the case where the test result is a number, refers to the way this number is presented. The presentation may be in absolute terms, which is called *criterion-referenced* testing, or in relative terms, which is called *norm-referenced.* The absolute terms refer to the content area, for instance, "the pupil answered 70 percent of the exercises correctly," while the relative terms refer to the population of testees, for example, "the pupil's performance was in the upper 10 percent level" or "the pupil's performance was at the 90th percentile."

In a CAI system, both initial placement and mastery checking are clearly criterion-referenced, because their purpose is to achieve optimal decisions for an individual according to her actual knowledge, and comparison with other students is irrelevant.

In summary, in this section we deal exclusively with criterion-referenced cognitive achievement testing.

Initial-Placement Algorithms

When dealing with courseware that may cover several years of school curriculum, it is crucial to build into the system the algorithms that will place every student at an appropriate initial condition.

More specifically, following our presentation of courseware topologies as structures formed by instructional blocks, the purpose of an initial-placement algorithm is to identify at which instructional block (or blocks) a student should start her learning process.

We assume, in what follows, that for every instructional block there is a testing component. This condition is naturally fulfilled in those blocks where mastery is tested in isolation—at the end of the instructional process, as in the TICCIT system. It is not so when the mastery assessment is embedded in the instructional dialogue, and for these cases we assume that a test is defined ad hoc for every instructional block. The easiest situation refers to Testing and Practice systems, because the instructional blocks consist of exercises only, and the same exercises may be used for practice and for testing. It is clear that the design of an initial-placement algorithm is very much dependent on the courseware topology. Nevertheless, many requirements of such an algorithm may be expressed in general terms:

1. The student should be placed within the courseware structure in such an instructional block (or blocks) that the instructional traversal may proceed unhindered or, in other words, so that the student instruction may progress smoothly.
2. Such a placement must be efficient, in the sense that the student should be placed in the most advanced position possible within the structure (satisfying requirement 1).
3. The placement should be safe, in the sense that it ensures that the blocks *not* to be presented to the student are known by her (or that there is a high probability of mastery).
4. The algorithm itself should be optimal (or quasi-optimal), in terms of minimizing the student time required to complete the placement process.
5. The algorithm should be stable, meaning that students with similar knowledge should be assigned placements that are near (within any reasonable metric). A particular case is that of the same student tested twice (test-retest), where we expect essentially the same placement. A testing process with this property is called *reliable*.
6. The algorithm should have content *validity*, a condition that must be checked by appropriate external verification. Validity refers to the property of a test to adequately reflect the knowledge, or lack of it, of the testees in the areas it is designed to cover.
7. The algorithm should be *replicable*, that is, not dependent on local conditions.

The identification of the initial placement is very much dependent on a global pedagogical strategy, including the level of mastery required to finish each instructional block and the level of challenge or of freedom for exploration allowed by the courseware.

Too high a placement—contradicting requirement 1—would generate an unduly hard learning process. Too low a placement—contradicting requirement 2—would waste the student's time, forcing her to traverse instructional blocks whose contents she already knows.

The satisfaction of point 4 may be accomplished only by means of the type of testing known as *adaptive,* or *tailored.* This is an important point, worth expanding on. In conventional testing we usually find a group of students who are presented with a fixed set of exercises. This *fixed* testing lends itself to both criterion-referenced and norm-referenced grading. Its major drawback is that for criterion reference, that is, for judging of mastery levels, it does a very poor job for the population in the lowest

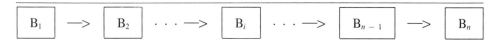

Figure 9.1. Sequence Structure

and highest quartiles. Adaptive testing was devised to solve this shortcoming. Rather than presenting a preset sequence of items, exercises are selected and presented according to an ongoing evaluation of the testee's performance during the test. For further information on computerized adaptive testing, see Hambleton & Swaminathan (1985), Lord (1971,1980), Lord & Novick (1968), Urry (1977), and Weiss (1983).

A safe strategy for the school environment is to tie the teacher into the process, asking for her control of intermediate test results, comparing them with her personal student evaluation. It may be necessary for her to "talk to" students with erratic performance, and retest them. It is clear that any testing algorithm decides on the basis of student performance, and not on the basis of student knowledge.

(Topology-dependent analyses are presented in the following sections.)

Sequence Structure. The *sequence* topology was described in Chapter 8, page 138, using the structure shown in Figure 9.1.

This structure expresses a basic pedagogical decision: the instructional blocks are to be traversed in linear order, starting from block B_1 and ending with B_n.[1]

In terms of an initial-placement algorithm, it is not enough to know that this linear structure reflects a sound decision. The critical point is whether this structure results from a logical necessity (i.e., each block is a prerequisite of its follower) or from a pedagogical decision (i.e., the author feels that this is a preferred study sequence). A mix of logical and pedagogical reasons is also possible.

Logical Sequencing. Let us start with the case where the sequence structure results from logical necessity. In this case, lack of mastery in a block ensures lack of mastery in all the followers, which is a strong aid in terms of the algorithm design. Let us formalize the conditions, because this will help us in the following analyses.

To simplify our language, let us call *subject i,* the knowledge content of the material taught by B_i. A student may be tested on her mastery of subject i and the result of this test will be expressed as

$$PER_i$$

meaning: "student performance at block i." The mastery requirements may be different at each block. Let us use the expression

$$REQ_i$$

to express the mastery requirements at block i.

---

[1] As previously mentioned, this refers to the basic canonical traversal, while the actual dynamic traversal depends on each student.

Let us define also a Boolean variable $MAST_i$, meaning "mastery at block i," and a metric for the comparison of performance and requirements such that:

$$MAST_i \text{ is true if } PER_i \geq REQ_i$$
$$MAST_i \text{ is false if } PER_i < REQ_i$$

Using now "$\rightarrow$" for "logical implication" and "$\sim$" for "negation" or "not," we may add precision to our original definitions, using the terms just defined.

- DEFINITION 1: B_i is a prerequisite of B_j if $\sim MAST_i \rightarrow \sim MAST_j$
- DEFINITION 2: The structure $B_1, \ldots, B_i, \ldots, B_n$, shown in Figure 9.1, is *logically sequenced* if B_i is a prerequisite of B_{i+1} $(1 \leq i < n)$.
- PROPERTY 1: In a logically sequenced structure:

$$\sim MAST_i \rightarrow \sim MAST_{i+1} \ (1 \leq i < n)$$

- PROPERTY 2: In a logically sequenced structure,

$$\text{if } 1 \leq i < j \leq n, \text{ then } \sim MAST_i \rightarrow \sim MAST_j$$
(We will spare the proof by complete induction.)

Property 2 is logically equivalent to:

$$MAST_j \rightarrow MAST_i \text{ for every } i < j \ (1 \leq i, j \leq n)$$

meaning that mastery in a block ensures mastery of all its predecessors.

The purpose of the initial placement algorithm may be now clearly defined: Find the block g $(1 \leq g < n)$ such that:

a) $MAST_g$ is true
b) $MAST_{g+1}$ is false

If g is found, the sequence is partitioned into two classes, as shown in Figure 9.2. In effect, mastery at block g ensures mastery of all its predecessors, and lack of mastery at block $g + 1$ ensures lack of mastery of all its followers. Such a g may not exist, in two distinct cases:

1. $MAST_1$ is false. In this case none of the blocks are mastered. In terms of the algorithm the student must start learning at B_1, but there is an external condition that the algorithm cannot test, which is whether the student has mastered the prerequisites of the course.

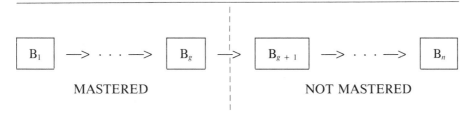

Figure 9.2. Sequence Partitioning

2. $MAST_n$ is true. In this case the student has mastery of all the blocks in the sequence and should study something else.

When g does exist, the student starts studying at B_{g+1}. This placement satisfies the conditions 2 and 3 of our algorithm requirements, that is, this is the most advanced placement possible, and mastery of all the predecessors is ensured. However, condition 1, which requested a smooth instructional process, cannot be ensured by the algorithm, and it is the author's responsibility. In effect, the algorithm checks necessary conditions, but it has no tools to check sufficiency.

Sufficiency, in this context, means that the student, having mastered B_1 to B_g, has learned all the prerequisites and has developed all the learning sets and learning tools required to learn B_{g+1}. It is a part of an author's trade to design the instructional sequence in such a way that sufficiency is satisfied at every block-to-block transition (at least, for an absolute majority of the learners). Nevertheless, when dealing with large models of knowledge, errors are possible. It is an exceedingly important advantage of working in a *complete* CAI environment, that those errors are detected by the statistical analysis of performance at the instructional block (or frame) level.

Let us move now to our condition 4 for initial-placement algorithms, which requires minimizing the testing time.

For the ideal case we are analyzing, where every instructional block is a prerequisite of its follower, computer science provides an optimal traversal strategy, known as binary (or bipartition or bisection or dichotomic) search.

BINARY-SEARCH ALGORITHM   A binary-search-based, initial-placement algorithm may be outlined as shown in the box.

Binary-Search Algorithm

1. Check mastery at the first block. If the student fails, then she must start the course at the first block—if at all.

2. If the student succeeds in 1, then check mastery at the last block. Success implies that the student has no need to study the course.

3. If the student fails at the last block we know that she mastered the first block but does not master the last. Then mastery is checked at the *middle* instructional block. This is the gist of the method: if the student fails, then the search moves to the lower half of the instructional block sequence; if the student succeeds, the search is restricted to the upper half.

4. Thus we return to a search interval where the student masters the first block but does not master the last one, the advantage being that the length of the interval has been halved. The process continues, by checking mastery at an instructional block that lies in the middle of the new search interval, and using the same criterion, the search interval is halved again.

5. This is a fast process. When the length of the search interval is 2, we are reduced to two instructional blocks: B_g and B_{g+1}, the first mastered, and the second not mastered. Thus the student must start learning at B_{g+1}

This algorithm presents a good example of the adaptive (or tailored or response-contingent) testing that was previously defined. Neither the binary search nor the testing algorithms that follow here are recommended for use in the classical paper-and-pencil environment.

Binary search is a very efficient algorithm, requiring approximately $\log_2 n$ iterations to find the student initial placement over an instructional sequence of n blocks (e.g., approximately 6 iterations for a sequence of 50 blocks, and 8 iterations for a sequence of 250). Unfortunately, this computer science search algorithm, perfectly valid when used with fixed data, becomes unreliable when applied in an instructional environment, because the student performance is not uniquely defined for each block, and may vary among testing instances. This variability arises because answering exercises is not a deterministic process, but rather a probabilistic one. For example:

- A testee may err in an exercise, even in a known subject. Conversely, lack of knowledge in a subject does not imply that a testee will answer incorrectly all the exercises she is presented with on this subject. In particular, for multiple-choice exercises with four choices, there is a 25 percent chance of answering correctly without reading the exercise. For Yes/No exercises, this probability increases to 50 percent.
- If a student performs below her real potential (because of fatigue, distraction, or a trivial error) at a certain instructional block, from then on the search will be confined to the preceding blocks.
- A very human consideration, that has no place in computer science, is that it is very "unfriendly" to the student to repeatedly increase and decrease the difficulty of the test items in large steps, and this feature may affect her performance.

The problems just mentioned may preclude satisfying some of the requirements we requested from an initial placement algorithm. In particular, reliability (condition 5) is directly affected.

INCREASING-DIFFICULTY BLOCK SEQUENCE A more robust (stable and reliable) and friendly algorithm may be defined if it is possible to assume that relative performance at B_i:

$$R_i = \frac{PER_i}{REQ_i}$$

defined as the ratio between performance and requirements, decreases when i increases (in statistical terms, to be specified in the following paragraphs).

In global terms this assumption is reasonable because, if we keep the requirements constant ($REQ_i = REQ_j$ for every i, j), it expresses the usual pedagogical progression from easy to difficult. In other words, if at a certain point in time we test the same student over different blocks, we may expect higher performance (or better scores), in the initial instructional blocks than in the more advanced ones. There may be exceptions, meaning that the global assumption may fail at particular blocks in the sequence where the contents, or the test, may be unusually easy or unusually difficult. Working in a complete CAI environment where long-term projects are feasible, it is possible to change the block requirements according to the statistical data collected on student performance at each block. By lowering the requirements when the exercises are difficult and raising them in the opposite case, we may "smooth" the relative performance curve.

This means that, in a mature system, we can approximate an ideal instructional sequence where the following condition holds:

$$\text{If } i < j \text{ then } R_i > R_j$$

This condition, to be understood in statistical terms, must satisfy two formulations:

1. **Weak**—for large populations: The average relative performance over a population P of p students satisfies (with high probability):

$$\text{if } i < j \text{ then } \frac{1}{p} \sum_P R_i > \frac{1}{p} \sum_P R_j$$

2. **Strong**—for individuals: For any given student tested at B_i and B_j there is a very high probability that:

$$\text{If } i < j \text{ then } R_i > R_j$$

It is pleasant to realize that this statistical condition is not orthogonal or unrelated to the logical prerequisites condition we have been assuming until now.

In effect, this *increasing-difficulty* condition is sufficient to prove that the logical-prerequisites condition holds. Let us do so.

Assuming that the increasing-difficulty condition is true, we want to prove that, for any given student,

$$\text{MAST}_j \rightarrow \text{MAST}_i \text{ for every } i < j$$

Proof: If MAST_j is true, this means that

$$R_j \geq 1 \text{ (Note that this is equivalent to: } \text{PER}_j \geq \text{REQ}_j)$$

The increasing-difficulty condition (in its strong form), says that:

$$\text{for every } i < j \text{ then } R_i > R_j \text{ (with high probability).}$$

Thus:

$$R_i > 1 \text{ for every } i < j$$

or, equivalently, MAST_i is true (with high probability) for every $i < j$ q.e.d.

Note that the thesis cannot have a higher degree of certainty than the hypothesis. If the *increasing-difficulty* condition would hold for every case, then the theorem would be absolutely true. When the condition is valid in probabilistic terms only, the same applies to the conclusion.

Before describing the more robust and friendly algorithm possible under the new condition, let us enter into some of the details of establishing mastery at a given instructional block. This is usually done by presenting a sequence of exercises to the student and counting the number of those correctly answered.[2] The number of exercises in such a testing sequence should be high enough to avoid incorrect decisions (at least for the majority of the students).

The problem of incorrect decisions appears because of the probabilistic character of exercise answering, which may be compounded by changes in probability for a particular student due to fatigue, lack of concentration, and similar perturbations. Everybody familiar with probabilistic phenomena knows that strange or abnormal sequences of events do happen, because the qualification of strange or abnormal refers to events that happen with low probability and not to those that do not occur at all. We cannot cope, within the testing processes, with extraneous psychological situations, but we can use statistical tools to determine an adequate minimum of exercises to be assigned in order to obtain a reasonably reliable assessment.

Because of this, the testing sequence for an instructional block may contain between 12 and 24 exercises (the exact number will depend on the statistical reliability required for the test and the psychometric properties of the exercises).

The initial-placement algorithm requires testing of many different blocks, so that a naive approach would result in an intolerably high number of exercises.

THE BLOCK-JUMPING ALGORITHM A different technique to improve efficiency characterizes the new algorithm (robust and friendly) whose description was postponed until this moment, when the presentation of the major difficulties related to standard testing algorithms has been completed.

We call this the *block-jumping algorithm* because its main idea is to abandon block-by-block testing and to change blocks, *within the same testing sequence,* according to ongoing results of the evaluation.[3]

This technique is valid only under the *increasing-difficulty* assumption and its essence is:

1. Select an initial block i to place the student, according to your best (informed/educated) guess.
2. Start testing at block i. If the student performance is below the block requirements, according to the partial results registered, continue testing at block $i - 1$. If student performance is above the block requirements, continue testing at block $i + 1$. If student performance equals the block requirement, continue testing at block i.
3. Repeat the branching structure described in step 2 at the block where testing is being performed. The block traversal will converge toward the blocks where relative performance is closest to 1.
4. Continue testing until stability is reached. This is reflected either in the fact that the student stays in a block g or that she oscillates between blocks g and

---

[2]Each exercise may have a different weight, but to simplify the presentation let us assume that exercise weights are equal.

[3]Although in a different context, this algorithm applies the ideas of the H-L and Robbins-Monro processes analyzed by Lord (1971).

$g + 1$. In both cases the student's initial placement (BEG) is $g + 1$ or, in other words, she should start studying at block $g + 1$, because she has mastery of block g and does not have mastery of block $g + 1$.

5. There are two extreme cases, not covered in 4. The student may fall below the first block, or she may "overflow" the highest block. In the first case, the student may start studying at the beginning of the instructional sequence (other prerequisites being satisfied), and in the second case, she is exempted from studying the course because she has mastery of its contents.

Some comments:

a) Moving to block $i - 1$ when the student is performing below the requirements at block i will raise her relative performance, because:

$$R_{i-1} > R_i$$

b) Similarly, if the student is performing above the requirements of block i, moving to block $i + 1$ will lower her relative performance.

c) In the situation described in a) we know that:

$$R_{i-1} > R_i < 1$$

but we do not know how the relative performance at block $i - 1$ compares with 1. If it is still less than 1, we move down to block $i - 2$. If it is equal to 1, we stay, and if it is greater than 1, we move back to block i.

d) A similar analysis applies to b).

e) In the ideal situation the algorithm converges, and does so efficiently because of the use of partial information to accelerate the traversal. The friendliness is reflected in the fact that there are no abrupt jumps in the difficulty of the test items, but rather there is a smooth and continuous change in difficulty, always from a block to one of its neighbors.

f) We now show robustness, in the sense that the system is capable of recovering from a "locally distorted" student performance.

Let us refer to Figure 9.3. Assume that a student, being tested at B_i has such a knowledge that, in normal performance:

$$PER_i > REQ_i \text{ (or } R_i > 1)$$

This means that, under normal conditions, the student should be upgraded to B_{i+1}.

Now suppose that, because of a distorted performance (distraction, non-relevant errors), the evaluation gives

$$PER_i^* \text{ such that } PER_i^* < REQ_i$$

In this case the student is moved to B_{i-1}, where testing continues.

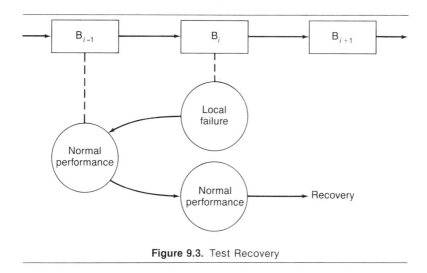

Figure 9.3. Test Recovery

Assuming now that the student recovers from her local failure,[4] her normal performance at B_{i-1} will satisfy the condition:

$$R_{i-1} > R_i > 1$$

so that the student will be upgraded to B_i. If performance is back to normal, the new testing at B_i will promote the student to B_{i+1}, and the recovery is completed.

g) A similar reasoning shows that if a student is upgraded, by chance, above her real capabilities, the probability weights will be biased against her so that she will return (with high probability) to her expected placement.

h) It is important to examine the influence of the deviation from the ideal *increasing-difficulty* condition at particular blocks. In other words, we want to examine the influence that unusually easy or unusually difficult blocks may have on student placement. Note that we are not talking about a temporary deviation in student performance (which was just analyzed) but about a structural defect in the sequence of block tests, particularly possible when there is not enough statistical data to correct the block requirements properly (early life of a course). It will help us to present, in Figure 9.4, our ideal plot of decreasing relative performance against increasing block numbers.

In correspondence with the two formulations that an increasing-difficulty sequence must satisfy, the plot may represent the relative performance of one student tested at successive blocks (strong formulation) or the average relative performance of a group of students tested over the same blocks (weak formulation). For convenience we have displayed a linear function, although any monotonically decreasing function would serve the purpose. Assuming that the

---

[4]Recovery is also possible after failure at several blocks.

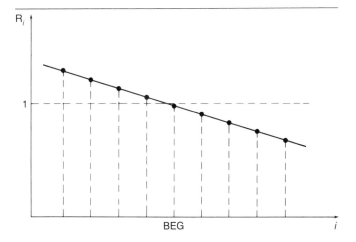

Figure 9.4. Increasing-Difficulty Block Sequence

plot refers to a particular student, the first block where $R_i < 1$ uniquely determines the student placement (marked as BEG).

Now let us plot, in Figure 9.5, a sequence with (structural) difficulty deviations, where we have distinguished two blocks: f (more difficult than the ideal) and g (easier than the ideal). Here f and g represent two types of deviations, not because g is easier and f more difficult than expected, but because B_f has switched classes, while B_g has not. In the ideal case, the student whose performance is plotted in Figure 9.5 would have shown mastery at B_f, if the block

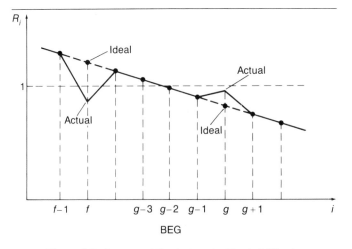

Figure 9.5. Structural Deviations in Block Difficulty

difficulty had matched the ideal (straight-line) plot. In the actual case, the student tested at f will show lack of mastery (there is·a switch from $MAST_f =$ true to $MAST_f =$ false). With respect to B_g, in both the ideal and the actual situations the student shows lack of mastery, so that there is no change in the classification of B_g. The importance of discriminating between the two types of deviations is shown next.

Case A: The student starts testing at an instructional block where the requirements are higher than her level of performance. The last stages of the placement algorithm will be:

$$Test\ B_{g + 1} \rightarrow MAST_{g + 1} = false \rightarrow move\ to\ B_g$$
$$Test\ B_g\ \ \ \rightarrow MAST_g\ \ \ = false \rightarrow move\ to\ B_{g - 1}$$
$$Test\ B_{g - 1} \rightarrow MAST_{g - 1} = false \rightarrow move\ to\ B_{g - 2}$$
$$Test\ B_{g - 2} \rightarrow MAST_{g - 2} = false \rightarrow move\ to\ B_{g - 3}$$
$$Test\ B_{g - 3} \rightarrow MAST_{g - 3} = true \rightarrow BEG = g - 2$$

Case B: The student starts testing at an instructional block where the requirements are below her level of performance. The last stages will be:

$$Test\ B_{f - 2} \rightarrow MAST_{f - 2} = true \rightarrow move\ to\ B_{f - 1}$$
$$Test\ B_{f - 1} \rightarrow MAST_{f - 1} = true \rightarrow move\ to\ B_f$$
$$Test\ B_f\ \ \ \rightarrow MAST_f\ \ \ = false \rightarrow BEG = f$$

The difference between cases A and B is very clear. In the first case the deviation in difficulty at B_g did not affect the logical decision, so that the student placement coincided with the ideal case. On the other hand, in case B, showing lack of mastery at B_f stops the algorithm, with an incorrect assignment. The placement error, a consequence of the structural deviations from the ideal design plus the random disturbances in student performance, can be bound as shown in Figure 9.6.

We can see the ideal relative-performance plot and its intersection (marked with a circle), with the horizontal $R_i = 1$, which determines BEG. If we assume that d is an upper bound of the total deviation (sum of structural deviation plus student local disturbance), then the two lines parallel to the "ideal" determine a band that bounds the actual measure of relative performance (R_i). This means that the intersections with $R_i = 1$ (marked by small squares) may displace the result of the placement algorithm to be as low as BEG − or as high as BEG +.

ADVICE The best results with this algorithm are obtained if:

1. The (negative) slope of R_i has a (relatively) high absolute value.
2. The exercises and requirements for the testing sequences are updated with experience, in order to obtain a smooth increasing-difficulty sequence.
3. When in doubt, retest.

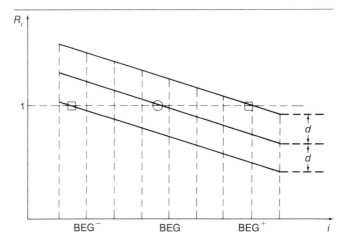

Figure 9.6. Maximum Placement Error

Pedagogical Sequencing. Until now we have been dealing with the case where the sequencing of blocks is uniquely determined by logical (prerequisite) conditions. We have already mentioned that, in other cases, sequencing may reflect pedagogical decisions only, or it may reflect a mix of pedagogical and logical reasons.

In terms of a placement algorithm, there is nothing to be done if the testing of mastery at a given block conveys no information with respect to predecessors or followers. In such a case each instructional block should have a built-in pretest; every student would start at the first block in the sequence and should traverse all the blocks. Instruction would be skipped at those blocks where the pretest shows mastery. In some cases, particularly for weak pupils, a review of those blocks that are critical for further instruction may be advisable when instruction is skipped.

Parallel-Sequences Structure. This structure, described in Chapter 8, consists of a set of sequences that are taught in parallel. Everything that was said with respect to the initial-placement algorithm for sequence structures applies individually to each one of the sequences in the set, but in addition, it is possible to make use of the design assumptions that characterize this structure to shorten the placement search. This is indeed necessary.

The description, just completed, of placement algorithms for isolated sequences makes it very clear that we are talking about time-consuming processes. If placement in a parallel-sequences structure, one that may contain more than 10 sequences, were to be done by repeating the algorithm sequence after sequence, the time requirements would be one order of magnitude above the search processes previously described.

An efficient solution was devised for the TOAM Testing and Practice courseware in Arithmetic, based on a curriculum design specifying that all the instructional blocks at a given level (irrespective of being indifferent topics) are taught in school during the same month at a specific class grade. Using the scope-and-sequence terminology used in American schools, the Arithmetic courseware comprises 15 topics, ranging in level from 1.0 (beginning of the first grade) to 7.9 (end of the seventh grade).

In terms of student placement this means that, although the final testing level may be different for each topic, levels will be generally clustered around the global average level. TOAM's placement algorithm uses this fact during an initial phase where the block-jumping algorithm is applied to all the topics simultaneously (in a round-robin fashion). Suppose that a student being tested at topic 6, level 4.0, fails; she is then moved to topic 7, level 3.9. Assuming she succeeds, she is tested at topic 8, level 4.0; if she succeeds again, she is moved to topic 9, level 4.1, and so forth.

At the end of this initial phase the approximate average level has been determined. This is a very important advantage because, in the second stage of topic-by-topic refinement, the starting level is near the final placement.

Let us give a feeling for the time requirements: the initial placement algorithm in TOAM Arithmetic requires eight 10-minute sessions to determine the global average, and four additional 10-minute sessions for the topic-by-topic refinement.

The control of nonrepresentative student performances is assigned to the teacher. At the end of the initial phase a class report is printed, and the teacher must check whether any student is placed below her expected performance (particularly when compared with her peers). If this is so, the teacher explains to the student the importance of her correct placement, and the initial phase is extended by two to four sessions. Note that we are concerned with low performances only; the constructed response in TOAM Arithmetic makes guessing statistically irrelevant.

At the end of the second phase the teacher compares each student's average with the average that student had at the end of the global placement phase. Irrespective of the within-topic displacements, the average should remain fixed. Any strong drop in level shows irregular performance and "conversation + retesting" is required.

A different design for a parallel-sequences structure can be found in Chapter 13, where the initial-placement algorithm for TOAM's Reading-Comprehension courseware is described.

Tree Structure. Probably the best example of testing within a tree-structured course has already been presented in Chapter 8 with the description of the "Prerequisites Mathematics Skills Course," and we refer the reader back to it. We will add that block-testing in this OISE's courseware, is shortened by using Wald's sequential-testing techniques (Wald, 1947).

Directed Graph. There is not much that we can add in general. When traversal is based on pedagogical considerations, every block should have a pretest, with the possibility of skipping instruction according to its results.

When prerequisite conditions do hold, a good strategy is to concentrate testing at strongly connected nodes.

Student Gain Assessment

Gain assessment is performed by comparing test results of the same learner at two separate points in time. The difference between the score at the final test and the score at the initial test determines the gain or progress. The score difference may be computed for a single student, thus providing that student's individual gain, or the gains may be computed for a group—a class, a whole grade, a school, or a district. Gains for a group are usually determined by averaging individual gains and computing statistical parameters that characterize the distribution of gains over the population.

For an educational institution's pedagogical purposes, the usual points in time selected for comparative testing are the beginning and the end of the school year or of a study period. Thus the computed gains reflect the instructional benefit accrued during an organizationally relevant period.

When comparing performances of the same population in two different moments of time, how is the first test related to the second test? The naive answer, striving for fairness, is that both tests must be equal. Actually, this is what is done in many cases. There is, of course, a methodological danger in this easy solution, and this is the possibility that a very specific "learning of the test" occurred during the first presentation, so that the second measurement incorporates not just the progress due to the instructional process but this extraneous test learning as well. This danger may be minimized by not providing feedback (i.e., the student ignores whether her answers are correct or incorrect), and by ensuring that a relatively long period of time elapses between the two presentations (e.g., beginning and end of the same school year). If these safeguards are not satisfied, the solution must be found in a different way.

The easiest, and most satisfying, solution from our standpoint refers to the case when the subject matter is supported by a Testing and Practice system that incorporates an initial-placement algorithm. In such a case we are dealing with adaptive testing, so that in each testing instance the student is presented with different exercises. The test score is, in this case, given by the student placement within the structure and, if the structure reflects a given metric, the gains are immediately computable.

When initial-placement algorithms are not available, we have to resort to standard testing techniques. This is an area where a wealth of bibliography is available, which we are not going to summarize in this book. Good references are Anastasi (1976) and Thorndike and Hagen (1985). From a CAI standpoint, we are interested in computerized testing and, in particular, in on-line testing. Computerized testing is associated with the idea of a "Test and Question Bank," that is, a repository of questions and tests repeatedly used, allowing for collection of statistics and for teacher selection and/ or construction of questions and tests, to satisfy the specific needs of a class studying a given subject. For a classic in this area, see Lippey, 1974. The concept of a bank refers to a very rich collection of questions, which provides an answer to the problem of avoiding repetition of the same questions by allowing for the construction of equivalent tests on the same subject. The goodness of the equivalence is very much dependent on the validity of the statistics that accompany each question and that define parameters such as difficulty and discrimination power. In a well-designed bank the teacher may define a test by specifying, for each type of question:

- A Boolean combination of topics
- Average difficulty (a range)
- Number of questions to be presented
- Their position in the test
- Weight for the test grade

For tests already in the bank, it is possible to compute also the discrimination power for each question.

In their first generation, Test and Question Banks were used to produce printouts of the tests, which were then given to the students in a classical paper-and-pencil test situation. There was, for the teacher, an additional advantage: multiple-choice exercises would be scrambled differently for each student, and numerical exercises with random values would be presented with different values for each student. The teacher would receive, of course, a table of the correct results expected from each student.

Today, the reduction in the price of terminal time allows for on-line testing, where the administration of the test to a student may be done at a computer terminal, with the grading automatically performed at test end. In the school of the near future, a teacher will bring her class to a computer lab, will select a test that all the pupils will take on-line simultaneously, and at the end, will receive a report indicating each pupil's grade and the topics where difficulties were detected. The report will also provide the average and standard deviation of the grades for the whole class and a summary of the topics in which a large proportion of the pupils didn't reach satisfactory results, pointing to the need for remedial instruction in the class. Where self-paced courses, or individualized instruction methods are implemented, tests may be taken at student request. A recent description of such an environment may be found in Gwinn and Beal (1987–88).

Within a complete CAI facility, and if our predicament about separation of instructional content from pedagogical strategy is applied, it is possible to build a Test and Question Bank quite cheaply. In effect, the same questions being used in the CAI courses may be used in the bank, and the performance statistics collected during the instructional process may be used as initial values for the bank utilization. As an example, from the almost 13,000 questions that constitute TOAM's courseware in Reading-Comprehension, 4,000 were selected for a bank in this subject. Today, teachers may select topics and grade levels, and build tests for on-line examination, enjoying all of the benefits previously described.

CONTINUOUS EVALUATION

As we have already mentioned, the main advantage of a CAI system lies in the possibility of making appropriate instructional decisions on the basis of a student model that is continuously updated by the student activities that take place during the student's learning process. We distinguished, in the student model, between the relatively fixed psychological parameters relevant to the instructional process and the variable state of the student knowledge, which instruction is trying to improve. To allow for a continuous assessment of the student learning process, we use two types of state variables to reflect student knowledge:

1. Situation variables, which usually describe mastery (or degree of mastery) over the components of the knowledge model, and which are dependent on its topology and internal representation.
2. Dynamic variables, which measure performance over a relatively short period of time (usually a computer session or a lesson, whichever is the shorter), to give the present picture of the student's proficiency. Dynamic variables store information on the number of exercises presented for a given task, the number of correct responses, latency (i.e., student's response time), and so forth.

The continuous evaluation of the student activity allows, without any need for external or ad hoc testing, for the satisfaction of two kinds of requirements essential in the design of instruction: the possibility of establishing a student's mastery over a certain topic or task, in order to switch the instruction to another area, and the possibility of diagnosing a student's misconception or lack of understanding, in order to provide remedial help. These will be the topics of the next sections.

Mastery Checking

Mastery Redefined. Let us consider a student who has finished the initial-placement test and starts studying a particular instructional block. If the author and the algorithm have done their best, we may assume that the student is capable of learning this block, but has not reached (yet) the required level of mastery.

And now a question: Should the mastery requirements for advancing to the next instructional block coincide with those defined for the placement algorithm?

The (surprising?) answer is no.

The reasons for this redefinition of mastery are to be found in three different areas:

1. The shape of the learning curve
2. The differences between short-term and long-term memory
3. The objectives of testing

We are familiar with learning curves from Chapter 5. Their well-known shape (see Figure 9.7) shows that initial plateau (which may not appear if the student has already acquired the learning sets necessary for the task being learned), the high-rise section, and the asymptotic approximation to "perfection."

In terms of cost-effectiveness, the best (short-term) result is obtained if we stop instruction at point B, where the ratio between performance and investment is maximum. But, in reality, we are interested in performance not immediately after instruction, but rather after some time has elapsed since the instructional process, and the student has to apply her knowledge. In this situation the investment in overlearning starts to pay off.

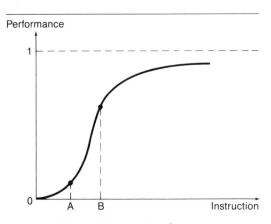

Figure 9.7. Learning Curve

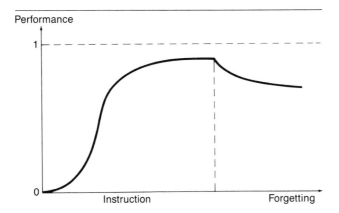

Figure 9.8. Learning-Forgetting Curve with Overlearning

In effect, forgetting curves have an initial sharp decline and then a slow asymptotic behavior. The initial degradation may be diminished by overlearning.

Because of these considerations, a combined learning-forgetting curve, for a student whose instruction included overlearning, looks like the one shown in Figure 9.8. Note that the horizontal axis in this graph requires an appropriate selection of "instruction units" (instructional resources and activities) and "forgetting units" (a weighed sum of elapsed time and interference).

On the other hand, optimizing the short-term instructional investment results in a very fast forgetting process (Figure 9.9).

Now, back to the differences in mastery requirements. When we test a student for initial placement, the assumption is that we are testing knowledge as internalized in her long-term memory. However, when we test a student for mastery of a block she is presently learning, we are still on the learning curve.

Then, if our long-term expectation is that a student should perform above REQ, we will not "graduate" her when reaching that level during instruction because, as we

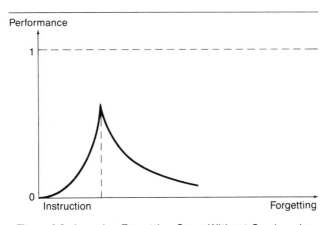

Figure 9.9. Learning-Forgetting Curve Without Overlearning

said, this would produce a forgetting curve of the kind marked with an X on Figure 9.10. What we do is raise the requirements to REQ⁺ so that, when "graduating" at this level, her forgetting curve will be shaped as the one marked with a Y on the same figure.

An interesting example of an ad hoc, but well-thought out, mastery checking algorithm, is found in Koffman (1972), previously mentioned in Chapter 8, page 136. The courseware described teaches concepts in circuit design. Koffman measures knowledge of a concept over an arbitrary linear scale (assigning it a level between 0 and 3). The initial values for the parameters of the student model are determined according to external testing and/or class standing. The level of each concept in the course is updated by an algorithm after each question that deals with it. It is worth mentioning that level decreasing and increasing are not symmetrical processes. Level stability is also measured and stored for each concept. Pedagogical decisions are based on these concepts levels.

> "Each concept is evaluated based on a number of factors such as the time elapsed since its last use, the stability of its current level, the sign and magnitude of its most recent level change (negative changes are weighed more heavily), and its relevance to other concepts as determined by the number of branches of the tree connected to it" (Koffman, 1972, p. 384).

An interesting feature of Koffman's approach is that when a student reaches mastery in a concept, not only will the system cease querying on this topic, but it will also provide the compuptional services related to its use "free of charge." For example, a student who has to solve a problem on Karnaugh maps and has level 3 (mastery) in Truth Tables, will have the truth tables done for her by the program.

Performance Measures. Until now we have referred to the comparison of performance with requirements, without actually describing how performance is measured or how the requirements are specified. The implicit assumptions, indeed valid for basic skills, is that we compare percentages of correct answers. Although in practice this is true, there is no need, particularly in a computerized environment, for such a restriction.

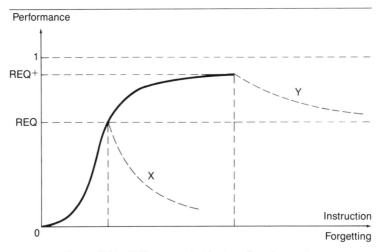

Figure 9.10. Differences in Mastery Requirements

Another possible measure of performance for basic skills is that of response time or latency, that is, how long it takes the student to perform a task (e.g., to answer an exercise).

This is particularly important when we try to determine an appropriate amount of overlearning, because in the asymptotic section of the learning curve the improvement in percentage correct is very small and thus hard to measure, with the danger of making an incorrect decision because of measurement errors. However, according to Judd and Glaser (1969) there is a strong improvement in student response time as a function of overlearning and this performance index may provide a more accurate and robust tool for establishing mastery.

It is clear that this refinement imposes burdens on the system. Note that mastery criteria like "85 percent correct" or "92 percent correct" may be implemented as soon as a course is prepared for its first trial run. Decisions based on latency measures, on the other hand, require a reliable statistical database, to determine normalized latency values and to establish suitable requirements.

When performance is measured over several dimensions, the judging mechanism must take this into consideration. Following are two examples from personal experience.

1. In the SMILE system, the performance index is a weighted average (with positive and negative weights) of the normalized values of the percentage of correct answers, the number of times remedial help is requested, and the time invested in the learning of each frame. The normalization is done with respect to statistical data collected during student instruction.
2. In TOAM's touch-typing course, two parameters are the basis for decision: speed, measured in characters per minute, and precision, measured as the percentage of correct key-presses. The decisions at the end of each lesson are based on the mapping of the student's performance on the Cartesian plane shown in Figure 9.11.

In the touch-typing courseware, two levels of requirements are established: a very demanding one and a minimum to get by. According to the most demanding, a student should have a speed of S_2 characters per minute, with a percentage of at least P_2 correct key-presses. The minima are determined by S_1 and P_1. If a student satisfies the higher requirements (zone 1 in the figure), she will pass with a highly commendatory message. But the system is also somewhat lenient, in the sense that if a student performs above the higher requirement in only one of the dimensions, she will receive a passing grade if, in the other dimension, her performance is above the minimum (zones 2 and 3). Furthermore, it is possible to pass with an adequate mix above the minima, even if neither of the high requirements are achieved (zone 4). In all the other zones (from 5 upward) the student must repeat the lesson. The message provided by the system is a function of the zone, e.g., "Your speed is good, try to reduce the number of errors", corresponds to zone 6.

Diagnostics

The purpose of diagnostics is remediation. From a systems design standpoint, we have to strike a balance between the effort invested in reaching a very precise and detailed diagnosis, and the instructional support that we can provide once the diagnostic proc-

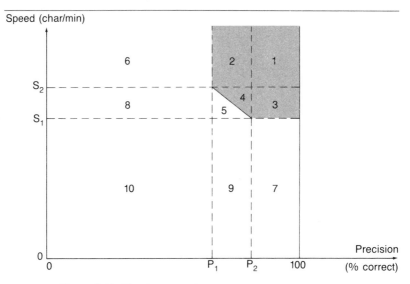

Figure 9.11. Touch-typing Courseware Performance-Map

ess is completed. These considerations apply to any of the models that have been described in Chapter 4. An important design factor is whether the remediation will be provided as part of the CAI process or externally.

External Remediation. This case is the most frequent when CAI serves an auxiliary purpose (as opposed to being autonomous), and it is possible to count on the teacher as a valuable instructional resource. The importance of this distinction, again from a systems design standpoint, is that if the remedial instruction is to be provided by the teacher, it is enough to identify the type of exercises where the student is having difficulties, or to list the concepts being misunderstood. The assumption, in this case, is that the teacher will sit down with the student, present her with an appropriate task to perform, ask the student to talk aloud while performing it, ask relevant questions, and thus gather the exact information required to correct the misconception and provide the most appropriate remedial instruction, as a better-tailored alternative to the instruction initially provided.

We resort to our paradigm of auxiliary CAI, the Testing and Practice systems, to provide a concrete example of this type of computer-diagnosis plus teacher-remediation interaction. For simplicity, let us assume a linear sequence topology. Thus, if a student reaches mastery of the instructional block B_i, she will be promoted to B_{i+1}. As already mentioned, there is no assurance that the student will, in every case, be able to cope with the requirements of B_{i+1}. If not, one of two things may happen: either the student fails totally or she fails partially. In the first case, which shows total lack of instruction about the subject $i + 1$ (or lack of preparedness for it), the symptom detected by the CAI system is that the student answers incorrectly all the exercises presented upon entrance to B_{i+1}. There is no need for prolonging this situation: a short sequence of failures (e.g., three exercises) prompts the system to suspend practice at B_{i+1} and to report the problem to the teacher.

The second case, partial failure, is detected by lack of progress after a reasonable period of instruction. The main assumption of Testing and Practice systems is that a well-graded set of exercises, integrated with appropriate class activities (explanations, discussions, etc.), will promote a steady flow of student progress. Then, if a student gets "stuck" in an instructional block, without reaching mastery after practicing for a period that greatly exceeds the expected time assigned for this activity, there is a specific difficulty or misconception that requires teacher attention. In this case the report to the teacher is issued without suspending the student practice.

On-line Remediation. Autonomous CAI is more demanding than auxiliary CAI, because the system has to provide not only the diagnosis but also the treatment. Diagnostic techniques may be classified into immediate and developmental. The first type, immediate diagnosis, is defined by the fact that no student history is used: the last student response allows for the detection of a misconception and, consequently, for its treatment. This simple process is the most widely used, and it is smoothly served by the structure presented in Chapter 8 when address-oriented programming techniques were described.

In effect, each one of the expected incorrect answers presumably corresponds to a certain bug or misconception. When a student answer is identified with an expected incorrect answer, the corresponding message and branching are designed to provide the required treatment. The minimum treatment is given by the provision of an error message, with the hope (actually fulfilled in many cases), that the student will correct herself. This minimum treatment is usually complemented by the presentation of the correct answer, in the case of a second or third mistake in the same exercise. A step above this consists of the presentation of a guiding message. A further investment may result in the design of a remedial loop, to review the instruction of the topic being taught or to provide an alternative explanation.

Developmental diagnosis is used when immediate diagnosis is unreliable or impossible. Its essence is to record the student performance over a set of tasks, in order to detect behavioral patterns that reflect misconceptions (à la Brown and Burton, 1978) or misrules (à la Sleeman, 1982), or even misuse or lack of use of tools that should integrate the student's repertoire. It is very clear, particularly in the learning of complex tasks, that just one incorrect instance does not allow for a categorical judgment. The case of the lack of use of tool is the strongest example. If the task was amenable to solution using other tools, the lack of use of the optimal tool on one occasion does not prove that the student will not use it on others. We expand on this area, providing a detailed example of developmental diagnosis, in Chapter 13 where we describe the methods used by Burton and Brown (1979) in their analysis of WEST players' performance.

Finally, let us point out that the additional sophistication required by the developmental diagnosis, as compared with the immediate one, is not necessarily reflected in a different type of student treatment. Once a misconception has been identified, the instructional process required to correct it is independent of the diagnostic method. The difference in practice is, usually, that developmental diagnosis allows for a finer and more precise analysis, which is reflected in the messages that may be presented to the student and in the specific remedial processes that may be designed.

SUMMARY

Assessment is the basis for sound decision making. This applies both to CAI, where the pedagogical model is constantly making decisions in terms of student placement, progress, traversal, remediation, enrichment, advice, and so on, and to the class situation, where the teacher must do the same on a much larger and more complex scale.

Computerized assessment may be done at discrete stages (like the beginning and end of a school term) or in a continuous fashion, as an integral part of the CAI process.

The discrete case corresponds to testing, which is performed for two main purposes: to determine an appropriate initial placement for a student when she starts her interaction with a piece of courseware and to find out whether instructional gains accrued as a result of the interaction. Initial-placement algorithms were described in detail and the conclusion reached that it is possible to develop very efficient algorithms if the instructional materials satisfy certain conditions. Initial-placement algorithms are essential for any large courseware structure. Testing may be easily accessible to the teacher, if she is provided with a Test and Question Bank, where she may define the contents and characteristics of a test, assign it on-line to her whole class, and receive an immediate printout with an analysis of student and class strong and weak points of knowledge.

Continuous evaluation serves two purposes: the determination of whether a student has mastered a certain topic, to allow for the continuation of instruction in other topics, and the detection, or diagnosis, of student difficulties to provide for remedial help. This help may be accessible on-line, or it may be provided by the teacher or other external sources. The mastery criteria should be sufficiently demanding, so as to provide a certain insurance against quick forgetting.

CHAPTER 10

Instructional Administration

All through my life things were too many.
—Jorge Luis Borges, *In Praise of Darkness* (1974)

Instructional administration is usually considered a boring area, related to things that must be done but nobody likes to do. The situation could be very different, and we hope that computerization will help in creating new administrative functions, tightly embedded in the instructional process. These functions should enable the teacher, with a minimum of paperwork (or data entry), to prescribe instruction differentially to every learner, according to individual situation and performance and balancing the curriculum priorities with the learner's preferences. In direct dialogue with a learner, the system could provide him with advice on what instructional units are available (in the sense that he masters their prerequisites) within the program of studies he is registered in, with comments in terms of adequacy to the learner's preferences or learning style.

The development of such a system requires a large investment, which starts by structuring curricula in terms of possible combinations of instructional units that must be indexed at least according to contents, instructional style, prerequisites, and average learning time. While these ideal systems are not available, we should strive for introducing as many pieces as we can, within our computerized systems, that are compatible with our long-term objectives.

SCHOOL ADMINISTRATION

Our purpose is to concentrate on the instructional administration related to the CAI facility. We are not going to deal with the standard administrative aspects of registration, attendance, tardiness, grades, grade reporting, and the like, which are outside the scope of this book. The data we are going to use are organized in interrelated files, whose records may describe classes, students, courses, or a whole school. To exemplify with a concrete scenario, we assume an elementary school whose student population is divided into classes, each student belonging to one class only. Each student may learn at a different pace, and thus different students within the same class may be registered in different CAI courses.

File Structure

Our method is to proceed in a top-down fashion in the selected scenario, presenting a file structure (among many possible) at school, class, and student level. We have selected a hierarchical organization for our data structure. Due to the increasing popularity of relational database management systems (RDBMS), we have recast our school data structure in terms of tables that could be used in a RDBMS. To avoid the repetition of data, fields in certain records contain pointers to records in other files. Nevertheless, some redundancy has been left, for the sake of readability and reliability.

The symbol "(*)" is used to denote a multiplicity of records of the same type. With these comments in mind, we can present the organization of the top level of school data in Figure 10.1.

As we can see, the information has been divided into two categories. The first one, which we have called "permanent," refers to stable administrative data that does not change according to an educational cycle. Of course, this data may be updated when required. The second category defines the school organization, built around classes. This data is usually updated at the beginning of each school year.

For each class there is a field containing a pointer to class data, in terms of students and courseware, that constitutes the second level in the structure. This class data structure is presented in Figure 10.2.

```
Permanent data
    School name
    School address and phone number
    School district
    Personnel
        Principal
            Name
            Address and phone number
        Secretary
            Name
            Address and phone number
        Guidance counselor
            Name
            Address and phone number
        Nurse
            Name
            Address and phone number
Functional organization
(*) Class
        Grade
        Teacher
            Name
            Address and phone number
        Room number
        Pointer to student and courseware records
```

Figure 10.1. School Data Structure (Top Level)

Teacher name
Class grade
(*) Student
      Student id
      Pointer to student record
(*) Courseware
      Name
      Parameters
      Activities
      Messages
      Pointer to courseware record

Figure 10.2. Class Data Structure

The starred components in the class data (indicating multiplicity) refer to the students in the class and to the courseware used for their instruction. In each of these records there is a pointer field that will lead us to a third level of information. In each courseware record there are several fields (see box below).

We look at the courseware record more closely later in this chapter. The student record, which brings us to the third level in this data structure, is presented in Figure 10.3.

Ideally, instructional decisions should be a function of every student's parameters and of his educational history. The record described in Figure 10.3 gives a feeling for the components that may be considered when selecting units, forming study groups, or determining whether mastery requirements have been achieved. In the student record we again find the distinction between relatively stable permanent data, and the dynamic data that is updated in every study session. It is worth noting that two of the components in the permanent data are planned for updating: the pedagogical parameters may be refined according to the student performance within the CAI system, and the educational history incorporates the data corresponding to every course the student completes at the system. The dynamic data segment contains the information related to every course the student is presently learning at the system. The performance parameters may be defined specifically for a particular student learning a particular course

---

PARAMETERS: The courseware may be tailored to the class requirements by setting parameters that, for example, may define active units or topics, may establish the required level of mastery for each unit, may determine the time assigned for each session, student options, and so forth.

ACTIVITIES: The teacher may specify activities common to all the pupils studying a piece of courseware, such as taking a quiz or getting a homework assignment when a certain unit is finished.

MESSAGES: The teacher may send messages to all the learners, specifying priorities, informing about bugs or difficulties recently discovered, or establishing discussion meetings for certain groups or topics. Under certain conditions students may be allowed to use this facility to send messages to their peers or to the teacher.

Permanent data
  Administrative
    Student id
    Name
    Address and phone
    Parents' names
    Parents' addresses
    Birthdate
  Pedagogical
    Learning-style parameters
    Proficiency parameters
    Personality parameters
  Educational history
    (*) Courseware
        Name
        Starting date
        Finishing date
        Performance data
        Grade
Dynamic data
  (*) Courseware
        Name
        Pointer
        Starting date
        Performance parameters
        State variables
            Situation variables
            Dynamic variables

Figure 10.3. Student Record

and provide an additional level of tailoring. The teacher may establish global parameters (for all the students) for a given course, as was previously mentioned, but may refine them for any individual student. An example may be the time allotted to respond to an exercise, which may be increased for students with learning difficulties.

The state variables, of which the student has a set for every course, consist of situation variables and dynamic variables, following the distinction that was introduced in Chapter 9. To give concrete examples of each type, let us consider a course with a parallel-sequences structure. For each parallel sequence, a situation variable defines at which instructional block the student is learning, and for each instructional block a set of variables registers the activities accomplished and the corresponding performance parameters. Dynamic variables store, for instance, the number of exercises presented in the last session, how many of those were correctly answered, and how many of the remaining were not answered within the allotted time. The contents of both situation and dynamic variables are used in reporting. The situation variables allow the student, when he signs on, to continue working at exactly the same point where he left off, because the student model is initialized using the values stored in the situation variables.

Data Collection and Processing

Standard programs and formats may be used for data entry. The critical component of data updating that refers to the student state variables must be performed on-line, accompanying the instructional process. For reasons of computational efficiency, it is usual to perform real-time updating of the student-model state variables in the main (random-access) memory and to update the student record on disk, according to the values of those state variables, at the end of each session. Similarly, courseware statistics are collected in real time, and courseware-statistics records on disk are updated at session end. In addition to the instructional administrator, it is very important to train the teachers in the use of the Administration facility programs that allow them to set parameters and activities, to communicate with the learners, and to request the reports that will be described in the next section.

Reports

The reports on student and class performance should be produced at two levels: a detailed one for the teacher, and a general one for the school principal. The teacher reports must provide the basis for the assessment of the instructional activity, in terms of progress and difficulties, and the teacher should plan his further steps in class as a function of this assessment. The principal's reports must provide a means for global supervision of class progress.

Class-Status Report. We begin by providing a concrete example of a class-status[1] report for a teacher; it is for a parallel-sequences structure case, that of the TOAM Arithmetic course. As seen in Figure 10.4, this class-status report is divided into three sections: headings, individual data, and summary data.

The headings section contains the data that identifies the class, the subject and the date, and the column headings for the second section.

The second section presents the individual data, with one line assigned to each student. This arrangement, when feasible, is very convenient, because it allows for easy scanning in the two dimensions: horizontal, to get all the data for one student, and vertical, to check the performance of the whole class on a specific topic or feature.

Let us analyze the information provided in the different columns, for each individual student.

The first two columns display the student identification: number and name. The next two columns display information related to dynamic variables:

- R/T = Right/Total, presents the number of exercises answered correctly and the total number of exercises presented in the last session.
- O/W = Time-Out/Wrong, presents the number of exercises that were not answered within the allotted time and the total number of exercises answered incorrectly.

---

[1]The qualifier "status" is to distinguish this report from the class "progress" report, described later in this chapter.

Number	Name	R/T	O/W	SE	AV	1	2	3	4	. . .	14	15
12	Sally	28/32	1/4	45	3.2	3.4^	H	3.3	3.1	. . .	3.0	L
24	Johnny	18/27	6/9	42	4.2	4.0	H	4.1*	4.3	. . .	4.2	L
36	Mike	31/34	0/3	46	6.4	6.3	H	H	H	. . .	6.6<	6.4
CLASS AVERAGES				44	4.6	4.6		3.7	3.6		4.6	6.4

SCHOOL: x
CLASS: t
STUDENTS
SUBJECT: Arithmetic
TEACHER: y
DATE: u

Figure 10.4 Class-Status Report in TOAM Arithmetic

The next column (SE) presents the number of sessions (10 minutes each in TOAM Arithmetic) the pupil has worked with this courseware since the beginning of the school term.

The last 16 columns present the student level in each one of the 15 topics that characterize the parallel-sequences structure of this course, as well as the student's average level over all the active topics (AV). This is the main information conveyed by the situation variables. Each sequence of exercises, corresponding to a specific topic, starts at a minimum grade level and ends at a maximum grade level. For instance, topic 2: Addition and Subtraction up to 20, starts at grade level 1.0 (the beginning of the first grade) and ends at grade level 2.9 (the end of the second grade). Topic 15: Divisibility, Factorization and Powers, starts at level 4.3 (the third month of the fourth grade), and ends at level 7.9 (the end of the seventh grade). Now we are ready to make a first pass over the report data.

Sally, student number 12, was presented with 32 exercises in the last session and answered 28 correctly. From the 4 exercises wrong, she answered 3 incorrectly and did not answer 1 of them within the time limit. Sally has completed 45 sessions, and her average level is 3.2. With respect to the subset of topics presented, we may see that she is working at level 3.4 in topic 1, at level 3.3 in topic 3, at level 3.1 in topic 4, and at level 3.0 in topic 14. The "H" under topic 2 stands for "High," meaning that she has already finished this topic. The "L" under topic 15 stands for "Low," meaning that she is still working below the entry level for this topic. A similar analysis may be performed for Johnny and Mike.

You may see that some of the topic level entries are flagged. The meaning of the flags is as follows: Sally has the entry 3.4^ under topic 1. The "^" indicates that she reached mastery at level 3.4, was promoted to the next instructional block in the sequence of exercises for topic 1 (level 3.5), and failed there drastically (e.g., she incorrectly answered the first three exercises she was presented with). Then a tactical retreat is called for. Sally was returned to level 3.4, and the teacher is notified by this report that she has to prepare Sally to cope with the difficulties of level 3.5.

Johnny has the entry 4.1* under topic 3. The "*" indicates that this topic has been closed by the pedagogical model. The reason for the closing is that Johnny, after reaching mastery of the exercises at level 4.1, was promoted to level 4.2 and, like Sally in the previous example, failed and was returned to level 4.1, with the corresponding teacher notification on the report. Time goes by, Johnny completes (among all the other exercises he is receiving for the different topics), a new mastery-testing sequence in topic 3 and, as predictable, shows mastery. So, he is promoted to level 4.2, and he fails again. Down goes Johnny, the teacher is notified, and the cycle continues. At some point in this seesaw, the pedagogical model decides that:

1. It is totally useless for Johnny to continue practice of topic 3 at level 4.1.
2. The teacher must help Johnny.

At this point, topic 3 is closed until the teacher provides guidance to Johnny and re-opens topic 3 (using an appropriate system command).

Mike has the entry 6.6< under topic 14. The "<" indicates that Mike is having trouble at this level. This is detected by the pedagogical model because too many mastery-testing sequences have been presented to Mike without his reaching mastery. This is, again, a call for teacher help.

It is important to note that the flags add a dynamic component to the static description provided by the levels presented in the report. In addition to *where* the student is, the flags provide information on *how* he is performing. This dynamic information is presented only when critically needed.

Another type of information that may guide the teacher in helping the student appears under the O/W heading. Johnny has "timed-out" six times: six out of nine exercises were judged wrong because he did not answer within the allotted period. The teacher may increase Johnny's time-factor performance parameter, thus allowing him a longer period of time in which to answer each exercise, and follow up his performance during the next sessions to see whether it improves. Note that this performance parameter is local to the Arithmetic course, while learning-style parameters are global to all the courses.

The class-status report provides a wealth of information to the teacher, who should use it to provide assistance, remedial help, explanations, and guidance to every student as needed. Furthermore, the teacher may profit from this information to plan appropriate instructional activities for the students in the class and to organize groups of students who may learn a topic together or jointly develop a project or receive a common explanation. This is auxiliary CAI at its best. The system designer should be careful when designing this type of report, in the sense that an information overload may antagonize the teacher—who will then ignore the whole report.

Progress (or Pacing) Report. The class-status report describes the situation of every student at a given period of time. A complementary type of report may be produced to describe the students' progress in a given period, usually since the beginning of the school term. The general structure of this report is similar to the one presented on Figure 10.4, with the exceptions that the R/T and O/W will not be present and that the topic entries will not be levels but rather the difference in levels between the present situation and the one that existed at the reference point. When progress reports are desired, the system must store copies of the student records with the data they contained at the required reference instances.

A less sophisticated, but very practical way of recording the students' progress, is for the teacher to manually fill out a "Progress Chart," like the one presented in Figure 10.5. Each pupil's average level at month's end is obtained from a corresponding class-status report.

P R O G R E S S   C H A R T

Subject: ARITHMETIC

School _____   Teacher _____

Year _____   Class _____

Pupil		Pupil's average level at end of month									
Number	Name	Sep	Oct	Nov	Dec	Jan	Feb	Mar	Apr	May	Jun

Figure 10.5. Progress Chart

Student Report. The data stored in the student record allows for individual reporting. For instance, using the educational history information, it is possible to print or to display a report where, for each piece of courseware, a line would be printed under the appropriate column headings, showing name, starting date, finishing date, interaction time, grade. We have listed interaction time as the only data pertaining to performance, but if the system is organized in such a way that performance on different concepts is quantifiable, then this information would be printed also. It is possible for the teacher to indicate a time period, and only the courseware studied during this period would be listed.

This report allows the teacher to follow up on a student's performance at the CAI facility in general and to decide whether the activity is satisfactory or whether it is below expectations. If the instructional blocks can be assigned weights (in some conventional unit), the teacher can establish a target for each student (the number of units by a certain date), and the system could report on students who are performing below teacher expectations. The teacher expectations can be rationalized by making use both of courseware statistics (particularly in terms of the distribution of the time required to learn each instructional block) and of each student's educational history.

Reporting to the Principal. Usually a school principal does not deal with 30 students but with 30 classes. The information reported should allow for supervision and for provision of guidance to the teachers, without reaching the level of detail presented in the class-status report. An illustration is presented in Figure 10.6, which is an example of a TOAM Arithmetic principal's report. The report contains global statistical information about class performance, plus a histogram presenting the pupil-level distribution. Each "*" corresponds to a pupil, and it is printed in correspondence with the pupil's level. The example presents real data, resulting from the activity of a fourth grade in an underprivileged area, at the end of the initial placement period just after the TOAM system was installed. The level dispersion is typical for this type of population.

HISTOGRAM REPORT

Subject: Arithmetic

School: x   Teacher: y

Class: 4 C   Date: u

No. of pupils: 26   LEVEL

Average no. of sessions: 12   Average: 2.77
                                                            Standard deviation: .56

LEVEL DISTRIBUTION   2.0   !**
                         2.1   !*
                         2.2   !
                         2.3   !**
                         2.4   !**
                         2.5   !***
                         2.6   !**
                         2.7   !*****
                         2.8   !*
                         2.9   !*
                         3.0   !*
                         3.1   !*
                         3.2   !*
                         3.3   !
                         3.4   !
                         3.5   !*
                         3.6   !*
                         3.7   !
                         3.8   !
                         3.9   !
                         4.0   !*
                         4.1   !
                         4.2   !*

Figure 10.6. Principal's Report

Similarly, pacing information may be compressed for presentation to the principal, using the data described in the section, "Progress Report."

Test Reports. The integration of tests within a CAI facility was described in Chapter 9. In terms of the data structure we described, there is no need for additions, because test results may be stored in the "Educational history" segment of the student record (Figure 10.3). Each test is considered a different piece of courseware. In terms of reporting, the possibilities vary according to what the system knows about the questions themselves.

In the most trivial case, the system knows nothing about the questions, and the information stored for each student is which questions were correctly answered and which were not. In this situation the test report may be built as a table (students versus questions), where each entry would show success or failure. In addition, average percentage correct may be printed for each student and for each question. If each question were assigned a different number of points, then the total points each student gets would also be printed.

In TOAM's Test and Question Bank, the questions are indexed according to a tree of topics. Furthermore, each expected incorrect answer is indexed in terms of the topics presumably not known by a student who selects such an answer. The teacher may assign weights to the questions and then, in addition to the information previously described for a simple report, the system will print another table (students versus topics) describing the students' performance for each topic that appeared in the indexing of the questions. The average over topics shows the teachers which topics were learned by the class and which were not, thus facilitating review decisions. The individual performances provide the data for specific remedial treatment.

The IMS Plus System for reading management marketed by Ginn and Co., maintains among its files the following three:

1. A Skills file, with a list of teaching objectives
2. An Inventory file, with an inventory of teaching materials
3. A Resource file, where skill objectives are cross-referenced with teaching materials

The system also includes a battery of tests, where the test items are associated with skill objectives so that, after a test is given, the system can display or print which skill objectives remain to be mastered by every pupil and can then assign to every pupil the teaching materials required to learn the missed objectives.

Table Structure for a RDBMS

Figure 10.7 shows how the school data structure could be organized using a relational database management system. Familiarity with RDBMS is assumed. For a bit of variety we have switched the environment to high school, so that classes have several teachers, lectures are given in different rooms, and different students in the same class may have different schedules. The focus is thus not on classes but rather on courses. A course has a teacher, an assigned meeting place, and a group of students. Viewed from the student's standpoint, each day of the week is divided into periods, and for each period the student is assigned to a course. The primary-school concept of a class has vanished. Scheduling of students is done individually, partly by computer and partly by hand, and it is usually impossible to satisfy every personal desire.

Our attempt here is not to provide a complete structure description but rather to give the reader its flavor.

The names of the tables are printed in capital letters, followed by the field (column) headings of the different records (rows). Some fields may be followed by the word *unique,* indicating a one-to-one correspondence between the data in this field and the object it is associated with.

PERSONNEL

Personnel id (unique)
Name
Position (e.g., principal, secretary, teacher, . . .)
Address
Phone number

COURSE PARAMETERS

Course name (unique)
Course level
Number of credits
Type (regular, honors, advance placement, remedial)

COURSE SCHEDULE

Course name (unique)
Teacher's personnel id (unique)
Room number (unique)
Day
Hours

COURSE REGISTRATION

Course name (unique)
Student id (unique)

STUDENT PERMANENT DATA

Student id (unique)
Student name
Address
Phone number
Birthday
Biological father's name
Address
Phone number
Biological mother's name
Address
Phone number
Active father's name
Address
Phone number
Active mother's name
Address
Phone number

Continued on next page

Figure 10.7. School Data Structure for an RDBMS

STUDENT PEDAGOGICAL PARAMETERS

> Student id (unique)
> Pedagogical parameter name
> Pedagogical parameter value

STUDENT EDUCATIONAL HISTORY

> Student id (unique)
> Courseware id (unique)
> Starting date
> Finishing date
> Interaction time
> Grade

STUDENT MEDICAL DATA

> Student id (unique)
> Vaccinations
> Allergies
> Special medicines
> Family doctor
> Person other than family to notify

Figure 10.7. *(Continued)*

COURSEWARE ADMINISTRATION

Information about courseware must provide support in two important areas: assignment of appropriate courseware to each student and courseware improvement. Part of this information is defined by the authoring team, and part is collected by the system during the instructional process.

File Structure

The courseware data is usually distributed in several files. We begin by presenting, in Figure 10.8, a possible structure for the records of a top-level courseware file.

The record is headed by the courseware name, and followed by three components used for matching this courseware to prospective learners. The first one gives a broad definition of the population, which could be specified, for instance, in terms of class grades. The second refers to the student history. The prerequisite courses may be defined in terms of courseware studied on-line, but they may also include courses studied outside the CAI system, if provision is made for the up-to-date recording of student activities. The prerequisite conditions may be stringent or may be recommendations related to the student's pedagogical profile.

The courseware is divided into units of interaction with the learners. Each unit has two "filtering" components, followed by pointers to the additional courseware files. The Library contains the actual programs and content data required for the in-

---

Courseware name
Target population
Prerequisite courses
Prerequisite conditions
(*) Unit record
      Prerequisite units
      Population parameters
      Pointer to Library
      Pointer to Statistics file
      Pointer to Interaction file

Figure 10.8. Courseware Record

---

structional interaction. The Statistics file records usage data in terms of number of students and, for each student, the interaction time and the options or answers selected within a standard frame structure. The Interaction file is used for nonstandard structures and stores protocols of student-system dialogues.

Information Usage

The first possibility that we mentioned, with respect to utilization of the data stored in the courseware records, is that of matching courseware to students. In the school of the future, the student record presented in Figure 10.3 will be fully defined for each student, with its data being updated all along the instructional process. A system pedagogical model will monitor the student record and, when pertinent, will suggest the study of the courseware units that match the student profile and whose prerequisites have been satisfied.

The second possibility is that of making use of the statistical information collected in order to improve the courseware. This is being done in the schools of today,[2] and it is critical for large courseware structures.

The initial-placement algorithms for sequence structures, presented in Chapter 9, were based on the "increasing-difficulty" condition. This condition is expressed in terms of a diminishing success rate when a student population is tested over successive blocks in the sequence, at a given moment in time. An alternative view is that, in order to reach the same level of success, each new block in the sequence requires additional instruction. Paradoxically (in appearance), the performance statistics for the successive blocks in a sequence structure that satisfies the increasing-difficulty condition, collected from students who are learning all along the school year, should show an average rate of success that fluctuates within similar bounds. Needless to say that when the first versions of the TOAM courseware in Arithmetic, or Reading Comprehension, or English as a Foreign Language (EFL), with thousands of exercises each, were field-tested, the rates of success exhibited more peaks and valleys than plains. The process followed at C.E.T. was to sort the statistics and provide the development teams with

---

[2]This is feasible only when the developer keeps links with the schools. It is very hard to do for off-the-shelf lessonware.

the "ten percent tails," meaning the harder 10 percent and the easier 10 percent among the exercises. Note that while an exercise with 30 percent of correct answers may be frustrating, an exercise with 100 percent of correct answers presents no challenge whatsoever. These exercises were reworked or repositioned in the grade structure, and a new version was field-tested. After five years of iterating this process, a relatively "smooth" version was obtained. As a help for the multiple-choice exercises, used in Reading Comprehension and in EFL, the authoring teams received a printed report indicating the distribution of answers over all of the distractors. Wrong answers that attract too many students are carefully analyzed, and the wording of the exercise or the distractor is changed accordingly.

An additional statistic that may be used to check difficulty in the case of exercises, and the most important one for expository materials, is the average interaction time. This applies particularly to reading time, normalized according to the text length. As reported in Osin (1976), the statistical detection of difficult frames (which considered interaction time, utilization of system help, and wrong answers in the case of exercises) pointed to a frame where a line was missing because of a typing error.

When complex interactions are allowed, the statistical analysis is less relevant, and it is customary to store the protocols of all the dialogues. If natural-language interaction is used, the system stores all the unresolved student inputs, which are then used by the developers to refine the language-processing algorithms.

HISTORICAL RECORDS

There is no need to keep on disk all the student and courseware data collected over the years. At the beginning of each school year part of this data may be stored on magnetic tape, retaining only one year of historical data. If the situation in terms of magnetic disk space is critical, the decision may be even more stringent, keeping on disk only the information related to the current year. Although prices for magnetic tape storage are much lower, a reasonable limit applies also. The decisions on what to store and what to purge are different from the school standpoint and from the developer standpoint. The courseware statistical data used for courseware improvement by the development team, for example, is not used by the school. This is the type of data that the school will not store and that the developer will purge once it has been used and the courseware has been modified accordingly.

The opening of a new school year requires the registration of the permanent data of new students and teachers, while the information of students who finished or ceased their studies and that of teachers who left is transferred to tape. In addition to this, class or subject registration must be performed for every student, and classes or subjects must be assigned to the teachers.

Having historical records of student performance over several years allows for longitudinal studies, where the pattern of student progress in different courses may be analyzed. For example, it is important to have more research in the area of performance correlation between topics, as well as on whether the classical student classifications (like low achiever, average, or high achiever) are robust over time.

Another important consideration for keeping historical records is that they make possible a "time-series" experimental design, where the introduction of new methods or materials may be evaluated in terms of the changes it produces over the previously registered rates of progress (Campbell & Stanley, 1963).

SYSTEM ACCESS

In the complete instructional facility we envision, students have access to resources that coexist with data files where student performance data and student grades are being stored. This potentially dangerous situation asks for a hierarchy of privileges, guaranteed by different levels of passwords, in such a way that students have access to the subset of the resources required for instruction, teachers have access to an additional subset, with the possibility of assigning values to certain student and courseware parameters, instructional administrators have access to even broader resources, particularly in reference to statistics reports, and finally, the system programmers have the widest access to the system. Automatic registration, preferably at a very secure level, of all the interactions related to sensitive information, may add another level of safety to the system.

SUMMARY

Instructional administration is the purpose of the Administration facility introduced in Chapter 7. In the current chapter we gave you a detailed description of the files and processes required to provide pedagogical support to students and teachers, and statistical information to the decision makers and the development team. For clarity of presentation, school administration and courseware administration were presented in separate sections. The third section described the storage of information over long periods of time, and the fourth closed this chapter with considerations related to system access. The language and the examples in this chapter referred to a school environment, but the main ideas may be applied without difficulty to an industrial, commercial, or military situation.

PART IV
System Implementation

Pedagogical theories, and the algorithms which express them, must find a concrete representation in the instructional materials that are the result of the design process we have been analyzing. Form serves function, and Chapter 11 is devoted to the form of the instructional dialogues. Chapter 12 describes the tools of the trade for building computerized instructional materials, and Chapter 13 provides some concrete examples of final products that illustrate the concepts presented in this book.

CHAPTER 11

Student-System Interface

The greatest intellectual challenge of our time is not how to design machines that behave more and more like humans, but rather, how to protect humans from being treated more and more like machines.
—Philip W. Jackson, "The Teacher and the Machine,"
Horace Mann Lecture (1967)

This is a chapter about media, by which we mean information-delivery technology.[1]

Computers deliver information, but they also possess a property shared by few other media: they are information-processing machines. A strong dichotomy exists between, on the one hand, media that present information to humans and, on the other hand, media with which humans interact. Computers belong to the second class, and what gives CAI its distinguished status when compared with other methods of instruction, is precisely its being based on interactive media. We agree with Schramm's (1977, p. 12) assertion that there are no instructional media, only media that can be used for instruction; but every medium has different intrinsic possibilities and requires specific treatment for these possibilities to be fulfilled.

Nobody will deny that students can learn from poorly written and ugly screens and that they may do so even if they have to endure headaches or stiff necks produced by wrongly designed terminals, but our task is to create an environment that will not only instruct, and do so efficiently, but will also educate by example in such relevant areas as good taste, intellectual style and respect for another human being. With this objective in mind, in this chapter we try to provide sound advice on several aspects of the learner-computer interaction. When possible, this advice is derived from psychological principles; when not, from controlled experience. If neither of these sources was available, we carefully weighed whether to tell you our opinions or to refrain from doing so.

Let us clarify that we will not expound on the media selection considerations that were presented in Part II. We assume here that a stage was reached, in the instructional design process, where CAI was selected as the optimal process for a given instructional objective, after due consideration of the possible alternatives. In this chapter we analyze the physical, functional, and esthetic aspects related to the human-computer interaction.

---

[1]*Media* has several dictionary meanings, including its popular use as "mass communications."

207

A CAI student terminal has a variety of information-delivery possibilities (visual, aural, or mechanical), which may reach the learner in different packagings (written or spoken text, graphics, animation, music, film, robot activities, etc.). The terminal may also have a variety of devices to allow for student input (keyboard, pointing devices, voice, sensors, etc.). We try to provide guidelines for the development of a fruitful instructional dialogue, trying to optimize the usage of the input/output devices.

In the absolute majority of cases, the information is presented on a visual-display unit (VDU), and learner input is received via a keyboard. There are variants, like multi-terminal displays, simulator consoles, different display technologies, and various input devices. Although the bulk of our description is devoted to standard equipment, we also review alternatives, trying to provide decision criteria for their selection.

INTERACTION LANGUAGES

In this section we analyze the types of dialogue that may arise between the learner and the computer by following the possible paths presented in Chapter 7 (Instructional facility). The dialogue starts when the student executes a log-in procedure by issuing a command, followed by the student-identification parameters (name or number, eventually a password). The system checks the input parameters and issues either a validation response or an error message.

In case of error, the student may reenter her parameters. When the access is validated, and according to the system organization and student status, the student may be assigned (by the pedagogical model—PM) to a given instructional unit, or the student may be allowed to use computational resources as she wishes.

The student determines which resources to use in two possible ways (or a combination of the two):

1. SELECTION: The computer presents a set of possibilities (by way of menus, icons, or labeled[2] keys), and the student selects one.
2. GENERATION: The computer presents a prompt, and the student types a command and, if required, its parameters (which may be prompted also).

This dichotomy is important because the design of the interaction for the case where a student selects an option is very different from that required for the case when she must generate an input.

According to the student's input, she may be presented with an instructional unit or with access to tools or other computational resources. In the first case the system will usually display explanations and exercises, and the student will answer with commands or answers to exercises or requests for advice. In the case of tools or similar resources, each one is provided with an ad hoc language, through which the user may operate the tool or the resource, enter data, or request advice.

It is the designer's responsibility to assure that the instructional dialogue is conducted in such a way that the learner always knows at which level she is, and what the options and expectations are. The purpose of the instruction is expressed in objectives

---

[2]A labeled key is a special-purpose key, with a command engraved in it (e.g., HELP, BACK, ERASE).

over a certain area of knowledge, and we should strive not to add extraneous tasks like the learning of a complex interaction language.

The main design problem arises from the contrast between human flexibility and computer rigidity, and it is clear that the computer side is usually the guilty partner in unsuccessful dialogues. It is not by chance that the interface terminology is computer-centered. As Nickerson (1986) remarks:

> Thus when we use the terms *input* and *output* in this context, we almost invariably mean input to the computer and output from the computer. The challenge for human-factors people, however, is to assure that output from the computer constitutes suitable input for the person and, conversely, that input to the computer is something that is convenient for the human to put out. (p. 89)

In the scenario just described, we may identify the following types of computer output: prompts, menus, icons, validation messages, error messages, execution acknowledgment, results of command execution, help or advice messages, explanations, and exercises or tasks assigned to the student.

Student inputs belong to one of three categories: commands, answers, or free input. Commands (or requests, to use a more polite form of expression), prompt the computer to provide a service or to change the interaction style; answers are student responses to exercises; and free input is input that is not meant to be "understood" by the computer program handling the interaction (i.e., it is not evaluated by the computer). A typical example of free input is a text created by a student using a computer editor.

In the following sections we analyze commands and answers separately—free input is not dealt with.

The system expectations differ for the different types of input. For instance, when the system is waiting for a command, this is what the student must provide—unless she makes a mistake; on the other hand, when the system is waiting for the answer to an exercise, it may allow the student to enter a command (e.g., a REVIEW command). To avoid a command being incorrectly judged as an answer, a clear system distinction must be provided between answers and commands.

Student Commands (or Requests)

As Card, Moran, and Newell (1983) point out, instead of "operating" a computer we must "communicate with" a computer, if we are to take advantage of the possibilities inherent in this media. Communication may be smooth and elegant, avoiding unnecessary failures, if the designer has a good model of the user and helps the user in developing a correct model of the computer.

The major problem in developing "a good user model" is that users come in many models, from the most sophisticated to the most naive. The best approach is to allow for different types of interaction according to the user's preferences. Of course, this requires a larger investment, and when the user population belongs largely to a certain type, the decision may be to design the interaction procedures with this type in mind, thus optimizing the investment. In most cases, the distinction between sophisticated and naive users separates merely the permanent (or at least frequent) users from the casual or occasional, reminding us that one of the main differences between expert and novice behavior is simply practice.

In general terms, there are two golden rules the designer should keep in mind:

1. CONSISTENCY: The same word should have the same meaning in different situations and the structure of similar interactions should follow a constant format. This is reflected, for instance, in our recommendations on functional areas.
2. FRIENDLINESS: The interaction should be designed in such a way as to be easy to use and its language easy to learn. Help should be easily available. The messages to the user should be comprehensible and conducive to positive or corrective action. User errors that lead to catastrophic results should be filtered. Friendliness may lack a formal definition, but in essence, all the advice we provide in this chapter tries to help in developing friendly systems.

Commands to a system, like other inputs, can be specified in two ways: by generation (typing a command defined within a command language), or by selection (from a menu, from a set of icons, or from a set of labeled keys).

In general, command languages are more adequate for experts, and selection methods are more adequate for novices. Selection methods are easier to use because all the options are explicitly presented to the user, thus placing a lower load on the user's memory: only recognition is required, not recall. Commands are fast to use, and so are selection methods when the selection may be done in one step. On the other hand, there are many cases where the selection of an option may require the traversal of several menus, while a single command could have achieved the same result in a much shorter time. In favor of menus it must be said that the initial time investment required to learn a command language is higher than that required to be able to navigate in a menu-driven system. Also, when returning to a system after a period of inactivity, it takes longer to remember commands than to be able to select options.

Command languages are more error-prone than selection methods, so the designer's attention should be focused on designing messages for error treatment and prevention. Since an ounce of prevention is worth a pound of cure, it is useful to ask for the confirmation of commands with irreversible effects. A typical "tragedy" is to mistakenly delete a file that contains the fruits of many hours of work, and this risk may be diminished by asking the user: "Are you sure you want to delete file x.y?" In terms of error treatment, different users may require a different level of detail in the messages. Probably the best approach is to design error messages at two levels. The first level, which is always presented, will suffice for the expert user most of the time. When this explanation is not enough, the user may ask for the second level also (which is what novices will usually do). Another possibility for tailoring the messages is to have different versions for different user profiles, which may be selected, for instance, in a log-in file.

The third way of selecting commands, by pressing labeled keys, is very much CAI-oriented. Several systems were designed with special keyboards, where fixed keys were assigned to a variety of commands (for an example, see Figure 11.1). The advantage is twofold: first, the distinction previously mentioned between commands and answers is immediately obtained; second, no special language or menu structure is required. The disadvantage is also twofold: functionally, because the number of commands that can be entered this way is small and, economically, because special equipment has to

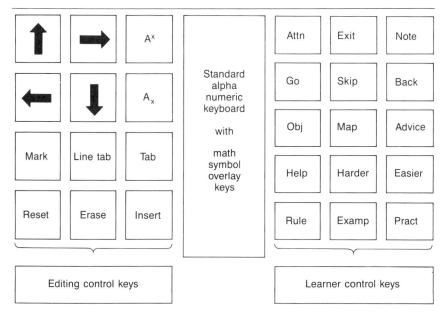

Figure 11.1. Keyboard Layout with Special Keys (TICCIT) (From C. V. Bunderson, 1973, The TICCIT Project: Design Strategy for Educational Innovation, ICUE Tech. Rep. No. 4, p. 16.)

be built, instead of buying mass-market products. We may argue that the education market is big enough to justify the investment in special purpose hardware (PLATO, TICCIT, and TOAM systems were originally built on this assumption), but present business reality provides no examples to support this thesis.

A compromise may be reached with standard commercially available equipment, using general-purpose function keys instead of labeled keys. Programmable function keys (usually labeled as PF*n* or F*n,* where *n* is an integer) may be assigned different meanings within various environments, and this justifies the term *soft keys,* that refers to keys whose functionality is defined by the software, as opposed to *normal keys,* whose meaning is engraved in their surface. The number of options grows considerably when the function keys are used in conjunction with other keys; a keyboard with 10 function keys, which may be used also with ALT, SHIFT, and CONTROL, provides 40 ad hoc functions for each application.

This compromise is not equivalent to labeled keys, because the user must remember which function corresponds, for instance, to F5. In fact, if no memory support is provided, soft keys are just aliases for command names, with no advantage except for the fact that they require just one key-press, and with the disadvantage that they have no mnemonic value. Paying a price, it is possible to approximate the advantages of the labeled keys. One way of doing it is to use a plastic overlay on the keyboard, which assigns to each soft key the name of the function it represents; another way is to display a menu—usually a horizontal one in the lower part of the screen—where each function is associated with a function key.

Student Answers

Student answers to exercises are classified with the purpose of providing different kinds of system feedback to the learners.

Answers may be separated into two categories: expected and unexpected. For expected answers, the author defines all the correct and incorrect inputs that her knowledge or experience may suggest. This definition may be done algorithmically or by listing the specific answers. For each correct or incorrect answer, the author must define an appropriate computer response. Knowing students (and authors), we also know that unexpected answers may appear. These unexpected answers may be of diverse types, requiring dissimilar system responses.

The system must include answer-processing routines for every type of expected answer. These routines are presented in Chapter 12, along with a more detailed taxonomy of student inputs.

DISPLAY DEVICES

Physical Aspects

The most widely used VDU (visual-display unit) is a cathode-ray tube (CRT), and the fact that the same technology is used in a popular mass media (TV) has benefited the educational (and administrative) world in terms of quality and price. Structurally, this device consists of a glass enclosure (see Figure 11.2), where the (approximately flat) display area is internally covered by phosphor. The phosphor, when "bombarded" by electrons "shot" from an electron gun that scans the display area, lights up, and this is what we see on the screen.

The dots that may be lighted on the screen (called *pixels*—short for *picture ele-*

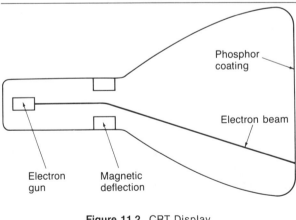

Figure 11.2. CRT Display

ments), constitute a rectangular grid whose resolution (or density) is limited by physical constraints but, within the ranges we are interested in, is very much a function of the price we are willing to pay. For home TV the number of horizontal lines on the screen is 525 according to the U.S. (NTSC) standard, and 625 according to the European (PAL) standard. This resolution is attained in two consecutive screen scans, with alternative (interlaced, in the technical jargon) horizontal lines. Humans do not feel the TV presentation as a sequence of discrete screens but rather as a continuous display, due to the persistence of the visual sensation on the retina.

Interlacing is not used for computer VDUs so that, if TV-like equipment is used, the resolution will be half of what we have become accustomed to in home entertainment. Furthermore, not all the scanned lines are employed (because of distortion effects at the borders), so that a long-time school favorite like the Apple II was designed with a resolution of 192 lines × 280 pixels/line. This is usually described as 280H × 192V, where H stands for Horizontal and V for Vertical. This relatively poor resolution is felt in jagged diagonal lines (an effect called "staircasing") when presenting graphics, and in a limited capacity for text (24 lines of 40 characters each). It is worthwhile to compare it with a pre-PC technology designed for CAI—that of the PLATO system. The square (plasma) display screen in the PLATO terminal, which appeared at the beginning of the 1970s, had a resolution of 512 × 512 pixels. When the Macintosh appeared in the market in 1984, its screen had a resolution of 512H × 342V. In 1987 the marketing of the Macintosh II started, with a resolution of 640H × 480V.

A comparison with the de facto standards established by IBM shows a low-resolution CGA[3] card with 320H × 200V pixels, and a medium-resolution EGA card with 640H × 350V pixels. The resolution for the VGA card, which characterized IBM's PS/2 family, coincides with that of the Mac II. To be fair in this comparison, there is an additional element that must be considered: the PLATO and Macintosh resolution correspond to monochrome presentation, all the rest to color presentation. Color requires a much higher investment, because each color pixel is composed of three physical dots, each on a different basic color (the RGB technology controls separately, for each pixel, the intensity of red, green, and blue, whose mix provides the color of the pixel).

The decision whether to use monochrome or color VDUs cannot be taken lightly. For the same resolution, which determines the readability of the screen, a color display may cost three or four times as much as a monochrome. Furthermore, the circuitry is more complex and its maintenance more delicate. For this reason, when most of the activity is in characters (letters and numbers), as happens typically in administrative activities, monochrome is used much more than color. It is not by chance that Apple's Macintosh was launched as the ideal office terminal with a monochrome display or that Apple's founder Steve Jobs was able to present his NeXT computer, in 1988, still with a monochrome display (although with gray levels). Monochrome is preferred when a higher resolution is required (more text or complex graphics), as with the workstations frequently associated with artificial intelligence projects, which have a typical resolution in the order of 800 × 1200 pixels. The range of terminals commonly encountered varies, therefore, from a display of about 50,000 pixels (Apple II), to about 1,000,000 (AI workstation, like Symbolics).

---

[3]CGA (Color Graphics Adapter), EGA (Enhanced Graphics Adapter), and VGA (Video Graphics Array) are the names of electronic boards (cards) that implement different display standards.

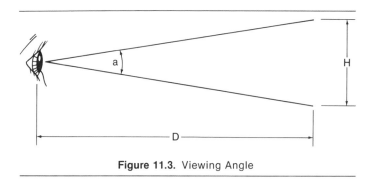

Figure 11.3. Viewing Angle

Resolution is one of the factors influencing visual aspect, but not the only one. Two additional factors are the size of the screen, and the distance between the observer and the screen. The geometry of the situation is depicted in Figure 11.3.

What actually determines our internal image of an object of height *H,* is the angle *a* at which it is perceived, which is a function not only of the height *H,* but of the distance *D* as well. To give a concrete example of how all of these variables interact, let us consider the problem of fusing the horizontal scan lines. If we sit at a recommended distance from our TV set, we do not see the horizontal lines as separated; rather, they are fused, providing a cinema-like quality. In this situation, the distance *H* between lines is equal to the height of the screen divided by the number of horizontal lines (525 in the United States), and the recommended viewing distance is 8 feet. In the instructional situation the height of the screen is typically half that of a home TV screen, and the viewing distance is 1.5 feet. A little bit of arithmetic shows that a vertical resolution of 1400 lines is required if we want to keep the aspect ratio of the TV situation. Fortunately we are very resilient, and we probably work with a different level of expectations in the two situations mentioned, because the resolution provided by the Mac II and the VGA card allows for a very pleasant presentation of texts and graphics.

Screen Design

Having previously described the components of the student-system dialogue, we now provide some advice on how to present such a dialogue on a computer-terminal screen. Although we tend to conceive the dialogue in terms of a computer presenting information on the screen, and a student answering by typing on a keyboard, the fact is that both the computer output and the student input are presented on the screen, because the input typed by the student is echoed on the display.

Functional Areas. All the types of information that were previously mentioned may appear on the screen at the same time: explanations or questions presented by the system (text and graphics), student answers to exercises, system feedback to student answers, student commands, and system responses to student commands, including error messages. The student may get lost among so many types of data presented in a variety of instructional situations. To help her we suggest two measures: the first is to add still another type of information, defining the student status; the second is to organize the information on the screen into functional areas.[4]

Each functional area should be identifiable by its location, its display characteristics (color, font, etc.), and its structure, when feasible. Size may change according to the application and the particular instance. A clean and simple partition is suggested, and consistent usage is essential. Thus the student focuses her attention automatically in the area where the currently active information is displayed.

We propose five areas: main workspace, student answer, student command, system response, and status.

1. Main Workspace. In the typical CAI dialogue, explanations or questions would be presented by the system in this area. Both text and graphics may appear. In terms of size, this is the largest area on the screen. If the student is working in free-input mode, this would be the area where input is displayed (e.g., a report being typed by the student). The main workspace may be structured differently according to presentation type. In science courses, for instance, a fixed subspace may be designated for diagrams or graphs; for multiple-choice exercises, a zone may be assigned to the question text, while the student options may be presented in a different zone (or window), differentiated from the text area by color, font, or graphic structure.

2. Student Answer. When a question has been asked, the cursor moves to a fixed functional area where the student answer is echoed. The exception to this condition arises when the input location is defined by the question itself, as in the case of arithmetic operations where each digit in the answer is placed according to a given algorithm, or in some types of cloze exercises, where the answers are typed directly into given blank spaces.

3. Student Command.

- If labeled or function keys are defined for the commands, no special functional area is required on the screen. The student receives feedback through the execution of the command, which may be echoed by the system also.
- If icons are used to represent commands, they are usually grouped in strips along the screen borders. It is good practice to highlight an icon when selected.
- If menus are the way to select commands, it is possible to organize them in the classical vertical list structure, or in the bar style popularized by Apple's Macintosh. Also here, the item selected should be highlighted.
- If the command has to be typed by the student, a functional area should be reserved for echoing the student input.

4. System response. Two possible responses may be assigned to the same functional area. The first is the system feedback to a student's answer; the second is a system message in response to a student command—an acknowledgment, an error message, or a request for additional information.

---

[4]The concept of functional areas is very well presented in Heines (1984).

5. Status. This information is useful for the student, the teacher, and the development team (for debugging purposes)[5]. Status information may be:

- Personal: Student identification (name, number, class).
- Topological: Where in the courseware structure the present interaction is taking place.
- Pedagogical: Whether the information on the screen is a direct explanation, a response to the student's request, or feedback to the student's answer to an exercise.
- Time: Time elapsed since the beginning of the session or, in some cases, time remaining for completion of a task (e.g., a test).
- Performance: For example, number of exercises presented and number of exercises solved correctly.

In Figures 11.4 and 11.5 we present two different examples of screen layout, which show the consistent use of functional areas, with icons for the provision of system services. The screens were designed for the third generation of TOAM systems, using MicroSoft Windows® as the presentation interface.

Icons must be selected for their expressive power, and their use should be consistent across the different types of interactions allowed by the system.

The use of functional areas allows the student to develop adequate reflexes. She will learn to look naturally for the expected information in a specific screen location and will be able to scan the screen intelligently when looking for additional data. On the other hand, this technique for screen design cannot help, and even has negative effects on, one of the classic problems affecting CAI designers: the small amount of information that can be presented on a typical screen. In effect, assigning fixed areas for different functional purposes diminishes the area available for the main presentation. A solution to this problem is to use dynamically "overlayed" windows (which became economically feasible only in recent years), instead of a static partitioning of the screen. In the overlay approach, where each new window may cover the preceding ones, it is possible to develop auxiliary dialogues without detracting from the area assigned to the main presentation. When the auxiliary dialogue ends, the overlayed windows disappear, and the main screen returns to its original state. Note that this advantage does not exist when the windowing system is organized in the "tiled" approach, where the screen is divided among non-overlapping windows.

Each overlay window may approach the size of the whole screen, but in this case the information on the successive windows is available sequentially and not simultaneously. It is not necessary, in an overlay windows system, to define each window with maximum size; successive windows may be disjoint or may overlap, according to the designer's or the user's decision, and may be opened and closed at will. When the information of different windows need not be presented simultaneously, overlapping successive windows provides a powerful metaphor of the instructional process, because each window represents a stage in the human-computer dialogue. Any stage may be reviewed and reconsidered by the learner by bringing its window to the foreground.

---

[5]In the TOAM system, teachers are instructed to copy the status information—which occupies the upper line on the screen—every time that something abnormal occurs or if a student complains about what she thinks is incorrect or unfair treatment of her input.

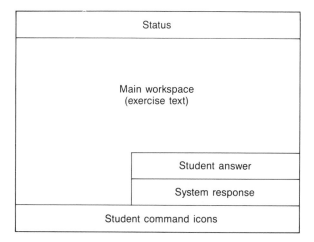

Figure 11.4. Functional Areas for Exercise Presentation

Text Presentation. There are no recipes for the creation of bright and clever explanations, but many good pieces of advice have been published that may help in avoiding the pitfalls frequently found in existing lessonware.

We have selected the following items, paraphrased, from Steinberg (1984) and Shneiderman (1987):

1. Be precise. Define the terms used. Avoid ambiguities.
2. Be explicit. Do not expect the student to know or to be able to add information you are not conveying.
3. Attune the reading level. The vocabulary and the syntax being used must be appropriate to the level of the learners.

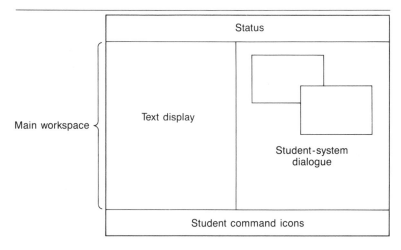

Figure 11.5. Functional Areas for Guided Reading

4. Avoid information overload. Design for minimal memory load on the user. When possible, make references within the same screen.
5. Keep the learner active. Ask frequent questions.
6. Be consistent. Terminology, abbreviations, formats, should all be standardized and controlled.
7. Help the learner. Present data neatly organized and with comprehensible labels.

and we add:

8. Try to focus each screen on one specific concept or idea.
9. Avoid gimmicks, distractors and baroquism. Clarity of design and simplicity of expression will convey your message more effectively than any mix of letter sizes and shapes, colors and noises.

Let us move now from style to some technical aspects. For a recent survey see Mills and Weldon (1987).

1. *Presentation speed.* Today's technology allows for the instant presentation of a complete screen. It is possible to display in bursts all the information required between student actions. The old discussions about optimal relation between student reading speed and presentation speed are remnants of teletype technology, with its (now) unbearable slowness. Every page on a textbook is printed before the student starts reading it, and nobody thinks that this has deleterious effects. Furthermore, movement is a distractor, so that being forced to read while text is being added to the screen can only be harmful:
2. *Fonts.* Be as near as you can to the excellence of the printed typography. For the moment it is necessary to compromise, because the resolution of the printed media is one order of magnitude above that of the standard screens. Nevertheless, reject gross limitations, like working in uppercase only. Lowercase letters should be designed with true descenders (e.g., g, p, y). For more information on this topic see Spencer (1969).
3. *Line structure.* Two elements help in readability: larger separation between lines and relatively long lines. If you have no control on line separation, consider writing with double spacing between lines. The optimal line length seems to be one that accommodates about 10 to 12 words or 60 to 70 characters (Spencer, 1969, p. 35). Experiments comparing lines covering the whole screen width with lines covering one third or two thirds of the screen width favored the longest line (Duchnicky & Kolers, 1983).
4. *Attention-getting devices.* This is one area where the computer display has a clear advantage over the printed media. In static terms, the screen has the usual possibilities for highlighting as are present in books, but the dynamic features characteristic of the computer environment add a dimension not available in print. The dynamic features are particularly useful for remedial loops, where the student attention may be focused on a particular expression by highlighting it during the remedial explanation. A list of attention-getting or highlighting devices follows. Their availability depends on the hardware being used, but this type of restriction will be clear to the reader (e.g., color cannot be used in monochrome screens).

a. *Fonts*. Present technology provides you with a variety of types, and you can build your own if a character generator is part of your development facility. It is possible to just change the font (e.g., italics, bold), but it is possible also to change the type size, for a stronger effect. Nevertheless, do not get carried away: it is not recommendable to use more than three or four fonts on a given display.

b. *Color*. Areas on the screen can be displayed over a different background color, or isolated words or expressions can be displayed with a different color alphabet. Again, not more than four compatible colors should be displayed simultaneously.

c. *Gray levels*. This and the following point are the substitutes for color used in monochrome displays. By changing the intensity of the electron gun it is possible to obtain different levels of brightness (or equivalently, of gray). In order to use this feature the displays mut be very well adjusted. In any case, do not use more than 2 levels of gray in standard equipment. Sophisticated cards, like VGA, support 16 levels of gray.

d. *Inverse video*. In this mode (also called "reverse video") the characters and the background switch colors (or intensity, actually, because this is typically a monochrome feature).

e. *Blinking*. The text is switched on/off alternatively. This is a very dominating tool, and its use should be carefully weighed. Shneiderman (1987) recommends a frequency of between 2 and 4 Hz.

5. *Dynamic text*. There are cases where information has to be presented in a relatively small window, in which case sequencing in time substitutes for sequencing in space. This is the situation, for instance, when we want to make a comment preserving essentially the whole screen. Diverse methods have been studied:

a. *Paging*. Paging refers to presentation of text in blocks; when the reader finishes a "page," the next page is presented; it is usually possible for the reader to page back and forth. Intuitively, the best situation is to read long pages, but Duchnicky and Kolers (1983) have shown that the number of lines presented in a window may be reduced to 4 without affecting reading speed (compared with 20-line pages). With less than 4 lines, reading speed diminishes.

b. *Scrolling*. Scrolling describes the presentation of text without page boundaries, that is, the text is organized as a long sequence of lines. Usually a fixed number of lines is displayed on the screen (or on a given window), and the user may shift the lines being presented. In normal scrolling the upper line disappears while a new lower line is displayed. In "smooth" scrolling, the jumps are not a line at a time, but rather a raster line at a time (i.e. the width of the electron gun scan). Users prefer paging to scrolling, and no advantages were found in using scrolling instead of paging. If it is to be used, then smooth scrolling is preferable to line-by-line (Mills & Weldon, 1987).

c. *"Times Square."* This is horizontal scrolling, named after the famous one-line display of news in New York City. The text enters from the right side and disappears at the left side, presenting a fixed length of characters to the reader. There is consensus in qualifying this as the worst of the methods.

d. *Rapid Serial Visual Presentation*. RSVP has lost its French etiquette meaning and has gained a new one among text-display researchers. Text is presented a few words at a time in a fixed space, each chunk replacing its predecessor. RSVP has the advantage that no eye movements are necessary, the eyes being focused all the time in the same place. The presentation speed may be adjusted by the reader (Muter et al., 1988). Optimal window size, in terms of reading comprehension, seems to be around 12 characters, that is, two or three words (Cocklin et al., 1984), which gives this method an advantage when the available space is minimal. Juola, Ward, & McNamara (1982) showed that, for equivalent reading rates, comprehension in the RSVP mode was the same as or only slightly below that obtained in page mode. Not all the studies performed reached the same conclusion (Mills & Weldon, 1987), but this is a line of work worth pursuing, because it shows that very unorthodox methods may succeed, even if they go against our intuitions.

Menus. The books by Shneiderman (1987) and Heines (1984) each contain a full chapter on menus, and we refer the reader who wants an in-depth analysis of this area to them. Following are some guidelines for their design.

Menus provide the learner with a direct and explicit selection procedure. We have placed menus within the commands techniques because it is in this context that the complexity of the situation requires nontrivial design considerations. A multiple-choice exercise may be also considered as a menu, but exercises deal with a very small number of options, and there are no technical problems with their display.

When the number of options is very high, the usual strategy is to build a tree of menus. The two contrasting dimensions in the design of the tree are breadth versus depth. A larger breadth (more elements for selection on the screen), results in a lower depth (fewer menus to navigate). On the other hand, the search over a long list is more prone to error or distraction and requires more time per menu. Several researchers seem to coincide in recommending about eight items per menu. This rule has to be applied intelligently, because the logical structuring of the tree, that is, the separation of items into coherent families, is equally important to menu size. Also to be considered is that a small departure from this rule may save another level in the structure. For instance, if we have 80 items for selection, we can organize them in two levels, by placing 9 or 10 items in some menus. By limiting each menu to 8 items we would require three levels.

The menu item names (or labels) should be carefully selected to avoid ambiguities and to help the user in the decision process. Nevertheless, selection errors may occur, and one of the friendliest tools that may be provided is an item that allows for the return to the previous menu (the father in the tree of the present menu node). In many cases of deeper menus, it may help to have also, as one of the menu options, the possibility of returning to the root (the initial or main menu). These "reverse direction" items may be distinguished by a different color or font. To this "lifesaver" device belongs the option of getting a graphical representation of the tree, highlighting the node where the user is presently located (or lost).

The classical structure of the menu items is as a list, but (at least) two other options are available:

1. *Embedded menus.* In this presentation mode, a coherent text is displayed on the screen, with words or expressions highlighted, as can be seen in Figure 11.6. These highlighted expressions are the menu items, and pointing to any of them will result in a support action (usually an explanation will be received by the

EVENTS: ANSCHLUSS   Page 2 of 7

The victorious ***Allies*** disapproved of such
a union and specifically forbade it in
both the ***Treaty of Versailles*** and the
Treaty of St. Germain-en-Laye. Austrian
nationalism remained weak throughout
the interwar period (1918-1939). During
these years, ***Austria***, like ***Germany***, gave
rise to a number of right-wing and
fascist political movements. Indeed,
Adolph Hitler's own ***Nazi*** Party had
a sizable Austrian branch. In 1934,
Engelbert Dollfuss, a member of the
Christian Social Party, destroyed the
First Republic's fragile parliamentary
democracy and established a right-wing
dictatorship.

Next Page   *Previous Page*   ***Return to FREUD, SIGMUND***

Figure 11.6. Embedded Menu (From L. Koved, & B. Shneiderman, 1986, Embedded menus: Selecting items in context, *Communications of the ACM* 29 (no. 4): 313. Copyright 1986 by the Association for Computing Machinery. Reprinted by permission.)

learner). Their advantage is twofold: from the user's standpoint her action is performed within the learning task, without the need of switching to another environment; from the designer's standpoint there is no need to invest in the intellectual effort we requested, in terms of defining well-balanced taxonomies, with appropriate names for each option. Embedded menus are not a general tool, and explicit menus will still be used in a majority of cases, particularly when dealing with large taxonomies, but this is a tool that may provide high user satisfaction when the instructional situation lends itself to it (see Koved & Shneiderman, 1986). The pointing action may be done by using a pointing device, like a mouse, but simpler methods may suffice, like moving the cursor through the use of the arrow keys.

2. *Pull-down menus.* As popularized by the Macintosh, it is possible to select a menu item, and to open it into a submenu. We think that a verbal explanation will not do justice to this type of feature. Most probably the reader has experience with this type of environment; if not, we strongly suggest "playing" with a Macintosh (or any personal computer with a similar window/icon/menu environment).

A final practical note refers to the selection mechanism offered to the user. The system may allow for keyed input or for pointing, but even if a pointing device is available, it is safer to allow also for selection from the keyboard. There are three standard ways of performing the selection: (1) by consecutively numbering the items and requesting the user to type the item number; (2) by assigning a letter to each item (usually its initial), to be typed by the user; (3) by allowing the user to move the cursor (using the arrow keys or any other keys selected) until it points to the item, and then hitting the RETURN or ENTER key.

The last mode is the least prone to error but the slowest. In the comparison between numbers and letters, the numbers are conceptually simpler, but the letters have a couple of points in their favor: they may serve as a mnemonic and, from the designer's standpoint, they may be assigned as a fixed-item parameter, irrespective of position in the menu (this is relevant when variable menus are generated by the system as a function of availability of options or of user parameters). A limitation of the letters is that more than one item may have the same initial and compromises have to be made to solve this type of collision (usually by typing a full word or enough letters to cancel the ambiguity).

Graphics and Animation. The use of graphics and animation may enrich presentations and make them more attractive to the learners. The limitation for their extended use has usually been an economic one, both in terms of equipment requirements and in terms of investment in their development. The development cost of a graphics-based display may be one order of magnitude above that of a text-based display, and an animation-based display may be one order of magnitude above that of a graphics-based one.

In every case, the golden rule is that the addition of graphics or animation should be the result of a design process whose conclusion is that the instruction of the topic being taught will benefit from it and not the result of a search for gimmicks or selling features.

Color. The use of color in graphics (and animated graphics) is governed by artistic considerations and by the inspiration of the graphics designer, thus falling outside the scope of this book. We concentrate on the use of color as relates to screen layout, windows, and text presentation.

Color may serve several purposes:

1. To enhance the "personality" of the different functional areas
2. To distinguish between different types of information
3. To establish a link between related pieces of information
4. To highlight important or critical messages
5. To aid in the comprehension of complex displays

To attain those purposes, color must be consistently and conservatively used. New designers get intoxicated by the richness of possibilities. Experienced designers work with compatible palettes, using usually not more than four colors per display. The combinations of background color with text (foreground) color should have enough contrast (do not use yellow on white!) but should not "shout." A norm whose validity is clear from a physical standpoint is to avoid the combination of red and blue. These colors are on the two extremes of the visible spectrum and require different focusing, thus straining the muscles of the eye. A norm of a different class altogether is to use the colors according to the culture of the users: many colors have connotations learned from real life (those of the traffic lights, for instance) and it is wise to use them accordingly.

As an example of a professional approach to color design, you may wish to consult the recommendations prepared by IBM (1987) for developers who work within IBM's S.A.A. (System Application Architecture). Each type of screen layout is supported by a palette. The palettes define background and foreground colors for each functional area or window in the layout. The palettes are named according to their predominant background color as: black, blue, cyan, and white. The moderation in the use of color can be seen in the fact that, when successive windows are overlayed, instead of presenting each in a different palette, only two alternating palettes are used.

White is frequently used as background, which returns us to the reading conditions we are used to in the printed media. Blue characters on white background is an excellent selection: first, for contrast reasons, and second, because blue is one of the three physical constituents of the color pixel and assigning blue means that only one electron gun is required, thus providing a much cleaner line than in the normal case, when red, green and blue are mixed.

For messages, yellow and red are used according to usual conventions: yellow for warning and red for a critical condition.

Before we get carried away by the beauty of color, let us remind ourselves that, for the same resolution, monochrome displays are cheaper, less bulky, and easier to maintain. There are color-dependent tasks where instruction is clearly improved by— and in certain cases almost impossible without—the use of a color VDU. In some other cases, and the TOAM courses in Arithmetic and Reading Comprehension are representative examples, the subject of instruction is not related to color, and in terms of cost-efficiency the reasonable decision is to design and market those courses for monochrome terminals.

A last warning: A significant proportion of the potential users have some type of color blindness, so that, whenever possible, discriminatory information, in terms of shape or background "texture," should be included as a color substitute.

ADDITIONAL PRESENTATION POSSIBILITIES

Videodisc

It comes naturally to mind that, having a TV screen for display, it is possible to present to a learner films produced using the same cinematographic techniques that have such a powerful impact in modern culture. The only request, from an instructional design standpoint, is to allow for student input, in order to preserve the central concept of the existence of an instructional loop.

The present videodisc technology answers to both requests. A videodisc may store a filmed sequence that may be presented to a student under her and the author's control. Furthermore, videodisc overcomes the limitation of videotape that hindered its possible instructional use: disk is a direct-access storage medium, while tape is a sequential storage medium. The result is that videodisc allows for very fast access to every frame (screen image)—independent of its position—while videotape has a relatively slow access time, that grows with the distance between the reading-head position and the required information, thus reaching limits that are incompatible with interactive instruction.

Today's standard videodisc includes 54,000 frames per side, plus audio. Each frame is accessible under computer control, and the videodisc may be displayed in motion or still modes. While motion usage is still relatively expensive, generic videodiscs with large collections of frames are available in such different areas as biology and art (e.g., the Washington's National Gallery of Art collection is available on one videodisc).

Instructional usage requires that the student station be provided with a videodisc player. To allow for a dialogue with the learner, either videodisc frames are overlayed with computer-produced texts and graphics, or two displays are used: one for the videodisc presentation, and the other one for the CAI dialogue.

Although the use of the full possibilities of videodisc would be ideal in subjects like history or geography, its cost[6] has made its utilization much more frequent in training than in general studies. A worker may get a filmed demonstration of how a component is assembled and, upon request, may be presented with a view from behind or from below. An employee may be trained in dealing with different types of customers. An executive may be trained in aural comprehension of a foreign language, by being confronted with a filmed interlocutor who engages her in the types of interaction that most probably would appear in a planned trip. In a course developed at C.E.T.'s Training Division, whose purpose is to raise the workers' awareness of safety procedures, the trainees "participate" in discussions between workers (personified by actors). When a trainee supports a position, the course presents her with a sequence reinforcing or rejecting it.

For a successful educational experience at the university level (irrespective of cost), see Smith, Jones and Waugh (1986). Since the humanities are usually underrepresented in CAI investments, it is particularly interesting to find a videodisc application in the teaching of art history (O'Connor, 1988–89).

Audio

Having a videodisc, audio comes very naturally into use.[7] This was not the situation with classical CAI, partly because the storage of sound is very demanding in terms of memory (some 8 Kbytes per second when using data-compression techniques). The price reduction in magnetic disk storage, the development of facilities for sound editing and compression, and the supply of boards for computer-controlled playback have made it presently possible to consider audio as an alternative channel for communication with the learner.

Audio requires additional hardware (a playback board and earphones), as well as

---

[6]Cost refers not only to the additional expenses for the student terminal but also to development costs, which are much higher than for standard CAI.

[7]Although the time matching between picture and audio requirements is not always easy.

more magnetic storage and a new class of personnel (professional speakers). Is it worth it?

In many cases it is. The clearest case is that of the learning of foreign languages, where the classical textual presentation may be strongly enriched by listening to dialogues, and by providing—upon learner request—the pronounciation of words or expressions. A second case is that of initial reading, and even more so for special populations where the text being read may be heard at the same time. In training situations, when the trainee is performing a complex task in an already cluttered display, verbal comments are ideal. The same applies when the trainee is engaged in a task that keeps him out of the terminal. Finally, it may allow for computer-assisted training in cases where the reading level of the trainee is very low.

A general case where CAI may gain from verbal explanations is that of short feedback comments accompanying students' activities. The messages should be clear and unambiguous, preferably selected from a fixed set, not only because of cost but also because, contrary to what happens with written text, they disappear once presented.[8] Thus, every effort should be made during the design stage to ensure that the messages are immediately understood by the learners. Whether the additional cost is worthwhile for this usage has to be decided case by case.

Mechanical

The computer output may be given in terms of commands that change the setting of electromechanical devices, thus allowing for computer-controlled experiments. To fit our conception of instruction, those commands should be under the control of an expert model. In practice, mechanical output is very unusual, and a frequent substitute is instructional simulations, which allow for student exploration without physical risks.

On the other hand, the accessibility of low-price robots opens interesting possibilities. Although LOGO's turtle, the most famous robot in the educational environment, was almost universally replaced by a much less attractive triangle on the screen, there is now a LOGO/LEGO product that allows children to build mechanisms activated by computer commands.

INPUT POSSIBILITIES

Input devices can be found in a variety of sizes, shapes, and functions, each one with different advantages and disadvantages in performance and price. Also, for a comparison of various input devices in terms of efectiveness, see Albert (1982), and Card, English and Burr (1978). This section presents the main features of each type.

Standard Devices

Keyboard. This is not only the most popular input device, it is the only one that appears consistently in every CAI terminal, while the other devices are optional. Its standard use is for text entry, but it may be used for pointing, by displacing the cursor on

---

[8]A command may be added for relistening.

the screen until it is over a selected area and then hitting the ENTER key. Special keyboards have been designed for instructional use, with labeled keys assigned to different pedagogical commands, as was shown in Figure 11.1. Modern keyboards have a set of function keys, that may be programmed for different actions, depending on the instructional environment. The combination of the keyboard with another input device has the disadvantage that the user has to take at least one hand off the keyboard (and this requires careful repositioning of the hand/s); an additional disadvantage appears when another object has to be grasped, as in the case of the light pen or the mouse—this does not happen with the touch screen.

Mouse. The mouse has become the most popular pointing device. Its displacement over the table (or any other surface) causes the displacement of the cursor over the screen. There are some initial adaptation problems, mainly due to the necessary mapping between different planes, the horizontal of the table and the vertical of the screen. On the one hand, left is left and right is right, but on the other hand, mouse toward the user means cursor down on the screen, and mouse away (forward) from the user means cursor up.

There is an "edge" effect also: for instance, if the mouse is moved toward the user and reaches the edge of the table before the cursor reaches its destination at a lower section of the screen, the user has to raise the mouse, replace it over the table at a further position, and restart the movement. The experience shows that, except for very extreme cases, the learners adapt rather quickly to the interaction.

Once the mouse has been used to place the cursor over the target, the user presses a mouse button, which indicates that this is her selection. There are one-, two-, and three-button mouses, according to the manufacturer's preference.

Trackball. This is a stationary, upside-down, mechanical mouse. The "belly" of the mechanical mouse is a ball that moves by friction when the mouse is displaced over the table. The trackball allows the user to move the ball directly, by rolling her palm or fingers over it. It is the preferred device for graphic designers, and its efficient use requires a higher degree of expertise than that demanded for the mouse. For instance, the ball may be hit and it will continue its movement because of inertia until it stops because of friction or because the user stops it. It is very fast, when used by proficient users, and it does not suffer from an "edge" effect. On the other hand, it is more expensive than a mouse. One advantage it has over the mouse is that it requires much less desk area.

Touch-Sensitive Screen. There are two devices where pointing does not require any mapping effort. They are the touch-sensitive screen and the light pen. The touch-sensitive screen detects the position of a finger when it touches the screen. The physical implementation may be done with an actual thin transparent screen on top of the terminal screen and with an embedded mesh of very thin wires, or by different methods, like the placement of a frame containing a strip of infrared emitters on two adjacent sides, with matching infrared detectors on the two opposite sides. In the first case, the finger pressure causes a short circuit between perpendicular wires, thus determining its location. In the second case, the finger interrupts the infrared rays, and the interrupted cells determine the coordinates of the finger location. Other methods are based on radarlike techniques.

Irrespective of its physical implementation, this device is the simplest conceptually and may be used with users who have minimal computer sophistication.

There are some drawbacks: its price is the highest among input devices, its resolution is relatively low, it is prone to errors due to the inclination of the finger (the designer must separate the target areas in order to avoid this problem), and the screens must be frequently cleaned because they get smudged by the users. Furthermore, the touch screen, and the light pen—discussed next—limit the distance between user and screen to an arm's length.

Light Pen. This is not a flashlight, as its name could suggest. It is, rather, a pen-shaped device with a lens at its tip, able to detect the presence of light. When the user places the tip over the screen, the light pen detects the passage of the electron gun when it lights the area pointed to by the light pen. Based on the timing of the electronic scan, the system computes the actual coordinates of the position where the lighted pixels were detected. The price of the light pen is one order of magnitude below that of the touch screen, but it has several disadvantages: as noted, it may be used to point only to lighted areas, it may provide an extraneous signal, it is uncomfortable to use over extended periods of time because of the arm-hand position, it is not well designed ergonomically to point perpendicularly to a vertical screen, and finally, small children tend to insert it in their ears, and the wax thus deposited over the tip prevents its functioning. Light pens are functionally better than touch screens in one aspect: their resolution is much higher.

Light pens have a switch that may be used for single action or for continuous action (to be used, for instance, when defining a path on the screen).

Graphic Tablet. The graphic tablet consists of a board and a stylus or a puck connected to the computer. The system is able to detect the position of the stylus over the board, and thus it may be used for such varied purposes as entering an answer to an exercise, entering the complete contour of a map of a country, or entering positioning data that defines a piece of machinery.

Speech. Speech recognition devices have been developed, able to recognize a restricted vocabulary (usually up to 100 words), after being "trained" by the user. The use for CAI is very limited, but training applications where the user gets her hands dirty (car mechanics, for instance) do benefit from the fact that the trainee may get explanations (visual or aural) by issuing vocal commands. Another situation where speech may provide a unique solution is that of physically impaired users who cannot make use of their limbs.

Special Devices

Many special devices have been developed for impaired learners, in each case according to the physical capabilities of the user. We do not delve into this issue.

ERGONOMICS

The study of the relationship between individuals and their work or working environments should be used to improve the learning environment of students. After all, we do agree with Williams James's idea that education is not a preparation for life, education is a part of life.

Environment

The student stations, in a CAI facility installed in a school, may be distributed over all the classrooms or concentrated in one classroom or laboratory. When they are concentrated, it is possible to prepare the room for its intended use. There are two global points worth mentioning: lighting and relative position of the stations. The VDU screen is a source of light, so that the considerations used for lighting a desk that will be used to write on, or to read printed materials, are not valid here. In a CAI classroom the lighting has to be indirect (typically toward the ceiling), and the windows must be curtained. These two measures are very important in order to eliminate, or at least to diminish, the most bothersome factor related to work at a computer station, which is the light reflected on the screen. The layout of the stations should minimize distracting effects. If stations are aligned as shown in Figure 11.7, the distance between students should be at least 4 feet. When stations are too close, there is a tendency for the children, particularly small ones, to take a look at what happens at the neighboring screens. Worse than that, it is not unusual to find children who hit any key at a neighboring station, the type of joke that produces not only an undesirable error but also a change in the concentration and aggressiveness of the fellow neighbor.

Two additional layouts, which are better in view of this problem, are presented in Figure 11.8. Fifteen-inch-high separation panels will interrupt the eye-to-eye contact without creating a cage feeling.

Student Station

American and European standards have been developed[9] for VDUs, and their recommendations are a good basis for the design of the student station. Nevertheless, those standards were developed for adult populations, whose variance is much lower than that of school-age learners. This is critical when the table and seat heights are considered; the relative heights for a 7-year old are very different than those for a 12-year old. Card, Moran & Newell (1983) recommend a head inclination of 20 degrees for physical comfort and an additional lowering of the angle of vision toward the screen of 15 degrees below the horizon. This adds to a 35-degree downward inclination, which demands very different arrangements for different child heights. A costly solution may be implemented using tables and seats of variable height. C.E.T.'s experience with this solution was not positive, because of the inordinate amount of time that children devote to height adjustments. Furthermore, the office chairs that were used for this experience had the usual rotating capability, which was enjoyed by the learners, creating a perpetual-motion environment.

In our opinion, the best compromise is to have fixed table and seat heights, allowing for comfortable legroom for the tallest students and providing a stairlike footrest, to avoid hanging legs that do not reach the floor. The thighs should be approximately

---

[9]American National Standard for Human Factors Engineering of Visual Display Terminal Workstations (July 1986) and Ergonomics Recommendations for VDU Work Places, European Computer Manufacturers Association (ECMA, TR/22, March 1984).

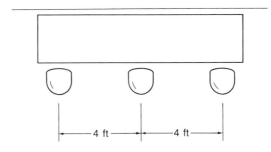

Figure 11.7. Contiguously Aligned Student Stations

horizontal. The additional condition is to have tilt-adjustable VDUs, in order to have the screen frontally facing each student.

Other recommendations:

1. The distance between the eyes and the screen should be about 20 inches.
2. Flicker (perception of periodic light variations) should be avoided. The present tendency to use a refresh rate of 70 Hz takes care of this problem.
3. Antiglare screens should be standard.
4. The screen should present, primarily, dark characters displayed against a light background.
5. The minimum height for an uppercase letter should be 3.7 mm, and the width/height ratio should lie between 0.67 and 0.75.
6. The character matrix should be at least 14 pixels high and 9 pixels wide. From those, an uppercase letter should have available at least 9 pixels in height and 7 pixels in width. For lowercase letters there should be space for true descenders.
7. The characters should be in sharp focus throughout the entire screen.
8. The terminal must not emit any disturbing noise.
9. The power consumption must be so low that fan cooling is not required.

The keyboard could require a complete chapter. We are stuck, for historical reasons, with what is called a QWERTY layout, whose design was defined by the attempt to avoid the old typewriter letter-levers banging into each other. There are no redeem-

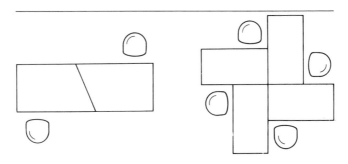

Figure 11.8. Two Examples of Student Station Layouts

ing features in terms of assigning the best positions (in terms of access time) to the most frequently used letters, nor in terms of mnemonics (an alphabet-ordered keyboard would avoid the random searches that characterize novice users). For an attempt to substitute the standard keyboard with a novel artifact, see Gopher and Raij (1988).

SUMMARY

In this chapter the theme changed from the high-level concepts presented in previous chapters (organization, taxonomies) to the concrete aspects of learner-computer interaction.

The first section described the languages that students use as input to the computer in two possible functional situations: issuing commands to obtain computer services and answering exercises within an instructional dialogue. Diverse forms of command specification were analyzed, distinguishing between labeled keys, general-purpose function keys, menus, icons, and typing of commands within a command language. Guidelines for the design, as well as pros and cons of these diverse forms, were discussed. Student answers were classified into expected (correct and incorrect) and unexpected. Treatment of answers is dealt with in Chapter 12.

The second and third sections were devoted to computer output, with the second section concentrating on visual display. The physical aspects of visual-display units (VDUs) were described first, followed by advice on screen design. This advice covered aspects of screen organization (with emphasis on the use of functional areas), text presentation in different forms, menu structures, and use of graphics, animation, and color. The third section succinctly described the possibilities opened by videodisc, audio, and mechanical output.

The fourth section covered a variety of input devices: the ever-present keyboard, the increasingly used mouse, the professionally preferred trackball, the intuitive (but expensive) touch-sensitive screen, the simple, direct, and problematic light pen, the multipurpose graphic tablet, and even speech and special devices.

The last section was devoted to ergonomics, a topic which unfortunately is ignored in too many cases.

CHAPTER 12

Courseware Development Tools

The effort of using machines to mimic the human mind has always struck me as rather silly. I would rather use them to mimic something better.
—Edsgar W. Dijkstra, On the Cruelty of Really Teaching Computer Science, *Communications of the ACM* (December, 1989)

The instructional materials have been written, the graphics and audio effects have been defined, the student-system interaction has been analyzed, the input/output instruments have been selected, and the instructional strategy has been planned. What remains is only to feed the computer with all the instructions and data that will allow for the student-computer instructional dialogue to take place.

How to do this is the subject of this chapter.

AUTHORING LANGUAGES AND AUTHORING SYSTEMS

Courseware production requires the integration of the computer programs that perform the following functions:

- Maintain the student-computer dialogue in each instructional block
- Determine the student path along the instructional blocks
- Collect interaction data and execute the required pedagogical administration
- Facilitate the usage of the system resources accessible to the student

Every computer is delivered with general-purpose programming languages (GPPLs), which allow the users to write the procedures that will satisfy their needs. The critical point, from a courseware author's standpoint, is whether, in addition to these GPPLs, the programming environment includes special-purpose facilities that help in the production process. The main reason for the development of these special-purpose facilities is that the logical constructs that appear in the GPPLs are optimized toward algorithmic design, but are relatively poor for handling the dialogue structure that characterizes instruction.

The first authoring facilities (from the early 1960s), provided *authoring languages* (ALs) that allowed for the easy coding of dialogues, following the structure described in Chapter 8 under "Address-oriented CAI." PLANIT may be taken as an example of these ALs. We want to differentiate the concept of authoring language from that of *authoring system* (AS). An AL provides the facilities for easy dialogue definition. An AS must provide support for all the functions required for courseware development, previously described, plus the standard services available in a software development environment in terms of project management, file handling, updating of versions, etc.[1]

According to our definitions, every AS includes an AL. Although it is conceivable that a gray area may exist where an enriched AL may be hard to distinguish from an impoverished AS, we think that the conceptual difference is important and helps the prospective author in his selection process. We would like to see a general adoption of these definitions, changing the existing situation of ambiguous usage.[2]

Powerful authoring systems are essential for the efficient production of courseware—so much so that professional development groups use hardware with more computational power for the development than for the delivery of courseware (Separated authoring was described in Chapter 7 under the section with that title.) As examples we may mention products offered by Authorware, Inc., whose Course of Action is used to produce courseware on a MacII with delivery on a regular Macintosh or an IBM PC; by Control Data Corporation, with development on a Cyber computer and downloading to a MicroPlato station, and by WICAT Systems, whose AS includes two components (WISE and SMART) running on proprietary hardware and producing courseware that may be downloaded to a stand-alone IBM PC or run on WICAT's time-sharing systems.

Every courseware function that can be performed by a standard component of the AS justifies careful developing and extensive debugging. Once such a component reaches a high level of reliability, every course that uses it will enjoy this reliability without additional cost. Consider, for instance, the collection of student answers and response times to be used for formative evaluation of the courseware. If the AS (in this case maybe an AL also) provides this function, the author has to worry about the dialogue only; on the other hand, if an author is using a GPPL it is his responsibility to determine the variables that will collect this information, write in each case the corresponding assignment statements, define the file structure that will record the information, and write the file-handling statements that will store the data collected.

In an environment where many courses are produced, the usage of standard components is reflected in large savings in programming and debugging time. Additional economic benefits accrue if the same development component may produce delivery modules for hardware from different manufacturers.

Why, then, are ASs or ALs not universally used?

Because every AS or AL imposes substructures or constraints on the programming environment. In many situations, particularly when developing courseware that is pedagogically oriented toward open activities of the learner, a GPPL may provide a cleaner and better structure and should be used without hesitation.

From time to time, another AS purports to have solved the limitations of its predecessors. In the initial and naive years of CAI the proliferation of authoring languages

---

[1]Authoring environment is sometimes used as a synonym for authoring system.
[2]For a different set of definitions, which we do not support, see Kearsley, 1982 (p. 429).

was so great, that Zinn (1971) mentions that more than 40 had been developed (''and the differences among them are not very great in most comparisons'' [p. 17]), while the 1973 Index to Computer-based Learning already listed 93. The Canadians, trying to impose some order over the chaos created by their southern neighbors, established a standard (ACIT, 1972), that gave birth to NATAL–74 (the NATional Authoring Language—Brahan et al., 1976). Although the majority of those 93 languages have died of natural causes, Locatis and Carr (1985) reported having identified more than 60 available authoring systems ''and undoubtedly more will appear'' (p. 29).

FUNCTIONAL COMPONENTS

Let us present, in Figure 12.1, a schema that describes, in very general terms, human-computer interaction. A specialized instance of this diagram was shown in Figure 7.1, when the Instructional facility was analyzed.

The cycle described in the figure starts either in the left upper corner or in the right lower one and continues until the system or the user (the student in the CAI case) decides to stop it. The following sections describe standard software components (usually present in the main authoring systems commercially available) that relate to the four processes presented in Figure 12.1. The styles for author control of these components may be classified using the interaction-language taxonomies presented in Chapter 11.

The power of an AS is not dependent on its operating style. What can be said is that menu-driven systems are easier to use for authors without programming experience. It is clear that such an author will not be able to use a QUEST feature such as the possibility of writing an external procedure in a Pascal-like programming language, to be called from a QUEST frame. To be blunt: sophisticated interactions require, in any AS style, programming support.

Presentation

The ''Presentation'' label that appears in Figure 12.1, and that gives its title to this section, must be understood in a very general sense as including visual information on

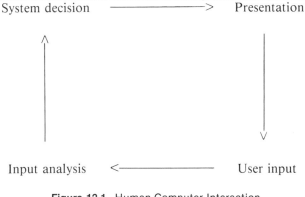

System decision ————————> Presentation

Input analysis <———————— User input

Figure 12.1. Human-Computer Interaction

> Three examples of authoring systems exhibiting different authoring styles are:
>
> cT, a command language developed at Carnegie Mellon University as an outgrowth of Micro-Tutor, a PLATO language developed at the University of Illinois. (Bruce and Judith Sherwood, who are the main figures behind the development of cT, moved from the University of Illinois computer-based Education Research Laboratory—where the PLATO system was developed—to the Center for Design of Educational Computing, at Carnegie Mellon.)
>
> QUEST, a menu-driven system inspired in WISE, the WICAT authoring language, and implemented for the IBM PC. (Vardell Lines, from Allen Communications, developer of QUEST, was originally with WICAT Systems.)
>
> Course of Action, an icon-driven system, implementing in a Macintosh ideas of OCD3, the authoring system developd at Control Data Corporation. (Authorware, Inc., which produces and markets Course of Action was founded by émigrés from CDC.)

the screen, the sound that may accompany it, and mechanical actions that may take place under computer control. Our discussion begins with the visual medium, which is the most widely used in instructional delivery and to which most of this section is devoted.

Display. Organizing the contents of a screen to be displayed consists of determining the texts and the graphics[3] that will be presented to a learner. The screen design considerations were discussed in the previous chapter. The screen production tools, to be described now, merit another dichotomy: authoring languages where the display is defined by language commands and authoring languages where the display is defined in a special-purpose editor.

Let us present a couple of examples, starting with one taken from Sherwood and Sherwood (1988).

The program:

```
unit       sample
at         140,100
write      This
           is an
           example
           that combines
           text and graphics
draw       125,58; 125,198; 323,198; 125;58
```

will produce the display presented in Figure 12.2.

The explanation of the commands is:

unit   Provides the name of the unit

at   Determines where the cursor will be positioned to start writing the text. The two arguments that follow are the x and y coordinates, starting from the left upper corner. The units may be assumed in pixels.

---

[3]In this context, we consider animated graphics and filmed sequences to be included in the term *graphics*.

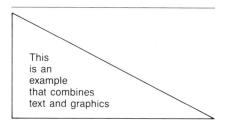

This
is an
example
that combines
text and graphics

Figure 12.2. cT Display Example

write   Defines the text to be written, in content and organization.

draw   Defines a polygonal, whose successive vertices are determined by the pairs of coordinates.

The same display would be obtained, in C.E.T.'s TOAM3 Authoring System (still under development), by issuing the command:

display sample

where "sample" is the name of a graphic object, which is built in a WYSIWYG ("What You See Is What You Get") editor.

We think that the separation between the "script," defined by the commands, and the "objects," defined in a WYSIWYG editor, is beneficial in terms of productivity and updating.[4] Nevertheless, an authoring language must provide the option of a command-defined display, to take care of the cases where the display changes according to variable values that are a function of the student input.

Irrespective of language style, the tools for display organization should include the following components:

TEXT FUNCTIONS
1. Selection of fonts (style and size) from the system library
2. Creation, storage, and usage of user-defined fonts
3. Text positioning
4. Text rotation
5. String concatenation
6. Selective erase
7. Special effects: changes in intensity, color, or blinking
8. Embedding within the display of computed values of program variables. A cT example, from the same source, is:
   write   The area is < |show, 13.7w| > square miles.
   which, for a value of w = 5, would print:
   The area is 68.5 square miles.
9. Embedding of system functions, like DATE.
10. Formatting

---

[4]To improve productivity, cT offers the option of automatic program generation, performed by the system while the author defines the display using a mouse.

GRAPHICS FUNCTIONS

11. Preparation of static graphics
12. "Import" of static graphics produced by standard packages
13. Preparation of animated graphics
14. "Import" of animations produced by standard packages
15. Integration with videodisc frames or sequences

Not all of these features are available in every authoring language, and it is up to the prospective author when selecting an authoring system to decide how important a feature that is missing is, according to his needs. Windowing environments provide easy-to-use tools to define windows (size, positioning, resizing, stacking—foreground/background—etc.) and menus (bars, pull-down, pop-up, etc.).

Sound. There are several methods for computer-controlled sound presentation, which differ according to contents (speech, music), to storage method (compressed audio, phonemes), and to fidelity (which affects the number of Kbytes required for each second of sound).

Let us start by describing a general-purpose system. The process starts (ideally) at a studio where the sound is recorded. The recording must include all the utterances required in the courseware, and the musical and sound-effect segments that will be presented to the students. The output is stored in analog form in a magnetic tape. Unfortunately, access time in a magnetic tape is very slow, because the tape is a sequential device. The solution is to digitize the sound and store it in a magnetic disc, which is a direct-access device. In this form we can reach every sound segment directly, without having to scan its predecessors (as in the tape). The analog-to-digital transformation is a well-known process and many firms provide the necessary hardware. There are electronics boards that can be connected to a PC slot and will do the job. From a user's standpoint, the main consideration is the price to be paid for fidelity, in terms of disk storage. High-fidelity recordings of music, for instance, reproduce frequencies of up to 20 KHz (20,000 cycles per second). For digital storage, the sound has to be sampled and (according to Nyquist theorem) the faithful reproduction requires sampling at twice the maximum frequency. Thus, if we use a byte to store the information of each sample, and we want to reproduce frequencies of up to 16 KHz, we need 32 Kbytes per second. This is not an exaggeration: studios that edit high-quality sound may work with rates of 100 Kbytes/second (!). It is clear that CAI cannot afford this rate but, fortunately, we can relax our demands without hurting the hearing sensation too much and, furthermore, there are engineering techniques for data encoding (pulse code modulation, delta modulation) that significantly compress the amount of storage. Thus, an efficient process can bring the storage rate down to 4 Kbytes/second. Hearing the stored sound requires a reverse process. The digitized and compressed audio has to be decoded (decompressed) and transformed back into an analog signal that will reach the earphones of the learner. There are electronics boards that perform both the encoding and decoding functions. Some of these boards allow for direct encoding from microphone input, storing the output on disk.

The usage within the dialogue program, that is, playing the sound to the learner, is done by a subroutine call, where an argument identifies the record, on the disk file, where the sound segment is stored. There is, usually, another argument to establish the pitch. The output of the digital-to-analog conversion is fed into a loudspeaker (or earphones, in a class environment).

If the sound required is only speech, further savings are possible. Special compression techniques have been developed, by modeling the vocal tract (linear predictive coding), that require only 1,000 bits (not bytes) per second. At a lower-quality level, it is possible to synthesize speech using phonemes, at a rate of 100 bits/second. A good survey of this topic can be found in Sherwood, 1979.

As well as generating sound from text (using grapheme-phoneme translation schemes), the computer may produce music starting from musical notation, if a music synthesizer is connected via an appropriate interface card. This capability has been extensively used for the teaching of music (e.g., Hofstetter, 1986).

Outside the realm of CAI, but worth mentioning for completeness, are the machines that may scan printed text and produce voice output. The Kurzweil machines are extensively used for reading to the blind.

Electromechanical Output. This type of presentation is not standard in authoring languages.[5] If the student terminal has slots available, it is possible to connect a transducer that will control an external device based on the values of program variables, calculated during the interaction. This type of interaction is usually programmed in a general-purpose programming language.

User Input Analysis

We begin by analyzing the tools necessary in an authoring system to cope with the functional diversity of student inputs. Later we look at the implications from a modal (device and response type) standpoint.

Functional Taxonomy. Student inputs may be classified as shown in Figure 12.3. The handling of commands was described in Chapter 11, "Student Commands (or Requests)." Here it suffices to say that it is very important for the authoring system to include the option (to be enabled or not, as an author's decision), of allowing for student commands in every stage of the instructional dialogue. This means that a student confronted with a task may utilize system resources, according to his personal strategy, in order to perform it. For instance, while working at a reading or writing assignment, the student should have access to an on-line dictionary; in solving a physics problem, access to a calculator seems appropriate. The facility that takes care of student commands should be transparent to the author when writing the scripts for the individual dialogues.

Moving to the treatment of answers, note that there are two dichotomies that are orthogonal: expected-unexpected on the one hand, and correct-incorrect on the other hand. The first one is the most important in terms of creating a smooth interaction.

---

[5]The reason for this is that very few instructional experiences have been developed using this type of output. In the near future, the field that seems to be expanding is the other side of the coin: input of physical measurements through adequate probes. Bob Tinker, at his TERC Laboratory in Cambridge, Massachusetts, pioneered this field, and in 1989 IBM presented its Personal Science Laboratory (PSL), a complete toolkit with probes, a control unit, and the programs to interface it to the IBM PC and PS/2 computers.

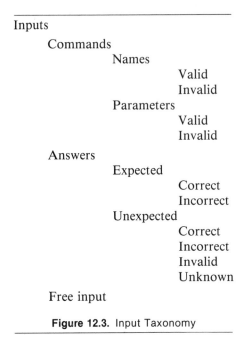

Figure 12.3. Input Taxonomy

The expected answers are those the author is able to predict, and for those a specific system response may be precisely defined. The unexpected answers may be accidental or may reflect an author's failure in not being able to predict them. Any authoring system should include the automatic recording of unexpected answers, to be analyzed by the authoring team so as to separate the irrelevant answers from those that should be incorporated into the expected group and treated properly.

Even when the system includes the facilities that will reduce the frequency of unexpected answers, such answers must be treated as long as they exist. The system response should be dissimilar according to their type. A classification of unexpected answers follows:

1. **Correct.** This type of unexpected answer may only happen when the author forgot to consider a correct answer. This is the most unpleasant situation in the whole educational dialogue, and utmost efforts should be invested in order to avoid it. Its net result is that a correct answer entered by the student will not be recognized as such by the system, and the student may get an (incorrect) error message.

2. **Incorrect.** The author may exert his option to define some but not all of the possible incorrect answers, if the set of correct answers is perfectly defined. In this situation, every unexpected answer that is consistent and not correct is incorrect. An ad hoc error message should be stored for this type of answer.

3. **Invalid.** When the answer is invalid or inconsistent with the exercise requests, it is a poor strategy to treat it as an error. In most cases it shows a distraction or the accidental hitting of a key. Typical cases may be that of answering with a letter when a numeric answer is expected or making an out-of-range menu

selection. In these cases the system should ask for the retyping of the answer.[6] An internal counter may be kept, within the student model, to be activated for diagnostic use if it exceeds a predefined bound, that is, if a student makes too many of these errors.

4. Unknown. If, in the author's opinion, the expected answers complete all the correct and incorrect possibilities, then any valid answer that does not match an expected answer must be treated as unknown. No judgment may be issued, and the student must be asked to reformulate his answer.

The AS or AL should provide the author with the possibility of defining a system response for each one of the categories just analyzed, and also for a special category of expected answer, not previously mentioned: the no-answer. In effect, an author should be allowed to determine a time limit for the student to answer and the system response if this limit is exceeded. This is called a "time-out" or "time-limit" feature.

Modal Taxonomy. Let us assume, to provide a concrete frame of reference, that the student input comes from a keyboard. When appropriate, we refer to other input devices.

The simplest input mode is that where each input consists of precisely one character. This mode is the easiest for students to learn and imposes a minimum of demands in terms of input activity. It is worth expanding on this point. When the expected input is of an unknown number of characters, the system stores the string of characters being typed by the student in a buffer, until a SEND command is issued by the student (in most systems, hitting the RETURN key). Allowing for human errors or hesitation, a friendly system will provide editing capabilities to handle the input string: the student may delete characters, move the cursor, insert characters, retype, and so forth. This friendliness has a price: editing is a metalanguage over the subject matter language (where the real objective resides), and it has to be learned as any other language. In order to benefit from the fact that in single-character input the length is known, the AS should include the option of declaring this type of mode and analyzing each character as soon as it is pressed, without the requirement of a SEND command.

Single-character input is simple and easy to learn. Is it useful? Very much so. All the commands in PLATO, TICCIT, and SMILE require just a single key-press; menu selection may be done with one character; multiple-choice exercises may be answered in this way; even the long constructed responses required from the pupil in C.C.C.'s and TOAM's Arithmetic exercises are analyzed character by character. An example of this last type of interaction is presented in Figure 12.4.

In the vertical addition exercise shown, a blinking question mark asks the pupil which digit should be written in that specific position. If the pupil types the correct digit, the blinking question mark moves to the left, asking for the next digit, until the exercise is completed. If the pupil types an incorrect digit, it is displayed in reverse video, until corrected by the pupil. If the pupil makes three errors, the system displays the correct answer. For an efficient pupil-computer interaction where each digit is

---

[6]These facilities are very well developed in data-entry systems, where the typist gets immediate feedback on any data that is invalid for the present field, or that is inconsistent with the values of previously entered fields (e.g., entering a character different from an "F" or an "M" in the sex field will be rejected as invalid; a declaration of "pregnant" will be rejected as inconsistent if the sex field has an "M").

246	246	246	246
+ 135	+ 135	+ 135	+ 135
?	?1	?81	381
(a)	**(b)**	**(c)**	**(d)**

Figure 12.4. Vertical Addition Exercise

checked independently, the pupil should type the digits only. It would be most irritating to be forced to hit the RETURN key after each digit.

There is a price to be paid for the benefits of the single-character mode: it does not allow for corrections.

Authoring systems should provide the option of single-character input but, of course, in many situations multicharacter answers are required from a student. In the very distant future we may expect that the student input will be written in natural language, without limitations, and that the CAI system will have a natural-language front end that will parse and interpret the input correctly. For the moment, what we can expect from authoring systems or languages is much more modest and usually based on the presence or absence of key-words. The student-produced string is compared with the expected answers written by the authors. Options that help in raising the authors' productivity are:

1. Ignore capitalization (the system should reduce the expected answers and the student input to lowercase).
2. Allow for misspelling (for prestige reasons, this option applies only to the student input). The implementation is much simpler than that of a general-purpose spelling checker, which requires a large dictionary. In a CAI environment the possibility to be considered is whether a word present in the input is a misspelling of—that is, is close in some metric to—a word present in one of the expected responses. If you want to develop your own misspelling routine, some sources of inspiration are Szanser (1969); Tenczar and Golden (1972); Durham, Lamb, and Saxe (1983); Pollock and Zamora (1984); and Rosenthal (1984).
3. Allow for synonyms (see Tenczar & Golden, 1972).
4. Define word families, using wild-card characters (usually the same symbols used in text editors: "?" for any one character and "*" for any contiguous string of characters).
5. Define irrelevant (noise) words, that may be deleted from the student input.
6. Ignore extra words (if the input string includes all the required key-words, the answer is considered correct, even if it includes additional words).
7. Remove extra blank spaces (only one space is retained between words).
8. Ignore punctuation (all the punctuation marks are erased).
9. Ignore word order (the order of appearance of the keywords is not taken into consideration).

Considerable "natural-language processing" can be done with these relatively simple tools. Do ignore the "clever" counterexamples which show that such a system will accept nonsensical answers. The answers in those counterexamples are written by developers, not by students.

Let us move to mathematical input. We should consider two types: numeric and algebraic. For the comparison of numeric values, the AS should offer the option of establishing a certain tolerance, either absolute or relative. Algebraic comparison is more demanding, but we are entering the era where powerful symbolic algebraic manipulators may be incorporated into the system tools, thus providing a solid foundation for comparison and analysis of algebraic expressions. Until now, the comparison of the student algebraic input with an expected answer was done by assigning the same set of random values (within specified ranges) to the variables in the two expressions, evaluating them, and verifying whether the same value was computed for the two expressions. Although equality of values of the expressions for one set of values of the variables does not ensure equivalence, lack of equality does ensure lack of equivalence. In practical terms, the use of real random numbers gives a high degree of certainty to the test. If you want more certainty of equivalence, use two sets of random values!

When the AS has the capability of checking algebraic equivalence, it should include the author option of specifying that the student answer may not include operators or variables. Otherwise, if you ask a student to evaluate an expression, it is possible to produce a correct answer just by retyping the expression.

An important case appears in the teaching of the physico-mathematical sciences, where answers may be composed of a numeric part and a magnitude part, that is, an answer may consist of a number (or an algebraic expression) followed by the physical units the number refers to. A correct answer may be expressed in many different ways, according to the way the student selects the units. This author is not aware of any AS or AL that provides an ad hoc solution to this problem. For the treatment of this type of answer, see Karr and Loveman, 1978.

Enough for keyboard input. Let us consider now the treatment of pointing devices.

The main requirement is for the AS (or AL) to have two system variables that store the coordinates of the screen location pointed to by the student. The programming treatment should be the same irrespective of whether the pointing was done with a finger (on a touch-sensitive screen), a light pen, a mouse, or any other pointing device. If we call x_p and y_p the two system variables that store, respectively, the x-coordinate and the y-coordinate of the pointed location, then the decision as to whether the student pointed to a certain area or object is usually done by defining a rectangle, with its sides parallel to the axis, that closely covers (maybe with some compromises) the area or object in question. This rectangle defines an x-range and a y-range. If x_p and y_p belong, respectively, to these ranges, the student "hit" the target. Icon-oriented authoring languages, like Course of Action and Iconauthor, provide direct facilities for the definition of "hot zones" (i.e., target areas) by using a mouse.

The AS should provide the following features:

1. Selecting an object. This is a direct and clean way of answering a whole family of questions, without resorting to a multiple-choice intermediate stage.
2. Moving an object by pointing to it and then pointing to its new location. A double option should be available: placing the object exactly where shown by the student or placing it in a location predetermined by the author, if the student points near enough to it. This is the technique used to build laboratory

apparatus or electric circuits, for example, by selecting the components from a collection of objects presented on the screen and placing them in their appropriate positions.

3. Similar to feature 2 but "dragging" rather than "moving" the object to its final destination. With a mouse, this is usually done by keeping the pointing button down until the destination is reached.

4. Defining a line or a path. This may be done by a continuous trace, or by drawing segments between consecutive points selected by the student. This option has a large variety of applications, ranging from technical design to military tactics. If the student-defined path has to be compared with expected alternatives, the AS should include facilities for the author definition of paths, and contiguity criteria to determine which author alternative, if any, the student is following.

An interaction area where pointing is becoming more and more popular is that related to student commands. The functional area of student commands may be implemented by displaying a set of icons, where each icon represents an action to perform or a tool to work with. The screen image of each icon must be carefully designed, with strong expressive power, able to convey the purpose of the icon, thus constituting an effective mnemonic that helps to guide the student during the interaction. When the pictorial image of an action is hard to design, it is always possible to create an icon by drawing a shape (usually a rectangle or an ellipse) labeled with the name of the action to be performed. Mixed-modality icons, that is, those composed of a graphic design and a label, were rated as distinctively more meaningful than other alternatives in an experiment conducted by Guastello, Traut, and Korienek (1989). Pointing techniques have also revitalized the topic of Hypermedia, which merits a separate treatment.

System Decisions

Actually, the title is misleading; what we really mean is system implementation of author decisions or student commands. In terms of an AS, we are concerned with the facilities offered to authors and students to express themselves. These facilities may exist at a global (course) level, or at a local (frame or unit) level. It is easier to standardize requests at a local level; at a global level the tools available usually reflect the pedagogical philosophy of the AS developers.

Global Level. Let us describe the features required to define different types of instructional strategies.

The simplest strategy that comes to mind is that of the test or exam. The AS should offer the options of selecting questions from a question bank, either by parameters (e.g., topics, difficulty) or by direct search from a catalog. The author should be able to decide on presentation order, on the amount of time assigned to the test, and on the type of report preferred. From then on, the system may control the presentation without additional requirements from the author.

A widely utilized instructional strategy is that of Testing and Practice. Taking C.C.C. and TOAM as examples, an author who wants to organize courseware according to this conception has to build the exercises that cover the parallel-sequences structure defined in Chapter 8. All the global decisions are taken care of within the system, including the testing algorithm and the traversal decisions, which are a function of the student performance.

Tutorial instruction may be exemplified, in two different modalities: learner-directed and author-directed. In the first case the traversal decisions are left to the student, so that the authoring task is that of building and labeling the frames; the AS just implements this learner-directed interaction. In the second case, branching is very much an author's responsibility, and the AS provides a group of commands to cope with it. In cT, these commands are: next, back, jump, do, imain, outunit and menu, and by their use the author determines the student traversal among the units, either as a function of the student's answers or as a result of his requests.

The strategies presented until now are usually implemented with discrete granularity, that is, the courseware is built as a structure of frames (or units, just a semantic difference). Simulation, the next strategy analyzed in terms of authoring support, is the paradigm for continuous granularity. Concepts and algorithms behind the building of models and the running of simulations were presented in Chapter 8 under "Modeling and Simulation." What are the requirements from an authoring system, if we want to implement those algorithms?

1. Possibility of writing programs in a convenient programming language
2. Having the resources to define the required number of input, output, and state variables
3. Being able to build the state-transition function (which defines how the state of the model evolves with the events)
4. Being able to build the output function (which defines the output as a function of the state of the model and its parameters)
5. Having the capabilities for generating output in the preferred output format

Local Level. At this level we analyze the tools available for the design of the learner-computer dialogue in its concrete and final expression. The structure of the program that controls such a dialogue is:

1. Initialization of system, content and student variables.
2. Presentation segment.
3. Reception of student input.
4. Analysis of student input and classification into a category.
5. System response according to input category. This part may be formalized as a Pascal case statement:

```
CASE input-category OF

     input–category–1   :   system–response–1;

     input–category–2   :   system–response–2;

     ...............................

     ...............................

     input–category–n   :   system–response–n;

END
```

6. Updating of system, content, and student variables.

7. IF dialogue-continues THEN go to 2
ELSE store system and student variables, and finish.

We have dealt, in previous sections, with parts 2, 3, and 4. What are our requests, in terms of an AS, for parts 1, 5, and 6?

1. Availability of content and student variables, and accessibility of system variables. Student variables should be of two types: local, to program the interaction within a frame, and global, to allow for pedagogical decisions based on the student's history.

2. Preprogrammed patterns of interaction, where the authoring task is reduced to providing data. Consider, for instance, *cloze* type of exercises: the student is presented with a text or a diagram with blanks, holes, or missing parts (missing pieces of information). The student's task is to assign to each blank its corresponding piece of information. To be concrete, let us assume a text with missing words. The text will be displayed with a small rectangle in the place of each missing word. The cursor will stop in the first rectangle, and a choice of words will be presented to the student. If the student makes a correct selection, the word jumps into place, replacing the rectangle, and the cursor moves to the second rectangle. If the student makes a mistake, the word will not jump into place, and a corrective comment will be displayed. Cloze exercises are very frequently used. Instead of being forced to program this fairly complex interaction, the author should provide the AS with the text to be presented, a code denoting the placement of the missing words (or fragments), and the multiple-choice sections for each missing word, including the comments to be presented for each incorrect answer. The whole interaction should then be handled by the AS without additional author intervention.

3. Automatic collection of student responses and latency times.

4. Possibility of including special keys (or icons) under student control, with author-defined responses.

5. Possibility of calling external subroutines, written in full-fledged programming languages (thus enjoying the use of complex data structures, function libraries, and a variety of control statements). This is particularly relevant when the author wants to develop his own *exercise generators,* that is, programs that generate a variety of exercises derived from a common pattern, by random selection of parameters. The ranges for this random selection may be governed by student performance, thus providing a controlled and graded path for the instruction of a topic. A seminal work in this field was written by Uttal et al. (1969), and additional ideas may be gathered from Koffman (1973), and from Palmer and Oldehoeft (1975). We will quote Koffman (1973), to give a flavor of these powerful ideas:

Problem generation for the concept which teaches how to form truth tables for arbitrary logical expressions is controlled by a probabilistic grammar. A probabilistic grammar is a formal language in which each rewrite rule is assigned a probability of being applied. Part of the grammar for generating logical expressions follows:

Rewrite Rule	**Probability**
R1: A → (A * A)	P1
R2: A → ~A	P2
R3: A → P	P3
R4: A → Q	P4
R5: A → R	P5
R6: A → S	P6

Rule R1 states that whenever A appears in a logical expression, it can be replaced by (A*A). The symbol A is considered a nonterminal symbol, as it appears on the left-hand side of a rewrite rule. The symbols P,Q,R,S are terminal symbols and serve as variables in the final expression. Replacing A by (A*A) or ~A, would increase the length and complexity of the expression generated; whereas, application of R3-R6 replaces the nonterminal symbol A by one of the terminal symbols. The probability of rule R1 being applied (P1) is directly proportional to a student's LEVEL in this concept and inversely proportional to the current length of the logical expression. (p. 186)

SUPPORT FACILITIES

In this section we discuss facilities that we consider important within our conception of CAI, although they are not always present in available authoring systems.

Information Retrieval

Courseware that encourages student exploration of the instructional materials must provide the tools that allow for this exploration. There are three main kinds of search tools: those based on the techniques of classification and indexing, those based on direct links between information pieces (Hypermedia), and those based on direct searches of words in the original texts.

Classification and Indexing. The classical library-style information search is supported by several tools. The main tool is a classification of all the world knowledge as a tree structure; dominant in the field are the Library of Congress (LC), the Dewey, and the Universal Decimal Classification (UDC). Let us concentrate on books, to simplify the wording and provide a concrete scenario, and let us assume that the LC classification has been adopted.

Under this assumption we will find the books in the library placed on stacks, and ordered according to a depth-first linearization of the LC classification tree. The reader who looks for books in a specific subject, will first search, in the LC Classification Outline, for the identification of his subject of interest, and will then go to the stacks, to find out which books are located there. Every library has two additional tools to help the reader: a title catalogue and an author catalogue, both alphabetically ordered. These catalogues provide the LC classification of each entry, thus allowing for another way of reaching the stacks. Not every library has another very powerful search tool, which is a *key-word catalogue*. Key-words are not classification headings, but rather important words that appear in the texts that would be classified under those headings. A key-word catalogue assigns, to each key-word, the classification headings to which it could possibly be associated.

Things should be made easier for the reader, an endangered species in this era of direct attack on the senses. Every library in the future should have what research libraries have managed to have today: a computerized facility, where the reader may present an inquiry as a Boolean combination of classification headings and key-words, and get the listing of the books that answer his request.

This is precisely what we would like to have in every CAI facility, both for author and for student use. This requires every instructional block to be indexed according to a subject matter classification, to pedagogical parameters, and when possible, according to a key-word list. The pedagogical purpose of the indexing demands an additional classification, according to the instructional event the block is designed to serve. Further indexing could register information on presentation style.

It immediately comes to mind the way a student may benefit from all this indexing: according to his requests, the delivery system may present the instructional blocks apropriate to his individual needs. Less immediate is the fact that development teams may increase their productivity by avoiding a useless repetition of efforts. A large library of instructional blocks would serve a population of authors, and when a course is to be developed, the first step would be to search in the library for the blocks that match the courseware requirements. Also, during the development process, having all the instructional materials indexed, allows for the authors to check and revise, following a specific cross-section of the instructional blocks, in order to ensure completeness and consistency. Today's practical limitations to the implementation of these ideas come from two different directions: (1) from a student's standpoint, where the main problem is the availability of instructional materials and of terminal time; and (2) from an author's standpoint, where the main problems are the lack of standardization and the lack of materials interchange.

Having made such an investment in indexing, which provides such a wealth of information, it is tempting to use it by creating a pedagogical model able to reach its own decisions in terms of pedagogical organization of the instructional blocks. A first attempt, based on information-retrieval techniques was done by Osin (1976); a more sophisticated approach, using artificial intelligence techniques, is described by Russell (1988). For an example, see Chapter 13, "SMILE in Electricity and Magnetism."

Hypermedia. Vannevar Bush, President Roosevelt's science advisor, invented (1945) the *memex,* consisting of an annotated microfilm library of text and graphics, where the user could create his own labeled links between any two pieces of information. Bush's invention was never implemented, but he would have been undoubtedly happy playing with the Macintosh implementation of his dream, known as HyperCard— which does much more than he ever hoped for. The substitution of a microfilm environment for a computer-based one allows the user in a hypermedia[7] environment to navigate from document to document until satisfied, following direct links between the documents and, furthermore, allows him to create his own documents, links and

---

[7]The term *hypermedia* is being used, instead of the more usual *hypertext,* because the information being linked does not have to be just text. It may include graphics, sound, videodisc sequences, and so forth.

labels. These documents may consist of text, graphics, or programs, thus expanding the field of applications well beyond the standard information retrieval.

Conceptually, the database of information in a hypermedia system resembles Quillian's semantic memory model presented in Chapter 8, when Carbonell's SCHOLAR system was described. Instead of the common organization of information in linear form (booklike), the alternative is to have chunks of information as objects in a database. These objects are called *planes* in Quillian's model, *frames* in the ZOG/KMS hypermedia system (Akscyn, McCracken, & Yoder, 1988), *notecards* in the NoteCards system (Halasz, 1988) and *cards* in Apple's HyperCard (Apple, 1987). For generic properties, we are going to use the term *node* to refer to any one of these objects. Hypermedia objects have no implicit order—they are nodes in a graph, and authors and users may establish links betwen them that allow for different traversal modes, according to the user's needs and preferences.

Besides the structuring of information as a database of linked nodes, the additional element that characterizes hypermedia is the heavy reliance on pointing as the main user activity to specify the navigation in the database. It is convenient to think about the presentation of nodes in terms of windows. Every time that a node has to be displayed, a window is opened for this purpose. Each window contains control *buttons,* labeled tokens, icons, or hot zones (the terminology is still fluid), to be pointed at. When such a pointing area is selected by a user, it activates a link to another node or information object, thus producing the opening of another window. The pointing area is called the "source" of the link, and the node pointed at by the link is called its "destination."

In the case of nodes whose contents are to be displayed on the screen, their size and the size of the windows where they are presented is a design decision. In Apple's HyperCard, each card fills a screen on a Macintosh Plus, while on a Macintosh II it appears in a window that leaves some room in the edges. In the ZOG/KMS system the screen is divided in two vertical windows, each covering half a screen; the nodes may fit one or the two windows—the second case is particularly useful when dealing with large diagrams or tables. In the University of Maryland Hyperties project the nodes are short articles (50–1,000 words typically), while in the Symbolics Document Examiner the nodes are the pages from the 12-volume manual of the Symbolics LISP (Conklin, 1987). Usually the nodes are designed to be fully displayed on one window; in the case of articles that exceed a window—like in the Hyperties case—either a paging or a scrolling mechanism has to be provided within the window. The ZOG/KMS approach implements a simple but well-engineered conception: by presenting two pages it is possible for the user to look simultaneously at the source of the last link activated, and at its destination. More complex interactions, where the user wants to look simultaneously at several small windows, are not solved by the two half-screen designs, and the systems that cope with this problem provide the tools to reposition and resize the active windows, and even to close a window temporarily and replace it by an icon on the screen.

Figure 12.5 presents a NoteCards screen. This sophisticated system, developed at Xerox PARC, is one of the richest in options. The nodes in the system may be of different types (text, graphics, animation, video, and even actions—an action being a program that is executed when the node is selected).

As can be seen in Figure 12.5, each notecard has a header—its title—and may

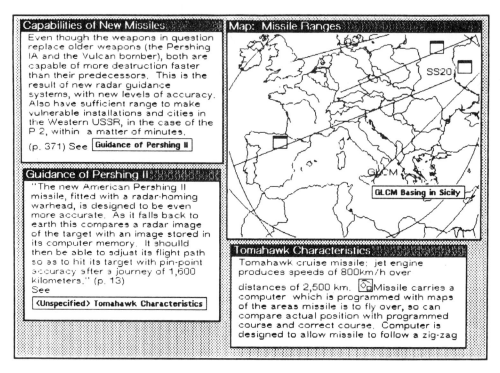

Figure 12.5. A NoteCards Display (From F. G. Halasz, 1988, Reflections on NoteCards: Seven Issues for the Next Generation of Hypermedia Systems, *Communications of the ACM*, 31 (no. 7): 837. Copyright 1988 by the Association for Computing Machinery. Reprinted by permission.)

have several link sources. In the screen presented, the user read the notecard on "Capabilities of New Missiles," pointed at the label "Guidance of Pershing II," and got the corresponding notecard. From this card, by pointing at "Tomahawk Characteristics," the destination node was displayed. This notecard includes an embedded icon that represents graphic objects (third line, before the word "Missile"), and by pointing at it the "Missile Ranges" map was displayed.

Navigation through author-determined links is probably the most frequent way to traverse a hypermedia database, but it limits very drastically the exploration possibilities. NoteCards—and some other systems—offer two additional options: Boolean searches and hierarchical strutures. Boolean searches are usually performed over strings; in the context we were examining, for example, a user can request all the nodes that contain simultaneously the words "missile" and "radar." Hierarchies are supported in NoteCards by special nodes called *fileboxes*. A filebox is a card in which other cards and fileboxes can be filed. Storing fileboxes into fileboxes allows for the definition of tree organizations of the notecards. The exploration of a hierarchical structure is supported in NoteCards by a browsing mechanism. Figure 12.6 presents a browser in action. Clicking on any one of the labeled rectangles causes the corresponding notecard to be displayed.

The instructional uses of hypermedia are most varied. A student reading a text

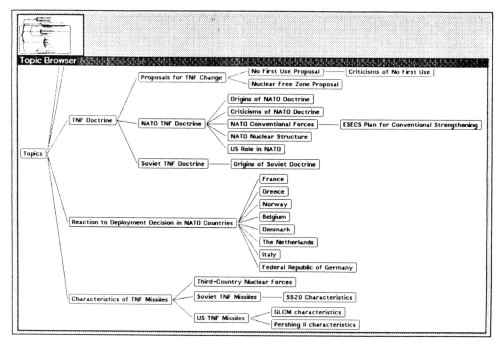

Figure 12.6. Browser of a Filebox Hierarchy (From F. G. Halasz, 1988, Reflections on NoteCards: Seven Issues for the Next Generation of Hypermedia Systems, *Communications of the ACM,* 31 (no. 7): 839. Copyright 1988 by the Association for Computing Machinery. Reprinted by permission).

may point at any difficult word and a window will open to explain it (if the author thus provided). A complex machine may be shown, and pointing at each one of its parts will result in this part's being enlarged, with each component labeled. Point at a label and an explanation of how the component functions is displayed. Response time is critical for the success of the application. The difference between an immediate switch from window to window, or a sluggish display of screens, is the difference between a motivating environment and a frustrating one.

The reader may remark that these possibilities existed before the hypermedia boom. The difference is that this boom provided the developers with very efficient tools for building the database, establishing the links, drawing the pointing areas, defining system responses attached to these areas, and more. Apple, the great communicator of Xerox PARC ideas, provided a quantum leap to the field by bundling Hyper-Card with every Macintosh being sold today. HyperCard provides a general-purpose tool, which is important from our standpoint because one of its applications is in the field of instruction. The types of activities that Apple has preorganized for HyperCard users are very mundane and can be recognized in Figure 12.7, which presents the Home Card, the jumping-off point for explorations.

Every icon in the Home Card identifies a named collection of cards, usually of the same type, which is called a *stack*. Cards in a stack are circularly organized,

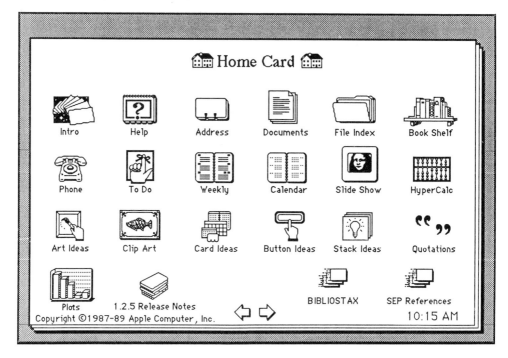

Figure 12.7. Hypercard's Home Card (From *HyperCard User's Guide* © 1988 Apple Computer, Inc. Used with permission.)

and the pictorial representation of this structure is a Rolodex file, as can be seen in one of the cards of the "Address" stack, presented in Figure 12.8.

Starting from the first card, it is possible to go through the whole stack one card at a time by pointing at the forward arrow (the arrow pointing to the right, between the "holes" of the Rolodex card), until back at the first card—by pointing forward from the last. At any point it is possible to go to the preceding card in the stack, by pointing at the left arrow. The curved arrow at the lower right is used to return to the previous card (the last card seen), irrespective of the stack structure.

Searches for specific words or strings are supported, as are editing facilities for changing existing cards or adding new ones. HyperCard is designed in such a way that it may be enjoyed by users at every level, from the computer naive to the experienced professional. At the easiest level the user may fill existing stack structures with the data she is interested in, and may create new stacks by copying their structure from existing ones. For each new stack an icon is added to the Home Card. The computer professional may program activities behind every button or, for that matter, behind every object in the system, either by using HyperTalk, an ad hoc language for this system or by linking with programs written in other high level programming languages (Goodman, 1987, 1988). A look at the first card of the Help stack (Figure 12.9) gives a feeling for some of the options available.

HyperCard has opened a new market, and stack developers have proliferated, delivering a variety of information stacks in many different fields. It is frequent to find HyperCard applications running at conferences, and providing information from

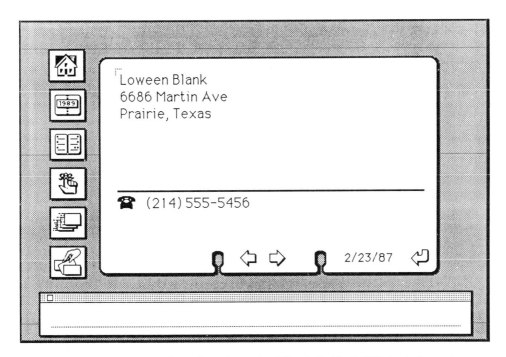

Figure 12.8. An Address Card (From *HyperCard User's Guide* © 1988 Apple Computer, Inc. Used with permission.)

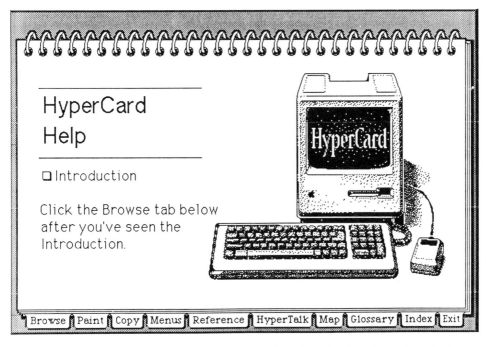

Figure 12.9. First Card in the Help Stack (From *HyperCard User's Guide* © 1988 Apple Computer, Inc. Used with permission.)

lectures to restaurants. In the instructional field, workshops and applications have been presented at the National Educational Computing Conference (taken as an example of an important forum in this area) since 1988.

There is another feature of hypermedia that is not usually present in other systems: the student may be given the use of authoring tools, thus allowing for the possibility of personal notes and of personal structures, that is, the student may establish his links between documents, recording an individual path that matches a line of thought. These personal nodes and links are stored in the database, providing, according to system criteria and to the user's decision, either for a private annotated structure or for an addition to the public domain.

A comment in another dimension: In most cases the nodes are written specifically for the application; when the corpus of data is preexistent (e.g., Symbolics LISP manual), the investment required for the development of the application is in the links only.

Coming back to the issues involved in the development of instructional materials, the conceptual framework for authoring classical CAI is very different than the one we find in hypermedia. CAI units are built along a line of thought developed by the author; students may deviate from this main line for remedial or exploration purposes, but they return to it. Not so in hypermedia materials, where no preferred sequence exists, and different students may navigate along different subsets of the database, according to their inclinations. Of course, in instructional hypermedia authors may suggest a preferred path to students.

A case study of hypermedia is analyzed in Chapter 13. The reader interested in more technical details is referred to the July 1988 issue of the *Communications of the ACM,* which is devoted to this subject. For a good tutorial see Conklin, 1987.

Direct Word Searches. While working with a text editor,[8] the user frequently wants to look for a particular word or string of characters. The editor accomplishes the search by moving character by character over the text, looking for an exact string match. Even with computer speeds, this type of search is feasible in small documents only. If a search is to be performed over a large database, a preprocessing of the database texts is needed in order to accelerate the search. To give just an example, suppose that we have a file containing all the federal laws, each divided into paragraphs. In a time-consuming process, which is done only once, the text file is scanned and a secondary file is built, where every word that appears in the text file is stored in alphabetical order, and indexed according to the law and paragraph where it occurs. Thus, when a user wants to see all the laws where the word "cocaine" appears, the system quickly finds this word in the secondary file (which is ordered), either by a binary search or by hash coding or by any other method valid with ordered keys. At this point all the occurrences may be listed, at the law or paragraph level, according to the user's request. The request may be expressed in terms of more than one word. For instance, the user may want to find all the laws where the words "cocaine," "medical," and "use" appear in the same paragraph. The system will respond by providing the set of laws and paragraphs that satisfies this request.

We are not aware of CAI systems where the user is provided with search tools that allow him to look for words or combinations of words that define his present interests

---

[8]"Word processor" is just a pompous and misleading name for the same thing.

within the courseware he is studying, and we hope that these tools will be available in a nondistant future. On the other hand, it is not necessary to wait in order to enjoy the use of prepackaged databases of general use. As an example, Microsoft Bookshelf® is a CD-ROM that stores, in its version 1.0, 10 major reference works including: The American Heritage Dictionary, Bartlett's Familiar Quotations, The Chicago Manual of Style, Roget's II Electronic Thesaurus, and the U.S. ZIP Code Directory. The same CD-ROM contains all the auxiliary files and the search programs. Searches are performed in a matter of seconds, and the programs allow for the references to be cut and pasted to several popular PC text editors.

Conclusions. The three information retrieval methods presented have different strengths and weaknesses. The strength of the first one, classification and indexing, is its conceptual power and generality. The strength of the second one, hypermedia, is its immediacy and user friendliness. The strength of the third, direct word search, lies in its efficiency. The instructional use is different for the three methods in several aspects. The first two can be embedded within the courseware, and may be defined by the authors. The third one, in today's reality, can be used as an external tool only, except for the very few cases where the developer has such a large market that the production of a special-purpose CD-ROM is economically feasible.

In terms of software engineering the big advantage of indexing over hypermedia is that indexing can be performed locally for each instructional block, without having to consider its connections to any other block, while hypermedia links establish relations that may cease to be true if one of the pieces of information is changed. This is crucial when updating the database, particularly years after it was created. If indexing procedures are used, instructional blocks may be created, deleted, or updated, without affecting the traversal procedures. On the other hand, in a hypermedia environment these operations must consider not only the blocks being dealt with, but also all those linked to them. Worse than that, when a block is added, the responsible author would have to go over all the existing blocks to decide on possible links. These considerations do not apply to direct word-search methods. The powerful systems of the future will include all the options.

Instructional Administration

All the data collection and processing that was mentioned in Chapter 10 must be available to the authors without any programming on their part. It is advisable to set options so that the authors may decide which information is worth collecting and which not.

On-line Resources for Student Use

Ideally, an instructional facility should not limit the student possibilities, but rather act as an "intellectual amplifier." When the student is learning at his terminal, all the external resources required should be available on-line. In addition to the pedagogical benefit, there is an economic advantage worth considering in the present situation, where the scarcity of terminal-hours forces a tight scheduling of the terminals. A student who must interrupt the on-line dialogue to look for external support is wasting a precious resource. The author must be aware of the services provided on-line, to be able to design the instruction on the basis of its existence. For example, having a calculator or a dictionary available to the student within the courseware being produced, frees the author from some worries in terms of the difficulty of the arithmetic operations that must be performed or in terms of the need to provide explanations for difficult words. Thus, the authoring system should include a variety of on-line resources that may be called from the courseware and, hopefully, the capability of expanding those resources according to the author's requests. The author must have also the option of not allowing the use of certain resources from within the courseware, when this would defeat the purpose of the assigned instructional task.

General-Purpose Resources. Under this category we include dictionaries, encyclopedias, thesauri, text editors and graphics editors, calculators and algebra manipulators.

Communication Among Users. For many observers, there is a frightful image of a computerized educational system where students learn in isolation. The answer may be given at two levels. At the first level, courseware may be designed as a group activity, of which strategy, management, or economic games are good examples. To be able to develop such a courseware, the authoring system must allow for global variables that represent the information available to all the users, and that are upgraded with every individual user activity. At a second and more philosophical level, we may envision a community of scholars and students who may communicate without the limitations of physical distance. Existing electronic mail facilities are a positive step in this direction, and some pioneering projects have already shown the motivational impact of this technology. An International Symposium on Telecommunications in Education (Jerusalem, August 1989), was organized by the International Society for Technology in Education (ISTE), and it is enough to describe two of the projects presented, to give a feeling for the possibilities opened. The first (Morton, Mojkowsky, Roland, & Copen) is a joint effort of the New York State GEM (Global Education Model) project and the Soviet telecommunications organization, whereby students from American and Soviet schools develop joint research activities. The second (Lenk) is the Network Science project, developed by TERC (Technical Education Research Centers, Cambridge, Massachusetts); as an example of their activities, in the National Geographic Kids Network Acid Rain unit, elementary school students learn about the effects of acids, measure the pH in their rainwater, share these data with other student investigators throughout the United States, analyze national data, and share their conclusions with each other and with professional scientists.

Databases and Query Systems. Here we refer to specialized sources of information, a good example of which could be LEXIS, a database of laws and jurisprudence, which provides services to the legal profession of the United States. These query systems may be searched by any of the methods described under "Information Retrieval" in this chapter. Having them available, authors may asign search activities to students and question them about their findings.

Help. The AS should provide the students with technical support for the smooth operation of the Instructional facility, including all the on-line resources, without placing any burden on the authoring team. Help could be provided at three levels: a short message, a detailed message including examples, and human assistance via electronic mail.

Project-Development Management

A modern AS should include the software engineering tools that accompany the development of any large software project. Each software or courseware component should be identified in terms of author, date, functionality and dependence on other software or courseware components. The different versions of each component should be stored, to be retrieved if needed. Global changes over a whole course should be possible with one command. Procedure libraries must be available to all developers. Sequences of system commands of frequent or important use should be stored in well-identified command files.

Debugging

An important element for efficient development is the availability of debugging tools, of which the most important is the possibility of switching between author and student modes without delays. All the other debugging features (insertion of breakpoints, variable watches, tracepoints, counters, etc.) are common to all programming environments.

EVALUATION AND SELECTION

If you are an author looking for an AS, the most important stage lies entirely within your realm and not with the vendors. You have to know what type of courseware you want to develop, at present and in the near future. Once you have defined this crucial point, it is possible to start checking authoring systems, correlating their features to your requirements. The capabilities range is at least as extended as the price range, although you will discover that those two variables are not clearly related. Make your life easier by not spending your time studying ASs from companies that are not solidly established or whose future is uncertain. Your investment in courseware will be much higher than the price of the AS, and if you are going to build it around an AS you will need the support of its developer, and even such a working relationship that will allow you to ask for ad hoc features.

Some concepts for categorizing features in order to have weighted decision criteria can be found in Davidove (1987), Locatis and Carr (1985), and MacKnight and Balagopalan (1989). A piece of advice that comes from experience and that you are going to be grateful for, is the following: After your first selection of ASs on the basis of declared features, check how each feature that is important to you is implemented. In other words, check not only *whether* but also *how*.

After you finish your analyses, several possibilities are opened:

1. You found a system that answers all your requests for a reasonable price, backed by a good company, and with a contract that ensures service and updatings. Buy it!

2. None of the ASs provides the services that are central to your instructional conception. Use a general-purpose programming language and start developing the building blocks of your own authoring facility.
3. Something between 1 and 2. It is perfectly reasonable to use different ASs for different types of courseware and also to develop courseware from scratch, using a general-purpose programming language for specific applications. On the other hand, do not diversify more than strictly necessary. Gathering expertise in the efficient use of a development tool is a long-term enterprise, with a lot of practice involved.

SUMMARY

This chapter described the tools of the trade for the development of computerized instructional materials. It summarized the requirements for courseware production and proposed a standard for the distinction between authoring languages (AL) and authoring systems (AS). Three functional components of authoring languages and systems were distinguished, dealing respectively with computer output, input, and decisions. For output, a list of the functions required or desirable for the organization of visual displays was presented; sound was analyzed also, emphasizing the concepts behind the determination of the amount of disk storage required for an application. With respect to input, the main effort was invested in the study of the tools necessary to provide the students with a variety of input possibilities, and the system requirements to be able to analyze this input. A taxonomy of inputs was organized, based mainly on two dichotomies: expected-unexpected and correct-incorrect. System decisions were described at global and local level, at global level to implement different instructional strategies and at local level to produce a fluent dialogue with the student.

The next section described support facilities. It started with information-retrieval methods, analyzing three styles: classification and indexing, hypermedia, and direct word search. After describing these styles, they were compared in terms of their advantages and disadvantages, particularly in an instructional context. This analysis was followed by brief descriptions of the requirements for instructional administraton, on-line student resources, project-development management, and debugging.

The last section provided criteria to allow for the evaluation, by prospective developers, of the authoring languages and systems available in the market, looking for the most appropriate to the particular development needs.

CHAPTER 13

Paradigms

Going forwards and looking back are not contradictory actions.
—George Sarton, lecture, Harvard University (quoted by Max Rowe, 1975)

In this chapter we present real-world implementations that exemplify the ideas developed in the previous chapters. The small group of examples selected describes an assortment of very different applications. Variety, in addition to quality, was one of the criteria for selection, trying to provide paradigms for major instructional styles. Another important consideration for inclusion was in-depth knowledge, and this explains why the two first examples were selected. From another angle, the first, second, and sixth examples illustrate team development, while the third, fourth, and fifth examples correspond to one or two individual authors.

This is not a Hall of Fame list, and many famous and widely used pieces of courseware were not included. So, if you have developed courseware not described here, do not consider this a discredit.

TOAM'S TESTING AND PRACTICE
IN READING COMPREHENSION (RC)

Concise Technical Description

Armed with all our taxonomies, we can describe this courseware as follows:

- Paradigm: Courseware
- Subject: Reading Comprehension (in Hebrew)
- Extension: Course for grades 2 to 7
- Topology: Parallel sequences
- Locus of control: Author-directed (prescribed) interaction
- Instructional events: Testing and practice
- Function: Auxiliary
- Granularity: Discrete

- Programming technique: Information-structure-oriented
- Pedagogical intervention: Fixed

Knowledge Model

The matrix that describes the parallel-sequences structure of this course is presented in Figure 13.1. Each sequence, and there are 14 of them, contains the exercises for one topic, classified according to monthly activities for each grade. This is the "scope-and-sequence" classification used in American schools. One axis in the matrix defines topics, with range from 1 to 14, and the other axis defines level, ranging from 2.0 to 7.9, with increments of 0.1. The lowest level, 2.0, corresponds to the beginning of the second grade, and the highest level, 7.9, corresponds to the end of the seventh grade. Each additional tenth in the level corresponds to another "ideal" month in grade placement. For example, an ideal fourth grader should start at a level 4.0 and, after one month, move to level 4.1. After nine months she should reach level 4.9, and finish the fourth grade ready to start level 5.0.

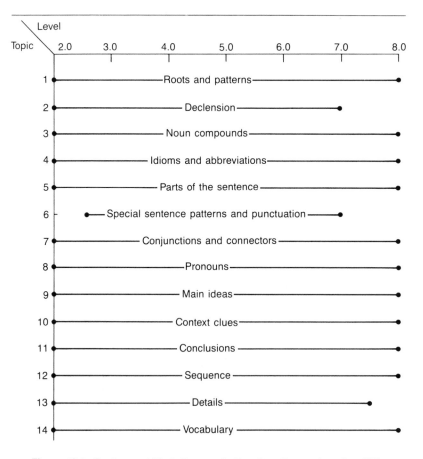

Figure 13.1. Topics and Their Ranges in Reading Comprehension (RC).

The exercises for each topic and level were written by the development team according to a certain conception of how Israel's Ministry of Education guidelines should be implemented. Topics 1 to 8 and 14 concentrate on Language Skills, while topics 9 to 13 concentrate on Thinking Skills. Not every point in the topic-level matrix is actually active, and the regions marked in Figure 13.1 show the active range for each topic. For each active point, the courseware includes a sequence of 15 exercises, organized as three 5-tuples (i.e., sequences of 5 exercises). The total courseware comprises more than 13,000 exercises.

The authors who wrote such a massive collection of exercises did not write programs. For each exercise they selected a pattern of interaction and placed the information required into a specific data structure, thus creating a frame. Each frame defines an individual instructional dialogue, where a context is presented, followed by one or more questions that test the learner's comprehension or skill. For each question a set of expected answers (correct and incorrect) is defined, each one followed by a system response (in this course, an author comment).

The data sructure that defines a frame is presented in Figure 13.2. In this case, for ease of reference, we have indicated repeated fields by writing in parentheses the number of times each field is repeated (*M, N, P*). Let us add some explanations.

1. Any frame has to be assigned its coordinates within the three-dimensional array that defines the course topology. The order of the coordinates is: topic, level, sequence number.
2. The context consists of text and graphics. It will stay on the screen while the different questions are presented.
3. The *M* questions are presented successively. The definition of each one starts with a set of parameters that characterize:
   a. The question pattern: it may be a simple multiple-choice (one correct answer), a plural multiple-choice (several correct answers must be identified), a fill-in (cloze), it may require the correct sequencing of several paragraphs, or it could be an open answer.
   b. The specific presentation for a selected pattern. For instance, if simple multiple-choice has been selected, the author has to decide on the number *Q* of choices

---

Frame
    Course-array coordinates
    Context
    Question (*M*)
        Question parameters
        Question text
        Correct answer (*N*)
            Expected answer
            System response
        Incorrect answer (*P*)
            Expected answer
            System response

Figure 13.2. Frame Data Structure

to present. The system will check that $N + P \geq Q$ and, for each presentation, will select one correct answer from the N available, $Q - 1$ incorrect answers from the P available, will permutate the Q answers selected, and will display them to the learner.

    c. The answer-processing algorithm. In this course this process was drastically simplified by defining one-character responses only.

4. The separation of the N correct answers defined for a question, from the P incorrect answers, serves two purposes:

    a. To emphasize that the set of correct answers cannot be empty $(N > O)$. Note, as an aside, that the set of incorrect answers may be empty, particularly when dealing with open answers. For one-character input it is very easy to list all the correct answers, so that all the unexpected answers may be treated as incorrect.

    b. The system response tends to be different for correct and incorrect answers. There is a standard component, a part of the AS, that provides congratulatory messages for correct answers and "try again" messages for the incorrect ones. What the author has to add, when considered convenient, are content-specific comments. This is more frequently done for incorrect answers, which should receive an explanatory comment.

5. By restricting the system responses to comments, we have avoided the writing of any programming segment within a frame. As previously mentioned, an author writes pure data.

6. A simpler frame structure, frequently used, is embedded in the one presented. If the CONTEXT is empty and $M = 1$, the structure defines a single question.

Student Model

The student model includes all the variables required for the decisions to be made by the pedagogical model. Referring to Figure 10.3, and concentrating on the dynamic data, we find:

1. Performance parameters.
    a. Time-factor, which allots more answer time to slow readers.
    b. Relief points, which relax the mastery requirements and may be used with low-proficiency pupils to speed up their progress a little.
2. Situation variables.
    a. Student level at each topic.
    b. For each topic-level point in the matrix, how many 5-tuples of exercises were completed (out of the three possible). This information is important because mastery checking is done at the end of each 5-tuple.
    c. For each point in the matrix, how many exercises were answered within the 5-tuple being presented.
    d. How many of the exercises in (c) were correctly answered.
3. Dynamic variables. This data refers to the present or last session:
    a. How many exercises were presented.
    b. How many of those exercises were correctly answered.
    c. In how many of the exercises counted as incorrect was the pupil timed-out.

Pedagogical Model

The pedagogical model (PM) operates according to different algorithms in the two successive stages of the instructional process: initial placement and practice.

The initial-placement algorithm (IPA) in a parallel-sequences structure was described, in Chapter 9, for TOAM's Arithmetic course. Unfortunately, the same algorithm cannot be applied to the RC course, mainly because a large proportion of the instructional blocks are not content-related, so that mastery in one block of a given topic has no implications over its predecessors or successors. Furthermore, the same exercise may present difficulties of different types to children according to their backgrounds. Even in the same instructional block, there may be a wide range of difficulty among the 15 exercises.

Nonetheless, in global terms the difficulty of the exercises increases with their level: more complex syntactic structures are successively introduced, the vocabulary becomes richer, the texts to be analyzed grow in length, and the situations presented have more dimensions to be considered. This global tendency to an increase in exercise difficulty was used in the testing algorithm, to find a region where the average proportion of correct answers was satisfactory: sufficiently high to avoid pupil frustration, but not too high, to preserve the pupil challenge. We established, in principle, the same requirement for RC as for Arithmetic: two-thirds correct. This responds to what we call the "ego repair principle"—for every frustrating error, the pupil is motivated by answering two exercises correctly.

The qualifier "in principle," stated in the previous paragraph, refers to the fact that there is a probabilistic difference, in terms of guessing a correct answer, between the exercises presented to the pupils in the two subjects mentioned: Arithmetic and Reading Comprehension. The constructed response in Arithmetic makes guessing extremely unsuccessful, while the multiple-choice structure (with 4 choices) of the majority of the exercises in RC yields, on the average, a 25 percent correct answer rate when answering randomly. Thus, assuming that the most frequent situation is that of multiple-choice exercises (with 4 choices), the requirement for RC was established at 75 percent correct. (See box.)

Using the notation established in Chapter 9, $REQ_i = 0.75$. The performance: PER_i, is not established at an isolated point in the matrix but rather as an average over a cross-section, at a given level, of all the blocks active at that level, thus measuring performance globally over all the topics. An initial sampling of the pupil's performance is done by taking cross-sections at the beginning of each grade: levels 2.0, 3.0, 4.0, and so forth, and for each one the relative performance: R_i, is computed. This sampling process continues in this form until $R_i < 1$ for two consecutive cross-sections. At this level we may safely assume that we have gone beyond the student placement level. Then, the density of the sampling is tripled but is concentrated on the last three grades covered, under the fair assumption that this additional sampling is being done in the region where the initial placement will be located. A typical result of these samplings is presented in Figure 13.3.

The cloud of R_i points resulting from the samplings is synthesized by determining the straight line that constitutes the best linear fit (BLF). The place where the BLF cuts the line $R = 1$ determines the student's initial placement level.

Note that no attempt is made to establish a different placement level for each different topic. In the given situation, all we have done is develop a method to start the

Guessing Correction

Let us assume that a test is composed of t multiple-choice exercises with n choices each. If a student answers c exercises correctly, i incorrectly, and does not answer the remaining r $(c + i + r = t)$, then her "gross" score would be: $G = c/t$.

Calling $a = c + i = t - r$, the number of exercises answered, it is possible to rewrite the gross score in the form:

$$G = \frac{c}{a} \times \frac{a}{t}$$

thus making explicit the fraction:

$$S = \frac{c}{a},$$

which provides the ratio of correct answers over all the student's answers, and which may be corrected (penalized) for guessing. Its corrected value is:

$$S' = S - \frac{1 - S}{n - 1}$$

With this correction, a student with a perfect score, $S = 1$, gets $S' = 1$, and a student who answers randomly and obtains: $S = 1/n$, gets $S' = 0$.

In the Reading Comprehension courseware, every exercise has to be answered, so that $a = t$, and the corrected net score for $S = 0.75$, $n = 4$, is $S' = 0.67$, which matches the Arithmetic requirements.

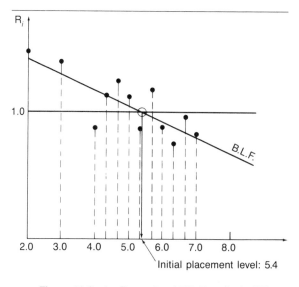

Figure 13.3. An Example of IPA Results in RC

pupil's practice at a reasonable level. The scattering of the R_i results for the different sampling levels shows another reason for our decision to develop a BLF-based algorithm. For the same requirements, local search methods could converge at many different levels, because the situation is very different from the ideal monotonically decreasing function that was sketched in Figure 9.4. On the other hand, the BLF method is based on the assessment of pupil performance over the whole course, so that the initial placement level thus determined is actually a global value, fairly independent of local distortions.

The initial placement level for each pupil is reported to the teacher who, when in doubt, may perform retesting.

When the student finishes the IPA and starts practice, the pedagogical model (PM) picks a topic randomly and displays the first available exercise from the sequence the student is following at her present level in the given topic. This random selection of topics continues until the practice session is completed (sessions are defined as 10-minute periods). Every time that a 5-tuple is completed for a given topic-level point, the PM checks whether mastery has been reached. The mastery criteria are: 100 percent correct for the first 5-tuple and 80 percent correct for the following 5-tuples. In other words, 5 out of 5 for the first check, and 4 out of 5 for the following. The reason for the change of requirements has to do with our belief in the importance of practice for long-term retention. A pupil is allowed to proceed with a minimum of exercises only if her performance is perfect. Otherwise, at least another 5-tuple will be presented. The sequence of 15 exercises provides three consecutive 5-tuples. If a pupil finishes the third without reaching mastery, the system will build another 5-tuple (or part of it) by repeating the exercises that were incorrectly answered by the student. It must be noted that, on a second opportunity, the exercises are much easier because the pupil was presented with the correct answer the first time she erred. The factors that make the second presentation not totally trivial are (1) the distractors for the same question may be different and a new permutation will be generated, and (2) some 200 different exercises may be presented before an exercise is repeated.

If the student performance is very poor (even in the first 5-tuple), this situation will be reported to the teacher, in a class report similar to the one presented in Figure 10.4. Some details are different; for instance, in the RC report, if a pupil is having trouble in a topic, the report will identify the 5-tuple where the pupil is working.

Field Implementation

The RC courseware is used in auxiliary mode in primary schools in Israel. Some 400 schools were using the TOAM system when this chapter was written, comprising about 100,000 pupils practicing with this particular courseware. The courseware is used mainly in grades 3 to 6, with the exercises for grade 2 (levels 2.0 to 2.9) providing activities for low achievers, and with the exercises for grade 7 (levels 7.0 to 7.9) doing the same for high achievers. The teachers involved receive training and support from C.E.T., with a TOAM instructor spending one day per month at each school. The courseware is accompanied by teacher's guides and by pupil activity booklets. These booklets are assigned individually (or in small groups) by the teacher, on the basis of the weekly computer report.

TOAM systems are installed under a leasing contract (which includes hardware, software, courseware, training, advice, and maintenance), signed by the local authorities or the parents' organization who pay for the system.

Development

We will not describe the complete development process. The point that we want to emphasize is that it is practically impossible to produce a perfect course, of such dimensions, in one stroke of genius. The development of the RC courseware was started by an academic team whose task was to define the topic-level matrix and to produce one exemplary exercise for each point in the matrix (about 900). The initial testing of those exercises was done at the C.E.T. premises with children from schools in the neighborhood and, after revisions and corrections, an authoring team was formed, with each member usually concentrating on only one topic in her writing, but reading and providing feedback on the exercises written by the other members of the team. When five exercises were written for each point in the matrix, a pool of typists and graphic artists entered the text and graphics defining those exercises. A first experimental version of the courseware was produced and subsequently tested in the field during a complete school year. The statistics obtained as a result of this year of experience allowed for two things: a revision of the matrix and the improvement (changes, deletions, replacements, displacements) of the first 5-tuple for every point in the matrix. This done, development continued with the second 5-tuple. A similar cycle, with school testing of the courseware that included 10 exercises for each point in the matrix, led to the writing of the third 5-tuple. The "completed" courseware is updated, and hopefully improved, every year, both in terms of exercises (after analyzing the performance statistics: percentage correct, distribution of answers over the different distractors), and in terms of algorithms and teacher reports.

SMILE IN ELECTRICITY AND MAGNETISM

The SMITH system (Osin, 1976) was renamed as SMILE, after too many inquiries about who Mr. Smith was. SMILE is an acronym for Structured Mixed-Initiative Learning Environment.

Concise Technical Description

> Paradigm: Courseware
> Subject: Electricity and Magnetism (in Hebrew)
> Extension: Course for Grade 10 (Vocational schools program)
> Topology: Sequence
> Locus of control: Mixed-initiative interaction
> Instructional events: Explication and practice
> Function: Auxiliary or autonomous
> Granularity: Discrete
> Programming technique: Information-retrieval-oriented
> Pedagogical intervention: Tutorial

Knowledge Model

The model of knowledge consists of a set of frames, indexed according to a tree-structured classification of topics. Each frame is a script for a dialogue, whose purpose is to provide instruction about certain topics. A frame may be indexed according to

1. Basic concepts
2. Electric circuits and signals
3. Electrostatics
4. Magnetism and electromagnetism
5. Components and systems
6. Units and measurements
7. Auxiliary topics

Figure 13.4. Electricity and Magnetism
Topics Tree—First Level

several topics. For organizational purposes, frames are organized into instructional units (similar to chapters in a book). The Electricity and Magnetism course comprises 22 units, each one with an average of 60 frames.

The first level of the topics tree for this course appears in Figure 13.4. The subject matter has been classified into seven main topics. Each one of these seven topics has up to nine "sons" or subtopics. The subtopics of topic 2, "Electric circuits and signals," appear in Figure 13.5. The whole tree has a maximum depth of four levels. For instance, 2.3.1.2 "Computation of current and voltage in a RL circuit," is a topic at the lowest level.

The usual information-retrieval approach to frame indexing would be to specify the topics (taken from a certain list) relevant to the frame. In this case this indexing of semantic content is not enough. SMILE is a teaching system and just knowing that a topic is mentioned in a frame is not enough to design an instructional process. It is also necessary to know why it is mentioned. In other words, the pedagogical reason for the presence of each topic mentioned in a frame must be known.

Under this approach, the indexing of a frame will not consist of a set of topic numbers: $(t_i, t_j, t_k, \ldots)$, but rather it will be a set of couples:

$$((t_i, q_i), (t_j, q_j), (t_k, q_k), \ldots)$$

where q_i is the pedagogical qualifier of t_i, q_j of t_j, and so forth.

SMILE recognizes six pedagogical qualifiers, described in Figure 13.6. The selection of the previous qualifiers was a design decision and survived extensive experience. The criteria used for the design of this taxonomy were:

1. The qualifiers should be easy to recognize and to apply and be linked to common educational practice.
2. The degree of discrimination should be enough to distinguish all the "impor-

2.1 Direct current circuits
2.2 Alternating current circuits
2.3 Electric signals
2.4 Transient phenomena
2.5 Connection of voltage and current sources
2.6 Network theorems

Figure 13.5. Subtopics of "Electric Circuits and Signals"
Topics Tree—Second Level

QUALIFIERS	FUNCTION
I	(Introduction) The frame introduces the topic.
N	(Necessary) The frame includes material considered essential, from a logical standpoint, for the presentation of the topic.
C	(Complement) The frame adds material for rehearsal or clarification of the topic.
E	(Exercise) The frame tests comprehension of aspects of the topic by including a question to be answered at the terminal.
P	(Problem) The frame tests deeper comprehension. Because of its instructional content, it demands time for thinking, reading, calculations, or project development and, consequently, it is assigned as homework. Correction and grading are performed by an instructor.
R	(Required) The topic is required for the teaching of other topics mentioned in the frame.

Figure 13.6. SMILE Pedagogical Qualifiers

tant'' instructional steps, but should not be artificially extended beyond practical use by the system.

The qualifier N refers to logical necessity, as opposed to pedagogical necessity. The author has other tools to force, in any given course, the presentation of frames that she considers pedagogically necessary, even if they are not logically necessary.

The knowledge model contains the following additional information about frames:

1. A precedence relation between frames, which establishes, for each frame, which frames are its logical predecessors. For instance, if frame f_i proves a lemma that is used in frame f_j to prove a theorem, then f_i logically precedes f_j. Similarly, if f_i is an exercise that tests comprehension of a topic explained in f_j, then f_j logically precedes f_i. The precedence relation is established between frames and not between topics. This is because the presentation of frames is always sequential, while topics are usually interwoven. As an example, consider the concepts "point," "straight line," and "plane" in Euclidean geometry, which cannot be presented independently.

2. A basic sequence of all the frames in a unit. From this basic sequence different subsequences of instruction are extracted in the actual teaching process. These subsequences will depend on each student's characteristics and performance. The basic sequence must satisfy the logical-precedence relation between frames (the AS builds the transitive closure of the relation based on the pairs defined by the author and checks that the basic sequence satisfies it). Usually, the logical-precedence relation will only determine partial orderings in the set of frames. We suggest the use of the following pedagogical criteria to complete the definition of the basic sequence:

a. Topics directly based on those the student already knows should be presented first.

b. New topics of instruction should be introduced in a smooth and continuous manner, that is, providing for topic contiguity in successive frames.

c. The presentation of each topic should begin with a set of introductory frames in order to activate recognition of related topics. Next, a set of necessary frames should be presented, followed by complementary frames, for rehearsal. Exercises must then be used to determine whether to continue or to provide remedial frames. Additional rehearsal is provided when new topics are introduced, because of the contiguity of topics in successive frames.

3. The extraction of subsequences from the basic sequence and the design of remedial loops are based on additional specifications, required to match the instructional material to each student's psychological profile. There are two types of specifications: levels, inherent in SMILE's conception, and tags, which are dependent on the author's pedagogical design; only levels are described here. The word "level" is used as an abbreviation for "level of additional pedagogical support." When an author does not want to write different material for different types of students, she still may obtain an efficient[1] presentation by classifying the frames according to levels.

Level–0 frames are all the essential frames that must be read by every student (e.g., all the N frames), some frames the author considers pedagogically necessary, and the exercises that ensure appropriate testing. For some students these frames are enough to provide instruction on the topics dealt with; there is no need for additional pedagogical support. Using the same term to classify students as well, these will be called "level-0 students." A certain confusion, which this comment tries to eliminate, may arise from the fact that the lower the level, the brighter the student—contrary to normal usage. This is because the level considered in this context is the level of required pedagogical support, and it is natural that the best students require a minimum of support, while the poorest students require a maximum.

The pedagogical assumption inherent in SMILE is that for not-so-bright students the same level–0 frames may be used if additional explanations are added, that is, if more introductory, complementary, and lower-difficulty exercises are provided in order to facilitate learning. This assumption is valid if the student population is not widely diversified (at least, not more than what is normal in secondary schools and university courses), and if the level–0 frames are designed with a clear vision of the whole student population.

To implement this level scheme after having defined the level-0 frames, the author's next step is to write a minimal set of frames that provides pedagogical support in some critical steps of the instructional sequence. These frames constitute level 1. Levels 2, 3, and so forth, are written according to the same criterion, that is, providing, step-by-step, additional layers of pedagogical support. The maximum level number that may be assigned in SMILE's present implementation is eight, but usually not more than four levels will be used.

4. Further information is contained in the frame data structure, which has many points in common with the TOAM Reading Comprehension frames described earlier in

---

[1]Efficient in the sense that it will not be boring for the better students nor unduly hard for the weaker ones.

this chapter, but which has some important additions also. The SMILE-frame structure is presented in Figure 13.7. Let us comment on the differences between this and the RC frame structure, shown in Figure 13.2.

a. A catalog number is used instead of the array coordinates, because the SMILE structure is of the sequence type.
b. The Pedagogically-Qualified topics field contains the indexing information, in terms of couples, as previously described.
c. The Frame-Predecessors field contains the catalog number of each frame declared as a logical predecessor.
d. If the frame is expository, it contains context but no questions.
e. When the learner answers incorrectly, a comment will be presented, and in addition, a remedial loop will be organized by the system, reviewing the set of topics listed in the Topic Failures field.

Pedagogical Model

The mixed-initiative interaction in SMILE is implemented in two different styles, guided and exploratory, which are student selected. In the first case, the interaction is controlled by a program called GUIDE, which presents the appropriate subsequence of each unit, and updates the student's activity record. In the exploratory style the program in charge of the interaction is called SOLO, and the student specifies the topics and the instructional events she is interested in. The present SOLO implementation allows for explication and practice in tutorial mode. In this style no updating is done on the student's record.

Although the set of student commands is the same under GUIDE or SOLO, the following description corresponds to guided activity, where the system has to make a more intelligent use of the available information, to produce correct pedagogical decisions. In both cases the student input will depend on whether she is presented with an expository frame or with an exercise.

```
SMILE-frame
    Catalog-number
    Pedagogically-qualified topics
    Frame predecessors
    Context
    Question (M)
        Question parameters
        Question text
        Correct answer (N)
            Expected answer
            Comment
        Incorrect answer (P)
            Expected answer
            Comment
            Topic failures
```

Figure 13.7. SMILE-Frame Structure

1. Expository frames

When the student finishes reading an expository frame (not an exercise), she presses a command key. The available commands and their effects are summarized in Figure 13.8.

2. Exercises

The student presented with an exercise is not forced to produce an answer when she is not sure. Guessing is not encouraged. In fact, the student may use any command described in the previous section (with the exception of ADVANCE).

When the student input is an answer to an exercise (as opposed to a command), GUIDE checks for correctness. The effect of a correct answer, with respect to the presentation sequence, is the same as that of an ADVANCE command. Furthermore, the student receives explicit approval as reinforcement. When the answer is not correct, a remedial loop is designed by the system, to review the topics that appear in the Topic Failures list defined by the author for the selected answer.

When the list of topic failures is not empty, the remedial loop will vary according to whether this is the first, second, or later presentation of the exercise, and to the topic coverage available in the frames. A minimal remedial loop would include only the frames that satisfy two conditions simultaneously: (1) they are qualified with an N under any one of the topics failed; (2) they are predecessors of the exercise. A maximum remedial loop would include any frame that teaches about the topics failed, and that precedes the exercise in the basic sequence.

Let us analyze now what use the PM makes of level information. Every student is assigned an initial level of pedagogical support. The relation between student level and the subsequence this level defines is very simple: SMILE will present, to any student of level i, all the frames with levels 0 to i, in the order they appear in the basic

COMMAND	SYSTEM ACTION
ADVANCE	Introduces the next frame in the sequence the student is presently following.
BACK	Presents the previous frame. Successive BACKs take the student back in the particular sequence she followed.
EXPLAIN	Presents frames at higher levels, not yet seen by the student, and finishes with the frame whose explanation was asked for.
REVIEW	This is the one command where the student must enter additional information, which defines a query. This query is entered as a Boolean function over the list of topics to review. GUIDE then presents a sequence of all the necessary frames covering those topics, up to the frame where the REVIEW command was issued.
SUSPEND	If a student is in a remedial or exploratory loop, this command returns her to the basic sequence. If she is in the basic sequence, the system closes the session, storing the student's updated history.

Figure 13.8. SMILE Student Commands

sequence. It is important to emphasize that this scheme defines an initial, static, subsequence. The actual presentation sequence, that is, the graph traversal, is determined by GUIDE according to the student's performance, her dynamically updated level, and her requests.

An example of well-designed interaction between level and content for the teaching of one topic is shown in Figure 13.9. Bars denote frames; their displacement in the *x*-direction corresponds to frame order in the basic sequence, and their displacement in the *y*-direction indicates frame level. The letter over each bar is the pedagogical qualifier of the topic being taught in the corresponding frame.

A level–0 student entering this segment of a unit would be presented the one frame with necessary information and her comprehension would be immediately tested with an exercise. If her answer is correct, this segment of the unit is finished (with only two frames presented). A level–1 student would start with an introductory frame, then would receive the necessary information followed by a complement (an example, for instance) and an easier exercise. Only when this exercise is correctly answered is the level–0 exercise presented. A level–2 student receives even more introductory and complementary frames.

When the necessary information is presented to a level–0 student she may ask for an explanation, and the preceding level–1 introductory material would be presented. If she asks for clarification when the exercise is presented, then the level–1 complement is displayed before her answer to the level–0 exercise is requested again.

Let us finish this section on the pedagogical model by emphasizing the freedom available to the student within SMILE's implementation. For example, a student presented with an exercise may ask for a review of some topics; while reading a review frame she may ask for a review of some other topics and, while in this new review, she may ask for further explanations or she may go back into the frame sequence she was following. When her doubts have disappeared or she thinks that she understands, or when further reading will not help her, she may switch back to the exercise and answer it.

Student Model

Referring again to the dynamic data of the student record sketched in Figure 10.3, SMILE has a performance summary for each unit the student has completed and a very rich description of the student traversal for each active unit, that is, for each unit the student has started and not yet finished. This description includes the status of the student with respect to any frame in the unit and the "historical" path the student is following. This path allows, for instance, for the implementation of the BACK com-

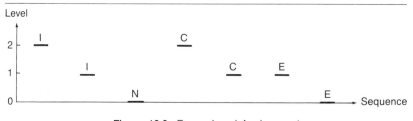

Figure 13.9. Frame-Level Assignment

mand. The support structure that allows for the mix of student commands and system-initiated remedial loops, is implemented as a stack. For every command or loop, a new state is pushed down into the stack and popped up when the treatment finishes.

Student performance at each frame is evaluated in terms of latency, usage of remedial commands, and in the case of exercises, in terms of answer correctness also.

School Activity

When a student is registered in a course, her attributes, including a teacher-assigned pedagogical-support level, are stored in a student directory. Then the student receives a user's manual and a course manual, and she is ready to start. The first unit in every course is a tutorial on SMILE usage.

Each unit is studied as a sequence of sessions at a terminal. The student determines the length of each session because she may terminate it when she pleases. The activity of each student at the terminal is recorded and stored in the administration file, so that when she starts a new session it begins at the same point of the instructional process where she left off. The average time required to study a unit in the "Electricity and Magnetism" course is about 90 minutes.

Evaluation of teacher and student satisfaction, through questionnaires and personal interviews, has been positive, but no serious summative evaluation has been attempted because the course is still in its developmental stage. The main difficulty we find is the resistance of teachers to part with some of their lecture time in favor of computer activities. The system is being used in auxiliary mode, with emphasis on practice (and remedial help when needed). In the traditional class organization, practice is student responsibility and is done mostly as homework. When practice at a computer lab is attempted, then we discover that students are not allowed to work in the computer lab without teacher supervision. Thus, either the teacher sacrifices part of the lecture time, or budget coverage is required for the added computer activity, which in today's tight budgetary situation has been hard to obtain.

HOW THE WEST WAS WON

Concise Technical Description

- Paradigm: Game
- Subject: Arithmetic
- Extension: Unit
- Locus of Control: Author-directed (prescribed) interaction
- Instructional events: Practice
- Function: Auxiliary or autonomous
- Granularity: Continuous
- Programming technique: Information-structure-oriented
- Pedagogical intervention: Coaching

General Description

In order to demonstrate the coaching technique, we have selected an example developed in the area of games. This allows us to concentrate on the pedagogical strategy, without being overwhelmed by the complexity of the subject matter (KM).

"How the West Was Won" is a game developed by Bonnie Anderson Seiler on the PLATO system. A personal computer version was developed later, under the name: "How the West Was One + Two * Three." Figure 13.10, taken from Paulson (1976), illustrates the terminal display.

The game is played by two players, one of which may be the computer. The players start at Tomb-Stone (position 0), and the winner is the first to arrive exactly at Red-Gulch (position 70). The number of steps each player advances in a move is the result of an arithmetic expression he/she/it builds by combining the values of three spinners randomly set by the computer for each move.

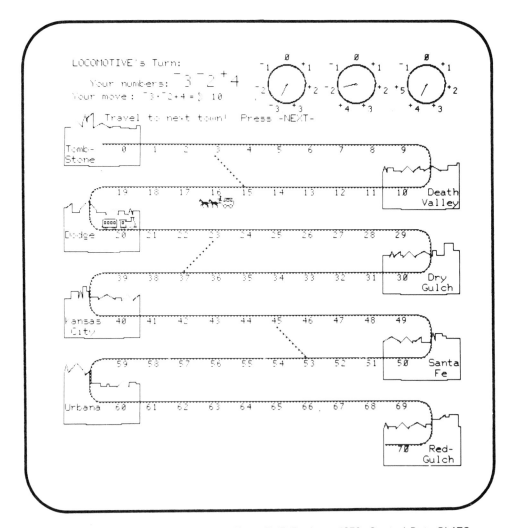

Figure 13.10. WEST Screen Display (From R. F. Paulson, 1976, *Control Data PLATO: System Overview.* pp. 5–13. Copyright 1976 by Control Data Corporation. Reprinted by permission.)

A player's initial strategy might be to maximize the value of the arithmetic expression, but the good player discovers very quickly that other options may be better:

- Landing in a town is rewarded with a jump to the next one.
- Landing on a shortcut means moving to the other end of it (e.g., landing in 23 moves the player to 37).
- Landing on the position occupied by the opponent (unless it is a town) "bumps" the opponent backward two towns.

Obtaining preselected results (i.e., having decided that a certain number of steps is advantageous, the player tries to form an expression that produces it) is much more demanding than just plugging the values of the spinners into fixed patterns.

You may well have observed that WEST has all the ingredients of a good educational game: adequate challenge; a nice mix of uncertainty, even suspense; and the possibility of playing it at different levels of proficiency, the player's sophistication progressing with experience. In fact, children love it. They may spend hours playing it at a terminal, which means that they practice arithmetic with pleasure, and their proficiency increases with their accumulated experience.

Does it?

This was the question raised by Cecily Resnick in her doctoral thesis (Resnick, 1975). The answer provides another example of the gulf that may exist between the expectations of the instructional designer and the actual results measured in the field.

Children do enjoy the game and their involvement keeps them at the terminal for hours. Nevertheless, they tend to become fixated into one strategy or even into one pattern, without any creative search, regardless of how many games they win or lose. This greatly reduces the educational value of the game. Burton and Brown (1976) took the challenge of reinforcing the educational strength of WEST without affecting the pleasure of the game, by introducing a COACH, a term coined by Goldstein (1977), in addition to the EXPERT embedded in the system.

The data structure and the training algorithm match the descriptions of those given in Chapter 8, except for the fact that the system is not sequencing the training over a set of tasks but merely providing training over a fixed task (playing WEST).

Assuming a student is playing against the computer, let us describe the highlights of the models used by Burton and Brown (1976).

Knowledge Model

The KM includes the "board" description, and an EXPERT, developed as a game component, to play the computer part.

The EXPERT was defined with a fixed strategy (strong, but subject to refinements), which consists of selecting, for each move, the arithmetic expression that maximizes the difference (delta) between the player's position and that of the opponent.

Due to the fact that there are only three spinners, it is possible to use a brute force algorithm: in each move, all the valid arithmetic expressions using the three given values are computed, and for each result the player's new position is determined, as well as that of the opponent. An expression providing maximum delta is selected as the player's move.

During the game, this algorithm is used in every move: When it is the computer's turn, it determines its move, and when it is the student's turn, the algorithm allows for an evaluation of her move.

Student Model

The evaluation of student performance is organized around "issues," each one defining a particular tool whose use is desirable. The system monitors whether the student uses:

1. Different ORDERing of the spinner values within the arithmetic expression
2. PARENtheses
3. Expressions leading to negative results, which may allow for a successful BACKWARD move
4. Special moves, like trying for TOWNS, BUMPing the opponent, or SHORT-CUTS
5. The subtraction operation (MINUS) and
6. The division operation (DIVIDE), both frequently neglected and often useful
7. A variety of operational PATTERNS
8. A STRATEGY allowing for evaluation of alternative expressions
   (The uppercase words or abbreviations are the code names used within the system to identify the different issues.)

The evaluation of issues is not trivial, because a student may have been using the spinner values in a fixed ORDER precisely because this order was optimal, and may have not used PARENtheses because there was no need for them. The solution to this problem, as developed by Burton and Brown, consists of analyzing the use (or lack of it) of the different issues within a classification of the possible moves according to their "quality." In a nutshell, a student weakness in an issue may be discovered because she is overusing it in poor moves or underusing it when it could be used to provide better moves.

Note the elegance of the solution, which allows for guidance related not only to the things the student did wrong, but also to those the student didn't do at all. As its quality measure of a move, the implementation uses the move's ranking within the sequence of all possible moves, ordered according to the maximum-delta strategy.

Coach Model

The principles of "let the student play" and "don't spoil the fun" sober the constructive criticism that the COACH could be tempted to utter at each move.

The COACH will not teach abstract rules but will rather look for concrete examples to make its point. The authors call it "Issues and Examples Paradigm."

To give an example of how the quasi-algorithm for coaching, presented in Chapter 8, is implemented in the WEST-COACH system, let us present the treatment corresponding to one of the steps of the instructional process (see p. 163): "If the move is poor and the coaching principles ask for it, advice is given."

- The COACH examines the list of issues where the student has weaknesses, and checks whether any of the possible better moves (remember that the student made a poor move) exhibits one of those issues. If this is so, the COACH selects the best of those moves (either in terms of issue importance or delta gain). Note that the COACH will not try to impress the student with the optimal move (in terms of maximum delta) but rather will present a move that exemplifies a tutorable issue.

- The alternative move is presented to the student with the option of adopting it. This increases the student's interest and favors the learning process.
- If none of the better moves exemplifies a weak issue, or if the student has no detected weakness, the COACH will say nothing. Under certain circumstances it could hint that better moves are possible and allow the student, if she wants, to substitute her expression.

The WEST-COACH program uses additional heuristics, some of which were presented explicitly in a later paper (Burton and Brown, 1979) and may be summarized as follows:

- Do not give advice in two consecutive moves.
- Applaud some of the student optimal moves.
- Do not give advice on an issue where the student has performed satisfactorily within the last three moves.
- If a good student has a weak issue, it is possible to give her advice in a good (but nonoptimal) move. (Poor moves are not frequent.)
- The example selected for advice must present a move clearly superior to the move selected by the student.
- If a student is about to lose, help her stay in the game.
- Give the student a chance to discover the game for herself. Do not tutor from the start.

The COACH will also present advice on request. This help is organized in four levels of increasing "directivity," to encourage the student to solve the problem by herself. Successive requests for advice (on the same move) will produce the following COACH responses:

1. Commenting on a weak issue whose use may produce an optimal move.
2. Presenting the set of all possible results.
3. Presenting the optimal result and explaining why it is optimal.
4. Presenting the optimal move (the arithmetic expression itself).

WEST is used in schools in its game form only. The coached version requires a much higher level of computer resources and was tested solely in laboratory conditions. Furthermore, modeling the coach was a brilliant pioneering effort, but practical application would require an additional investment in the more prosaic aspects of providing explanations in the areas where student weaknesses persist.

GRAPHS AND TRACKS

Graphs and Tracks is a simulation package developed by David E. Trowbridge, from the Department of Physics at the University of Washington (Seattle). Its purpose is to improve the students' insight of some concepts taught within the kinematics curriculum by providing a simulated laboratory where students can practice, in guided or free form.

This description is based on Trowbridge (1988, 1990).

Concise Technical Description

- Paradigm: Simulation
- Subject: Graphs of motion in one-dimensional kinematics
- Extension: Unit in the first-year introductory physics course
- Topology: Sequence
- Locus of control: Student-directed (free) interaction
- Instructional events: Practice, problem solving
- Function: Auxiliary
- Granularity: Continuous
- Programming technique: Information-structure-oriented
- Pedagogical intervention: Open, with help on request

Instructional Conception

Many physics students show errors and misconceptions when dealing with graphs that represent motion of objects (see research references in Trowbridge, 1988a). For example, a frequent error is not representing continuous motion by a continuous line, when graphing position versus time, and another is not recognizing that velocity has to be continuous. An attempt to cope with these difficulties resulted in the design of a sequence of laboratory exercises, in each of which students were shown a graph on paper and asked to build an apparatus with U-shaped aluminum channel segments, such that a steel ball rolling on it would reproduce the motion shown in the graph. Students used clocks and meter sticks to make measurements of clock readings, time intervals, positions, and displacements. Although instructive, this technique was very time consuming, only two or three experiments could be performed during a class period, and very limited time was left to think about the correspondence between real motions and graphs. An additional limitation was imposed by the number of teaching staff available to evaluate each student's work.

The information gathered from observations of what students do with activities in a laboratory-centered physics course, from reports of their responses to oral questions in individual interviews, and from studies of their responses to conceptually oriented written questions, motivated the development of a pair of highly interactive graphical programs, *Graphs and Tracks, Parts I and II*. In this simulated laboratory, no time is required for construction or measurements, and the students may concentrate on the cognitive aspects where the objectives of instruction are focused. There are no limits related to support staff, because the students may interact freely with the programs. The number of activities that each student performs is much higher, and those activities are selected by each student according to her perceived needs or interests.

Implementation

Graphs and Tracks was written in cT (from Carnegie Mellon University), and runs on Macintosh (Plus,SE,II) and Unix workstations (under CMU's Andrew operating system).

In Part I, "From Graphs to Motion," the student is asked to manipulate a set of sloping tracks (see Figure 13.11), by raising or lowering the track supports, so that the movement of a ball matches a set of given graphs (position, velocity, and acceleration). The student may switch among the graphs by clicking at their titles, which may also be seen in Figure 13.11.

The student also has to set the initial position and velocity of the ball; this is done by moving cursors over corresponding axes. Values are rounded to the nearest mark on the axis.

The target graph is dotted; every time the student "rolls" the ball, a set of graphs is generated and the one corresponding to the student selection (position, velocity, or acceleration) is displayed, so that the student may compare the result of her decisions with the desired target. In case of mismatch, help is available and, according to the student's preferences, she may ask for one suggestion only, for help on every move, or for no help at all. Help does not give the solution, rather, it focuses the student's attention on problematic areas, as shown in Figure 13.12.

Graphs and Tracks I includes 8 built-in examples: the first 4 fairly simple, the next 4 slightly more complex. The student may tackle them sequentially or by direct selection. In addition, teachers and students may add up to 20 examples, by experimenting and saving the more interesting ones.

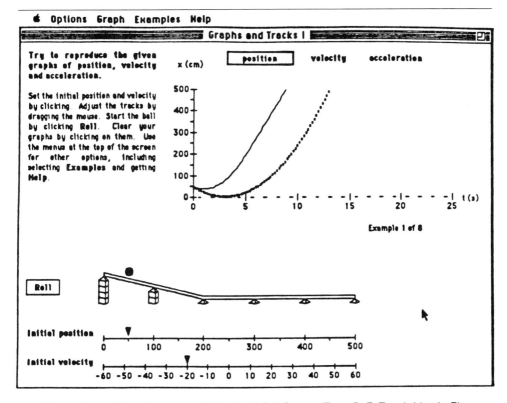

Figure 13.11. "From Graphs to Motion"—A Full Screen (From D. E. Trowbridge in *The Conference on Computers in Physics Instruction Proceedings,* edited by E. F. Redish and J. S. Risley, © 1990, Addison-Wesley Publishing Co., Inc., Reading, Massachusetts. Fig. 3, p. 287. Reprinted with permission of the publisher.

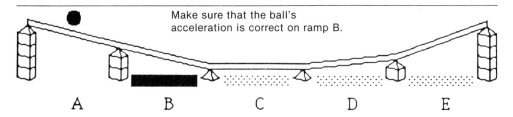

Figure 13.12. A Help Message (From D. E. Trowbridge, 1988, *Graphs and Tracks,* p. 6. Copyright 1988 by David E. Trowbridge. Reprinted by permission.)

In Part II, "From Motion to Graphs," the student is presented with a setting of the tracks and with a verbal description of the motion, and asked to graph (approximately) the position, velocity, and acceleration functions. Graphs are drawn by concatenating segments of different forms, selected from a palette of shapes. The segments may be edited, by pulling handles. "Free hand" is available also, but for single parabolic segments. A complete screen display may be seen in Figure 13.13.

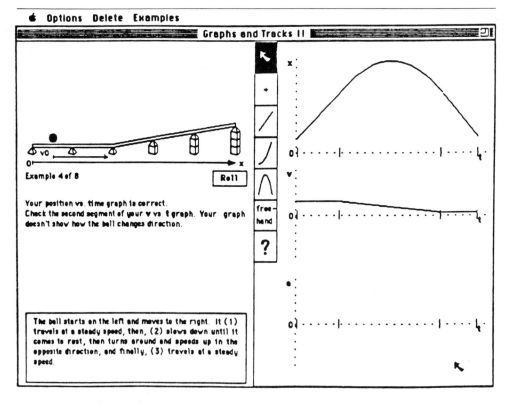

Figure 13.13. "From Motion to Graphs"—A Full Screen (From D. E. Trowbridge in *The Conference on Computers in Physics Instruction Proceedings,* edited by E. F. Redish and J. S. Risley, © 1990, Addison-Wesley Publishing Co., Inc., Reading, Massachusetts. Fig. 3, p. 287. Reprinted with permission of the publisher.)

The screen is split into two windows. The left one presents the exercise and the system responses, and the right one is the student's working area. In this particular example, the track setting appears in the upper part of the left window, and the verbal description of the movement in the lower part. In the middle part, there are system comments about the position graph (which is correct), and the velocity graph (which is wrong). When the student clicks on the "Roll" button, the system displays an animation of the ball motion.

Part II includes eight built-in examples also, and feedback is provided for common types of errors. This feedback does not provide tutorial explanations; it merely points to gross discrepancies between the student-produced graph and the system expectations.

Modeling and Simulation

This is an ideal environment for simulation. The laws of motion to be applied are well known and easy to computerize—some simplifications have been introduced for pedagogical reasons. The model is deterministic, so that no extraneous phenomena will interfere with the experiment being conducted. Differential and integral equations are used in this time-driven, continuous model, to compute the output functions. The initial conditions are determined by just eight values: six pillar heights and the initial position and velocity of the ball.

Guidance

There is no student model in this environment, so that guidance, feedback, advice, or help is provided solely on the basis of the last activity performed by the student, and not on the basis of her accumulated system history.

In Part I the main feedback is received by the student by just looking at the differences between the target graph, and the one that results from her selections. By establishing significant jumps between the values that may be selected by the student, both in pillar heights and in the initial values of position and velocity, the mismatch is easy to recognize. If help is requested from the system, it will focus the student's attention on specific track segments where the mismatch occurs, without additional guidance. This is an instructional decision that tries to foster problem-solving capabilities.

In Part II the student may request feedback by clicking on the question-mark icon. The system will check for correct graph segment types, correct signs and correct slopes, and, in Position versus Time graphs, it will also check for kinks that exceed some small change in angle.

THE GEOMETRIC SUPPOSER

"We have not done very well in traditional mathematics courses at conveying to our students an appreciation of the centrality of conjecture to the making of mathematics." This evaluation of a major instructional problem motivated Judah Schwartz and Michal Yerushalmy (1985) to develop the Geometric Supposer, a microworld for exploration of and inquiry into the world of plane geometry.

The following description is based on Schwartz and Yerushalmy (1985), Yerushalmy, Chazan, and Gordon (1987), and Yerushalmy (in press).

Concise Technical Description

- Paradigm: Microworld
- Subject: Euclidian (plane) geometry
- Extension: Open-ended
- Topology: Implemented as a sequence of independent units: Pre-Supposer, Triangles, Quadrilaterals, and Circles
- Locus of control: Student-directed (free) interaction
- Instructional events: Problem solving (exploration and guided inquiry)
- Function: Auxiliary
- Granularity: Continuous
- Programming technique: Information-structure-oriented
- Pedagogical intervention: Open

Instructional Conception

High school geometry is taught for two reasons: students should learn the properties of geometric entities, and they should develop the skills of deductive reasoning. Unfortunately, in too many classes the students' activity is reduced to memorizing proofs, whose need they do not see, of properties whose importance escapes them. The most creative part of doing mathematics, that of creating mathematical objects and exploring their properties, is usually absent from classroom practice.

The purpose that the Geometric Supposer tries to serve is that of helping the students create geometric objects and develop conjectures about their properties. Each geometric object is a particular instance of a class, and the students must be able to generalize their observations. The perception that observations and measurements are done on specific objects, while properties belong to classes of objects, provides the motivation for formal proofs.

The authors call for a "guided inquiry" instructional process, where the classical contents of the geometry courses are the basis for an integration of inductive with deductive reasoning, where empirical work is intertwined with conceptual work. Students can be active participants while learning, without sacrificing content coverage. This requires a major change in the role of the teacher, who, in this approach, must structure the class activities in a different form, must provide guidelines for inquiry, and must support the students' struggle to identify relevant properties from the wealth of information available. In contrast to a pure discovery approach, guided inquiry does not call for students to discover every theorem on their own; some theorems may be presented by the teacher, and students then investigate, at the computer, problems related to them.

Implementation

The Geometric Supposer is a set of programs written for Apple, IBM PC, and TOAM computers. Users can construct on the computer screen any shape that fits the canon of Euclidian geometry, that is, that can be built with straightedge and compass. The programs include supporting procedures to make measurements and making computations with the results of those measurements. A very important feature is the REPEAT command, which instructs the computer to repeat a user-defined process (building of a figure, measurements, computations), on another shape of the same family. This allows the student to investigate whether a conjectured property is valid in a particular figure only, or whether it is valid on all the cases, of the same family of figures, tested on the system.

The system is menu-driven, with the student selecting commands from a main menu or from any of its descendants in a tree of menus. The system records the commands and their parameters for any construction the student is doing, thus allowing for the REPEAT command just mentioned. The screen is divided into four functional areas (see Figure 13.14).

The lower part of the screen is assigned to the active menu; the central part is the main work area, where a figure is built or displayed; at the right of the main work area there are three small windows that display the last figures built by the user; the remaining area, to the left, is used for the display of the results of measurements and computations.

Course Integration

The integration of the Geometric Supposer within class activities is described here according to the model developed in a year-long evaluation study (1985–1986 school year), conducted at three secondary schools in three Boston suburbs. Classes met usually every day, for one class period. The computer activities could be performed in the same classroom or in a computer lab.

From the topics presented in the course, the teacher selects those that she feels are more appropriate for investigation with the Supposer. Students usually conduct their

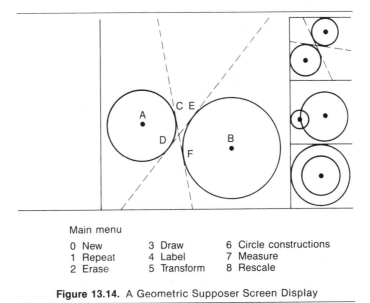

Main menu

0 New	3 Draw	6 Circle constructions
1 Repeat	4 Label	7 Measure
2 Erase	5 Transform	8 Rescale

Figure 13.14. A Geometric Supposer Screen Display

inquiry activities in groups of two or three. The conjectures generated by some groups, and the problems that are faced by others, are discussed in the classroom. For an example of the type of problem that may be posed, suppose that the class has studied a well-known property of the medians in a triangle: their intersection divides them in the ratio 2:1. The teacher may suggest a generalization of the concept of median, by dividing each side, not into two equal parts but rather into N equal parts. What happens then? Figure 13.15 presents the analysis of data for one case of $N = 3$, and Figure 13.16 presents the same for $N = 4$. Analyzing data for several cases, enunciating a correct theorem, first for concrete cases of N, and then generalizing and proving those theorems, is real mathematical work.

Developing conjectures gives a feeling of discovery, and in many cases students would post and sign conjectures for their classmates to prove. There are cases when students get disoriented or lost and, to help them, guidelines for conjecture making have been developed:

1. Make a construction and repeat it on several figures, looking for visual clues only.
2. Does anything strike you?
   Figures that may by congruent
   Figures that may be similar
   Segments that may be congruent
   Areas that may be the same
   Parallels
3. Write down the things that you are going to look for.
4. Gather numerical data.
5. Make a formal statement of conjectures.
6. Look for a convincing argument.

These guidelines must be treated in a flexible way. In reality, the discovery procedure is not linear, but rather iterative: For instance, a conjecture may guide the student in terms of what data to look for.

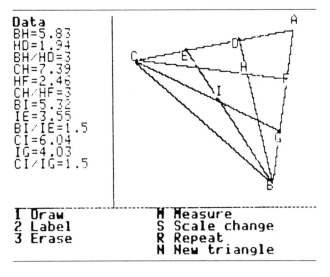

Figure 13.15. Median Generalization ($N = 3$) (From J. L. Schwartz and M. Yerushalmy, 1985, The Geometric Supposer: An Intellectual Prosthesis for Making Conjectures, *The College Mathematics Journal* [June 1985]: 60. Copyright by the Mathematical Association of America. Reprinted by permission.)

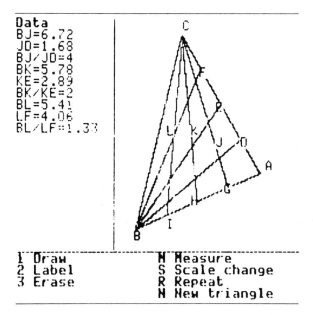

```
Data
BJ=6.72
JD=1.68
BJ/JD=4
BK=5.78
KE=2.89
BK/KE=2
BL=5.41
LF=4.06
BL/LF=1.33
```

```
1 Draw          M Measure
2 Label         S Scale change
3 Erase         R Repeat
                N New triangle
```

Figure 13.16. Median Generalization (*N* = 4) (From J. L. Schwartz and M. Yerushalmy, 1985, The Geometric Supposer: An Intellectual Prosthesis for Making Conjectures, *The College Mathematics Journal* [June 1985]: 60. Copyright by The Mathematical Association of America. Reprinted by permission.

The focus of the course changed along the year: at the beginning, conjecture making was the center, then it moved to plausibility arguments, and finally to proofs. Toward the end of the year, the students were assigned individual projects, to be presented with a full written report.

According to Yerushalmy et al. (1987), in the guided inquiry approach that we have presented:

> communication and discussion are fundamental. Using clear and precise language to communicate mathematical ideas is essential. Proof becomes the language of argument, and its utility is evident. In the context of discussion, teachers elicit opinions, acknowledge and value diversity, encourage creativity, build powers of argument, and facilitate resolution of different points of view. Students learn to listen, to respect the contributions of their classmates, and to communicate effectively with one another, not just with or through the teacher. (p. 85)

Evaluation

A formal study was conducted, comparing three high school geometry classes, where the Geometric Supposer was used as previously described, with three control classes that were selected by the school administrators to match the experimental classes in ability and academic level. The evaluation data were gathered as usual by a pretest and a posttest of all the students involved, but the data also included classroom observations, all the written student work on Supposer problems, notes from teachers' meetings and from interviews with teachers, teachers' written comments, and notes from interviews with students.

The tests themselves, and accompanying measurement criteria, were defined in order to evaluate the aspects that the work with the Supposer purports to improve: generalization skills (level, originality, correctness) and theorem-proving skills (argument generation). Generalization/conjecture performance was compared with a pretest consisting of four problems, and a posttest consisting of three problems. In the pretest, there was only one statistically significant difference between the two groups: the control group performed better than the experimental group on originality in problem 1. In the posttest there were two statistically significant differences, both in favor of the experimental group: the Supposer students produced higher-level generalizations on two out of the three questions and produced more arguments than the control group. This last aspect was reinforced by the findings of the argument/proof test, consisting of three problems, which was assigned as a posttest only; in this test the Supposer students made as many supporting arguments as the control students on two questions and more than the control students on the third. This is worth emphasizing, because the instruction of the control group focused on proofs, while the experimental groups worked more on informal argumentation.

Teachers' feelings may be summarized by a statement written by one of them: "I found working with the Supposer challenging, stimulating, and sometimes frustrating." Teachers recognize the positive impact on student learning style. Those teaching with the Supposer for the first time complained that they had received insufficient training. All of them declared that class preparation is much more time consuming with the Supposer, although this may be equated to the effort that must be invested when preparing a course for the first time.

Students had no problems in mastering the mechanics of the system. They enjoyed exploring and discovering; on the other hand, conjecturing presented real problems. Knowing what to conjecture about, discerning patterns and relationships, and generating conjectures, were all hard work. For some students, conjecture making was the province of "smart people." Not always was the classroom activity well integrated with the lab activities and, for some students, it appeared to be two parallel curricula. The change in intellectual demands was very clear: "It's different . . . You got to use your mind a lot . . . You're not just sitting back listening . . . You're doing the work." Through cooperation, which is not a hallmark of traditional math instruction, students gained new insights into what it means to be a member of a community of active learners.

As usual in microworlds or tools, we will not find models of knowledge, teachers, or students in the Geometric Supposer. This is not a hindrance for its use, if the rules of the game are clear and nothing is built on nonexisting features. For instance, the lack of a pedagogical model precludes on-line student guidance, but this guidance may be provided by teachers or student peers. The Supposer is a tool that performs a well-defined function, within an instructional design that includes knowledge and skill objectives and support infrastructure that comprises a teacher, a class, and the appropriate equipment.

BROWN UNIVERSITY HYPERMEDIA PROJECT

Brown University's Institute for Research in Information and Scholarship (IRIS), in collaboration with the university's English Department, has developed a hypermedia computational component to enhance the instruction of an introductory English literature course. The description presented here is based on Yankelovich, Landow, and

Cody (1987); Figures 13.17–13.19, however, represent more recent IRIS hypermedia work, and were provided through the courtesy of the IRIS staff.

Concise Technical Description

- Paradigm: Hypermedia
- Subject: English Literature from 1700 to the Present
- Extension: Semester course for majors and nonmajors
- Topology: Directed graph
- Locus of control: Student-directed (free) interaction
- Instructional events: Introduction, explication, problem solving
- Function: Auxiliary
- Granularity: Discrete
- Programming technique: Information-retrieval-oriented
- Pedagogical intervention: Open

Instructional Conception

The purpose of Brown University's course, "English Literature from 1700 to the Present," is to allow students to sample a wide range of great authors and important literary movements, providing them with a sense of the historical continuities of major literary forms and the traditions of the last few centuries. The present conception of a literature course places more emphasis on every student's developing an original view of the author's message transmitted by the text than on the learning of classical interpretations. To develop the critical-thinking skills required for this endeavor, it was decided to shift the emphasis from lectures to class discussions initiated and directed by students.

The analysis and discussion of a literary piece require background knowledge in terms of the interrelations of authors, their contributions, and the social, religious, political, intellectual, artistic, and technological contexts. Unfortunately, and due to the lack of literary experience of most students, lecture time concentrates upon the primary texts. The main idea of this project is to provide the background information as an on-line computerized resource that students may explore at ease, thus liberating them from the time-consuming library research that would be needed otherwise. In this environment students may pursue their own individual interests and bring their own discoveries and insights to the class discussions.

Implementation

A hypermedia environment, as described in Chapter 11, fits the designers' requirements extremely well. The software developed by the IRIS team is called Intermedia, and runs on networked high-resolution workstations. Intermedia includes four applications that were used to develop the materials for the English course:

- InterText, a word-processing program to create the formatted text to be presented at the windows,

- InterVal, to create and display chronological timelines,
- InterDraw, a structured graphics editor, used in conjunction with
- InterPix, a scanned image viewer, to create and display diagrams and bit-mapped images.

All the text documents were written specifically for the course. The initial database included 300 Intertext documents, 600 Interdraw documents (about 400 of these included InterPix images), and 75 InterVal timelines. These documents supplement the main reading and do not replace the books traditionally read in the course. The text documents fall into three categories: biographical sketches of authors, essays on particular aspects of an author, and brief explanatory essays on topics that relate to more than one author. The essays contain questions that either refer students back to the reading assignment or encourage them to follow links to discover the answers.

The Interdraw documents serve different purposes.

- Scanned images (portraits, photographs or drawings of authors' homes, evocative scenes, etc.) allow students to attach faces to names and to visualize the scenarios where authors lived and worked. Art reproductions allow students to juxtapose different art of the same or of a later or an earlier period.
- Overviews (e.g., Figure 13.17) include links to all the material in the database

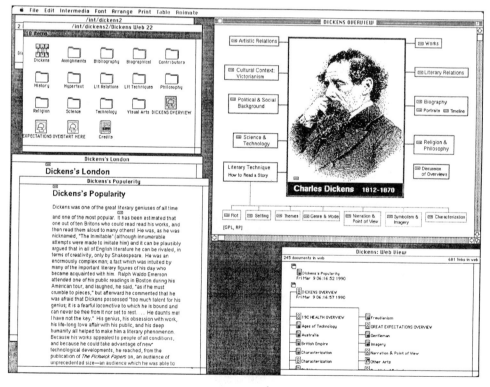

Figure 13.17. Dickens Overview (Copyright 1990 by Brown University. Provided through the courtesy of the Institute for Research in Information and Scholarship [IRIS].)

related to a given author. This graphical presentation shows the connections between an author and the surrounding world, thus emphasizing one of the main educational messages of the course.

- Literary-relations diagrams (e.g., Figure 13.18). The author's name appears centered in one window; above it are the names of people or movements that influenced that author; below it, those whom the author influenced; contemporary authors are placed to the right or to the left. The arrowheads on the side show the direction of the influence. Other windows in this diagram show further information on the author's literary relationships.

InterVal is used to create *timelines,* which supplement text and graphics documents. Timelines may be particular (e.g., events in an author's life) or general (e.g., British History). A student may juxtapose several timelines as a way to explore possible connections, influences and relationships (see Figure 13.19).

Two tools aid students in navigating through the database. Authors may add descriptive texts, called "link explainers" to the links, providing an indication of what is expected at the other end. Second, maps provide a graphical description of the database structure by showing the nodes and their links. Maps are available at global and local levels.

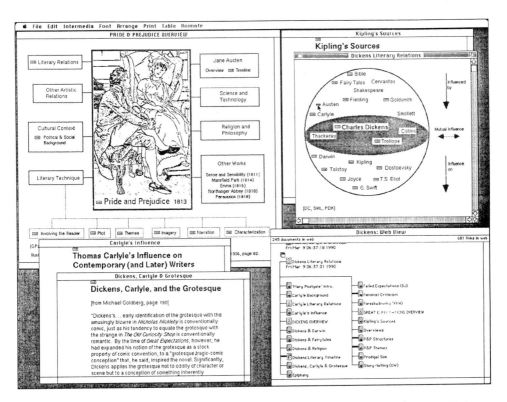

Figure 13.18. Dickens Literary Relations (Copyright 1990 by Brown University. Provided through the courtesy of the Institute for Research in Information and Scholarship [IRIS].)

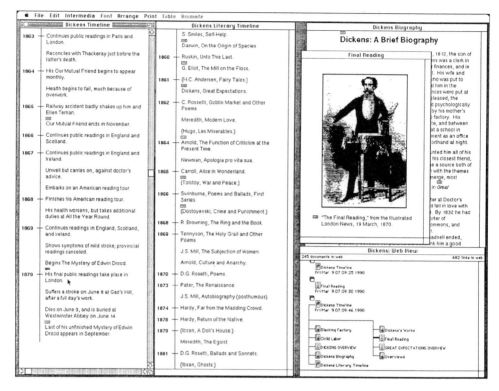

Figure 13.19. Dickens Timelines (Copyright 1990 by Brown University. Provided through the courtesy of the Institute for Research in Information and Scholarship [IRIS].)

Course Integration

The newly structured course has four components: (1) assigned readings, (2) student-directed class discussions, (3) writing assignments and examinations, and (4) hypermedia activities. Concentrating our attention on the fourth point, a student may use the hypermedia environment to read the background documents that were described, and to explore the database, either following the existing links or issuing Boolean queries. Furthermore, she may use the Intermedia tools to create her own documents, links, and even influence diagrams, which may be discussed by her peers. These activities will stimulate on-line dialogue, which will serve as a training ground for a much richer class discussion.

SUMMARY

The computerized instructional materials presented in this chapter, in addition to their intrinsic value, exemplify the taxonomies defined in this book. As a guide to the examples we will abbreviate the names of the instructional pieces presented as follows:

- RC: TOAM's Testing and Practice in Reading Comprehension
- EM: SMILE in Electricity and Magnetism

- WE: How the West Was Won
- GT: Graphs and Tracks
- GS: The Geometric Supposer
- HP: Brown University Hypermedia Project

The taxonomies are exemplified as follows:

- *Paradigms:* Courseware (RC, EM); Game (WE); Simulation (GT); Micro-world (GS); Hypermedia (HP).
- *Extension:* Course (RC, EM, HP); Unit (WE, GT).
- *Topology:* Sequence (EM, GT); Parallel sequences (RC); Directed graph (HP).
- *Locus of control:* Prescribed interaction (RC, WE); Mixed-initiative interaction (EM); Free interaction (GT, GS, HP).
- *Instructional events:* Introduction (HP; Explication (EM, HP); Testing (RC); Practice (RC, EM, WE, GT); Problem solving (GT, GS, HP).
- *Function:* Auxiliary (RC, EM, WE, GT, GS, HP); Autonomous (EM, WE).
- *Granularity:* Discrete (RC, EM, HP); Continuous (WE, GT, GS).
- *Programming technique:* Information-structure-oriented (RC, WE, GT, GS); Information-retrieval-oriented (EM, HP).
- *Pedagogical intervention:* Fixed (RC); Tutorial (EM); Coaching (WE); Open (GT, GS, HP).

PART V
Outlook

CHAPTER 14

The Decade Ahead: Looking into the Crystal Ball

The future lies ahead.
                    —Mort Sahl

Prognostication styles generally fall into three categories: *supportable and safe, way-out-on-a-limb,* and *obscure.* In the first class are those predictions that follow directly from the extension of a curve or from other rational projections of past changes. For example, various authors in a special issue of *Science,* on computers and electronics, projected through these means, trends for the 1980s in density of packing of microchips, hardware-software cost ratios, and other features of the computer industry, all of which were highly reasonable and most of which came true (*Science,* 1982).

The obscure approach is represented best in this millennium by Michel de Nostredame, better know as Nostradamus, a sixteenth-century French physician and clairvoyant, who is credited with predicting everything from Marie Antoinette's demise to guided missiles and atomic bombing. Nostradamus didn't predict any of these things directly however; instead, he wrote in obscure quatrains that have been interpreted quite generously, after the fact. The middle category, way-out-on-a-limb, is closest to what this chapter is all about. In this approach, radical departures from past trends are forecast, but with the obvious caveats (i.e., If such-and-such finally occurs, then we can expect. . . .).

We chose this approach not out of authorial license, but because we think it is informative of what technology might contribute to education, given certain social, educational, and technological changes. For those of you who have arrived at this chapter after careful study of all that has come before, we offer these projections as a reward for your patience and persistence. On the other hand, for those who jumped directly here from the Contents listing or from some intermediate point more closely located near the front than the back of the book, we offer these notions as an inducement to return to the unread chapters and partake of the technology that can lead to such a glorious future. Our plan here is to look ahead at development environments, delivery systems, and courseware, projecting what we might see in the next 5–10 years. First, however, we describe the social and educational changes that are necessary for this crystal-ball vision to come true.

SOCIAL CONTEXT

In industrialized countries the value of education, particularly of postsecondary education, has been increasing over the past decade and should continue to increase in the near future. With manufacturing shifting to the Far East, the industrialized countries of Europe and the Americas have begun to concentrate more on high-tech industries and services—occupations that require, for the most part, postsecondary education. In the United States, for example, of the 8 million jobs projected to become available between 1987 and 2000, only 1 million are projected in the low-skill category. This shift in employment opportunities will bring an increased willingness on the part of both government and private industry to invest in education, particularly in the teaching of technical skills. Concurrently, parents will be more willing to pay a high price for a college education for their children and will seek the best schools attainable, not just for engineering and science education, but for liberal arts as well. The higher price of educational technology will no longer be a barrier to its acceptance *if* its educational value can be demonstrated.

At the same time the industrialized nations will begin to assume a larger role in education for underdeveloped countries. Only part of this trend will be humanitarian; the other motivations will be (1) to assist in building an economic base so that major debts can be repaid, and (2) to raise the skill levels of cheap manpower so that they can operate the factories installed by large conglomerates. With emphasis on literacy, numeracy, and entry-level technical skills, educators will seek technological support for instruction. Teachers will be scarce, materials will need to be written in a variety of languages, and instruction will need to be delivered in remote areas as well as in the cities. Technology could be a cost-effective adjunct to human instruction under these conditions.

EDUCATIONAL CONTEXT

Due to its size, its wealth in natural resources, and the generally high educational levels of its citizens, the United States has been complacent about the quality of its schools. However, in the late 1980s several national and international assessments provided the shock waves that we hope will, in time, stir the country to reevaluate its educational system. The first was a survey of the literacy abilities of young adults, ages 21–26, that showed relatively few could cope with complex written materials (Kirsch & Jungeblut, 1986). An analysis of the implications of these results referred to the problem faced by the country as a "subtle danger" (Venezky, Kaestle, & Sum, 1987). Then, a 1989 evaluation highlighted U.S. ratings in the International Assessment of Educational Progress survey of math and science abilities in six different industrialized countries (Lapointe, Mead, & Phillips, 1989). In this survey, as the evaluation pointed out, U.S. 13-year-olds (the only age assessed) scored below the mean in both mathematics and science, trailing Korea, Spain, the United Kingdom, Ireland, and most of the Canadian groups in mathematics, and trailing Korea, the United Kingdom, Spain, and most of the Canadian groups in science.

In general, American students perform satisfactorily at the lowest levels of mathematics, science, or language arts. Where simple facts, problems, or vocabulary must be mastered, American students are both accurate and fast in responding. But when complexity levels increase, the relative performance of American students plunges. Over the coming decade we could see a major restructuring of American education to meet the problems revealed in these surveys.

Problem solving, particularly in mathematics and science, needs to be stressed in both elementary and secondary education. Instruction must no longer be driven by basal series that reduce the level of complexity of each subject area to what can be marketed nationally. Instead, teachers should become, as part of being good instructors, resource managers, drawing upon both print and electronic materials to teach a full range of skills in each subject area.

Instructional organization might also change, with a renewed emphasis on small groups, teams, and peer and cross-age tutoring. Secondary school education might become more extended and more distributed. Some students might complete the traditional four-year curriculum in three years, while others could take five or six years to do so, working part of the time and taking courses not only within educational institutions but also at work, recreation centers, government offices, and even at home. School-industry cooperation should increase, as should college-high school cooperation. Colleges might also become more involved with short courses and other forms of extension education, and industrial/business education could increase in scope and extent. Students could be tracked across time and location through a national student database that would record educational progress, diagnoses of skill strengths and weaknesses, and other relevant instructional/learning information. Modeled on the database for children of migratory farm workers that has been in place for over 20 years, this database would allow continuity of learning as students move around the country and in and out of schools and industrial training programs.

Scenario I—An Industrial Educational Program

Our first projected scenario is a small manufacturing plant, employing about 350 persons at various job levels. The company, Comtech, Ltd., holds patents on a new molding process for composites and makes a limited line of parts for the world aircraft industry. Its lowest-level workers receive incentives for finishing high school, including free courses partly on company time. Students study at workstations for some courses and have study partners who are often at other locations. The partners communicate on-line, through both electronic mail and voice communications, and often do mathematics problems and simulated lab experiments together. The workstations are tied into a regional high school network that supplies courseware, keeps student records, monitors progress, and provides on-line tutoring from other high school students and from volunteers in business, industry, and universities. Basic skills in literacy and in numeracy are monitored continually by the courseware, and when major deficiencies are detected, remedial work is recommended.

A student working on a science problem might be interrupted with a message saying that the system feels he should stop and work on qualifiers like "while," "during," and "until" before continuing. A specific lesson is also suggested. This conclusion is based on long-term monitoring of student responses, evaluated against a model that breaks tasks into basic skill components and then provides functions for deciding which of these skills might be lacking in particular wrong answers. In many cases the system is unable to diagnose the student's weaknesses completely and therefore recommends a live diagnostician, who might be routed on a house call, much like a plumber or washing machine repair person. In many places, full-time on-site instructors provide these same services.

Engineers and other technical specialists at this same plant also have workstations for continuing education. An international engineering network, connected via satellite, provides refresher courses on such topics as partial differential equations, qualitative analysis, and physical chemistry. Summaries of new methods and materials are available on a monthly basis from several research and development centers, with follow-up reading material in any one of 10 or so languages available for downloading. An on-site educational director tailors courseware to individual needs, selecting from courseware libraries around the world. User fees sustain this network, and new graphics and text interface languages allow courseware to be developed for a wide range of output devices.

Journal articles, available on-line, allow call-up of minicourses to explain different aspects of article content. For example, a reader might encounter some matrix algebra equations that he wants to understand better. A simple key-press brings up several options for explanations, including modules developed for different levels of mathematical expertise. After working through one of these, the reader can return to the point where he left off in the article. Similary, keying on any referenced work brings up not only the work, but reviews and comments published on the work and, for some works, voice recordings of the author, adding background and further explication.

All the workstations just referenced have high-quality, color graphics, good speech output, and some speech recognition ability, at least enough to recognize 100–200 commands and simple phrases (e.g., "Open window number six", "Print screen"). Optical storage units in the local network hold several billion characters of courses, reference materials, and student records. Processing power within workstations is in the 20–25 MIPS range, allowing fast animation of complex images. Less powerful units, many of which are the size of a large book, are available for use outside of work. These can be downloaded with homework of various types, and can connect through cable TV to local, national, and international networks. Adaptive devices allow users with a wide range of physical handicaps to make extensive use of the system.

Scenario II—A Middle School

Think-big Middle School is a typical American elementary school of the late 1990s. About 450 students in grades 4–6 attend classes in a remodeled factory building near the downtown area of a large city. Students are organized into study teams of 6–8 students each, with a volunteer team advisor drawn from parents, local businesspeople, or high school students. These advisors are generally available for about an hour each day, but can also be reached by telephone and through electronic mail. Most work in this school is centered on projects that integrate the main school subjects—language arts, mathematics, science, social studies, and art. However, separate skills are tracked by computer for each student and occasionally students work individually or in small groups on separate skills. Work sheets and boardwork still occur, although they are a minor feature in the instructional landscape.

Computers are used frequently for extra skill work, for advanced problem solving, and for access to library resources such as encyclopedias and dictionaries, although these latter items have now been combined on-line into knowledge stores where students can navigate through knowledge outlines to locate any desired level of description, definition, or visualization they might desire. Projects have been developed around a combination of print, on-line, and hands-on materials. Many require construction, tape recording, videotaping, or computer simulation. Courseware has been developed to teach some of the skills and procedures for these projects and to assist in recording, analyzing, and presenting data. An intelligent weather program, for example, tutors students on how to make simple measurements and observations about the weather. The resulting data are entered into the system and then organized and presented in various forms. One module assists in plotting weather maps for a region, using measurements of wind speed, temperature, and barometric pressure obtained from other student sites via a computer network.

As each student attempts to create an on-line weather map, the tutoring system is plotting its own map and comparing it to the student's. Where major deviations occur, the system provides feedback, tailored for the student's background level in the topic and his aptitude for the subject matter. Tutoring might include full lessons on both reading and plotting weather maps, using current maps from the area as exemplars. At the end of each day the system prints a summary for the instructors, stating what progress was made by each group and what problems are recurring. Suggestions are also made for specific skill practice. At a remote site, a cooperating meteorologist periodically reviews student work and sends his comments directly to the students involved. The students may visit a meteorology station or might participate in a teleconferencing session with one. Some students collaborate with partners located at other sites around the world, exchanging weather data and doing collaborative projects such as acid-rain monitoring.

The courseware involved in the school projects is highly adaptive to the skill needs of each group of students. Using project frames, the instructional system can vary the mathematical, language, and scientific skills involved, according to the skill curriculum of the school and the skill needs of the students. Some groups, for example, do weather maps requiring extensive computation, while others are given a more demanding communication task, requiring, for example, a script for a TV weather report. Projects that involve social studies skills—history, geography, civics, and so forth—are similarly adapted. An intelligent report analyzer does the first pass in evaluating student writing. The output from this system goes first to the student to allow rewriting. Then, a second analysis is done to assist the teacher in grading and in providing corrective feedback. All student writing skills are tracked on-line, and, using teacher-set criterion levels, homework is automatically generated to overcome specific skill weaknesses.

Teachers can draw on national and international courseware libraries for configuring courses. Courses and lessons are stored with reviews and comments from users, data gathered on-line on errors (if relevant) and on-average times for completing identifiable components. Schools and other educational institutions can contract with development groups to adapt registered courseware and to integrate different courses and lessons into a curriculum.

Scenario III—A College

South-by-Southeast University has a student enrollment of 26,000, of whom 5,000 are graduate students. All students are required to acquire a particular microcomputer; in addition, this same model is available for rental at a pittance. The university maintains a maintenance and replacement service provides, via a campus network, file storage, access to special processors (e.g., supercomputers), remote networks, and special databases (e.g., bibliographies, *Oxford English Dictionary,* North American museum holdings). Printers of various qualities are located at many sites on and off the campus, so that output can be routed at the student's discretion. Some courses, nevertheless, maintain their own instructional laboratories.

One such case is foreign languages, where pronunciation training is done almost exclusively with intelligent on-line systems. For introductory speaking courses, students sit in front of graphics monitors and attempt to imitate words they hear over earphones. As they speak, their vocal output is analyzed and displayed on the screen along with an analysis of the model voice. In one mode the display animates the vocal tract, showing the ideal positions of tongue, lips, glottis, and so forth, along with the corresponding positions for the utterance just made by the student. In another mode, frequency-time-intensity plots appear. In both cases the student can repeat the target word over and over, continually trying to shape his pronunciation until it looks like that of the native speaker. Where repeated errors occur, the system shifts to an aural discrimination mode to ensure that the student can discriminate the phonetic components that characterize the target forms. Periodically, reports are generated for the instructors, giving specific problems that students are having.

In physics, mathematics, statistics, and many other sciences, large data banks of problems are available, with intelligent tutors that assist students on-line. By indicating a course and assignment, a student can access a problem set selected by a course instructor, and receive on-line help in working the problems. For some problems, each student step is monitored and feedback given. For others, only expert comments are available, either as hints for solution strategies or as commentary on a stored solution. For most problems, important solution processes are keyed to instructional modules. For example, if a particular modern-algebra proof requires use of recursion, a link is made to a recursion-teaching program, with some selectivity in the level of sophistication of the instruction.

First-year English is also highly automated. All writing assignments are done on-line, with on-line writing tutors and semiautomatic evaluation of the finished product. Part of the tutoring process involves tagging components of the theme according to both syntactic and semantic functions. This is an interactive process wherein the system queries the writer for specific information that is used to construct both a grammatical and a semantic map of the work. The system then analyzes these maps and generates suggestions for how the writing might be improved. Dictionaries, encyclopedias, almanacs, atlases, usage guides, and a variety of other reference works are available on-line, as are samples of writing from famous novelists, short-story writers, essayists, and technical writers. Part of the tutoring involves suggestions for how these resources might be used to assist in writing. When needed, instruction is given on their use. Spelling and grammar checkers keep track of errors, accumulated across students, and periodically give short quizzes on the most common mistakes, primarily to sensitize students to areas in which they should work on their own to improve. Since all themes are saved on-line, some checks can be made for plagiarism.

In many courses that have a high reading load, key readings have been annotated by instructors, using a hypermedia system. In History 671—American Constitutional History, the Mayflower Compact, the Declaration of Independence, the Federalist Papers, the Constitution, Lincoln's Gettysburg Address, and many Supreme Court decisions have been treated in this way. Students who study these documents on-line receive comments on the texts, questions, suggestions for collateral readings, and hints at interpretation. Most of these are stored voice messages, but display text is also available. In some cases the instructor thinks out loud as he reads the text, modeling an expert reading; in other cases a more tutorial approach is used, with questions, suggestions for comparison and backtracking, and encouragement for notetaking, outlining, and the like.

Many other applications of on-line learning occur, including simulation of science laboratories, music training, statistics, and art history. All of these applications are supported by small professional staffs of coursewriters who are located within and supported by the separate colleges. For example, Arts and Sciences maintains a courseware center that specializes in hypermedia applications and document analysis. The Engineering College group is more oriented toward laboratory simulations and problem solving, and therefore serves not only its own interests, but those of certain Arts and Sciences departments, such as physics, mathematics, and astronomy. These latter departments have to pay a fee for these services, so that cost-benefit analysis has become crucial to instructional resource allocation.

Scenario IV—A Home

The McGurby home on Elm Street is one of several familiar types of American households, with two working parents, two teenage children, and a lot of appliances. Among the latter are two microcomputers, one that the parents use for their work and one that the children use for theirs. Both are medium-range machines: 5 mbyte of RAM, 80 mbyte hard disk, inexpensive laser printer, and fax attachment. Both computers can be connected to the cable network to download courseware, access large databases, or use electronic mail. (New cable technologies allow several separate transmissions to occur concurrently; from a single cable, one TV set can be connected to a selected TV channel while a computer connects to a remote databank.) Courseware can also be rented from the local video store, which carries a full range of materials for two or three popular computer formats.

For the children, courseware is a standard part of their curricular materials. Math practice problems, science laboratory simulations, English vocabulary and writing practice, and social studies databases are supplied by the school for home use. Additional courseware is available from the school library, covering music and art topics, technical skills such as automotive repair, and foreign languages. Some courseware even has take-home tests that are done on-line, and then returned to the classroom where they are graded by teacher-run programs. A school bulletin board is maintained 24 hours a day during the school year. It allows students, parents, and teachers to communicate on a variety of topics, including homework, school events, and personal matters (e.g., services available, items for sale, information needed).

For the parents, the computer is used primarily for work-related learning. Both parents bring home courseware from their companies: lessons on corporate procedures and products, on machine operations, and on specific skills like technical writing and geometry. One is involved with a highly complex printing machine for which a simulator panel has been developed for interfacing to standard microcomputers. The panel is a reduced version of the actual press panel; a simulation package has been designed along with it for training operators and repair specialists. On some days one or the other of the parents works at home part of the day as part of a distributed educational program that both companies have developed. Employees receive time off with pay to enroll in one job-related course during each six-month period. Some courses are done at a local university, some are done on site, and some are done on-line, using machines at home or at work. Merit pay increases are partially tied to successful completion of such courses, as are promotions.

The household also owns a CD-ROM player that can be be used either for music or for digital data. Most standard home resources such as encyclopedias and dictionaries are contained on optical disks and can be accessed through a single retrieval system that allows rapid lookup of words and phrases, synonym and spelling checks, and even limited graphic searches. A single disk holds a combined encyclopedia, dictionary, atlas, and almanac. Another, which is updated periodically, contains the contents of 10 newspapers from major cities around the world, plus 20 magazines (news, sports, business, etc.) This disk is used for various school assignments and for recreational reading. Some resources, such as the atlas, are accompanied by a book that has high-quality graphic plates but some, like the dictionary, are not.

ADVANCES IN SUPPORT TECHNOLOGIES

The wonders of automated instruction incorporated into these scenarios assume major advancements in certain support technologies: cognitive psychology, development environments, and delivery systems. For projecting improvements in delivery systems, no tarot cards are needed. The supportable-and-safe approach to prognostication yields, in the near future, 20–25 MIPS workstations with 8–16 megabytes of random-access storage and gigabytes of fast-access, backup storage. High-quality voice synthesis is available now, albeit at a cost slightly above what is needed for mass instructional use; voice recognition is out of its long Pleistocene and moving rapidly into practical utility. Coupled with increased capacity machines will be new networks for international and national educational cooperation, utilizing satellites, cable television, and voice-grade lines.

Psychological Base

One important barrier to improved courseware is the limited psychological base upon which most instructional development must draw. In spite of some promising new directions in cognitive psychology, the total activity in this field is presently too low to produce major improvements over the next decade in psychological models of learning and in approaches to instruction. But given the dismal state of science, math, and language arts achievement among American youth, we predict a major new effort to improve education in the United States, funded jointly by government and private sources. Technology, combined with better teacher training, holds the best hope for large improvements in achievement over the coming decade and therefore will be the focus of many new research and development efforts. Although basic research will continue on memory and learning, increasing emphasis will be placed on what Piaget called *instructional pedagogy:* the study of learning within ongoing educational environments. Instead of testing a new approach to fifth-grade mathematics with 5–10 students in a university laboratory, new methods and programs will be incorporated into regular classrooms and marginal gain or loss observed. In addition, through studies of student errors and of student explanations of their learning processes, deeper insights will be gained into how knowledge is acquired and used.

Much of this work will be theory-driven, drawing on models of cognitive development and of learning, but some will be more practice-based, where alternative approaches derived from expert practice are field-tested. Much of instructional development must be done without theoretical guidance; for instance, how many examples should be included for the first lesson in long division, whether or not to invoke a plumbing metaphor in introducing current electricity, selecting an appropriate graphic representation for the food chain. The decisions that come out of such considerations must be tested in live classrooms, but the testing must be done systematically so that the greatest generalization possible can be derived from the effort. We cannot fine-tune every program that is made available for use, but we can build a testing scheme that allows developmental knowledge to accumulate over time rather than to disappear with the demise of each development project.

DEVELOPMENT ENVIRONMENTS

The development environment of the mid–1990s will be radically different from what we now have. Courseware will be demonstrated first with rapid prototyping languages, similar to HyperCard, Smalltalk and C^{++}, but with generators for instructional paradigms, student-instructor dialogues, and different types of simulations. Smart editors for speech and graphics will also be available, along with systems for composing video displays from stored images (e.g., systems that generate animated scenes from static images). Development machines will include emulators or coprocessors for all of the common target machines. Model tryout sites (military, industrial, school, college, etc.) will be linked electronically to the development labs, allowing rapid formative testing of new ideas. Modular development of lessons and lesson components will allow configuration of some courses from available modules. Most target machines will have coprocessors especially for courseware produced according to new International Instructional Standards; graphics interfaces, using structural tagging similar to that specified by Standardized General Markup Language (SGML), will allow output to be adapted to a variety of different display (and speech) capacities.

Most importantly, a mass market for good, on-line instructional systems will encourage a wide range of producers, including textbooks publishers, universities, and even cooperatives composed primarily of elementary and high school instructors. With the International Instructional Standards, courseware will no longer become obsolete when particular machines go out of production. Courseware cooperatives, like EDU-COM, CONDUIT, and Kinkos, will assist in publicizing and distributing courseware, particularly that produced by small organizations. University programs will appear everywhere for training courseware developers, and computer science departments will offer instruction and encourage research in the design of courseware development environments and in authoring languages.

EPILOGUE

These fantasies could be continued for many more pages, but the general vision of the future we foresee should be clear by now. The causal chain that transports us from where we stand today to these elysian fields of endless instructional joy moves from national awareness of serious educational problems, to intensified research and development on instruction and learning, to new instructional systems that closely integrate technology with improved organizational and instructional methods. In parallel with this causal chain, hardware and software technology continue their current trajectory toward improved capabilities at lower costs, but with the addition of more systematic approaches to the development of large software systems. With all of these improvements, however, little will be gained without systematic development of instruction, which is what we hope this book has made more reachable.

Appendix
Compendium of Organizations and Publications in the Field of CAI

ORGANIZATIONS

AACE

Association for the Advancement of Computing in Education. Formerly the Association for Computers in Mathematics and Science Teaching (ACMST). Publishes several journals, including the *Journal of Computers in Mathematics and Science Teaching.*
P.O. Box 2966
Charlottesville, VA 22902

ACM/SIGCUE

Special Interest Group on Computer Uses in Education (SIGCUE) of the Association for Computing Machinery (ACM). Established in 1969; publishes a newsletter titled the *SIGCUE Outlook.*
ACM
11 W. 42nd St.
New York, NY 10036
(212) 869–7440

CONDUIT

A nonprofit consortium of the universities of Oregon, North Carolina, Dartmouth, Iowa, and Texas. Maintains a center that reviews and distributes courseware for college-level instruction.
CONDUIT Central
P.O. Box 388
Iowa City, IA 52440
(319) 335–4100

EDUCOM

A nonprofit consortium of colleges, universities, and other institutions, founded in 1964 to facilitate the introduction, use, and management of information technology. Publishes various newsletters and a journal (*EDUCOM Review*). Sponsors the EDUCOM Software Initiative (ESI) and the Educational Uses of Information Technology Project (EUIT).
EDUCOM
P.O. Box 364
777 Alexander Rd.
Princeton, NJ 08540
(609) 520–3340

ISTE

International Society for Technology in Education, a merged society of the International Council for Computers in Education (ICCE) and the International Association for Computing in Education (IACE). Publishes *The Computing Teacher, Journal of Research on Computing in Education,* and a newsletter (*Update*).
ISTE
University of Oregon
1787 Agate St.
Eugene, OR 97403
(503) 686–4414

MECC
Minnesota Educational Computing Corporation, a nonprofit organization founded in 1973 to promote the use of computers in the public schools. Now serves, among other functions, as a distributor of microcomputer courseware.
2520 Broadway Dr.
St. Paul, MN 55113
(612) 481-3500

NECC
A nonprofit consortium of organizations that sponsors a major conference (The National Educational Computing Conference) each year, generally in late June. The NECC Steering Committee can be reached through any of its cooperating societies (e.g., ACM/SIGCUE, EDUCOM, ISTE, IEEE Computer Society).

JOURNALS AND NEWSLETTERS

Classroom Computer Learning (established in 1980; issued monthly)
Pitman Learning, Inc.
19 Davis Dr.
Belmont, CA 94002

Computers and Education (established in 1976; issued quarterly)
Pergamon Press, Inc.
Maxwell House
Fairview Park
Elmsford, NY 10523

Computers in the Schools (established in 1964; issued quarterly)
Haworth Press, Inc.
10 Alice St.
Binghamton, NY 13904

The Computing Teacher (established in 1987; issued eight times each year)
ISTE
University of Oregon
1787 Agate St.
Eugene, OR 97403

Educational Communication and Technology Journal (established in 1978; issued quarterly)
Association for Educational Communications and Technology
1126 16th St., N.W.
Washington, D.C. 20036

Educational Computer Journal (established in 1981; issued bimonthly)
Box 535
Cupertino, CA 95015

Educational Technology (established in 1960; issued monthly)
Educational Technology Publications
140 Sylvan Ave.
Englewood Cliffs, NJ 07632

Electronic Learning (established in 1981; issued eight times each year)
Scholastic, Inc.
730 Broadway
New York, NY 10003

IEEE Transactions on Systems, Man, and Cybernetics (established 1971; issued quarterly)
IEEE Press
345 E. 47th St.
New York, NY 10017

Instructional Science (established in 1972; issued quarterly)
Elsevier Science Publishers
Postbus 2400
1000 CK Amsterdam
The Netherlands

Instructional Uses of School Computers (established in 1986; issued quarterly)
Center for Social Organization of Schools
Johns Hopkins University
3505 N. Charles St.
Baltimore, MD 21218

Interactive Learning International (established in 1985; issued quarterly)
John Wiley & Sons, Ltd.
Baffins Lane
Chichester, Sussex
England

International Journal of Man-Machine Studies (established in 1969; issued monthly)
Academic Press
Oval Road
London NW1 7DX
England

Journal of Computer-Based Instruction (established in 1974; issued quarterly)
Association for the Development of Computer-Based Instructional Systems
Miller Hall 409
Western Washington University
Bellingham, WA 98225

Journal of Computers in Mathematics and Science Teaching (established in 1981; issued quarterly)
JCMST
P.O. Box 2966
Charlottesville, VA 22902

Journal of Educational Computing Research (established in 1985; issued quarterly)
Baywood Publishing Co., Inc.
26 Austin Ave.
Amityville, NY 11701

Journal of Education Technology Systems (established in 1972; issued quarterly)
Baywood Publishing Co., Inc.
26 Austin Ave.
Amityville, NY 11701

Journal of Research on Computing in Education (established in 1987; issued quarterly)
ISTE
University of Oregon
1787 Agate St.
Eugene, OR 97403

MicroNotes on Children & Computers (established in 1983; issued six times each year)
ERIC Clearinghouse on Elementary and Early Childhood Education
University of Illinois
College of Education
805 W. Pennsylvania Ave.
Urbana, IL 61801

Pipeline (established in 1975; issued 2 to 3 times each year)
CONDUIT
University of Iowa
Box 388
Iowa City, IA 52244

SIGCUE Outlook (established in 1968; issued quarterly)
ACM Order Department
P.O. Box 64145
Baltimore, MD 21264

Software Review (established in 1982; issued semiannually)
Meckler Corporation
11 Ferry Lane W.
Westport, CT 06880

Technology and Learning (established in 1987; issued monthly)
Lawrence Erlbaum, Inc.
365 Broadway
Hillsdale, NJ 67642

Glossary

Address.   Label for a location in a computer memory where a specified amount of information can be stored.

ALGOL.   (*Algo*(rithmic) *L*(anguage.)) A high-level programming language, especially designed for scientific programming.

Algorithm.   A procedure defined as a finite sequence of well-defined and executable steps. The name *algorithm* is used to qualify a procedure in which all eventualities have been considered, so that its application always provides a result.

Applications program.   A computer program written to solve a specific data-processing or computational problem.

Artificial intelligence.   Qualifies the research and development of advanced computer programs, particularly those that perform sophisticated tasks that had been considered executable by humans only.

ASCII.   *A*merican *S*tandard *C*ode for *I*nformation *I*nterchange. (See also Character.)

BASIC.   (*B*eginners *A*ll-purpose *S*ymbolic *I*nstruction *C*ode.) An easy-to-learn, high-level programming language, developed at Dartmouth College in 1964.

Baud.   (From J.M.E. Baudot, Fr. inventor.) Rate of information transmission in bits per second.

Bit.   A *b*inary dig*it*.

Bit-mapped display.   A screen display technique in which each pixel on the screen is represented by one or more bits in memory. For a simple display, each point on the screen would be represented by a single bit. For color, multiple gray scale levels, blinking, and inverse, more bits are required for each screen point.

Boolean expression.   An algebraic expression that may include Boolean (i.e., logical) operators, variables, and constants, and whose evaluation provides either the value TRUE or the value FALSE.

Boolean variable.   A variable whose values may be only TRUE or FALSE.

Breadth-first search.   When traversing a tree, this method will explore all the brothers of a node, before moving to its descendants. (See also Depth-first search.)

Bug.   An irritating and hard to find error in a computer program. By extension, is also being used to refer to conceptual or reasoning errors.

Bulletin board (electronic).   A message-handling system that makes messages sent by a number of users available to other users as if they had been posted on an open bulletin board. Generally, a bulletin board manager controls access to the system and determines when to add or remove messages.

Bus.   A physical pathway within a computer for either data or addresses. In a simple microcomputer, a data and an address bus interconnect (in parallel) a microprocessor, memory, and input and output ports.

Byte.   A sequence of a fixed number of bits within a computer memory for storing data. In most computers, a byte consists of eight bits and therefore can hold 256 different patterns.

Disk.   Any of several forms of circular, rigid, rotating media for external storage. (See Magnetic disk, Optical disk.)

C.   A high-level programming language developed in the 1970s as the primary language of the Unix operating system. C is characterized by a high level of generality and a relatively low level of restriction.

C++.   An object-oriented language based on C.

Cache memory.   A very fast but generally small area of computer memory used for holding heavily accessed parts of a program or its data.

CAI.   Computer-assisted instruction.

CAL.   Computer-assisted learning.

CATO.   (*Compiler for Automatic Teaching Operation.*) An authoring language developed for an early version of PLATO, written in an extended Fortran.

CBE.   Computer-based education.

CBI.   Computer-based instruction.

CBL.   Computer-based learning.

CD-ROM.   (*Compact Disk Read-Only Memory.*) A read-only form of external memory for digitized data.

Central processing unit (CPU).   The part of a computer that contains circuitry for executing program instructions. Also called *central processor* or, in a microcomputer, a *microprocessor.*

Channel.   See *Bus.*

Character.   A unique sequence of bits within a byte. The ASCII standard character set defines the characters that will be printed or the terminal functions that will occur for each of 128 standard bit sequences.

Chip.   A small slice of semiconducting material on which one or more integrated circuits are formed. A microprocessor is usually contained on a single chip.

Code.   A name (i.e., a string of characters from a given alphabet) assigned to an object, a quantity, or an operation. In computer programs, every computer operation is defined by a specific code.

Command.   In a computer environment, the regular meaning of this word is specialized to indicate an instruction for immediate computer execution.

Compiler.   A program able to translate a computer program written in a high-level language to the machine codes the computer is able to execute directly.

COMPUTEST.   An early CAI authoring language from which PILOT descended.

Coprocessor.   A processor, usually dedicated to a specific function (such as mathematic computations), that operates in parallel with the main processor (CPU) of a computer.

Coursewriter.   An early CAI authoring language, developed at IBM.

CPU.   See Central Processing Unit.

Cursor.   A symbol on the VDU screen, indicating where the next character will be displayed. The symbol selected for a cursor is usually either a blinking rectangle or a blinking underscore. In graphics packages and in certain types of interaction, the cursor may be displaced by the user to specify a location or an object on the screen.

Database.   A collection of information, organized and formatted for computer access.

Data bus.   See Bus.

Data entry.   Input of data to a computer through keyboard, magnetic disk or tape, optical scanner, or other conversion device.

Data structure.   An arrangement of data according to a fixed pattern, in order to store information in a computer.

Debug.   To look for bugs with the hope of correcting them.

Depth-first search.   When traversing a tree, this method will explore all the descendants of a node before moving to its next brother. (See also Breadth-first search.)

Digital data.   Data represented by bits, bytes, or computer words.

Digitizer.   A device for transforming analogue information (e.g., pictures, sounds) into digital data.

Discrimination power.   Measure of a property of a question in a test, namely, how well the question discriminates between strong and poor students. In statistical terms, it is the correlation coefficient between the grade on the specific question and grade on the whole test.

Distributed processing.   A computational procedure in which two or more CPUs work on the same problem. Also, a configuration of computers that acts toward users as a single machine.

Download.   Any transfer of data or programs from a distant to a nearby machine or peripheral device, or from a larger to a smaller machine.

Ecological validity.   Demonstration of a psychological effect under natural, as opposed to laboratory or other controlled, conditions.

Editor.   Program used to create, organize, restructure, and store information (text, graphics, sound) in a computer environment.

Electronic blackboard.   A generally large, displayable writing surface, the contents of which can be transmitted electronically to other such devices. Used in teleconferencing.

Emulator.   Software or hardware able to execute, in a computer system, programs that were written for another computer system, usually a predecessor or a competitor.

Expert system.   An AI program able to perform an intellectual task at a level comparable to that of a human who is an expert in the field of the application.

File.   A collection of records, usually storing data of the same kind.

File server.   A device able to connect different computers, linked by a network, to a set of files, enabling the computers to receive and store information to and from the files.

Floppy disk.   A thin, flexible disk with magnetic surfaces on which digital information can be stored.

Formative evaluation.   Evaluation of innovative instruction, which is performed in parallel with its experimental implementation and whose purpose is to improve the instructional process being developed.

FORTRAN.   (*For*mula *Tran*slation.) A popular, high-level programming language used mainly in science and engineering. First specified in 1954.

Gigabyte.   One billion (10^9) bytes. Generally used as a measure of storage capacity and (more recently) of information transfer speed (gigabytes/sec).

Graphics editor.   Specialized editor, with commands that allow for the development of drawings, figures, or illustrations. (See Editor.)

Gray scale.   Gray is a mix of black and white. A gray scale is a set of grays linearly ordered, from black to white, according to an increasing proportion of white.

Hard disk.   A rotating stack of rigid disks with magnetic surfaces, used for information storage and retrieval. Also called Magnetic disk or Disk (Cf. Floppy disk.)

Hardware.   The physical components of a computing system, as opposed to its Software.

Hash coding.   Method used to accelerate information searches in large files, the essence of which is the direct calculation of an address from a string of characters (e.g., a name).

High-level programming level.   Languages such as Pascal, C, and FORTRAN whose instructions are problem-oriented rather than machine- (i.e., computer) oriented. By contrast, but seldom so labeled, are *low-level programming languages* such as *assemblers* whose instructions generally represent basic functions of the computer.

Histogram.   Representation of the distribution of a population, according to one variable, using bars to denote the relative sizes of the different subpopulations.

Icon.   Small figure, preferably with expressive and mnemonic powers, that appears on the screen and is pointed to in order to invoke an activity to be executed by the computer.

ILLIAC.   (*Ill*inois *A*utomatic *C*omputer.) An early digital computer, designed and constructed at the Digital Computer Laboratory at the University of Illinois in the early 1950s.

Individualized instruction.   System of instruction in which the program of studies is tailored to every pupil according to his or her capabilities and interests, but keeping a necessary common core. Pupils learn at different speeds, consistent with their possibilities. The teacher organizes class, group, and individual activities in conformity with needs and possibilities.

Information retrieval.   Search for information on storage media, according to a different criteria: by topic, by keywords, by specific strings, or by Boolean combinations over any of these. It is usually used when dealing with large databases.

Initialization.   Assignment of initial (starting) values to the variables of a program in order to run it under the desired conditions.

Input device.   Any device for transferring data or programs into a computer's memory: keyboard, mouse, magnetic disk, optical scanner, etc.

Input-output.   The processes of transferring data or programs into or out of a computer's memory.

Interaction mode.   In CAI, refers to the interaction between student and computer and, in particular, to the locus of control; i.e., who controls the interaction—the student or the computer program?

Interactive instruction.   Instruction in which the student is not a passive recipient, but rather reacts to the instructional process; the process changes according to this reaction.

Interpreter.   A program designed to execute, line by line, the statements of a program written in a high-level language.

Iteration.   Repetition of a set of instructions, each repetition is called a "pass" of the iteration. Usually each pass is performed after updating certain variables of the iteration. The iteration stops when a predetermined condition is reached.

Kilobyte.   One thousand (10^3) bytes. Used as a measure of data-storage capacity or data transfer speed (kilobytes/sec).

Laser printer.   A printer that uses a laser to produce clean, sharp images on paper. Generally, a laser printer can print any type style or graphic image that can be downloaded to its memory.

Lemma.   A simple (easy to prove) theorem that is proved before a complex theorem, and then used in the proof of the more complex theorem.

LISP.   (*List P*rocessing.) A high-level programming language, popular in artificial intelligence, that processes data in list structures. Developed at MIT around 1960.

LOGO.   (From Greek *logos,* meaning 'word,' but spelled as if an acronym.) A high-level, list-processing language designed at Bolt, Beranek and Newman, Inc., in 1967; used especially with children.

Log in.   Procedure required to start using a computer. In large systems, identity has to be established, usually controlled by a password.

Log out.   Procedure required to leave a computer. Files opened during the interaction are saved during the execution of this procedure. It prevents the next user of the terminal from using the account and resources of the previous user.

Loop.   Besides the usual dictionary meanings, used in programming with the meaning of Iteration.

Machine instruction.   An instruction that a computer is wired to execute.

Magnetic disk.   A type of disk on which data are stored as configurations within a magnetic surface.

Mail (electronic).   A communication protocol whereby messages are transferred from one user on a computer system or network to another without a direct connection between the correspondents. Electronic mail systems can store and forward messages and maintain user mailboxes.

Mass storage. Any memory system that can store and retrieve large volumes of data, generally several orders of magnitude more than what a computer's random access memory will hold. The actual size of the average mass memory continues to grow, however, with each new generation of computing systems. Present-day mass storage devices include magnetic disk, optical disk, tape, and a variety of other devices.

Megabyte. One million (10^6) bytes. Used as a measure of storage capacity and data transmission speed (megabytes/sec).

Memory (hardware). A physical system for storing and retrieving data or programs. A computer generally has a main (random access) memory plus some type of mass storage.

Menu. Sequence of options from which the user may select activities.

Microchip. See Chip.

Microcomputer. A small computer, built around a microprocessor. Also called a *personal computer,* as opposed to a *minicomputer, mainframe,* or *supercomputer.*

MIPS. *M*illion *I*nstructions *P*er *S*econd. Used as a measure of CPU processing speed.

Multitasking. Adjective characterizing operating systems in which several computer tasks or programs may be dealt with simultaneously.

NATAL. (*Na*tional *A*uthoring *L*anguage.) A CAI authoring language, patterned on ALGOL and developed under the sponsorship of the National Research Council of Canada in the early 1970s.

Network. A configuration of computers, storage units, and input-output devices, interconnected for rapid transmission of data and programs. In general, a network implies sharing of devices or computational responsibility among computers. Networks can be classed as either *local* or *long-haul,* depending upon the physical distances between devices.

Off-line. Activities performed independent of the central computer system. For example, data entry at a typist station.

On-line. Activities performed under control of a computer facility.

Operating system. Set of programs that provide the interface between the user programs and the physical facilities of a computer.

Optical disk. A mass-storage device that records data as pits in a rigid disk surface and uses a laser beam for data retrieval.

Optical scanner. A device for converting printed images into digital data, usually for computer storage and processing.

Output device. Any device for displaying or recording data transferred from a computer's memory: visual display unit, printer, floppy disk, speech synthesizer, etc.

Pascal. (Named after the French mathematician and philosopher Blaise Pascal, 1623–1662.) A high-level programming language developed in the early 1970s, primarily for scientific and engineering work, but since applied more generally.

Peer tutoring. System of instruction where students at the higher levels of ability help students at the lower levels.

Peripheral devices.   Those devices that do not perform computational tasks but rather are used in the transfer of data to and from the central processing unit. Examples: terminals, printers, disks, and tapes.

PILOT.   (*P*rogramming *I*nquiry, *L*earning *o*r *T*eaching.) An early CAI authoring language, based on COMPUTEST, that is enjoying a renewed popularity on microcomputers.

PLANIT.   (*P*rogramming *Lang*uage for *I*nteractive *T*eaching.) An early CAI authoring language, developed in the 1960s at Systems Development Corporation.

Plasma panel.   A display screen composed of a rectangular grid of minute cells, each filled with plasma. Each cell is traversed by an x-wire and a y-wire, and according to the x and y voltages determined by the computer, each cell may or may not be lit. The plasma panel on the PLATO IV terminal had 512×512 cells.

PLATO.   (*P*rogrammed *L*ogic for *A*utomatic *T*eaching *O*peration.) An early and influential CAI system, developed at the University of Illinois and marketed until recently by Control Data Corporation.

Plotter.   An output device for producing maps, graphs, and other plotted images.

Pointer.   A software link from one unit of information to another.

Procedural network.   An information representation scheme, based upon a graph structure, which shows goals and the actions required to reach them.

Procedure.   A named subprogram, which may be called from different points of a main program, as needed, to perform a specific task. The procedure may have parameters, which may be replaced by different arguments (values) in each call.

Production rule.   A transformation rule that defines how to evolve from one given string of symbols or characters to another, while preserving certain properties or satisfying certain conditions.

Query systems.   Systems or languages used with databases for specifying information searches and retrievals.

Random access memory.   Memory in which each storage unit can be accessed directly.

RDBMS.   See Relational database management system.

Read-only memory.   A type of memory that allows reading of its contents but not changing them through writing. Used to hold system routines and other protected data in microprocessors.

Real-time.   Characterization of computerized systems that must react to processes while they are taking place, usually with very severe requirements in terms of response time, which may be measured in thousandths of a second.

Record.   A set of related data belonging to an individual or to an instance in a data-processing environment.

Recursion.   Process defined by a procedure that calls itself, i.e., in the sequence of instructions that defines the procedure, a call to the procedure itself will appear. For a recursion to be executable, this calling process must be finite, i.e., it must stop after a certain number of iterations. This requires the procedure to be defined directly (i.e., without calling itself) for a given set of values of the calling parameters. Furthermore, the recursion process must ensure that this set of values is reached.

Relational database management system.   A system for storage, updating, and retrieval of information, with tools for queries and for reports. The qualifier "relational" reflects the way the data is structured, in records that contain n-tuples of related values.

Remote storage.   Memory other than a computer's main memory.

Resolution (display).   The number of pixels that can be displayed in a unit of length. Usually the length is taken as a whole side of the screen, thus measuring resolution as: "640 pixels over the horizontal length of the screen." Resolution may be different over the vertical and horizontal dimensions of the screen.

RISC.   (*R*educed *I*nstruction *S*et *C*omputer.) A simplified computer architecture that requires many complicated instructions that are hard-wired in some machines to be realized through software.

Secondary storage.   Mass storage that is usually slower, cheaper, and much larger than a computer's main memory.

Server.   In a networked structure, applies to a device (usually a computer) that supplies storage, communications, or printing services to the users of the network.

SGML.   (*S*tandard *G*eneralized *M*arkup *L*anguage.) A procedure for tagging the structural elements of a document, based upon internationally agreed standards.

Smalltalk.   A graphical, interactive programming environment developed at the Xerox Palo Alto Research Center (PARC) in the early 1970s.

Software.   Initially this term applied to the programs that computer manufacturers supplied with their machines, to facilitate their use. It was used as opposed to "hardware," which characterized the physical components of the equipment. Today it is used to refer to any type of computer program.

Spreadsheet.   A very popular type of computational program, in which data are organized in a matrix structure. The user may define how each cell in the matrix is computed as a function of input values or of the values of other cells in the matrix.

Structural tagging.   A document markup technique in which structural elements are tagged. (See also SGML.)

Subroutine.   See Procedure.

Summative evaluation.   An assessment of the implementation of an innovative instructional method or process, once it has reached a mature stage, as seen by its designers. The conclusions of a summative evaluation tend to recommend or to reject the extended application of the innovation considered.

Supercomputer.   A powerful and fast mainframe computer. The giant of computers.

System routine.   Procedure that serves as a function required by the operating system, and which is accessible to system and applications programmers.

Taxonomy.   Classification and naming of things in groups within a system, according to their similarities and differences.

Terminal.   Working station connected to a computer, usually with a keyboard as input device and a VDU as output device.

Text editor.   A software system for texts, with commands to enter, modify, displace, organize, search, store, and retrieve texts. See Editor.

Theorem.   Assertion whose validity is logically proved, based on a set of axioms and on theorems previously proved in the same way.

TICCIT. (*T*ime-shared *I*nteractive *C*omputer *C*ontrolled *I*nformation *T*elevision.) An early CAI system developed at the MITRE Corporation, the University of Texas, and Brigham Young University. It was built from standard hardware components.

TOAM. A multi-terminal CAI system developed at the Centre for Educational Technology in Tel Aviv.

Topology. (1.) Branch of mathematics. (2.) Frequently used, as in this book, to emphasize relations and contiguity among objects, without considering the content of the objects themselves.

TUTOR. A CAI authoring language developed in 1967 at the University of Illinois for PLATO III.

UNIX. A flexible and versatile operating system originally developed at Bell Laboratories in the late 1960s and early 1970s. Now the lingua franca of computing.

User interface. The devices and methods used to allow communication between a user (usually a human) and a machine (usually a computer).

Utility program. A program used to assist in the operation of the computer. Examples: sorting, conversion, printing.

Virtual memory. A technique for memory addressing that allows a program to be written for a larger memory size than actually exists on a particular computer. The operating system swaps program and data segments from secondary storage to main memory as needed.

Voice synthesis. The computer generation of voice from phonological components.

Window. In the context of a screen display, a rectangle in which a certain user-computer interaction takes place. The use of windows is particularly important when the user may switch between windows, each one corresponding to the execution of a different task.

Workstation. A powerful microcomputer.

References

Abelson, P., and A. Hammond. 1977. Electronics revolution. *Science* 195 (no. 4283):1087–1091.

ACIT Working Panel. 1972. *A functional specification for a programming language for computer aided learning applications.* Report No. NRC–13659. Associate Committee on Instructional Technology, National Research Council, Ottawa, Canada.

Adams, M. J. 1989. Thinking skills curricula: Their promise and progress. *Educational Psychologist* 24 (no. 1): 25–77.

Akscyn, R. M., D. L. McCracken, and E. A. Yoder. 1988. KMS: A distributed hypermedia system for managing knowledge in organizations. *Communications of the ACM* 31 (no. 7): 820–835.

Albert, A. F. 1982. The effect of graphic input devices on performance in a cursor positioning task. *Human Factors 24* (no. 1): 54–58.

Alderman, D. L. 1978. *Evaluation of the TICCIT computer-assisted instructional system in the community college.* Vol. 1, Final Report. Princeton, NJ: Educational Testing Service.

Alessi, S. M., and S. R. Trollip. 1985. *Computer-based instruction: Methods and development.* Englewood Cliffs, NJ: Prentice-Hall.

Alpert, D., and D. L. Bitzer. 1970. Advances in computer-based education. *Science* 167 (no. 3927): 1581–1590.

Anastasi, A. 1976. *Psychological testing.* 4th ed. New York: Macmillan.

Anderson, J. R. 1985. *Cognitive psychology and its implications.* 2d ed. New York: W. H. Freeman.

Anderson, T. H., and B. B. Armbruster. 1984. Studying. In *Handbook of research in reading,* ed. P. D. Pearson. New York: Longman.

Apple. 1987. *Hypercard user's guide.* Cupertino, CA: Apple Computer, Inc.

Atkinson, R. C., J. D. Fletcher, H. C. Chetin, and C. M. Stauffer. 1971. Instruction in initial reading under computer control: The Stanford Project. *Educational Technology Research Reports.* Englewood Cliffs, NJ: Educational Technology Publications.

Ausubel, D. P. 1968. *Educational psychology.* New York: Holt, Rinehart & Winston.

Baddeley, A. 1986. Working memory, reading and dyslexia. In *Communication and handicap: Aspects of psychological compensation and technical aids,* ed. E. Hjelmquist and L.-G. Nilsson. Amsterdam: Elsevier Science Publishers.

Barr, R. 1972. The influence of instructional conditions on word recognition errors. *Reading Research Quarterly* 7: 509–579.

Bartlett, F. 1932. *Remembering.* Cambridge: Cambridge University Press.

Becker, H. J. 1986. *Instructional uses of school computers: Reports from the 1985 national survey.* Baltimore: Center for Social Organization of Schools, Johns Hopkins University.

Becker, H. J. 1987. The importance of a methodology that maximizes falsifiability: Its applicability to research about Logo. *Educational Researcher* 16 (no. 5): 11–16.

Benjamin, L. T., Jr. 1988. A history of teaching machines. *American Psychologist* 43 (no. 9): 703–712.

Berliner, D. C. 1986. In pursuit of the expert pedagogue. *Educational Researcher* 15 (no. 6): 5–13.

Berlyne, D. E. 1960. *Conflict, arousal, and curiosity.* New York: McGraw-Hill.

Berlyne, D. E., and F. D. Frommer. 1966. Some determinants of the incidence and content of children's questions. *Child Development 37:* 177–189.

Bertin, J. 1983. *Semiology of graphics.* Madison: University of Wisconsin Press.

Bitzer, D. L., P. G. Braunfeld, and W. W. Lichtenberger. 1962. Plato II: A multiple-student computer-controlled automatic teaching device. In *Programmed learning and computer-based instruction,* ed. J. E. Coulson. New York: John Wiley and Sons.

Bitzer, D. and D. Skaperdas. 1970. The economics of a large-scale computer-based education system: PLATO IV. In *Computer-assisted instruction, testing and guidance,* ed. W. H. Holtzman. New York: Harper & Row.

Bloom, B. S., ed. 1956. *Taxonomy of educational objectives. Handbook I: Cognitive domain.* New York: David McKay.

Bok, D. 1985. Looking into education's high-tech future. *Harvard Magazine* (May–June): 29–38.

Brachman, R. 1977. What's in a concept?: Structural foundations for semantic networks. *International Journal of Man-Machine Studies* 9: 127–152.

Brahan, J. W., B. A. Colpitts, J. R. Goguen, A. M. Hlady, and R. A. Orchard. 1976. *NATAL-74—Definition and development of a course authoring language to meet national requirements.* Second Canadian Symposium on Instructional Technology, Quebec.

Brahan, J. W., and D. Godfrey. 1984. *Computer-aided learning using the Natal language.* Victoria, Canada: Press Porcepic, Ltd.

Brown, A. L. 1978. Knowing what, where, and how to remember: A problem of metacognition. In *Advances in instructional psychology,* Vol. 1, ed. R. Glaser. Hillsdale, NJ: Erlbaum.

Brown, J. S., R. R. Burton, and A. G. Bell. 1974. *SOPHIE: A sophisticated instructional environment for teaching electronic troubleshooting (An example of AI in CAI).* BB&N Report 2790. Cambridge, MA: Bolt, Beranek and Newman, Inc.

Brown, J. S., and R. R. Burton. 1978. Diagnostic models for procedural bugs in basic mathematical skills. *Cognitive Science* 2: 155–192.

Brown, J. S., A. Collins, and P. Duguid. 1989. Situated cognition and the culture of learning. *Educational Researcher* 18 (no.4): 32–42.

Bruner, J. S. 1960. *The process of education.* Cambridge, MA: Harvard University Press.

Bruner, J. S. 1966. *Toward a theory of instruction.* Cambridge, MA: Harvard University Press.

Bulkeley, W. M. 1988. Computers failing as teaching aids. *The Wall Street Journal,* June 6, 23.

Bunderson, C. V., and G. W. Faust. 1976. Programmed and computer assisted instruction. *Seventy-fifth yearbook of the National Society for the Study of Education.* Chicago: University of Chicago Press.

Burton, R. R. 1982. Diagnosing bugs in a simple procedural skill. In *Intelligent tutoring systems,* ed. D. Sleeman and J. S. Brown. London: Academic Press.

Burton, R. R., and J. S. Brown. 1976. A tutoring and student modelling paradigm for gaming environments. *SIGCSE Bulletin* 8: 236–246.

Burton, R. R., and J. S. Brown. 1979. An investigation of computer coaching for informal learning activities. *International Journal on Man-Machine Studies* 11: 5–24.

Bush, V. 1945. As we may think. *Atlantic Monthly* (July): 101–108.

Campbell, D. T., and J. C. Stanley. 1963. *Experimental and quasi-experimental designs for research.* New York: Houghton-Mifflin.

Campbell, J. 1972. *Myths to live by.* New York: Bantam Books.

Carbonell, J. R. 1970a. AI in CAI: An artificial intelligence approach to computer-assisted instruction. *IEEE Transactions on Man-Machine Systems* MMS–11(4): 190–202.

Carbonell, J. R. 1970b. *Mixed-initiative man-computer instructional dialogues.* BB&N Report No. 1971. Cambridge, MA: Bolt Beranek and Newman, Inc.

Card, S. K., W. K. English, and B. J. Burr. 1978. Evaluation of mouse, rate-controlled isometric joystick, step keys, and text keys for text selection on a CRT. *Ergonomics* 21: 601–603.

Card, S. K., T. P. Moran, and A. Newell. 1983. *The psychology of human-computer interaction.* Hillsdale, NJ: Erlbaum.

Carroll, J. B. 1963. A model for school learning. *Teachers College Record 64* (no. 8): 723–733.

Carroll, J. B. 1989. The Carroll model: A 25-year retrospective and prospective view. *Educational Researcher* 18 (no. 1): 26–31.

Case, R. 1978. Piaget and beyond. Toward a developmentally-based theory and technology of instruction. In *Advances in instructional psychology,* ed. R. Glaser. Vol. 1. Hillsdale, NJ: Erlbaum. 167–228.

Case, R., and C. Bereiter. 1984. *From behaviorism to cognitive behaviorism to cognitive development: Steps in the evolution of instructional design.* Occasional paper #2. Toronto: Centre for Applied Cognitive Science, Ontario Institute for Studies in Education.

Clancey, W. J. 1979. Tutoring rules for guiding a case method dialog. *International Journal of Man-Machine Studies* 11: 25–49.

Clancey, W. J. 1986. Qualitative student models. *Annual Review of Computer Science* 1: 381–450.

Clancey, W. J. 1987. *Knowledge-based tutoring: The GUIDON program.* Cambridge, MA: M.I.T. Press.

Clark, R. C. 1983. Reconsidering research on learning from media. *Review of Educational Research* 53 (no. 4): 414–459.

Clements, D. H. 1986. Effects of Logo and CAI environments on cognition and creativity. *Journal of Educational Psychology* 78 (no. 4): 309–318.

Cleveland, W. S. 1985. *The elements of graphing data.* Monterey, CA: Wadsworth.

Clifford, G. J. 1973. A history of the impact of research on teaching. In *Second handbook of research on teaching,* ed. R. M. W. Travers. Chicago: Rand McNally.

Cocklin, T. G., N. J. Ward, H. Chen, and J. F. Juola. 1984. Factors influencing readability of rapidly presented text segments. *Memory and Cognition* 12: 431–442.

Collins, A., J. Brown, and S. Newman. 1986. Cognitive apprenticeship: Teaching the craft of reading, writing and mathematics. In *Knowing, learning, and instruction: Essays in honor of Robert Glaser,* ed. L. B. Resnick. Hillsdale, NJ: Erlbaum.

Conklin, J. 1987. Hypertext: An introduction and survey. *Computer* 20 (no. 9): 17–41.

Conrad, R. 1972. Speech and reading. In *Language by ear and by eye,* ed. J. F. Kavanagh and I. G. Mattingley. Cambridge, MA: M.I.T. Press.

Corno, L. 1988. The study of teaching for mathematics learning: Views through two lenses. *Educational Psychologist* 23 (no. 2): 181–202.

Coscarelli, W. C., and T. M. Schwen. 1979. Effects of three algorithmic representations on critical thinking, laboratory efficiency, and final grade. *Educational Communication and Technology Journal* 27: 58–64.

Coulson, J. E., ed. 1962. *Programmed learning and computer-based instruction.* New York: John Wiley and Sons.

Coulson, J. E., and H. F. Silberman. 1962. Automated teaching. In *Computer applications in the behavioral sciences,* ed. H. Borko. Englewood Cliffs, NJ: Prentice-Hall.

Cox, L. S. 1975. Diagnosing and remediating systematic errors in addition and subtraction computation. *The Arithmetic Teacher* 22: 151–157.

Craig, F. I. M., and R. S. Lockhart. 1972. Levels of processing: A framework for memory research. *Journal of Verbal Learning and Verbal Behavior* 11: 671–684.

Crowder, N. A. 1963. Intrinsic programming: Facts, fallacies and future. In *Prospectives in programming,* ed. R. T. Filep. New York: Macmillan.

Cuban, L. 1986. *Teachers and machines: The classroom use of technology since 1920.* New York: Teachers College Press.

Dahl, O. J., and K. Nygaard. 1966. SIMULA—An ALGOL-based simulation language. *Communications of the ACM* 9 (no. 9): 671–678.

Davidove, E. A. 1987. Evaluation and selection of courseware development software. *Educational Technology* 27 (no. 7): 34–37.

Denham, C., and A. Lieberman, eds. 1980. *Time to learn.* Washington, DC: National Institute of Education.

di Sessa, A. A. 1982. Unlearning Aristotelian physics: A study of knowledge-based learning. *Cognitive Learning* 6 (no. 1): 37–75.

Dick, W., and L. Carey. 1978. *The systematic design of instruction.* Glenview, IL: Scott, Foresman.

Driver, R., and J. Easley. 1978. Pupils and paradigms: A review of literature related to concept development in adolescent science students. *Studies in Science Education* 5: 61–84.

Duchnicky, R. L., and P. A. Kolers. 1983. Readability of text scrolled on visual display terminals as a function of window size. *Human Factors* 25 (no. 4): 683–692.

Durham, I., D. Lamb, and J. B. Saxe. 1983. Spelling correction in user interfaces. *Communications of the ACM* 26 (no. 10): 764–773.

Ebbinghaus, H. 1913. *Memory: A contribution to experimental psychology.* Trans. H. A. Ruger & C. E. Bussenius. New York: Teachers College. (Original work published 1885)

Ellis, H. C. 1978. *Fundamentals of human learning, memory, and cognition.* 2d ed. Dubuque, IA: Wm. C. Brown.

Ericsson, K. A., and H. A. Simon. 1980. Verbal reports as data. *Psychological Review* 87: 215–251.

Feldhusen, J. P. 1963. Taps for teaching machines. *Phi Delta Kappan* 44: 265–267.

Ferguson, E. S. 1977. Nonverbal thought in technology. *Science* 197 (no. 4306): 827–836.

Feurzeig, W. 1965. Toward more versatile teaching machines. *Computers and Automation* 143: 22–25.

Fisher, L. M. 1988. PC makers campaign in schools. *The New York Times* (19 July): D1, D11.

Fitts, P. M., and M. I. Posner. 1967. *Human performance.* Belmont, CA: Brooks/Cole.

Ford, G. W., and L. Pugno, eds. 1964. *The structure of knowledge and the curriculum.* Chicago: Rand McNally.

Forrester, J. 1971. *World dynamics.* Cambridge, MA: M.I.T. Press.

Gagne, E. D. 1985. *The cognitive psychology of school learning.* Boston: Little, Brown & Co.

Gagne, R. M. 1965. *The conditions for learning.* 2d ed. New York: Holt, Rinehart & Winston.

Gagne, R. M., and L. J. Briggs. 1974. *Principles of instructional design.* New York: Holt, Rinehart & Winston.

Gagne, R. M., and L. J. Briggs. 1979. *Principles of instructional design.* 2d ed. New York: Holt, Rinehart & Winston.

Gagne, R. M., W. Wager, and A. Rojas. 1981. Planning and authoring computer-assisted instruction lessons. *Educational Technology* 21 (no. 9): 17–26.

Gentile, J. R. 1967. The first generation of computer-assisted instructional systems: An evaluative review. *AV Communication Review* 15: 23–53.

Gesell, A. 1928. *Infancy and human growth.* New York: Macmillan.

Glaser, R. 1976. Cognitive psychology and instructional design. In *Cognition and instruction,* ed. D. Klahr. Hillsdale, NJ: Erlbaum.

Goldsmith, E. 1984. *Research into illustration: An approach and a review.* Cambridge: Cambridge University Press.

Goldstein, I. 1977. *The computer as coach: An athletic paradigm for intellectual education.* AI Memo 389, AI Laboratory, M.I.T., Cambridge, MA.

Goodman, D. 1987. *The complete HyperCard handbook.* New York: Bantam Books.

Goodman, D. 1988. *Danny Goodman's HyperCard developer's guide.* New York: Bantam Books.

Gopher, D., and D. Raij. 1988. Typing with a two-hand chord keyboard: Will the QWERTY become obsolete? *IEEE Transactions on Systems, Man and Cybernetics* SMC-18 (no. 4): 601–609.

Gott, S. P. (1988–89). Apprenticeship instruction for real-world tasks: The coordination procedures, mental models, and strategies. *Review of Research in Education* 15: 97–169.

Guastello, S. J., M. Traut, and G. Korienek. 1989. Verbal versus pictorial representations of objects in a human-computer interface. *International Journal of Man-Machine Studies* 31: 99–120.

Gwinn, J. F., and L. F. Beal. 1987–88. On-line computer testing: Implementation and endorsement. *Journal of Educational Technology Systems* 16 (no. 3): 239–252.

Haith, M. M. 1971. Developmental changes in visual information processing and short-term visual memory. *Human Development* 14: 249–261.

Halasz, F. G. 1988. Reflections on NoteCards: Seven issues for the next generation of hypermedia systems. *Communications of the ACM* 31 (no. 7): 836–852.

Hambleton, R. K., and H. Swaminathan. 1985. *Item response theory: Principles and applications.* Dordrecht, The Netherlands: Kluwer.

Harrow, A. J. 1972. *A taxonomy of the psychomotor domain: A guide for developing behavioral objectives.* New York: David McKay.

Hawley, D. E. 1986. *Cost, effects and utility of microcomputer-assisted instruction.* Technical Report, Center for Advanced Technology in Education, College of Education, University of Oregon, Eugene.

Hayes-Roth, B., and P. Thorndyke. 1985. Paradigms for intelligent systems. *Educational Psychologist* 20: 231–241.

Heines, J. M. 1984. *Screen design strategies for computer-assisted instruction.* Bedford, MA: Digital Press.

Hofstetter, F. T. 1986. *The eleventh summative report of the Office of Computer-Based Instruction.* Newark: University of Delaware.

Hopp, J. C. 1985. Cognitive learning theory and classroom complexity. *Research in Science and Technology Education* 3 (no. 2): 159–174.

Houghton, H. A., and D. M. Willows, eds. 1987. *The psychology of illustration. Vol. 2: Instructional issues.* New York: Springer-Verlag.

Hudgins, B. 1977. *Learning and thinking: A primer for teachers.* Itasca, IL: F. E. Peacock.

IBM. 1987. *Systems application architecture-common user access: Panel design and user interaction.* SC26-4351-0. Boca Raton, FL: IBM Corporation.

Jackson, P. W. 1968. *The teacher and the machine.* Pittsburgh: University of Pittsburgh Press.

James, W. 1958. *Talks to teachers.* New York: W. W. Norton. (Original work published 1899)

Judd, W. A., and R. Glaser. 1969. Response latency as a function of training method, information level, acquisition, and overlearning. *Journal of Educational Psychology Monograph 60* (no. 4): Part 2, 1–30.

Juola, J. F., N. J. Ward, and T. McNamara. 1982. Visual search and reading of rapid serial presentations of letter strings, words, and text. *Journal of Experimental Psychology: General* 111: 208–227.

Kaplan, R., and F. G. Simmons. 1974. Effects of instructional objectives used as orienting stimuli or as summary/review upon prose learning. *Journal of Educational Psychology* 66: 614–622.

Karr, M., and D. B. Loveman III. 1978. Incorporation of units into programming languages. *Communications of the ACM* 21 (no. 5): 385–391.

Kearsley, G. 1982. Authoring systems in computer based education. *Communications of the ACM* 25 (no. 7): 429–437.

Kemeny, J., and T. Kurtz. 1984. In quest of true BASIC. *PC World* 2 (no. 12): 120–128.

Kirsch, I. S., and A. Jungeblut. 1986. *Literacy: Profiles of America's young adults.* Report No. 16-PL-02. National Assessment of Educational Progress, Princeton, NJ.

Klahr, D., and J. G. Wallace. 1976. *Cognitive development: An information processing view.* Hillsdale, NJ: Erlbaum.

Klausmeier, H. J., R. A. Rossmiller, and M. Saily. 1977. *Individually guided elementary education.* New York: Academic Press.

Koffman, E. B. 1972. A generative CAI tutor for computer science concepts. *Spring Joint Computer Conference, AFIPS Conference Proceedings, 40,* 379–389.

Koffman, E. B. 1973. Design techniques for generative computer-assisted instructional systems. *IEEE Transactions on Education* E-16 (no. 4): 182–189.

Koved, L., and B. Shneiderman. 1986. Embedded menus: Selecting items in context. *Communications of the ACM* 20 (no. 4): 312–318.

Krathwohl, D. R., B. S. Bloom, and B. B. Masia. 1964. *Taxonomy of educational objectives. Handbook II: Affective domain.* New York: David McKay.

Kulik, C. C., J. A. Kulik, and B. J. Shwalb. 1986. Effectiveness of computer-based adult learning: A meta-analysis. *Journal of Educational Computing Research* 2: 235–252.

Kulik, D., J. A. Kulik, and P. Cohen. 1980. Instructional technology and college teaching. *Teaching of Psychology* 7: 199–205.

Kulik, J. A., R. Bangert, and G. Williams. 1983. Effects of computer-based teaching on secondary school students. *Journal of Educational Psychology* 75: 19–26.

Kulik, J. A., and C. C. Kulik. 1988. Timing of feedback and verbal learning. *Review of Educational Research* 58 (no. 1): 79–97.

Lancaster, P. 1976. *Mathematics: models of the real world.* Englewood Cliffs, NJ: Prentice-Hall, Inc.

LaPointe, A. E., N. A. Mead, and G. W. Phillips. 1988. *A world of difference: An international assessment of mathematics and science.* Report No. 19-CAEP-01. Princeton, NJ: Educational Testing Service.

Larkin, J. H. 1983. The role of problem representation in physics. In *Mental models,* ed. D. Gentner and A. L. Stevens. Hillsdale, NJ: Erlbaum.

Lenneberg, E. 1967. *Biological foundations of language.* New York: John Wiley and Sons.

Levin, H., G. V. Glass, and G. R. Meister. 1984. *Cost effectiveness of four educational innovations.* Project Report No. 84-A11. Stanford, CA: Institute for Research on Educational Finance and Governance.

Licklider, J. C. R. 1962. Preliminary experiments in computer-aided teaching. In *Programmed learning and computer-based instruction,* ed. J. E. Coulson. New York: John Wiley and Sons.

Lindsay, P. H., and D. A. Norman. 1979. *Human information processing.* New York: Academic Press.

Lippey, G., ed. 1974. *Computer-assisted test construction.* Englewood Cliffs, NJ: Educational Technology Publications.

Little, J. K. 1934. Results of use of machines for testing and for drill, upon learning in educational psychology. *Journal of Experimental Education* 45: 22–27.

Locatis, C., and V. Carr. 1985. Selecting authoring systems. *Journal of Computer-based Instruction* 12 (no. 2): 28–33.

Lord, F. M. 1971. Robbins-Monro procedures for tailored testing. *Educational and Psychological Measurement* 31: 3–31.

Lord, F. M. 1980. *Applications of item response theory to practical testing problems.* Hillsdale, NJ: Erlbaum.

Lord, F. M., and M. R. Novick. 1968. *Statistical theories of mental test scores.* London: Addison-Wesley.

MacKnight, C., and S. Balagopalan. 1989. An evaluation tool for measuring authoring system performance. *Communications of the ACM* 32 (no. 10): 1231–1236.

Mager, R. F., and K. H. Beach. 1967. *Developing vocational instruction*. Belmont, CA: Fearon.

Malone, T. W. 1981. Toward a theory of intrinsically motivating instruction. *Cognitive Science* 4: 333–369.

Matz, M. 1982. Towards a process model for high school algebra errors. In *Intelligent tutoring systems*, ed. D. Sleeman and J. S. Brown. London: Academic Press.

Mayer, R. E. 1983. *Thinking, problem solving, cognition*. New York: W. H. Freeman.

Merrill, M. D. 1980. Learner control in computer based learning. *Computers and Education* 4: 77–95.

Merrill, M. D., E. W. Schneider, and K. A. Fletcher. 1980. *TICCIT*. Englewood Cliffs, NJ: Educational Technology Publications.

Mills, C. F., and L. J. Weldon. 1987. Reading text from computer screens. *Computing Surveys* 19 (no. 4): 329–358.

Minsky, M., ed. 1968. *Semantic information processing*. Cambridge, MA: M.I.T. Press.

MITRE Corporation. 1974. *An overview of the TICCIT program*. Washington: MITRE Corp.

Morton, R. P. 1976. The variety of TICCIT systems—An overview. In *Computer science and education*, ed. R. Colman and P. Lorton, Jr. New York: Association for Computing Machinery.

Murphy, R. T., and L. R. Appel. 1977. *Evaluation of the PLATO IV computer-based education system in the community college*. Final Report, Contract No. NSF-C731. Princeton, NJ: Educational Testing Service.

Muter, P., R. S. Kruk, M. A. Buttigieg, and T. Jin Kang. 1988. Reader-controlled computerized presentation of text. *Human Factors* 30 (no. 4): 473–486.

Nagel, L. W., and D. O. Pederson. 1973. *SPICE: Simulation program with integrated circuit emphasis*. Memo ERL-M382. Electronics Research Laboratory, College of Engineering. Berkeley: University of California.

Neill, S. B. 1989. *Only the best: The annual guide to highest-rated software, preschool-grade 12, 1990 edition*. New York: Bowker.

Neisser, U. 1976. *Cognition and reality*. San Francisco: W. H. Freeman.

Nickerson, R. S. 1986. *Using computers: Human factors in information systems*. Cambridge, MA: M.I.T. Press.

Norton, D. S., and P. Rushton. 1952. *Classical myths in English literature*. New York: Rinehart & Co.

O'Connor, R. J. 1988–89. Integrating optical videodisc and CD/ROM technology to teach art history. *Journal of Educational Technology Systems* 17 (no. 1): 27–32.

Oettinger, A. C. 1969. *Run, computer, run; The mythology of educational innovation*. Cambridge, MA: Harvard University Press.

Ohlsson, S. 1985. *Some principles of intelligent tutoring*. Learning Research and Development Center, University of Pittsburgh, Pittsburgh, PA.

Osin, L. 1976. Smith: How to produce CAI courses without programming. *International Journal of Man-Machine Studies* 8: 207–241.

Osin, L. 1984. TOAM: C.A.I. on a national scale. *Proceedings of the 4th Jerusalem Conference on Information Technology, IEEE*: 418–424.

Palincsar, A., and A. Brown. 1984. Reciprocal teaching of comprehension fostering and monitoring activities. *Cognition and Instruction* 1 (no. 2): 117–175.

Palmer, B. G., and A. E. Oldehoeft. 1975. The design of an instructional system based on problem generators. *International Journal of Man-Machine Studies* 7: 249–271.

Papert, S. 1987. Computer criticism vs technocratic thinking. *Educational Research* 16 (no. 1): 22–30.

Papert, S. 1980. *Mindstorms: Children, computers, and powerful ideas*. New York: Basic Books.

Patterson, C. H. 1977. *Foundations for a theory of instruction and educational psychology.* New York: Harper & Row.

Paulson, R. F. 1976. *Control Data PLATO: System overview.* St. Paul, MN: Control Data Corporation.

Pea, R. D., D. M. Kurland, and J. Hawkins. 1985. Logo and the development of thinking skills. In *Children and computers: Formative studies.,* ed. M. Chen and W. Paisley. Beverly Hills, CA: Sage.

Pea, R. D., E. Soloway, and J. Spohrer. 1987. The buggy path to the development of programming expertise. *Focus on Learning Problems in Mathematics* 9: 5–30.

Pea, R. D. 1987. The aims of software criticism: Reply to Professor Papert. *Educational Researcher* 16 (no. 5): 4–8.

Perkins, D. N., and G. Salomon. 1989. Are cognitive skills context-bound? *Educational Researcher* 18 (no. 1): 16–25.

Perkins, D. N., and R. Simmons. 1988. Patterns of misunderstanding: An integrative model for science, math, and programming. *Review of Educational Research* 58 (no. 3): 303–326.

Piaget, J. 1963. *The origins of intelligence in children.* New York: Norton.

Pollock, J. J., and A. Zamora. 1984. Automatic spelling correction in scientific and scholarly text. *Communications of the ACM* 27 (no. 4): 358–368.

Pressey, S. L. 1926. A simple device for teaching, testing and research. *School and Society* 23: 373–376.

Pressey, S. L. 1950. Development and appraisal of devices providing immediate automatic scoring of objective tests and concomitant self-instruction. *Journal of Psychology* 29: 417–447.

Pressey, S. L. 1959. Certain major psycho-educational issues appearing in the conference on teaching machines. In *Automatic teaching: The state of the art,* ed. E. Galanter. New York: John Wiley and Sons.

Psotka, J., L. D. Massey, and S. A. Mutter. 1988. *Intelligent tutoring systems: Lessons learned.* Hillsdale, NJ: Erlbaum.

Quillian, M. R. 1968. Semantic memory. In *Semantic information processing,* ed. M. Minsky. Cambridge, MA: M.I.T. Press.

Ragosta, M., P. W. Holland, and D. T. Jamison. 1982. *Computer-assisted instruction and compensatory education: The ETS/LAUSD study. The executive summary and policy implications.* Project Report Number 20. Princeton, NJ: Educational Testing Service.

Rath, G. J., N. S. Anderson, and R. C. Brainerd. 1959. The IBM Research Center teaching machine project. In *Automatic teaching: The state of the art,* ed. E. Galanter. New York: John Wiley and Sons.

Reid, J. M. 1969. *An adventure in textbooks, 1924–1960.* New York: R. R. Bowker.

Resnick, C. A. 1975. Computational models of learners for computer assisted learning. Ph.D. diss., University of Illinois, Urbana-Champaign.

Rickards, J. P., and G. J. August. 1975. Generative underlining strategies in prose recall. *Journal of Educational Psychology* 67: 860–865.

Romaniuk, E. W. 1978. *A summative evaluation of the CAI course "COMPS."* Report DERS-06-049. Division of Educational Research Services, University of Alberta, Edmonton.

Romiszowski, A. J. 1981. *Designing instructional systems: Decision making in course planning and curriculum design.* London: Kegan Paul.

Rosenshine, B., and R. Stevens. 1986. Teaching functions. In *Handbook of research on teaching,* 3d ed., ed. M. C. Wittrock. New York: Macmillan.

Rosenthal, S. 1984. The PF474: A coprocessor for string comparison. *Byte* (Nov.): 247–256.

Ross, S. M., and G. R. Morrison. 1988. Adapting instruction to learner performance and background variables. In *Instructional designs for microcomputer courseware,* ed. D. H. Jonassen. Hillsdale, NJ: Erlbaum.

Rowe, M. 1975. An international perspective on open learning and nontraditional study. *Proceedings of the Second National Conference on Open Learning and Nontraditional Study.* Lincoln, NE: University of Mid-America.

Russell, D. M. 1988. IDE: The interpreter. In *Intelligent tutoring systems: Lessons learned,* eds. J. Psotka, L. D. Massey, and S. A. Mutter. Hillsdale, NJ: Erlbaum.

Sakamoto, E. J. 1980. *The CAN/CAI course user's manual—Version II.* Toronto: Ontario Institute for Studies in Education.

Salomon, G., and H. Gardner. 1986. The computer as educator: Lessons from television research. *Educational Researcher* 15 (no. 1): 13–19.

Sarton, G. 1952. *A history of science: Ancient science through the Golden Age of Greece.* Cambridge, MA: Harvard University Press.

Scardamalia, M., and C. Bereiter. 1985. Fostering the development of self-regulation in children's knowledge processing. In *Thinking and learning skills: Research and open questions,* eds. S. F. Chipman, J. W. Segal, and R. Glaser. Hillsdale, NJ: Erlbaum.

Schoenfeld, A. H. 1982. Measures of problem-solving performance and of problem-solving instruction. *Journal for Research in Mathematics Education* 13 (no. 1): 31–49.

Schoenfeld, A. H. 1985. *Mathematical problem solving.* Orlando, FL: Academic Press.

Schramm. W. 1977. *Big media little media: Tools and technologies for instruction.* Beverly Hills, CA: Sage.

Schwartz, J. L., and M. Yerushalmy. 1985. The geometric supposer: An intellectual prosthesis for making conjectures. *The College Mathematics Journal* 16: 58–65.

Science. 1982. (Special issue on computers and electronics) 215 (no. 4534).

Sherwood, B. A. 1974. *The TUTOR language.* Urbana: C.E.R.L., University of Illinois.

Sherwood, B. A. 1979. The computer speaks. *IEEE Spectrum* (Aug.): 18–25.

Sherwood, B. A., and J. N. Sherwood. 1988. *The cT language,* Champaign, IL: Stipes Pub. Co.

Shneiderman, B. 1987. *Designing the user interface: Strategies for effective human-computer interaction.* Reading, MA: Addison-Wesley.

Shortliffe, E. H. 1976. *Computer-based medical consultations: MYCIN.* New York: American Elsevier.

Siegler, R. S. 1986. *Children's thinking,* Englewood Cliffs, NJ: Prentice-Hall.

Simon, H. A. 1979. *Models of thought.* New Haven: Yale University Press.

Skinner, B. F. 1954. The science of learning and the art of teaching. *Harvard Educational Review* 24 (no. 2): 86–87.

Skinner, B. F. 1963. Reflections on a decade of teaching machines. *Teachers College Record* 3: 168–177.

Slavin, R. 1983. *Cooperative learning.* New York: Longman.

Sleeman, D., and J. S. Brown, eds. 1982. *Intelligent tutoring systems.* London: Academic Press.

Sleeman, D. 1982. Assessing aspects of competence in basic algebra. In *Intelligent tutoring systems,* eds. D. Sleeman and J. S. Brown. London: Academic Press.

Smith, S. G., L. L. Jones, and M. L. Waugh. 1986. Production and evaluation of interactive videodisc lessons in laboratory instruction. *Journal of Computer-based Instruction* 13 (no. 4): 117–121.

Spencer, H. 1969. *The visible word.* New York: Hastings House.

Steinberg, E. R. 1984. *Teaching computers to teach.* Hillsdale, NJ: Erlbaum.

Stephens, J. M. 1967. *The process of schooling; A psychological examination.* New York: Holt, Rinehart & Winston.

Sternberg, R. J. 1985. *Beyond IQ: A triarchic theory of human intelligence.* New York: Cambridge University Press.

Stevens, A. L., A. Collins. 1977. *The goal structure of a socratic tutor. Proceedings of 1977 Annual Conference, Association for Computing Machinery,* Seattle, October: 256–263.

Stevens, A. L., A. Collins, and S. Goldin. 1979. Misconceptions in students' understanding. *International Journal of Man-Machine Studies 11:* 145–156.

Sugarman, R. 1978. A second chance for computer-aided instruction. *IEEE Spectrum* (Aug.): 29–37.

Suppes, P., and M. Morningstar. 1969. Computer-assisted instruction. *Science* 166 (no. 3903): 343–350.

Swets, J. A., and W. Feurzeig. 1965. Computer-assisted instruction. *Science* 150 (no. 3696): 572–576.

Swinton, S. S., M. Amarel, and J. A. Morgan. 1978. *The PLATO elementary demonstration educational outcome evaluation. Final Report: Summary and conclusions.* Submitted to the National Science Foundation. Princeton, NJ: Educational Testing Service.

Szanser, A. J. 1969. Error-correcting methods in natural language processing. *Information Processing* 68: 1412–1416.

Tenczar, P., and W. Golden. 1972. *Spelling, word and concept recognition.* C.E.R.L. Report X–35. University of Illinois, Champaign.

Thorndike, E. L., and R. S. Woodworth. 1901. The influence of improvement in one mental function upon the efficiency of other functions. *Psychological Review* 8: 247–261.

Thorndike, R. L., and E. Hagan. 1985. *Measurement and evaluation in psychology and education.* 5th ed. New York: John Wiley and Sons.

Tobias, S. 1982. When do instructional methods make a difference? *Educational Researcher* (April): 4–9.

Treisman, A. M. 1969. Strategies and models of selective attention. *Psychological Review* 76: 282–299.

Trowbridge, D. E. 1988. *Graphs and Tracks—Version 1.0 manual.* Center for Design of Educational Computing. Pittsburgh: Carnegie Mellon University.

Trowbridge, D. E. 1990. Applying research results to the development of computer assisted instruction. In *The conference on computers in physics instruction proceedings,* ed. E. Redish and J. Risley. Reading, MA: Addison-Wesley.

Trowbridge, J. E., and J. L. Mintzes, 1985. Students' alternative conceptions of animals and animals classification. *School Science and Mathematics* 85 (no. 4): 304–316.

U.S. Congress, Office of Technology Assessment. 1982. *Information technology and its impact on American education.* OTA-CIT–187. Washington, DC: U.S. Government Printing Office.

U.S. Congress, Office of Technology Assessment. 1988. *Power on! New tools for teaching and learning.* OTA-SET–379. Washington, DC: U.S. Government Printing Office.

Uhr, L. 1967. Toward the compilation of books into teaching machine programs. *IEEE Transactions on Human Factors in Electronics* HFE-8: 81–84.

Urry, V. W. 1977. Tailored testing: A successful application of latent trait theory. *Journal of Educational Measurement* 14 (no. 2): 181–196.

Uttal, W. R., T. Pasich, M. Rogers, and R. Hyeronimus. 1969. *Generative computer-assisted instruction.* Communication 243. Mental Health Research Institute. Ann Arbor, MI.

Uttal, W. R. 1962. On conversational interaction. In *Programmed learning and computer-based instruction,* ed. J. E. Coulson. New York: John Wiley and Sons.

Venezky, R. L., C. F. Kaestle, and A. M. Sum. 1987. *The subtle danger: Reflections on the literacy abilities of America's young adults.* Princeton, NJ: Educational Testing Service.

Venezky, R. L., and S. D. Pittelman. 1977. PRS: A pre-reading skills program for individually guided education. In *Individually guided elementary education,* eds. H. J. Klausmeier, R. A. Rossmiller, and M. Saily. New York: Academic Press.

Vygotsky, L. S. 1962. *Thought and language.* Cambridge, MA: M.I.T. Press.

Walberg, H. J., H. Keiko, and S. P. Rasher. 1978. English acquisition as a diminishing function of experience rather than age. *TESOL Quarterly* 12: 427–437.

Wald, A. 1947. *Sequential analysis.* New York: John Wiley and Sons.

Weinstein, R. S. 1983. Student perceptions of schooling. *Elementary School Journal* 83: 288–312.

Weiss, D. J., ed. 1983. *New horizons in testing: Latent trait test theory and computerized adaptive testing.* London: Academic Press.

White, A. L., and D. D. Smith. 1974. A study of the effects of varying student responsibility for instructional decisions in a CAI course. *Journal of Computer-based Instruction* 1(no. 1): 13–21.

White, B. Y., and J. R. Frederiksen. 1987. *Causal model progressions as a foundation for intelligent learning environments.* BB&N Report No. 6686. Cambridge, MA: Bolt, Beranek and Newman, Inc.

Willows, D. M., and H. A. Houghton, eds. 1987. *The psychology of illustration. Vol. 1: Basic research.* New York: Springer-Verlag.

Wittrock, M. C. 1981. Learning and memory. In *Psychology and education: The state of the union,* ed. F. H. Farley and N. J. Gordon. Berkeley, CA: McCutchan.

Wittrock, M. C. 1986. Students' thought processes. In *Handbook of research on teaching,* 3d ed., ed. M. C. Wittrock. New York: Macmillan.

Wright, P., and F. Reid. 1973. Written information: Some alternatives to prose for expressing the outcomes of complex contingencies. *Journal of Applied Psychology* 57: 160–166.

Yankelovich, N., G. P. Landow, and D. Cody. 1987. Creating hypermedia materials for English literature students. *SIGCUE Outlook* 19 (no. 3/4): 12–25.

Yankelovich, N., B. J. Haan, N. K. Meyrowitz, and S. M. Drucker. 1988. Intermedia: The concept and the construction of a seamless information environment. *Computer* 21 (no. 1): 81–96.

Yerushalmy, M. In press. Using empirical information in geometry: Students' and designers' expectations. *Journal of Computers in Mathematics and Science Teaching.*

Yerushalmy, M., D. Chazan, and M. Gordon. 1987. *Guided inquiry and technology: A year long study of children and teachers using the geometric supposer.* ETC Final Report. Cambridge, MA: Harvard Graduate School of Education.

Zeigler, B. P. 1976. *Theory of modelling and simulation.* New York: John Wiley and Sons.

Zinn, K. 1971. *Requirements for programming languages in computer-based instructional systems.* Paris: Organization for Economic Cooperation and Development.

Zinn, K. L. 1968. Instructional uses of interactive computer systems. *Datamation* 14 (no. 9): 22–27.

Index